Lecture Notes in Computer Science   8906

Commenced Publication in 1973
Founding and Former Series Editors:
Gerhard Goos, Juris Hartmanis, and Jan van Leeuwen

T0212836

Jan Hodicky (Ed.)

Modelling and Simulation for Autonomous Systems

First International Workshop, MESAS 2014
Rome, Italy, May 5-6, 2014
Revised Selected Papers

 Springer

Volume Editor

Jan Hodicky
NATO Modelling and Simulation Centre of Excellence
Piazza Villoresi 1, 00143 Rome, Italy
E-mail: jan.hodicky@seznam.cz

ISSN 0302-9743 e-ISSN 1611-3349
ISBN 978-3-319-13822-0 e-ISBN 978-3-319-13823-7
DOI 10.1007/978-3-319-13823-7
Springer Cham Heidelberg New York Dordrecht London

Library of Congress Control Number: 2014955627

LNCS Sublibrary: SL 3 – Information Systems and Application, incl. Internet/Web and HCI

Typesetting: Camera-ready by author, data conversion by Scientific Publishing Services, Chennai, India

Printed on acid-free paper

Springer is part of Springer Science+Business Media (www.springer.com)

Preface

This volume contains the papers presented at MESAS Workshop 2014: Modelling and Simulation for Autonomous Systems held on May 5–6, 2014 in Rome.

MESAS 2014 was a two-day workshop organized by the NATO Modelling and Simulation Centre of Excellence. The event gathered together, in plenary sessions and round tables, fully recognized experts from different technical communities in military, academia and industry. The aim of MESAS 2014 was to explore the possible use of Modelling and Simulation to integrate systems with autonomous capabilities into operational scenarios and to support coalition interoperability.

The community of interest submitted 50 papers for consideration. Each submission was reviewed by 3 Program Committee members. The committee decided to accept 46 papers to be presented during the workshop. The plenary session and round table discussions included an extra 5 invited presentations. Following a thorough review process, only 32 papers were recommended to be included into these proceedings.

September 2014   Jan Hodicky

MESAS 2014 Program Committee

General Chair

Francesco Langella — General Director of the Air Systems Procurement Agency, under the Italian National Armament Director, Italy

Technical Chair

Antonio Bicchi	University of Pisa, Italy
Marco Protti	Alenia Aermacchi, Italy

Members

Gianluca Antonelli	University of Cassino and Southern Lazio, Italy
Agostino Bruzzone	DIME University of Genoa, Italy
Wayne Buck	NATO Allied Command Transformation, USA
Andrea Caiti	University of Pisa, Italy
Alessandro Cignoni	NATO Modelling and Simulation Centre of Excellence, Italy
Andrea Cini	ITA Navy Institute for Electronics & Telecommunications, Italy
Andrea D'Ambrogio	University of Rome Tor Vergata, Italy
Emilio Frazzoli	Laboratory for Information and Decision Systems, and the Operations Research Center at the Massachusetts Institute of Technology, USA
Flavio Fusco	Selex ES SpA, Italy
Marco Garspardone	Telecom Italia Research Center, Italy
Jan Hodicky	NATO Modelling and Simulation Centre of Excellence, Italy
Pedro Jose Marron	Universität Duisburg-Essen, Germany
Jan Mazal	University of Defence in Brno, Czech Republic
Lucia Pallottino	Università di Pisa, Italy
Libor Preucil	Czech Technical University in Prague, Czech Republic
Paolo Proietti	MIMOS, Italy
Michal Reinstein	Czech Technical University in Prague, Italy
Bruno Tranchero	Alenia Aermacchi, Italy

MESAS 2014 Event Manager

Alessandro Cignoni, Simulation Based Acquisition Section Chief in the NATO M&S COE

MESAS 2014 Organizing Committee

Corrado Cacciatori - NATO M&S COE

Tiziana Cartechini - NATO M&S COE
Mattia Crespi - QBIT TECHNOLOGIES
Marco Giorgi - NATO M&S COE
Lucia Pallottino - University of Pisa
Paolo Proietti - MIMOS

MESAS 2014 Sponsors

COMMERCIAL SPONSORS

TECHNICAL SPONSORS

Inter-Domain and Multi-disciplinary Exchange of Knowledge within Modelling & Simulation and Robotics Communities of Interest

The Idea

At the beginning of 2012, Supreme Allied Command Transformation invited all Centres Of Excellence (COE) to explore their possible involvement for the integration of Autonomous Systems in the operational activities. In response to this request, the M&S COE became actively involved in a Study Group within the System Analysis and Study Panel of the NATO Science & Technology Organization entitled SAS 097: "Robotics Underpinning Future NATO Operations". Moreover, the M&S COE contributed to the Multinational Capability Development Campaigns (MCDC) 2013 and 2014 by participating to the Autonomous Systems (AxS) Focus Area meetings under the lead of ACT.

During ITEC 2013 in ROME, the Centre presented the information collected through SAS-097 and MCDC involvement. An example of the interaction between a simulated environment and a real robot was illustrated in what we called "a hybrid world" in which real and virtual robots cooperated to accomplish basic tasks.

In order to investigate further examples of how M&S can be applied to better integrate AxS into operational environments, the idea of MESAS was born: that is to create a Community of Interest focused on M&S in support of Autonomous Systems. The idea was further developed when we considered impacts to training, command and control interfaces and future AxS development.

The planning, organization and conduct of this workshop fit perfectly into the mission of the M&S COE, which provides support to NATO and Nations through collaboration with industry, academia and other organizations for research and experimentation of M&S tools and concepts.

The Way Ahead

The future of integration and interoperability is reliant upon the exchange of ideas, visions and fresh perspectives, as well as experience, know-how and frank and open dialogue amongst all stakeholders.

I think this workshop has proven to be a significant opportunity for high level debate on the topics I mentioned above and I believe this newly established Community of Interest will continue to enhance future M&S/AxS development.

NATO M&S COE Director
Col. Stefano Nicoló

MESAS 2014 Objective

Systems with Autonomous Capabilities are abbreviated with the acronym xSAC, where the x indicates the operational domain: ground, maritime, air, space and cyber.

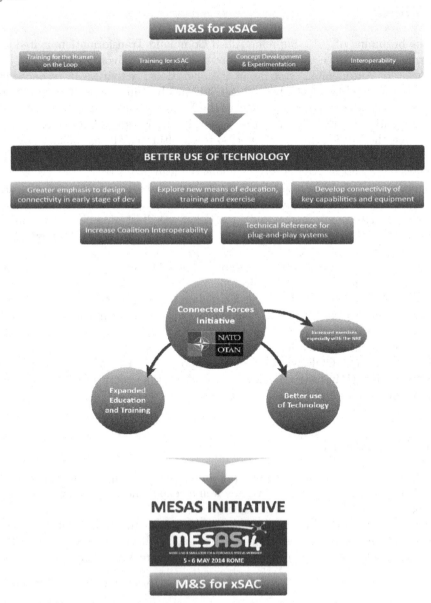

MESAS 2014 Organizer

NATO MODELLING AND SIMULATION CENTRE OF EXCELLENCE (NATO M&S COE)

The NATO M&S COE is a recognized international military organization activated by the North Atlantic Council in 2012, and is not under the NATO Command Structure. Partnering Nations provide funding and personnel for the Centre through a memorandum of understanding. Czech Republic, Italy and the United States are current members, but other nations are in consideration.

The NATO M&S COE supports NATO Transformation by improving the networking of NATO and nationally owned M&S systems, promoting cooperation between Nations and organizations through the sharing of M&S information and serving as an international source of expertise.

The NATO M&S COE seeks to be a leading world class organization, providing the best military expertise in modelling and simulation technology, methodologies and the development of M&S professionals. It will be the focal point of an integrated network of M&S training centres and other COEs promoting an interoperable, distributed M&S Service to all of NATO and Partnering Nations.

Key Objectives:

- Within 5 years, the NATO M&S COE will provide NATO and Nations a M&S framework composed of a Distributed Simulation Environment and Subject Matter Experts in M&S for Concept Development and Experimentation.
- Beyond 5 years, the NATO M&S COE will provide a persistent, distributed M&S framework among COEs, Nations, NATO training entities (JFTC, JWC) and key industry players, becoming the premier influential entity in M&S standardization.

NATO M&S COE with its M&S framework will become the glue for interdisciplinary military projects.

https://www.mscoe.org/

Table of Contents

Robot System

Military Application

Validation

Human-Machine Communication

Gazebo Simulator

Algorithm

A PLM-Based Approach for Un-manned Air System Design: A Proposal

Giorgio Bernabei[1], Claudio Sassanelli[1], Angelo Corallo[2], and Mariangela Lazoi[2]

[1] Dhitech Scarl, Lecce, Italy
{giorgio.bernabei,claudio.sassanelli}@dhitech.it
[2] Università del Salento, Lecce, Italy
{angelo.corallo,mariangela.lazoi}@unisalento.it

Abstract. In the ACARE's "Flightpath 2050 - Europe's Vision for Aviation", a declared objective is the seamlessly operation of the European air transport system through interoperable and networked systems allowing manned and unmanned air vehicles to safely operate in the same airspace. One of the crucial aim is to develop technological advances in civil applications and unmanned systems, in a more "designed to cost" and "electric" way. According to the above-mentioned vision, "occurrence and impact of human error is significantly reduced through new designs, training processes, technologies that support decision-making". In addition, CTNA is starting to move in this direction, in order to develop innovative technologies for unmanned airplanes. This paper proposes a technological architecture for innovation on UAS (Unmanned Air Systems) piloting systems. The design of a UAS adopting a Product Lifecycle Management (PLM) platform as repository for data-mining and decision support system is discussed; the vision is to manage the autonomous capabilities of the vehicle, based both on previously simulated scenario and on real-time calculation, to adapt the behavior of the vehicle on the real operational scenario. A further step could be the collaborative evaluation of the real operational scenario trough the integration of autonomous vehicles that interact and exchange own real behavior data. To manage this big amount of data, it is necessary to grant access to design data, through the access to the above-mentioned PLM platform. The advantages of this methodology is implicit in the point of view from which we approach the PLM data repository: the Product Data Record, that gathers data coming from all the phases of the life cycle of UAS, enables an on-time centralized data management. It allows companies to operate on a single, synchronized source for all product data, improving integrity and reliability and decreasing time and cost.

Keywords: product lifecycle management, modelling and simulation, unmanned air systems, model-based design, business process management.

1 Introduction

In the Europe's Vision for Aviation, a declared objective is the interoperability of air transport, with particular attention to unmanned vehicles as innovative driver for

J. Hodicky (Ed.): MESAS 2014, LNCS 8906, pp. 1–11, 2014.

further economic and technological developments related to passenger and freight transport. Nowadays, initiatives to promote and support the research and development on UAS (Unmanned Aerial System) are increasing. An example is the recent opening of Taranto-Grottaglie Airport, in Apulia, as the first European centre for experimentation, testing and certification of UAS. The described scenario suggest directions for important perspectives to study a new paradigm for the development and testing of technological solutions to support the aerospace industry.

The paper proposes a functional and a technological architecture for innovation on UAS piloting systems, adopting a PLM (Product Lifecycle Management) platform to support the improvement of their behavioral and control model.

It is part of a study started in a Community of Practice (i.e. an informal organization of people with different background around a topic of common interest) among the participants on the Italian Research Project KHIRA (Knowledge Holistic Integrated Research Approach) by the researchers working in cPDM Lab - Università del Salento and Dhitech Scarl. The project is in collaboration with national aerospace industrial players, aimed at innovate methodologies and technologies for an integrated management of data and information along the product lifecycle.

The proposal is based on the integration of the discipline of Modelling and Simulation, within the product lifecycle, extending its role to the management of autonomous capabilities of the vehicle, based both on previously simulated scenario and on real-time calculation, to adapt the behavior of the vehicle on the real operational scenario.

The next sections of the paper are a background section describing the main relevant issues on UAS, modelling & simulation practices and product lifecycle management. A further section describes the proposed architecture highlighting relevance and related proposed architecture. A final section of conclusions ends the paper.

2   Background

2.1   Un-manned Aircraft Systems

Unmanned Aircraft Systems (UASs) have only been in service for less than a century. UAS's history begins in 1922 with the first launch of an unmanned aircraft (RAE 1921Target) from an aircraft carrier (HMS Argus). Over the years UASs have been developed into the highly sophisticated machines in use today. Today UASs are indeed an important surplus to many countries air defenses. The drones used by the USAF in the 1940s were built for spying and reconnaissance, but were not very efficient due to major flaws in their operating systems. Thanks to the technological development, modern UAS's level of autonomy is considerably increased, inversely proportional to the vehicle commander. During the years, there has been indeed a switch from the remotely piloted vehicles to semi-automatic, automatic and autonomous vehicles [1].

The UAS's evolution enables them for many important applications including civil (e.g. Aerial photography, Agriculture, Coastguard, Conservation) and military use. In the military use, it is possible to distinguish among: navy (e.g. Electronic intelligence, Relaying radio signals, Shadowing enemy fleets), army (e.g. Reconnaissance, Surveillance of enemy activity, Monitoring of nuclear, biological or chemical (NBC) contamination) and air force (e.g. Long-range, high-altitude surveillance, Radar system jamming and destruction).

As UASs are used in a variety of applications, it is difficult to develop one classification system that encompasses all UASs. UASs can be classified according to two main aspects: performance specifications and mission aspects. The key specifications of a UAS include weight, payload, endurance and range, speed, wing loading, cost, engine type and power; these aspects are useful for designers, manufacturers and potential customers because classification enables these groups to match their mission expectations with the performance aspects of UASs and to easily chose the most suitable from the wide variety of UASs available [2].

2.2 Modelling and Simulations

In the aviation field, engineering challenges become more and more difficult to deal with, due to the ever-increasing technological complexity of the products; therefore, methodologies and tools that were adopted until a few years ago are no longer adequate to meet the new demands of the market. The Modelling and Simulation (M&S) is a powerful technology for prototyping, evaluation and design of systems that is used extensively in industry today [3]; it allows companies to accelerate time to market, improve product quality and reduce development costs. Modelling and Simulations provide information on the behavior of a system without realizing prototypes and without testing them in a real environment, so it is applied to confirm and validate, as analogue of physical testing; furthermore, the physical fidelity of the system models will greatly improve [4]. M&S is mainly adopted in the automotive and aerospace fields and uses models, technical knowledge, software simulators and a set of engineering tools to aid designers to make the right choices. The challenge of M&S is to ensure that outputs of simulations fit with the real behavior of the system in the operational scenario; this requires to engineers to evaluate the right boundary conditions and constraints and to conceptualize the reality [5].

For the purposes of this proposal, among the plethora of modelling and simulation approach, is taken into consideration the relatively new Model-Based Design (MBD) approach. Due to the complexity of big systems, traditional approach (i.e. programming or text-based models) are inadequate and not free-of-errors. MDB enables multi-domain simulation thought the use of graphical blocks that contains rules and libraries for the description of a system; modern MBD tools enables the simulation, code generation and test/validation, particularly useful for embedded systems. The result is both a model and a simulation environment where multi-body systems are described with blocks representing bodies, links, and forces in a parameterized way. Last, but not least, a system can be optimized by tuning design parameters [6].

2.3 Product Lifecycle Management

Producing complex and knowledge intensive products in this scenario requires that information about product and process is accessible to partners, suppliers and customers.

Consequently, the product lifecycle is fragmented among several actors and high level of integration and collaboration is needed. In this scenario the adoption of PLM approach and specific system finds its adequate context since the companies can build channels within the whole value network through which information and knowledge can be exchanged and go far beyond the traditional exchange of specifications, drawings and contracts. The tendency is to use a PLM strategy to integrate people, processes, business systems and information in order to manage the product development [7] and support its lifecycle.

PLM means Product Lifecycle Management and its value is increasing, especially for manufacturing, high technology and service industries [8]. In fact, today PLM is widely recognized as a business necessity for companies to become more innovative in order to meet current challenges such as product customization and traceability, growing competition, shorter product development and delivery times, globalization, tighter regulations and legislation. Being an innovative business, it doesn't simply mean creating innovative products, but it also means improving the processes a company uses to realize its products and how it supports them using innovative approaches for a complete product lifecycle [9].

Therefore, PLM is a holistic business concept [7]; it is both a business approach and a software solution that during the last years has evolved from a set of engineering oriented tools into an enterprise-level solution [10].

Figure 1 shows the main phases of the product lifecycle.

Fig. 1. Product Lifecycle phases

The core of PLM is the creation and storage of data related to engineering activities with the aim to guarantee an easy way to found, distribute and re-use all the information required for the activities execution. The main concept is to identify the package of information available in the company that constitutes its informative fundamental. This has to be available in an information system of data management and sharing. PLM is a technology of linkage among the systems used in the different organizational units. A PLM system help to globally manage all the technological resource and to guarantee an easier access for sharing information [11].

3   The Proposed Architectural Framework

3.1   Relevance of M&S in the UAS Lifecycle

Nowadays UASs represent the new frontier for the aeronautical sector. Even though during the last years enormous steps were done in order to increase the reliability and autonomy degree of their operating systems, a turning point has not yet been reached: too many flaws are still unresolved and in the meantime a lot of possible improvement are only in power.

Despite these explained critical points, technology level is now considered the key leverage to enable, support and manage innovation during the whole lifecycle of UASs. Product Lifecycle Management (PLM) system indeed, combining digitalization and virtualization, makes innovative processes more efficient and effective, linking the diverse phases of the product lifecycle through data and knowledge shared in a collaborative way. This infrastructure is today frequent and necessary dealing with complex products. The further step that this proposal aim to is the integration between Modelling & Simulation and PLM systems to support UASs innovation development. Though, considering their high technological content and the difficulties to ensure autonomous capabilities of the UAS control, the traditional scheme of PLM systems needs to be revisited. For this reason, the following PLM-M&S interaction diagram have been conceived (Figure 2).

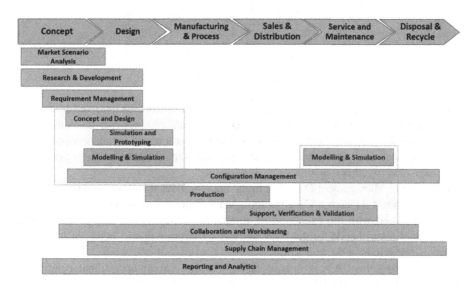

Fig. 2. Modelling & Simulation for UASs

It explains that to increase UAS's autonomy piloting system is necessary to involve the Modelling & Simulation systems not only in the initial phase of the product lifecycle, including concept, design and prototyping until manufacturing, but also in the utilization phase.

Therefore, M&S systems will be supposed to have a critical role also in operational activities as a support, verification & validation tool contributing to configuration management and collaboration & work sharing.

3.2   Functional and Technological Architecture

To implement the proposed scenario and process, it is designed the architecture that combines organizational database and organizational system in an organic and integrated infrastructure. In Figure 3 an overview of the Functional Architecture is given.

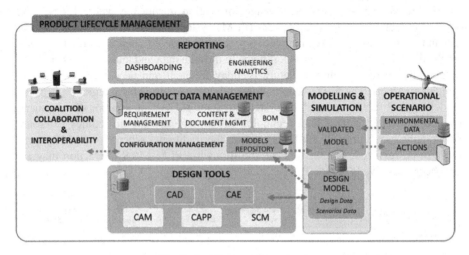

Fig. 3. Architectural Framework

The functional area called Design Tools includes the softwares involved in the engineering activities, such as CAD and CAE. The data produced in this phase are called design data. Information describing the scenario on which simulation and flight test are executed (e.g. environmental condition) are named scenarios data. Scenarios and design data together constitute a design model.

The Product Management Data functional area includes the storage and versioning of Design Models through a Configuration Management system. Model and Simulation is concerned with the execution of simulations based on the design model, the generation of control code for the UAV and the verification that its behavior is correct during its operations in the real world.

Finally, when the UAV is operational, if for the current operational conditions there are no validated models contained in the local Model Repository, remote archives maintained by allies can be consulted (Coalition, Collaboration & Interoperability functional area). Furthermore, a specific detail on the data and information flow core is provided; it is synthetized in the in Figure 4, with emphasis on the repositories.

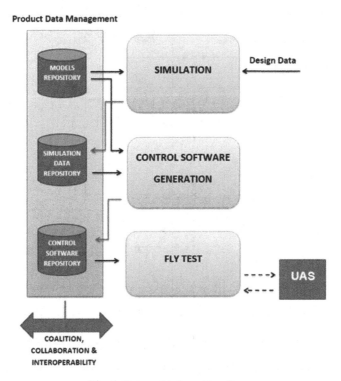

Fig. 4. Data and information flow

In the following section it is described the process, that is to say the set of activities, which constitute the foundation of this proposal. The process is modelled using the Business Process Management Notation (BPMN), which in a further implementation step allows the system to work in an automatic and integrated way.

Starting from the CAD and CAE data, the idea is to design the component-based model and to simulate and verify the behavior of the UAS. Once the system has been accepted, it is saved in the Model Repository that is used as references to control the real system. As this first model is based on assumed scenario and design data, it could be supposed that the UAS will act differently in the real environment, thus it could be necessary to test and validate the model through test campaigns.

Figure 5 shows the process for model testing and validation.

The validated model will be the starting point for UAS's piloting system development: M&S software are able indeed, at state of the art, to generate the control code. Whether, on real operational scenario, the environmental data are not the same of the data used in design, or UAS's behavior is not consistent with the designed/validated model, the M&S can act as a remote-brain. By broadcasting to PLM platform the information from the UAS, the PDM can retrieve the model of the vehicle (from the model repository), launch a new simulation and consequently generate the correct control code based on the real and updated data.

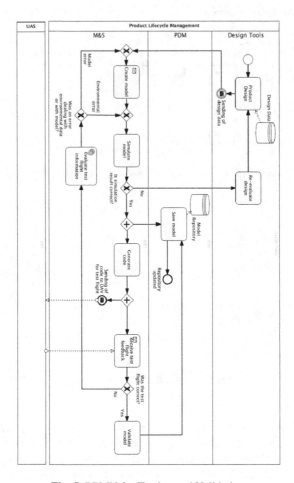

Fig. 5. BPMN for Testing and Validation

The new generated model, at the same time, will be stored in the repository that will act as knowledge base for further mission.

The Model Repository will be, on the other side, the knowledge-base for vehicles belonging either to the same family, so characterized by similar properties, or to a coalition: it will enable the system to gather critical data to adapt the behavior of the vehicle during the mission, or to accurately plan an operation based on the experience of other vehicles.

Figure 6 shows the process for operational scenario.

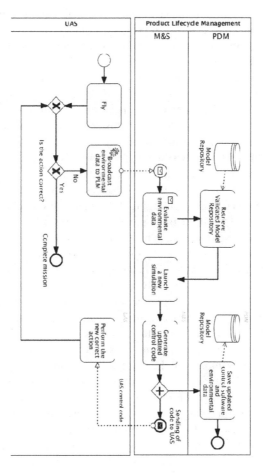

Fig. 6. BPMN for Operational Scenario

4   Conclusions

In this paper it has been firstly introduced the evolving framework of Un-manned
Aircraft Systems (UAS), than a context of both Modelling and Simulation (M&S)
systems and Product Lifecycle Management (PLM) approach was exposed. In the
core section we proposed a functional and a technological architecture that integrate
the discipline of Modelling and Simulation within the product lifecycle management
of UASs: this structure, based on the continuous updating/retrieving of data from a
multi type repository, is supposed to increase the capabilities of the vehicle in terms
of autonomous behavior in the real action. In particular, the functional architecture
explains that during the UAV lifecycle is necessary to extend the application of Modelling & Simulation systems also in the utilization phase: in this way these tools
will be critical also in operational activities as support, verification and validation,

contributing to configuration management and collaboration & work-sharing. Using the proposed architecture a model repository, composed of design model, validated model and control software sections, needs to be involved. It will used to store, update and retrieve knowledge during the different phase of the UAV's life: initially in terms of experience/heritage or hypothesized design and scenario data, than of generated control code and validated model, finally of collected operational flight data. The availability of these kind of data is important for two different issues. In the operational one, we have to highlight that with this solution the reaction to threats and unknown scenarios is committed only to the system, without an operator intervention. The repository, linked to M&S systems, from one side allows UAV to recognize the surrounding environment and, when necessary, make a query to obtain new orders and advices, from the other it permits to broadcast the new knowledge, collected during test and operational flights, enlarging the quantity of data accessible in the future. For the second issue, the strategic one, we have to underline that the companies involved in the UAV development can handle this knowledge firstly in the medium run, to customize and configure the product depending on customer's needs and expectations, and secondly in the long run, to redesign the product on the base of continuous improvement guidelines. A further advantage is the reachability and manageability of this experience by all the vehicles belonging either to the same family or to a coalition: it will represent an ever-increasing heritage enabling the system to have more accurate supporting system in real action, and designers and alliance partners to gather loads of data by different environments, scenarios and devices. So the advantages of this methodology is implicit in the point of view from which we approach the PLM data repository: the Product Data Record, that gathers data came from all the phases of the life cycle of UAS, enables an on-time centralized data management. It allows companies to operate on a single, synchronized source for all product data, improving integrity and reliability and decreasing time and cost.

Notwithstanding the reported advantages of the proposal, the next steps will be the more critical. In fact, the next future research will be focused on the development of the integration software based on a sort of middleware among the different systems involved and to identify a pilot-case in order to apply in a real context the described proposal. The application at a pilot-case will suggest feedbacks and improvements at the overall architecture and processes proposed in the paper.

References

1. Williams, R.: BAE Systems – Autonomous Capability Overview (2007), Presentation from `http://www.stfc.ac.uk/resources/pdf/richardwilliams.pdf` (accessed April 2014)
2. Arjomandi, M.: Classification of unmanned aerial vehicles (2006)
3. Ören: A Basis for a Modeling and Simulation Body of Knowledge Index: Professionalism, Stakeholders, Big Picture, and Other BoKs. SCS M&S Magazine, 40–48 (January 2001)
4. CIMdata, Data Challenges for Modeling and Simulation, Technical Report (2012), `http://www.pdteurope.com/media/4884/1_data_challenges_for_mo deling_and_simulation.pdf` (accessed April 2014)

5. DOD, Modelling and Simulation Body of Knowledge (2010), Report from `http://www.msco.mil` (accessed April 2014)
6. Simulink (2014), `http://www.mathworks.com/products/simmechanics/` (accessed April 2014)
7. Lee, T., Verstraeten, J.: Product lifecycle management in aviation maintenance, repair and overhaul. Elsevier Computers in Industry 59, 296–303 (2008)
8. Saaksvuori, I.: Product Lifecycle Management, 2nd edn. Springer (2008)
9. CIMdata, Product Lifecycle Management - Empowering the Future of Business (2002), Technical report from `http://www.cimdata.com/publications/pdf/PLM_Definition_0210.pdf` (accessed December 2011)
10. Garetti, T.: Product Lifecycle Management definizione, caratteristiche e questioni aperte (2003), Technical report from `http://coenv.it/bo/allegati/Files/23_definizione_plm.pdf` (accessed December 2011)
11. Grieves: Product Lifecycle Management: Driving the Next Generation of Lean Thinking. McGraw-Hill (2005)

A UAV-Based Visual Tracking Algorithm for Sensible Areas Surveillance

Pierluigi Carcagnì[1], Pier Luigi Mazzeo[1], Cosimo Distante[1], Paolo Spagnolo[1], Francesco Adamo[2], and Giovanni Indiveri[2]

[1] National Research Council of Italy - Institute of Optics, Arnesano (LE), Italy
pierluigi.carcagni@ino.it
[2] University of Salento, Lecce, Italy

Abstract. Unmanned aerial vehicles (UAVs) are an active research field since several years. They can be applied in a large variety of different scenarios, and supply a test bed to investigate several unsolved problems such as path planning, control and navigation. Furthermore, with the availability of low cost, robust and small video cameras, UAV video has been one of the fastest growing data sources in the last couple of years. In other words, object detection and tracking as well as visual navigation has recently received a lot of attention. This paper proposes an advanced technology framework that, through the use of UAVs, allows to supervise a specific sensible area (i.e. traffic monitoring, dangerous zone and so on). In particular, one of the most cited real-rime visual tracker proposed in the literature, Struck, is applied on video sequences tipically supplied by UAVs equipped with a monocular camera. Furthermore in this paper is investigated on the feasibility to graft different features characterization into the original tracking architecture (replacing the orginal ones). The used feature extraction methods are based on Local Binary Pattern (LBP) and Histogram of Oriented Gradients (HOG) . Objects to be tracked could be selected manually or by means of advanced detection technique based, for example, on change detection or template matching strategies. The experimental results on well known benchmark sequences show as these features replacing improve the overall performances of the original considered real-time visual tracker.

Keywords: LBP, HOG, visual tracking, spatial histogram.

1 Introduction

Many autonomous vehicles have been developed in last decades. In particular Unmanned Aerial Vehicles (UAVs) have achieved considerable attention in many fields for their great potentials. Diverse UAVs are designed from heavy to miniature in size, and more powerful and agile in capability. They are capable of taking versatile duties, especially when human intervention is boring, hard, dangerous or expensive e.g. hazardous zone or wide range reconnaissance, traffic monitoring, disaster relief support, military operations etc. [15][16]. This paper

J. Hodicky (Ed.): MESAS 2014, LNCS 8906, pp. 12–19, 2014.

proposes an advanced technology framework that, through the use of UAVs, allows to supervise a specific sensible area (i.e. traffic monitoring, dangerous zone and so on). In particular, a real-time object tracking system is presented. The proposed real-time tracking algorithm could be exploited to reconstruct people and vehicle movements and their interactions in order to prevent or immediately detect any action that could damage persons or things (e.g. access to forbidden areas, gathering, loitering, etc.). The first aim of the visual tracking is to estimate the state of the target, in a frame, along the execution of video sequences. There are many factors that affect the efficiency of a tracking algorithm, such as the variation of illumination, the presence of occlusions and the distinction of the object from the background.

One of the most innovative visual tracker algorithms proposed in the literature in recent years is Struck.

Struck (Structured Output Tracking with Kernels) [1] is a framework for adaptive visual object tracking that is based on structured output prediction. This architecture uses a kernelized structured output support vector machine (SVM), which is learned on-line to provide adaptive tracking. The application can work in real-time thanks to a budgeting mechanism which prevents the unbounded growth in the number of support vectors. However, challenging problems, like the similarity appearance measures and object changes appearance managing, remain still open. Often, the appearance of different objects and background in the scenes may be similar to the target appearance and this may influence its correct detection. This way, it is difficult to distinguish the features of the target object from those of the objects in the scene that are not targets. This phenomenon is known as cluttering. For these reasons feature representation is a critical aspect in tracking by detection algorithms.

In this work, we replace this feature characterization (haar-like) with different local feature-based method, such as LBP (Local Binary Pattern) [2], and HOG (Histogram of Oriented Gradients) [4].

LBP method has been intensively used as feature extractor in visual tracking: in [5] it is used for face description in order to achieve robust face tracking performance. The face is represented by the fusion of color and LBP cue. However, because only LBP cue is employed, the tracking method is not robust. In [6] a novel on-line feature selection mechanism based on mean shift tracking algorithm is described. Different features as gray level, Local Binary Pattern (LBP) and edge orientation are selected, but they are tested only with mean shift tracking algorithm.

An LBP-based tracking algorithm is described in [7]. This approach is based on two main steps: (i) LBP histograms of each image and target pattern are constructed; (ii) a similarity measure is calculated in order to find the best LBP-histograms matching. The idea is interesting because LBP is used to solve visual tracking; however, no tests have been done on tracking video benchmark.

In [8] several methods of pedestrian detection that use different local statistical measures such as uniform LBP and a modified version of HOGs are presented. Two extraction features methods are compared, but the results are presented only in the particular context of pedestrian detection.

Some HOG based tracking systems have been presented in literature: in [9] is proposed a real-time visual tracking system that delivers high performance under difficult situations. The system is based on HOG within the on-line boosting framework. The comparison, however, is done only with Haar-based tracking system.

In [10] a detection and tracking algorithm for pedestrian is presented. It is based on HOG and SVM as detector and particle filtering as tracker. Experiments show that using HOG as features gives better pedestrian detection results.

Generally speaking, in this paper we investigate on the feasibility to replace haar-like feature descriptors in struck architecture, in order to improve the overall detection and tracking performances of this very popular algorithm. The performances are evaluated on the most important video benchmark sequences. The obtained results confirm that replacing the feature extraction mechanism gives better results in the algorithm architecture with respect to the classical one.

The paper is organized as follows. In section 2 there is a brief explanation of the feature extraction methods actually used in the considered framework. Experimental results are described and discussed in Section 3. Conclusive remarks and future perspectives are given in Section 4.

2 Visual Feature Representation

In Struck is straightforward to use different image features by modifying the kernel function used for evaluating patch similarity. Main results are obtained using simple Haar-like features for image representation. In the original struck algorithm, six different types of Haar-like features have been used. In particular a grid at two scales is used instead of random locations. This choice 1) limits the number of random factors in the tracking algorithm; 2) compensates the fact that feature selection is not performed.

Haar-like descriptors have been replaced by Local Binary Patterns (LBP) and Histogram of Oriented Gradients (HOG). In the following subsection these descriptor are briefly described.

2.1 Local Binary Patterns

The LBP operator proposed in [2] is a powerful tool for describing the texture of images. The original LBP operator labels the pixels of an image by thresholding the 3×3 - neighbours of each pixel with the center value. If the neighbor is higher it takes the value 1 otherwise it takes the value 0. Finally the thresholded neighbor pixel values are concatenated and considered as a binary number that becomes the label for the central pixel (Fig. 1(a)). The main limitation of the basic LBP operator is its small fixed spatial area which can not capture the larger texture. So the LBP operator is extended to use different sizes [11]. Bilinearly interpolation of the pixel values and the use of circular neighbours make any scale and number of pixels in the neighbours possible (Fig. 1(c)).

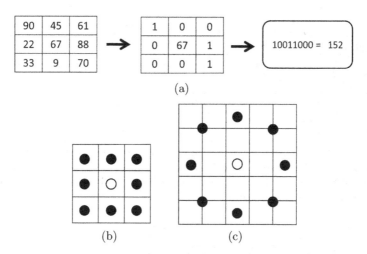

(a)

(b)   (c)

Fig. 1. LBP labeling procedure (a) and two examples of neighbouring pixels: $LBP_{1,8}$ (b), $LBP_{2,8}$ (c)

2.2 Spatial Histograms Representation for LBP Operator

Putting all features into a single histogram, all spatial information is discarded. Spatial information is very useful, so it has to be incorporated into the histogram somehow. The representation proposed by [13], is to divide the LBP image into grids and build a histogram of each cell seperately, in order to model local texture variation of the patch. Then by concatenating the histograms the spatial information is encoded (not merging them), as shown in Fig. 2. In this work spatial histograms have been applied to LBP operators, both interpolated and not.

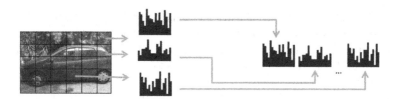

Fig. 2. Spatial histogram

2.3 Histogram of Oriented Gradients

Histogram of Oriented Gradients (HOG) [4], is a well known feature descriptor based on counting the occurrences of gradient orientation in localized portions of an image. This method is based on evaluating well-normalized local histograms of image gradient orientations in a dense grid. Local object appearance and shape

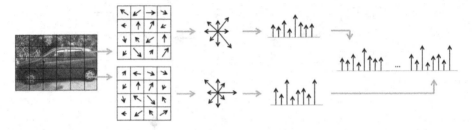

Fig. 3. HOG extraction features representation. Image is divided in cells. Each cell is done of $N \times N$ pixel. We compute the orientation of all pixel and construct the histogram of orientation of the cell. Finally all orientation histogram are concatenated to construct the final features vector.

can often be characterized rather well by the distribution of local intensity gradients or edge directions, even without precise knowledge of the corresponding gradient or edge positions. The implementation requires that the image window is divided into small spatial regions, called cells, and for each cell is accumulated a local 1-D histogram of gradient directions or edge orientations over the pixels of the cell. The combined histogram entries form the representation. For better invariance to disturb, it is also useful to contrast-normalize the local responses before using them. This can be done by accumulating a measure of local histogram energy over larger spatial regions, named blocks, and using the results to normalize all of the cells in the block. The normalized descriptor blocks represent the HOG descriptors (Fig. 3).

3 Experiments

In order to compare different feature extraction methods, some changes have been made to the original architecture. Public available Struck source code[1] has been integrated into a wider framework hosting LBP and HOG descriptors. For LBP, an available on-line[2] implementation has been used. The VLFeat library[3] is used for HOG operator.

Three sequences (Fig. 4), taken from PETS 2009[4] , were used to evaluate several object tracking methods. The sequences that are used for evaluation, have manually annotated ground truth data. These particular sequences are typical of UAVs equipped with a moncular camera.

An overlap measure is used to compare the output of an algorithm to ground truth values. This measure equally penalizes translations in both directions and scale changes as shown in [14].

---

[1] http://www.samhare.net/research/struck
[2] http://www.bytefish.de/blog/local_binary_patterns/
[3] http://www.vlfeat.org
[4] http://www.cvg.rdg.ac.uk/PETS2009

(a) pedestrian2   (b) pedestrian3   (c) car

Fig. 4. PETS2009

A result is considered true positive (TP) if the overlap is larger than a threshold ω. A result is counted as false negative (FN) when the algorithm does not produce some results for a frame even though an entry in the ground truth database is present. In the opposite case, a false positive (FP) is counted. A true negative (TN) is considered in cases when there is no either an algorithmic output nor an entry in the ground truth database for each single frame. In the end, false negative (FN) and a false positive (FP) are counted if the overlap is lower than a specific threshold ω. After processing a video sequence, *recall* and *precision* are calculated.

The performances of algorithmic output depends on the threshold ω that defines the bounding box overlap between the algorithmic result and ground truth values. Recall and precision of each video sequence are calculated for three threshold (ω) values: 0.75, 0.50 and 0.25. When ω decreases both recall and precision increase. Of course, in table 1 we report the best results (bolded), obtained for $\omega = 0.25$.

Regarding interpolated LBP, have been chosen the following configurations of radius and neighbours (*radius,neighbours*): (1,8), (1,10), (2,8), (2,16). Furthermore LBP, both interpolated and not, has been applied to the samples patches by means of both spatial histograms and not. Grid dimensions chosen for the spatial histograms have been of 2×2, 3×3, 4×4.

Regarding HOG, standard parameters as in [4] have been chosen. For Struck architecture have been set: a tracker search radius of 30 pixels; a SVM regularization parameter of 100; a SVM budget size of 100. For haar features, a gaussian kernel with $\sigma = 0.2$ has been used; for HOG and LBP, instead, an intersection kernel [1].

LBP gives better results in all sequences. It should be noted that spatial histograms improve the detection performance for the LBP descriptor. In sequence *"Pedestrian3"* HOG gives the worst results (respect than LBP and Haar) due to poor texture content of the tracked patch.

The aim of this work is threefold: to compare the discriminative power of the different local-based feature descriptors; to improve performances on well known visual tracking architecture (Struck); to evaluate the improved visual tracking architecture by means video sequences typical of moving camera visual tracking systems like Unmanned Aerial Vehicles. We have not rigorously measured the computational load. A qualitative assessment of the computing time tell us that, even if the computational burden is grown, the performances remain close to real-time (Intel I7 processor based system).

Table 1. Comparison between obtained results. For any pair of values, the first one refers to *precision*, the second one to *recall*. Label *LBP* refers to original LBP operator. LBP_{int} refers to the interpolated version one. Subscripts 2×2, 3×3, 4×4 denote which type of spatial histogram the best result refers to. With subscript *whole* we intend that the best result is obtained without applying any kind of spatial histogram but using the entire patch. *Radius* and *neighbors*, valid only for interpolated LBP operator, are denoted respectively in apexes.

	LBP	LBP_{int}	*HOG*	*Haar*
Pedestrian2	$\mathbf{(0.77/0.98)}_{4\times4}$	$(0.76/0.96)^{2,8}_{4\times4}$	$\mathbf{(0.76/0.97)}$	$(0.21/0.26)$
Pedestrian3	$\mathbf{(0.85/1.0)}_{3\times3}$	$\mathbf{(0.85/1.0)}^{1,8}_{4\times4}$	$(0.28/0.33)$	$(0.57/0.67)$
Car	$\mathbf{(0.79/0.87)}_{whole}$	$(0.79/0.86)^{2,8}_{whole}$	$(0.67/0.73)$	$(0.64/0.70)$

4   Conclusion

UAV systems are increasingly used in the field of video surveillance. In this work, a well known visual tracking architecture has been proposed to be used in the context of video surveillance by means UAV systems. The original tracking architecture has been improved replacing original feature characterization methods with local feature-based visual representations. The improved visual tracker has been evaluated by means of video sequences typical of moving camera visual tracking systems like UAV. Preliminary results show that some improvements are possible. LBP, joined with spatial histograms, in Struck architecture works better than Haar-like feature descriptors in all tested sequences. Future work will be addressed to study different classification algorithms which are more suitable for each feature characterization.

References

1. Hare, S., Saffari, A., Torr, P.H.S.: Struck: Structured output tracking with kernels. In: 2011 IEEE International Conference on Computer Vision (ICCV), pp. 263–270. IEEE (2011)
2. Ojala, T., Pietikäinen, M., Harwood, D.: A comparative study of texture measures with classification based on featured distributions. Pattern Recognition 29(1), 51–59 (1996)
3. Jun, B., Choi, I., Kim, D.: Local transform features and hybridization for accurate face and human detection. IEEE Trans. Pattern Anal. Mach. Intell. 35(6), 1423–1436 (2013)
4. Dalal, N., Triggs, B.: Histograms of oriented gradients for human detection. In: IEEE Computer Society Conference on Computer Vision and Pattern Recognition, CVPR 2005, vol. 1, pp. 886–893. IEEE (2005)

5. Wang, C.-X., Li, Z.-Y.: A new face tracking algorithm based on local binary pattern and skin color information. In: International Symposium on Computer Science and Computational Technology, ISCSCT 2008, vol. 2, pp. 657–660 (2008)
6. Yi, S., Yao, Z., Liu, J., Chen, J., Liu, W.: Robust tracking using on-line selection of multiple features. In: 2012 Spring Congress on Engineering and Technology (S-CET), pp. 1–5 (2012)
7. Rami, H., Hamri, M., Masmoudi, L.: Article: Objects tracking in images sequence using local binary pattern (lbp). International Journal of Computer Applications 63(20), 19–23 (2013)
8. Brehar, R., Nedevschi, S.: Local information statistics of lbp and hog for pedestrian detection. In: International Conference on Intelligent Computer Communication and Processing (ICCP), pp. 117–122. IEEE (2013)
9. Sun, S., Guo, Q., Dong, F., Lei, B.: On-line boosting based real-time tracking with efficient hog. In: International Conference on Acoustics, Speech and Signal Processing (ICASSP), pp. 2297–2301. IEEE (2013)
10. Xu, F., Gao, M.: Human detection and tracking based on hog and particle filter. In: 2010 3rd International Congress on Image and Signal Processing (CISP), vol. 3, pp. 1503–1507 (2010)
11. Ojala, T., Pietikainen, M., Maenpaa, T.: Multiresolution gray-scale and rotation invariant texture classification with local binary patterns. IEEE Transactions on Pattern Analysis and Machine Intelligence 24(7), 971–987 (2002)
12. Jun, B., Choi, I., Kim, D.: Local transform features and hybridization for accurate face and human detection. IEEE Transactions on Pattern Analysis and Machine Intelligence 35(6), 1423–1436 (2013)
13. Ahonen, T., Hadid, A., Pietikäinen, M.: Face recognition with local binary patterns. In: Pajdla, T., Matas, J(G.) (eds.) ECCV 2004. LNCS, vol. 3021, pp. 469–481. Springer, Heidelberg (2004)
14. Hemery, B., Laurent, H., Rosenberger, C.: Comparative study of metrics for evaluation of object localisation by bounding boxes. In: Fourth International Conference on Image and Graphics, ICIG 2007, pp. 459–464 (2007)
15. Office of the Secretary of Defense, USA: Unmanned Aerial Vehicle (UAV) Roadmap. 2005-2030, [R] (August 2005)
16. Campoy, P., Correa, J.F., Mondrag6n, I., Martinez, C., Olivares, M., Mejias, L., Artieda, J.: Computer vision onboard UAVs for civilian tasks. Journal of Intelligent and Robotic Systems 54(1- 3), 105–135 (2009)

A Cloud Based Service for Management and Planning of Autonomous UAV Missions in Smart City Scenarios

Gabriele Ermacora[1], Antonio Toma[1], Stefano Rosa[2], Basilio Bona[2],
Marcello Chiaberge[3], Mario Silvagni[1], Marco Gaspardone[4] and Roberto Antonini[4]

[1]Politecnico di Torino, DIMEAS, Turin, Italy
[2]Politecnico di Torino, DAUIN, Turin, Italy
[3]Politecnico di Torino, DET, Turin, Italy
{gabriele.ermacora,antonio.toma,stefano.rosa,basilio.bona,
marcello.chiaberge,mario.silvagni}@polito.it
[4]Telecom Italia S.p.a., Turin, Italy
{marco.gaspardone,roberto1.antonini}@polito.it

Abstract. Cloud Robotics is an emerging paradigm in which robots, seen as abstract agents, have the possibility to connect to a common network and share on a complex infrastructure the information and knowledge they gather about the physical world; or conversely consume the data collected by other agents or made available on accessible database and repositories. In this paper we propose an implementation of an emergency-management service exploiting the possibilities offered by cloud robotics in a smart city scenario. A high-level cloud-platform manages a number of unmanned aerial vehicles (quadrotor UAVs) with the goal of providing aerial support to citizens that require it via a dedicated mobile app. The UAV reaches the citizen while forwarding a real-time video streaming to a privileged user (police officer),connected to the same cloud platform, that is allowed to teleoperate it by remote.

Keywords: UAV, smart city, cloud robotics, open data, shared knowledge, navigation, path planning.

1 Introduction

At the dawn of cloud robotics [8] [9][10] many and interesting applications are possible exploiting the power of this technology [11][12]. Moreover the number of applications that see UAV as interesting devices for environment monitoring is growing. Indeed users can access to services built by fetching data from UAVs, such as telemetry or video streaming. As this paper illustrates, these services, which are part of the IT architecture, can be accessed via web or other devices, such as smartphone applications. A real security problem in a urban context is proposed as a test case in this paper; urban spaces monitored by cameras are not an efficient way to decrease crime rates since criminal events e.g., theft, robbery, rape tend to occur in unmonitored zones. Thus the aim of this test case is to apply this cloud architecture, based on ROS [1] [2], to crime prevention. In the case of aggression the user requests the emergency

J. Hodicky (Ed.): MESAS 2014, LNCS 8906, pp. 20–26, 2014.

service from the IT architecture, by providing GPS coordinates and an identification number. The IT architecture organizes a UAV to reach him/her for offering monitoring and support. In the meantime a police officer will use the service to see the current position of the UAV, its telemetry and video streaming from its camera. When UAVs are required for search and rescue or emergency interventions:

1. User sends a request to the service.
2. The request is automatically forwarded to the platform.
3. The platform transforms the request into a mission in a lower level language message.
4. Depending on the mission the message will be deployed to either a single or a swarm of UAVs

2   Interfaces

In this paper two interfaces to service are presented:

- A user-side interface which requests help and assistance from the UAV;
- A police-side interface for monitoring and management

The first interface is a mobile application running on an Android smartphone. It acquires GPS coordinates and phone ID when the user request for help. Then it sends these data (GPS coordinates and phone ID), over HTTP protocol, through a GET request to the server of the cloud platform. An example of the GET request could be:
http://fsc/request/?gps=45.674524,7.398732&cell=32308937642&command=takeoff

Fig. 1. Android application

The second interface is addressed to the police force. The officer accesses all the information about the UAV collected by telemetry and video streaming via a web browser. In this way he/she can know the actual position of the UAV, displayed on a map embedded in the web page. Information about remaining estimated time and distance for mission accomplishment are also made available. In addition, the video streaming from the UAV camera can offer assistance to the person in emergency.

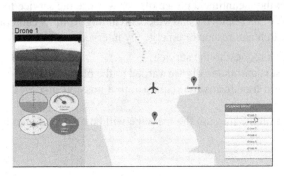

Fig. 2. Web browser GUI

3   The Cloud Platform

The cloud platform mainly consists of three layers :

- Front End which contains APIs to build new services;
- Application which contains all specific applications (the so called "remote brain"), that support APIs above;
- Adaption which contains adapters and drivers to connect different robots, and abstracts their basics functionalities to the above applications and APIs.

The platform is based on ROS framework [2], as showed in Figure 3, where gray boxes represent ROS nodes. The platform context is composed by two additional layers:

- Robots which contains all robots. They are connected to the platform through specific ROS nodes, named drivers and adapters (Adaption Layer);
- Services which contains all services exploiting APIs exposed by the platform (Front End Layer).

In order to have the cloud platform more robust and resilient we add the following managing elements:

- WatchDog System (WDS): to manage ROS nodes and represent the node status;
- Message Discovery Function (MDF): to enable or disable APIs according to ROS messages.

4   The Agents

The first validation-tests of the overall system have been conducted using a quadrotor as agent. Three different products are used in the validation of the proposed architecture:

Parrot AR.Drone: The AR.Drone [3] is a commercial low-cost quadrotor solution, fully equipped for remote control via smartphone. It features a front HD camera and the flight stability is ensured by a mother board (running a real-time linux-based operating system) and a navigation board interfaced with the on-board sensors (two cameras, ultrasonic range finders, gyroscopes and accelerometers).

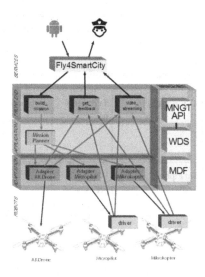

Fig. 3. The cloud platform architecture

Mikrokopter: Mikrokopter [4] is a complete auto-pilot designed for the control of generic multi-rotor platforms. It features two different boards: the Flight Control board guarantees vehicle inherent stabilization and altitude-hold function, the Navi Control board adds a set of GPS/Compass based autonomous navigation functions (waypoint navigation, come-home function, position hold mode). The Flight Controller relies on Atmel ATMEGA644 board running at 20MHz, and interfaces with the main inertial sensors (3-axis accelerometer, three gyros, one barometric sensor). Mikrokopter allows the user to take external control of the UAV (i.e., bypassing the radio controller) by means of a dedicated serial protocol.

Micropilot 2128: uPilot 2128 [5] is an auto-pilot board embedding all the peripherals needed for a stable and autonomous quad-rotor flight. This auto-pilot is specifically addressed to professional use and applications, this is reflected by its higher price and its market segment. Though Micropilot uses a completely closed-source software, it offers some tools allowing the user to write his own code. These functions come with an add-on product called "Xtender" [6]; Xtender provides a dedicated dynamic linking library that acts as a intermediate layer between the user code and the autopilot software. Using the functions encoded in the library the developer is able to get access to several low-level parameters of the auto-pilot and can modify their values. Due to Micropilot's high price and to its relatively young support to multi-copters when compared to other solutions on the market, it is not so common to find academic works that use this hardware.

Notice also that AR.Drone is a commercial ready-to-fly quadrotor while Micropilot and Mikrokopter are just two different models of autopilot electronic boards; in order to fly these require a mechanical frame, four or more motors, the same number of ESCs (Electronic Speed Controllers) and a battery. However since the ROS interface has to communicate directly with the autopilot, from a functional point of view the ROS architecture is not impacted by the general architecture of the agent, therefore this has not been described in detail.

Table 1. Quadrotors features and integration status in ROS environment

	Market	Command	Telemetry link	Autonomous navigation	SDK	ROS support
AR.Drone	Videogames /Hobby	Smartphone (via wifi)	Wifi (TCP/UDP packages)	☹	☺	☺
Mikrokopter	Hobby/ Photographer	Radio controller	UART (Custom Serial Protocol)	😐	☹	😐
Micropilot 2128	Professional applications	Radio controller	UART (Custom Serial Protocol)	☺	☺	☹

The three architectures offer growing functionalities, but also growing difficulties in implementation. Table 1 summarizes their main features and their integration status in ROS environment.

5   Conclusion and Future Work

In this paper we propose a test case for cloud robotics for emergency management and monitoring service. We apply emerging technologies such as web services and mobile applications to use robotics in the proposed cloud architecture. In the future work we intend to improve the cloud robotics platform enhancing the concept of robustness and resilience. In particular we intend to apply the multi-master robot concert technology [7] enabling ROS container multiplicity. We are testing the architecture in a real smart city environment with LTE connectivity. Then we want to exploit Open Data from the Internet in order to plan a flight according to obstacles present in the environment and information regarding LTE signal strength and availability. A preliminary simulation of the path planning exploiting Open data is in Figure 4.

In figure 4 there is the path computed by the platform according to LTE signal strength and obstacles present in the environment using a simple A*. The platform finds a path (in purple) .Waypoints are calculated with radiuses. Starting from the first point of the path it calculates a radius from the point to the nearest no fly zone (both physical obstacle and LTE low signal). With the calculated radius it draws a circle (in Figure 4 is in blue) that intercepts the path finding the next waypoint. This procedure continues for any waypoint.

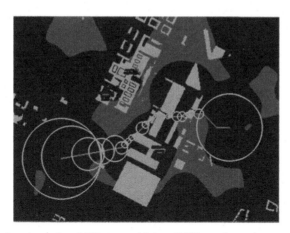

Fig. 4. Path planning simulation. LTE areas with low RSSI are shown in grey. Obstacles shown in white, free space in black. Waypoint are shown with associated radiuses in blue.

Acknowledgment. This work is in collaboration with Telecom Italia S.p.A. in the project Fly For Smart City.

References

1. Quigley, M., et al.: ROS: an open-source Robot Operating System. In: ICRA Workshop on Open Source Software 3(3(2)) (2009)
2. http://www.ros.org
3. http://ardrone2.parrot.com/
4. http://mikrokopter.de/en/home
5. http://www.micropilot.com/
6. http://www.micropilot.com/products-xtendermp.htm
7. http://www.robotconcert.org/wiki/Main_Page
8. Mell, P., Grance, T.: The NIST definition of cloud computing (draft). NIST special publication 800.145 (2011): 7
9. Goldberg, K., Kehoe, B.: Cloud Robotics and Automation: A Survey of Related Work. Electrical Engineering and Computer Sciences University of California at Berkeley
10. Sanfeliu, A., Hagita, N., Saffiotti, A.: Network robot systems. Robotics and Autonomous Systems 56(10), 793–797 (2008)
11. Chibani, A., et al.: Ubiquitous robotics: Recent challenges and future trends. Robotics and Autonomous Systems (2013)
12. Kamei, K., et al.: Cloud networked robotics. IEEE Network 26(3), 28–34 (2012)

Using Virtual Simulation Environments for Development and Qualification of UAV Perceptive Capabilities: Comparison of Real and Rendered Imagery with MPEG7 Image Descriptors

Georg Hummel and Peter Stütz

University of the Bundeswehr Munich, Werner-Heisenberg-Weg 39,
85577 Neubiberg, Germany
{georg.hummel,peter.stuetz}@unibw.de

Abstract. When it comes to more autonomous unmanned aerial vehicles, enhanced sensory and perceptive capabilities need to be integrated and qualified for mission scenarios of larger scale. In this context, recent developments in embedded technologies now allow the use of onboard image processing on such airborne platforms. However, the acquisition of mission relevant imagery and video test data necessary to develop and verify such processing algorithms can be complicated and costly. Therefore we are interested in the usability of commercial-of-the-shelf virtual simulation environments for generation of test and training data. To yield general acceptance, the relevance and comparability to real world imagery needs to be investigated. We pursue a multi-level approach to analyze differences between real and coherently simulated imagery and measure respective influence on image processing algorithm performance, taking into account typical visual database and rendering benchmarks such as level of detail, texture composition and rendering details. More specifically, in this paper we analyze corresponding real and synthetic footage using image descriptors from the content based image retrieval domain introduced in the MPEG7 standard. This allows us to compare the appearance of images in regard to specific image properties without disregarding their overall content. In future work it is planned to apply and evaluate the test subject, a computer vision algorithm on real and synthetic imagery. These evaluations are compared to allow detection of specific image properties influencing the performance of the test subject and therefore will help in identifying differences in the synthetically generated image. The results will provide insight on how to specifically trim image generation methods to reach equal processing performance with both image sets, mandatory to justify usage of synthetic footage for algorithm development and qualification. . . .

Keywords: virtual environment, modelling, validation, qualification, UAV, MPEG7.

J. Hodicky (Ed.): MESAS 2014, LNCS 8906, pp. 27–43, 2014.
© Springer International Publishing Switzerland 2014

1   Introduction

In today's security applications perceptive algorithms are often used to detect and track objects of interest. The recent technology boost in miniaturization of embedded systems, electrical powered engines and rechargeable batteries empowered the use of such algorithms also on unmanned aerial vehicles of smaller size. Relevant scenarios are described in [1–3]. Popular use cases are object detection and tracking or aerial mapping. To develop such algorithms usually a wide range of varying video footage is necessary to achieve a generalized model of the outside world within the algorithm. However the acquisition of relevant footage (holistic missions, or complex scenarios) can become costly. Additionally the acquired footage will be limited by the environmental requirements to perform a staged live scenario (i.e. weather, location, duration). Szeliski proposes a three step approach to test new computer vision algorithms [4]:

- Test on clean synthetic data (very abstract data, stimulating the mathematical model)
- Test on synthetic data with added noise, to evaluate the performance as a function of noise level.
- Test on real-world data, from a wide variety of sources, to test it against real-world complexity.

We suggest to also use *virtual environments* providing synthetic data additionally to real-world data in step three to increase the often limited variety of existing data sets for special applications i.e. airborne perception [5]. There are several possibilities to create synthetic images reaching from functional realism over photo-realism to physical realism [6]. Since increasing the level of realism is accompanied by an increase of costs (computation time and modelling effort), the question "which level of realism is necessary?" is raised. In [5] we define several requirements towards an virtual environment for testing of perceptive algorithms. These lead us to the selection of a serious gaming commercial-of-the-shelf virtual environment mainly utilized for education and training of governmental or military personal [7]. Using this environment we demonstrated the feasibility to use synthetic data with several perceptive algorithms, initially solely designed on real-world [3][8] or synthetic data [9, 10]. Similar evaluation approaches have been employed for image based vehicle assistance system in the automotive domain using vehicle simulators [11–13]. These use the output of the assistant system directly as comparison metric and therefore quality measure of the synthetically generated data set. In [12] this however emphasizes the modelling quality and placement accuracy.

Taking aforementioned investigations into regard, we believe that testing the actual *performance* of the algorithm will yield results less sensitive to modelling and allow direct evaluation. Therefore we developed a multi level approach to investigate differences in performance of perceptive algorithms between synthetic and real world data (see Fig. 1). Further more this approach shall provide insight in which image properties critically influence the performance of the perceptive

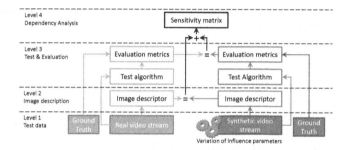

Fig. 1. Multi-level computer vision algorithm evaluation concept

algorithm (also referred to as test algorithm) and how these image properties can be altered by configuration of the virtual environment. On Level 1 the test data and the correlating ground truths are generated. The *real* video stream is derived from video footage recorded in the real world environment and contains scenes of interest for the test object. To create a correlating *synthetic* stream, the best practise is to record camera position, attitude and altitude together with the real world imagery. Using this data, several synthetic video streams now can be created with diverging image properties using a configurable virtual environment. Both video stream types are accompanied by ground truth which is often created manually via labelling in case of synthetic imagery however it can be directly extracted from the virtual environment. Ground truth refers to additional background information gathered from the real world environment such as the current camera position, position of objects of interests, type, colour or number of objects in the mission scenario. This information helps to improve the quality of the synthetic environment and is necessary to evaluate the performance of the test algorithm (i.e. number of found detections against all possible detections). On Level 2 the images of each video stream are processed using *image descriptors* [14] which produce meta data to be compared. This meta data is dependent to the properties a specific descriptor describes. The difference between two images of the different sources can be numerically computed by comparing the meta data sets of several image descriptors resulting in a list of image properties and their numerical distance. On this level the influence of different configuration parameters of the virtual environment on specific image properties can be extracted. On Level 3 the test algorithm is fed with each video stream and its performance is evaluated against the ground truth generated on level 1. It should be mentioned, since ground truth is algorithm specific, it needs to be adapted to each type of algorithm tested. Likewise each algorithm has its specific performance metrics for evaluation. The computed algorithm performance is then compared between the two image sources, which displays divergence in quality of the synthetic image to achieve real world performance. On level 4 this result is then combined with the image property distances for the specific parameter set of the virtual environment to an entry in the sensitivity matrix. This matrix, completed after several iterations with different virtual environment parameter sets, should allow following conclusions:

- Identification of the virtual environment parameter set closest to the real world results.
- Recognition of the sensitivity of test algorithms performance towards specific image properties. Allowing identification of modelling, texturing, rendering and/or post-processing components influencing these properties, leading to (near) real world test results.
- Providing the validation to use synthetic data to assess the performance of tested algorithm by demonstrating equal performance with both image source types.
- Therefore deriving the most relevant design factors necessary to evaluate tested algorithms may leads to conception of an virtual environment most suitable for proposed application.

Chapter 2 now discusses the implementation of level 2 of the multi level evaluation approach,while Chap. 3 describes the generation of test data. Chapter 4 gives a detailed explanation of conducted experiments as well as their evaluation. In the final chapter achieved results are discussed and next research steps are pointed out.

2   Comparison of Real and Synthetic Footage

On level 2 the comparison of real and synthetic footage is performed enabling a numerical impartial characterization of the image. Several Methods exist to compare images in literature. In the *image synthesis domain* perceptually based image quality metrics are used [15]. Three of these methods are compared in [16]. They focus on comparison in the frequency domain and need image registration to compensate misalignment in modelling qualities. These methods allow detection of small differences in images taking the *human perceptual vision system* into regard. Differing from that, we are interested to find and describe features or image properties on which *image processing algorithms* rely on to extract their useful information. Thus, the conducted investigation for suitable comparison methods leads to the *visual image retrieval domain*, where features are derived by basic image content descriptors from the original image. These features are then compared using distance functions. Therefore *image descriptors* according to the MPEG7 standard for visual content description [14] have been selected as comparison metric, since they are more focused on image content properties then usual image comparison metrics. The MPEG7 standard defines descriptors used for content based image retrieval using audiovisual content as search query to find similar content. These descriptors are intended to be used as standardized header bits of i.e. images to support identification, categorization and filtering [17]. For images and video the content can be described by shape of objects, object size, texture, colour, movement of objects and camera motion. The standard only defines the semantics and the syntax of the descriptors, however the extraction of the features as well as the definition of similarity between images are not defined [17]. Level 2 of our approach uses the Image Descriptor process to apply MPEG-7 descriptors, which can be categorized in colour, texture, object size movement and shape descriptors, on images to compute the descriptions and save them to XML files. Each process uses all currently implemented colour and texture descriptors (see section 2.1 and 2.2). Others such as shape, object size and movement descriptors are not used (however may be considered for later phases) since our test scenario is not containing objects and camera motion is already predefined through test flight meta-data as depicted in Fig. 2.

Each of these image descriptors defines a specific abstract image property which allows categorization of its content while disregarding pixel based similarity. The following chapters provide an overview for each employed descriptor for an detailed discussion please refer to [18].

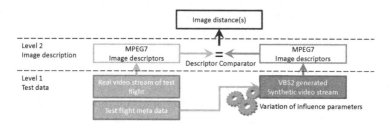

Fig. 2. Implementation of the Multi-level test approach using MPEG7 descriptors

2.1 Colour Descriptors

In image and video retrieval colour is one of the most widely used features. The two used image sources, real and synthetic, are 3 channel RGB colour images. To describe their properties the following four descriptors are utilized:

The *Colour Structure Descriptor* (CSD) expresses the global colour features as well as the local colour structure by using an 8x8 pixel kernel to count contained colours as depicted in Fig. 3. The kernel is sweeping over the image describing the local colour structure at 64 uniformly distributed locations. For images with a resolution greater than 640x480 sub-sampling is used to cover the image uniformly [19].

Therefore the CSD can discern images that have the same global color features but different distribution of colour among the image. Thus it reacts to the quality to textures used in the modelling process and local differences (missing objects, agricultural fields in different vegetation stages) between real world and synthetic images.

The *Scalable Colour Descriptor* (SCD) is basically a global colour histogram in HSV colour space and separates it into 256 bins. The bin values are non-uniformly quantized to an 11-bit value to reduce the size of the descriptor. Haar-Transformation is used to reduce the amount of data even further [18].

The Distance between two colour histograms is calculated by matching Haar co-efficients with the Manhattan distance (L1). Therefore this descriptor evaluates the difference in colour composition between two images. The example in Fig. 4 the colour distribution of three images based on this feature the left and the middle image show higher similarity.

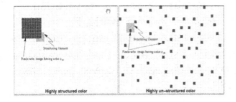

Fig. 3. Example for structured and un-structured colour distribution[14]

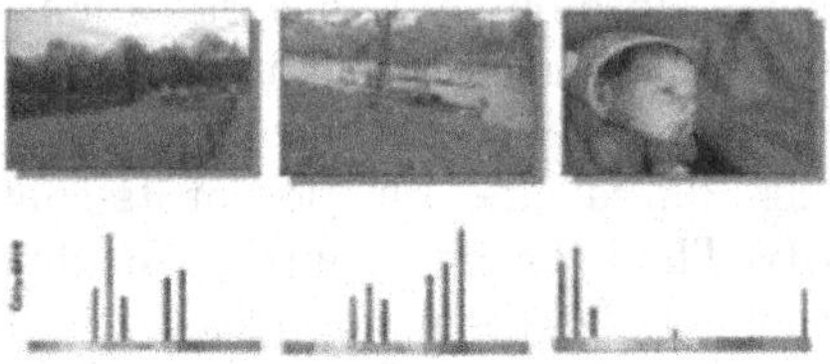

Fig. 4. Three example images and their colour distributions[17]

The resolution invariant *Colour Layout Descriptor* (CLD) presents the spatial distribution of colour in the YCbCr colour space. As depicted in Fig. 5 the descriptor separates the image into 64 blocks (8x8) and computes the average colour for each block as its representative colour. Encoding of the result is performed by zigzag scanning the image and performing a discrete cosine transformation.

Spyro concludes in [21] the CLD to be an effective descriptor for sketch-based image retrieval, content filtering and visualization. In our context this descriptor allows us to compare the sources by spatial differences in colour representation.

The *Dominant Colour Descriptor* (DCD) is a very compact descriptor extracting up to eight colours dominating the images colour composition, the area the color covers in percentage and variance as well as the spatial coherency of dominant colours [21]. The Distance is calculated via the Colour Distance Measure presented in [22], which calculates the Euclidean distance (L2) between the colours identifying the closest related colour and multiplying the result with the difference in percentages for each colour. The DCD allows non-location based comparison of dominant colours and their amount of appearance.

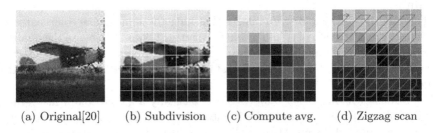

(a) Original[20]   (b) Subdivision   (c) Compute avg.   (d) Zigzag scan

Fig. 5. The four steps of the colour layout descriptor (CLD)

2.2   Texture Descriptors

In the domain of content based image retrieval the term texture is defined as visual patterns with possibly homogeneous properties that result from multiple colours and intensities in an image [17]. These peculiar patterns provide powerful means for similarity matching. In this paper we use two descriptors defined in the MPEG-7 standard, the *Edge Histogram Descriptor* (EHD) and the *Homogeneous Texture descriptor* (HTD).

The scale invariant *Edge Histogram Descriptor* also known as the non-homogeneous texture descriptor captures the spatial distribution of edges similar to the CLD. The Image is divided in 16 equal blocks and edge orientation is calculated for 5 different categories as depicted in Fig. 6 The resulting 80 bins (5 x 16) are useful for image matching of images containing non-homogeneous textures. This Descriptor allows spatial comparison of inhomogeneous textures (edges) distributed among the image.

a) vertical edge   b) horizontal edge   c) 45 degree edge   d) 135 degree edge   e) non-directional edge

Fig. 6. The five types of edges extracted from the edge histogram detector [14]

The *Homogeneous Texture Descriptor* expresses the amount of structure inside an image by directionality, coarseness, regularity of patterns, etc. Since the descriptor focuses on structures it is well suited for similarity matching in texture data bases or in general of repetitive patterns in images. The information is calculated by converting the image into the frequency domain and separating the resulting frequency image into 30 different channels as depicted in Fig. 7. For each channel the energy and energy deviation are calculated. The conversion in the frequency domain introduces the requirement of an image of at least 128 x 128 pixel for the HTD being able to be computed.

2.3   Descriptor Comparator

The major task of the *Descriptor Comparator* in Fig. 2 is to compare real and synthetic image pairs using the six previous mentioned descriptors. The DCD distance metric has been implemented according to the example of [22], while for all other descriptors the implementation of the Low level feature extraction library is used [23]. This Library is adapted from the XM reference software [24]. Additionally a *total distance* measure D(A,B) is introduced. This measure emphasizes whether only one or more descriptors display high similarity and is computed by taking the root of the sum of the square distance dx for each descriptor:

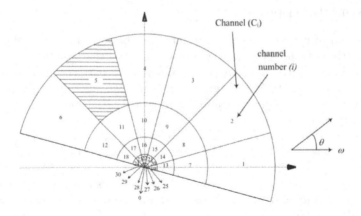

Fig. 7. Segmentation of the frequency domain according to displayed layout for feature extraction [14]

$$D\left(A,B\right) = \sqrt{\sum\nolimits_{1 \leq x \leq 6} d_x\left(A,B\right)^2} \tag{1}$$

3   Test Data Generation

To test this approach test flights were conducted to generate real world test data. In our test scenario an unmanned aerial vehicle is reconnoitring a given area on the test flight site of the University of the Bundeswehr Munich. The utilized UAV technology demonstrator *Graphite*, an electric motor glider is equipped with autopilot, processing modules and two cameras, with one camera is facing downwards while the other has a first person view as depicted in Figure 8. Further technical details of the demonstrator can be found in [25].

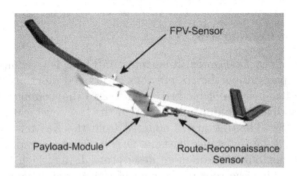

Fig. 8. The UAV technology demonstrator graphite and its payload [25]

The reconnaissance sensor has a resolution of 1920x1080 at 30Hz. The images are directly stored onboard the aircraft in full quality and resolution using a data distributed architecture (DDS) [26]. The processing architecture additionally allows recording of the current aircraft attitude, velocities, accelerations, altitude and location in sync to the image recording. The lens has a horizontal field of view of 75. The test flight recordings used in this paper where con-ducted on September 2012 at dawn about 6:40 am CET. The weather conditions where sunny with partial overcast. The experiment was conducted this early due to increased GPS performance.

In Fig. 9 the route of the UAV is depicted in red. Test flight was performed over terrain that can be categorized in different types as debris, infrastructure, vegetation and buildings. Each category is related to aerial images of varying complexity (i.e. fields have low complexity) and therefore are expected to yield differing distance measures. Therefore the evaluation will take these categories in consideration.

To generate the corresponding synthetic imagery, we use virtual battle space 2 (VBS2) from bohemia simulation [7]. The computer graphics rendering is performed via the *Virtual Reality 3* Engine based on the DirectX 9 (Shader Model 3) rendering pipeline. Summarized this pipeline first computes the scene as wire frame model from the cameras perspective. Afterwards an illumination model is applied to calculate the lighting of the Scene followed by employment of textures, shadow- and mapping techniques to increase the graphical quality before providing the image to the output device (a more detailed description can be found in [27]).

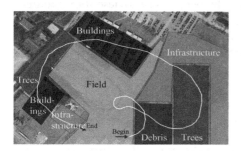

Fig. 9. Test scenario location, flight route and terrain categories

Fig. 10. University of the Bundeswehr Munich. Left: Modelled terrain database. Right: Aerial image.

A geo-referenced terrain database of the test flight environment has been modelled including buildings, fences and vegetation. The terrain database was generated using aerial images with a resolution of 0.2m/pixel and a digital surface model (DSM) with a grid resolution of 25m. The resulting database has a ground texture resolution of 1m/pixel and a grid spacing of 7.32 m. As commonly done, the buildings wire frame models were modelled using construction blueprints, and textured using rectified photographs and areal imagery [28]. The buildings were placed using the underlying ground texture as template. The accuracy of the database was tested by several reference points. Terrain size was fixed to 15 x 15 km to cope the diminishing accuracy of the flat earth model used in the virtual environment at large terrains. A comparison between terrain database and real world is depicted in Fig. 10.

Finally a mission scenario is created within the virtual environment to calibrate the terrain database towards the flight recordings. Additionally a model of the aircraft is used to simulate the aircraft shadow. A birds-eye view camera with 75 horizontal FOV (same as real camera) is attached to the model. Weather and time are set accordingly to produce similar lighting conditions using the engines hemispherical ambient lighting model. Different synthetic data streams are generated by changing the rendering configuration. Table 1 presents the eight different data sets and corresponding configuration parameters. The data sets have been named after the analysed configuration parameter. The *default* dataset is the basis of this evaluation. Here all configuration parameters have been set to the highest possible value, while high dynamic rendering has been disabled. The Output Resolution is set to 1920x1080 to correlate with the real world stream. The configuration parameter *texture detail* sets the quality of object and terrain textures. Low settings lead to blurry textures. The quality of objects and the line of sight distance where the level of detail (LOD) of an object is increased is set with the *object detail* parameter. This parameter does not affect buildings modelled in this terrain database since only one LOD has been defined. *Screen Space Ambient Occlusion* (SSAO) [29] is a global illumination technique approximating the object exposition to a light source dependent on its occlusion by other objects. To measure the behaviour the descriptors to images missing high frequencies/sharp and crisp details the *render resolution* (low RR) has been reduced to 50% (960x480). After rendering, the engine resizes the image back to the output resolution of 1080.

Table 1. List of synthetic image data sets and their configuration. Most parameters can be configured from highest (5) to lowest (1) quality. 0 indicates a disabled feature. Settings different from *default* are highlighted in bold.

Synthetic Image Datasets	Virtual Environment Parameters				
	Texture Detail	Object Detail	SSAO	Render-Resolution	HDR Quality
Low Render-Resolution	5	5	5	**540**	0
Default	5	5	5	1080	0
Low Texture	**1**	5	5	1080	0
Low Object	5	**1**	5	1080	0
No SSAO	5	5	**0**	1080	0
HDR	5	5	5	1080	**5**
No Objects	5	**0**	5	1080	0

Precision of high dynamic range (HDR) lighting can be set via the *HDR Quality* parameter. For each setting a correlating image stream was generated. For the generation of stream *No Object* all 3D-Objects on the terrain database have been removed, leaving only the surface model textured with aerial imagery.

4 Experiments

In a first step recorded meta data is replayed in the synthetic environment to achieve a corresponding virtual image stream. Now as depicted in Fig. 2 both streams are provided to the MPEG7 image descriptor process. Before that, the video streams are converted into image datasets to simplify the off-line processing and feature computation. The descriptors for these datasets are computed and saved in XML format. Now the descriptor comparator process is used to manually define the exact counterparts of the real world images.

After definition of image pairs the distance between the pairs is computed according to Chap. 2.3. Each evaluation consists of 1000 image pairs compared by MPEG7 descriptors. Therefore the results for each image dataset are statistically evaluated by computing the arithmetic mean distance of all descriptors per real world-synthetic result data set. The dispersion is represented using standard deviation . The measures indicate higher similarity with lower values, comparing the same image will result in the distance 0. Before evaluating a real video stream against its synthetic counterpart, real images of different similarity are compared against each other to demonstrate a reference values for high and low correlations. The chronologic order of images from the real world data set *real* depicted in Fig. 11 is given from reference frame t (recorded at 30Hz). The Fig. 11c) is the sub-sequent frame, while Fig. 11a) has a distance of 10 frames to Fig. 11b). The last Fig. 11d) was shot 22.033 seconds prior to t. The results listed in Tab. 2 depict descriptor values for high correlation in case of images with high overlap and low correlation for images with no overlap. As shown, already small spatial changes can result in high differences for descriptors taking the image layout into regard (CLD, EHD). The spatial independent descriptors CSD, SCD, DCD and HTD show only small differences in this case. The measure D(A,B) provides an overall distance indication. Note that values above 1 are possible but indicate low correlation.

Table 2. Real world data set images compared to (comp. to) each other demonstrating example results for high (1st and 2nd row) and low (3rd row) correlation

Image Pairs (Figure 11)	D(A, B)	CSD	SCD	CLD	DCD	HTD	EHD
t comp. to t+1	0.10	0.02	0.01	0.06	0	0.01	0.08
t comp. to t+10	0.49	0.05	0.03	0.45	0	0.03	0.18
t comp. to t-668	1.03	0.39	0.13	0.52	0.70	0.18	0.32

| (a) t+10 | (b) t | (c) t+1 | (d) t-668 |

Fig. 11. Example Images of the real world image dataset *real* dependent to reference frame t (30 Hz)

Now we compare the virtual dataset *default* against the real world data set (Fig. 12). The columns indicate the arithmetic mean of 647 compared image pairs, which is also indicated in white inside the column. The standard deviation is depicted by black error indicators. $D(A,B)$ as well as all specific descriptors show that while similarity exists a significant distance is measured. Especially the standard deviation value of DCD depicts that the distance is varying vastly over the duration of the test flight.

The results are now explained using significant sample images in Fig. 13. The image pair Fig. 13ab) depicts a scene of low complexity from the terrain category *field*. The simulated image consists of the ground texture, the overlaid surface texture and a small amount of vegetation objects. The race track is not modelled but contained in the background texture. Numerical results of aforementioned image pair is shown in Tab. 3 attest high correlation with a total distance $D(A,B)$ of 0.41. In both images the grass fields are the main objects providing uniformly coloured regions leading to a low CSD distance, since it is measuring the structure of colour in the colour distribution.

After examining the sample for a high correlation the comparison of the image pair Fig. 13cd) is discussed. These images show the same location of a highly complex scene depicting a concrete surface accompanied by a thick mixed forest. Such a scene typically puts high demand on a virtual environment. The first visible difference is the over exposed nature of the real image stemming from an automatic aperture in the camera. Secondly the forest in September is already

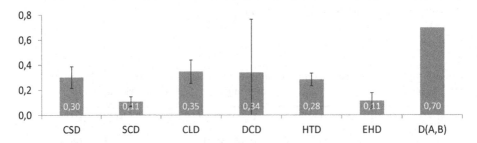

Fig. 12. Comparison of synthetic data set default against data set real. The error indicators display the standard deviation.

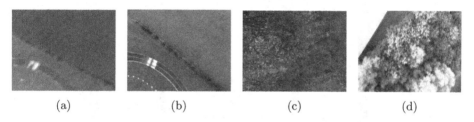

(a)   (b)   (c)   (d)

Fig. 13. Example Image Pairs representing good (a & b) and bad (c & d) correlation of default synthetic images (left) and real world images (right)

changing colours, which is not considered in the terrain database. Additionally modelling misalignments (big trees, covering the concrete surface underneath) increase the discrepancy in this sample. These three effects lead to poor performance in all colour based descriptors. Measured HTD distance can simply be explained by the absence of the concrete surface and its homogeneous pattern in Fig. 13c). Likewise the missing boundaries of aforementioned surface lead to 0.19 in EHD distance. Thus these examples demonstrate the dependency of comparison results to texture, alignment, modelling and camera effects.

The following investigation uses the six different synthetic data streams (Tab. 1) to identify the influence of rendering engine settings to the comparison. Terrain modelling, scenario settings and camera model remain unchanged. Comparison results of data set *default* with data set *real* are subtracted of the following comparison to emphasize the differences. Thus negative values yield higher correlation, and positive values lower correlation. The scale has been scaled to distance difference in percentage. The results in Fig. 14 show the generally low influence of rendering engine settings to image properties analysed by used descriptors. Maximum influence appears by disabling *SSAO* leading to a 4.1 percent lower DCD distance, due to more isochromatic textures (less shading applied). Other interesting effects are the investigations of *low render resolution*. Due to reduced resolution and post-render resizing the textures should be of low frequency letting the HTD benefit. Marginal changes of HTD distance demonstrate that homogeneous patterns in the synthetic stream are of lower frequency than 360Hz employing the Nyquist-Shannon sampling theorem [30]:

$$f_{max} = \frac{ImageWidth}{2} \tag{2}$$

Table 3. Sample comparisons between images of dataset *real* and synthetic dataset *default*, showing high correlation (1st row) and low/no correlation (2nd row)

Image Pairs (Figure 13)	D(A, B)	CSD	SCD	CLD	DCD	HTD	EHD
13a) comp. to 13b)	0.41	0.18	0.09	0.25	0.18	0.09	0.15
13c) comp. to 13d)	0.99	0.57	0.18	0.55	0.44	0.31	0.19

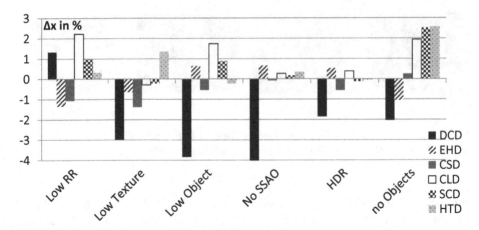

Fig. 14. Results of several synthetic-real world data set comparisons using data set default as reference. This diagram shows the influence of rendering engine settings in percentage.

Other datasets as *Low Texture* or *Low Object* where expected to influence by comparison by reducing the quality of textures and models. Reduced complexity allows the DCD to lower its distance. Other descriptors such as HTD and CSD react to the low texture quality differently. While the structure is becoming more similar by using blurred textures the HTD has more difficulties finding similar patterns (patterns in ground and object textures are blurred). Utilizing *HDR lighting* did not yield significant changes in the measurement. Ultimately the *no Objects* data set may be the most interesting due to producing the most particular changes of all datasets. First it needs to be mentioned that the overall distance D(A,B) is almost identical to the *default* data set (+0.1%) with significantly less standard deviation (-33%). Thus meaning a scene with 3D-objects can correlate more with real world images, in the case models with correct textures, placement and dimensions are used. Therefore models can also introduce higher distances than without any 3D-objects at all, which eventually discourages the use of geo-typical models for this kind of investigation.

Aforementioned results showed that distance measurements using MPEG-7 descriptors is dependent to the complexity of the scene, therefore the comparison of *default* with *real* is segmented in the terrain categories introduced in Figure 9. The results of this investigation are depictured in Fig. 15 confirming the dependency of measurement distance to terrain categories. Since Scenes containing fields are of low complexity and mostly isochromatic the correlation between real world fields and their synthetic counterpart is high. The next categories with high similarity are debris and infrastructure. Here usually complexity (number of object) is low as well while these two categories have more prominent texture features. While debris textures are of non-homogeneous irregular nature, infrastructure textures are homogeneous with high gradient edges (street boundaries). These three categories show small standard deviation values for almost all descriptors, with the highly colour and colour diversity dependent DCD being an exception. High complexity scenes such as buildings are dependent on correct alignment of objects and textures (CLD) as well as employment of colour true, geo-specific textures (HTD, DCD, EHD). Scenes containing trees suffer under the consequences of geo-typical modelling (as used in this terrain map), and seasonal based colour differences.

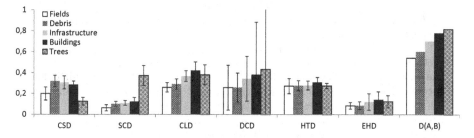

Fig. 15. Comparison of synthetic data set default against data set real, segmented into categories of terrain. The error indicators display the standard deviation.

5   Conclusions and Future Work

Employing MPEG-7 descriptors allows measurement of disparity between real world and synthetically generated image data sets. The presented approach has been investigated using aerial reconnaissance as use case. The differences in appearance regarding colour and texture could be numerically measured and correlated to image properties / rendering properties. Several interesting results have been identified; for example usage of geo-typical objects can reduce the similarity in relation to use no objects at all. Therefore, careful consideration in which objects to model should be taken. One of the next steps will be employment of a common computer vision algorithm on tested datasets. It is important to point out that the MPEG-7 distance measurements do not indicate the performance of computer vision algorithms on the data sets, but will help to identify which properties of the image the algorithm is sensitive to. Thus this method enables identification of weighing values for specific image properties, which influence the performance of computer vision algorithms. Furthermore we intend to apply changes to the modelled terrain database and analyse the improvements using acquired results as a priority list. Additionally the introduction of additional image descriptors measuring features such as spatial distribution of gradients or luminance would complete the image comparison method.

References

1. Erman, A.: AWARE: Platform for Autonomous Self-Deploying and Operation of Wireless Sensor-Actuator Networks Cooperating with AeRial ObjEcts. In: Proceedings of IEEE International... (2007)
2. Ollero, A., Lacroix, S.: Multiple eyes in the skies: architecture and perception issues in the COMETS unmanned air vehicles project. Robotics & ..., 46–57 (June 2005)
3. Hummel, G., Russ, M., Stütz, P., Soldatos, J., Rossi, L., Knape, T., Utasi, Á., Kovács, L., Szirányi, T., Doulaverakis, C., Kompatsiaris, I.: Intelligent Multi Sensor Fusion System for Advanced Situation Awareness in Urban Environments. In: Aschenbruck, N., Martini, P., Meier, M., Tölle, J. (eds.) Future Security. CCIS, vol. 318, pp. 93–104. Springer, Heidelberg (2012)
4. Szeliski, R.: Computer vision: algorithms and applications (2011)
5. Hummel, G., Stütz, P.: Conceptual design of a simulation test bed for ad-hoc sensor networks based on a serious gaming environment. In: International Training and Education Conference 2011, Cologne (2011)
6. Ferwerda, J.: Three varieties of realism in computer graphics. Proceedings SPIE Human Vision and Electronic... SPIE 5007, pp. 290–297 (2003)
7. Morrison, P.: White Paper: VBS2 Release Version 2.0. Technical report, Bohemia Interactive Australia, Nelson Bay, Australia (2012)
8. Hummel, G., Kovács, L., Stütz, P., Szirányi, T.: Data Simulation and Testing of Visual Algorithms in Synthetic Environments for Security Sensor Networks. In: Aschenbruck, N., Martini, P., Meier, M., Tölle, J. (eds.) Future Security 2012. CCIS, vol. 318, pp. 212–215. Springer, Heidelberg (2012)
9. Hummel, G., Smirnov, D., Kronenberg, A.: Prototyping and training of computer vision algorithms in a synthetic UAV mission test bed. In: 52nd Aerospace Sciences Meeting, pp. 1–10 (2014)
10. Russ, M., Stutz, P.: Airborne sensor and perception management: A conceptual approach for surveillance UAS. In: 2012 15th ... Information Fusion (FUSION), pp. 2444–2451 (2012)
11. Nentwig, M., Miegler, M., Stamminger, M.: Concerning the applicability of computer graphics for the evaluation of image processing algorithms. In: 2012 IEEE International Conference on Vehicular Electronics and Safety (ICVES 2012), pp. 205–210 (July 2012)
12. Nentwig, M., Stamminger, M.: Hardware-in-the-loop testing of computer vision based driver assistance systems. In: Intelligent Vehicles Symposium (IV... (Iv)), pp. 339–344 (2011)
13. Hiblot, N., Gruyer, D.: Pro-SiVIC and ROADS. A Software suite for sensors simulation and virtual prototyping of ADAS. In: Proceedings of DSC, pp. 277–288 (2010)
14. Yamada, A., Pickering, M., Jeannin, S.: Text of 15938-3/FCD Information Technology–Multimedia Content Description Interface–Part 3 Visual. Tech. Rep. (2000)
15. Chalmers, A., McNamara, A., Daly, S.: Image quality metrics (July 2000)
16. Rushmeier, H., Ward, G., Piatko, C.: Comparing real and synthetic images: Some ideas about metrics. Rendering Techniques' ... (1995)
17. Sikora, T.: The MPEG-7 visual standard for content description-an overview. IEEE ... Circuits and Systems for Video Technology 11(6), 696–702 (2001)
18. Manjunath, B., Ohm, J.R., Vasudevan, V., Yamada, A.: Color and texture descriptors. IEEE Transactions on Circuits and Systems for Video Technology 11(6), 703–715 (2001)

19. Buturovic, A.: MPEG 7 Color Structure Descriptor for visual information retrieval project VizIR 1. In: Interface, pp. 7–8 (2005)
20. Wang, J., Li, J.L.J., Wiederhold, G.: SIMPLIcity: semantics-sensitive integrated matching for picture libraries. IEEE Transactions on Pattern Analysis and Machine Intelligence 23 (2001)
21. Spyrou, E., Tolias, G., Mylonas, P., Avrithis, Y.: Concept detection and keyframe extraction using a visual thesaurus. Multimedia Tools and Applications 41(3), 337–373 (2008)
22. Ma, W.Y., Deng, Y., Manjunath, B.S.: Tools for texture / color based search of images (1997)
23. Bastan, M., Cam, H., Gudukbay, U., Ulusoy, O.: Bilvideo-7: an MPEG-7-compatible video indexing and retrieval system. IEEE MultiMedia, 62–73 (2010)
24. ISO/IEC: Information technology – Multimedia content description interface –. Part 6: Reference software 15938-6:20 (2003)
25. Böhm, F., Schulte, A.: UAV Autonomy Research–Challenges and advantages of a fully distributed system architecture. In: International Telemetering Conference, ITC 2012, pp. 1–10 (2012)
26. Boehm, F., Schulte, A.: Scalable COTS Based Data Processing and Distribution Architecture for UAV Technology Demonstrators. In: European Telemetry and Test Conference, ETC 2012... (2012)
27. Bender, M., Brill, M.: Computergrafik. Hanser (2003)
28. Hanke, B.: 3D-Modellierung des Geländes der UniBwM für einen UAV Simulator. Bachelorthesis, University of the german federal armed forces (2013)
29. Bavoil, L., Sainz, M.: Screen space ambient occlusion. NVIDIA Developer Information (2008), http://developer.download.nvidia.com/SDK/10.5/direct3d/ Source/ScreenSpaceAO/doc/ScreenSpaceAO.pdf
30. Shannon, C.: Communication in the presence of noise. Proceedings of the IRE 86(2), 447–457 (1949)

Plume Tracking by a Self-stabilized Group of Micro Aerial Vehicles*

Martin Saska, Jan Langr, and Libor Přeučil

Dept. of Cybernetics, Czech Technical University in Prague
{saskam1,kaslzden}@fel.cvut.cz, preucil@labe.felk.cvut.cz
http://imr.felk.cvut.cz/

Abstract. A cooperative odor plume tracking approach designed for use with groups of micro-scale, autonomous helicopters in GNSS-denied environment is proposed in this paper. The designed method is based on a particle swarm optimization enhanced for efficient and fast cooperative searching for gas sources. The possibility of MAVs deployment in GNSS-denied environment is enabled by employed visual relative localization using onboard monocular cameras and identification patterns. In addition to constraints given by the relative localization (necessity of direct visibility and limited range of the system), MAV motion constraints and non-colliding multi-robot coordination are satisfied in the method. The developed method has been verified using a numerical model of smoke plume in various simulations and real experiments with a fleet of MAVs.

Keywords: chemical plume tracking, micro aerial vehicles, swarm intelligence, visual relative localization.

1 Introduction

Recent progress in Micro Aerial Vehicle (MAV) platforms and light-weight gas detectors allows us to consider utilization of multi-MAV systems driven by decentralized swarm principles for efficient localization of gas sources. Employment of simple swarm rules enables exploitation of swarm knowledge (information simultaneously gained by multiple MAVs equipped with on-board sensors) and to solve the given task much more efficiently than using a single, even better equipped, aerial vehicle. The decentralized swarm intelligent based approach significantly increases system robustness, mainly the tolerance to failures of team members, and substantially reduces communication requirements. Minimizing communication demands stands important for large MAV groups due to generally limited bandwidth and in cases where communication is denied, not allowed, or at presence of jamming. The proposed swarm stabilization approach relies on an onboard visual relative localization of team members and therefore the system is independent of external global positioning systems. This is beneficial in environments with limited or spoiled GNSS signals (forests, caves, urban and indoor

---

* This work was supported by GAČR under postdoc grant of Martin Saska no. P103-12/P756.

J. Hodicky (Ed.): MESAS 2014, LNCS 8906, pp. 44–55, 2014.

environment). Besides, under certain conditions the precision and reliability of GNSS is insufficient for stabilization of compact MAV groups. In our approach, the swarm as a whole is driven by the measured properties of the environment. It tracks the odor plume by a Particle Swarm Optimization (PSO) technique, while the mutual coordination between the swarm entities is ensured by the relative visual localization. Therefore, knowledge about the exact global position of swarm members is not necessary in this scenario. In the approach, each MAV is represented by one PSO particle and the function being optimized by the PSO is considered as the gas plume concentration. In the gas plume tracking, the highest concentration is usually near the source of the gas, in which we are interested in. The designed method is ready for use in numerous applications, such as localization of source of poisonous gases, pollutants, or fires; all in outdoor and indoor.

Various approaches for odor plume tracking and its source localization are well studied in robotics and artificial intelligent oriented fields. In literature, one can find plenty of techniques designed for smart stationary sensory nodes [4], for single mobile ground robots [7], [3], [12], for swarms of ground vehicles [8], [13], for aerial vehicles [1], [2] and even for swarms of aerial vehicles [11], which is the most related to this paper. The presented approach goes beyond these works mainly in the possibility of deploying of closely cooperating teams of MAVs based on onboard sensors only. Our swarming approach takes into consideration real-world limitations of MAV swarms, which is in contrast with the state-of-the-art methods, where these constraints given by real deployment of multi-MAV systems are usually omitted, since these works are often designed for holonomic dimensionless particles.

2 Particle Swarm Optimization

Let us first briefly describe the basic PSO method. The PSO technique is an optimization method developed for finding a global optima of nonlinear functions [5]. The method applies the approach of problem solving in groups, which is especially appealing for the deployment of cooperative swarms of MAVs. In PSO, each solution represents a point in multidimensional space (3D workspace of MAVs in our case). The solution is called "particle" and the group of particles (population) is called "swarm".

PSO algorithm uses two kinds of information, which is available to all particles, to achieve the global convergence. 1) Each particle knows its own experience - the best state found so far by the particular PSO swarm member. 2) A social knowledge is shared within the swarm - the best state found so far by any particle of the swarm.

In i-th PSO iteration, each particle is represented as a position vector $\mathbf{x}_i$ (pose of the corresponding MAV in our case) and has a corresponding instantaneous velocity vector $\mathbf{v}_i$ (it does not match to MAV velocity, which is controlled by a trajectory tracking mechanism separately). In each iteration, a velocity update rule is applied on each particle in the swarm as follows:

$$\mathbf{v}_{i+1} = w\mathbf{v}_i + c_1 r_1 (\mathbf{p} - \mathbf{x}_i) + c_2 r_2 (\mathbf{g} - \mathbf{x}_i). \tag{1}$$

The social knowledge (position of the best solution found so far - referred to as a *global best*) is denoted as $\mathbf{g}$ and the individual experience (position of the best solution found by the particular particle - referred to as an *individual best*) is denoted as $\mathbf{p}$. The parameter w is called inertia weight and during the optimization decreases linearly from w_{start} to w_{end}. The constance c_1 and c_2 are weights that influence preference of particles' own experience and the social knowledge. Variables r_j, where $j = 1, 2$, introduce a desired uncertainty into the optimization process, which is crucial for escaping from local extremes, and are obtained as

$$r_j = \begin{pmatrix} r_{j1} & 0 & 0 \\ 0 & \ddots & 0 \\ 0 & 0 & r_{jD} \end{pmatrix}, \tag{2}$$

where r_{jk}, $j = 1, 2$, $k = 1 \ldots D$, are random numbers from a uniform distribution between 0 and 1. D is dimension of the problem being optimized, in our case $D = 3$ since we consider MAVs flying in 3D space.

If any component of $\mathbf{v}_{i+1}$ is less than a threshold $-V_{max}$ or greater than $+V_{max}$ after applying the velocity update rule, the corresponding value is replaced by $-V_{max}$ or $+V_{max}$, respectively. Finally, a position update rule is applied in each PSO iteration for all particles:

$$\mathbf{x}_{i+1} = \mathbf{x}_i + \mathbf{v}_{i+1}. \tag{3}$$

3   PSO Algorithm Adapted for Odor Plume Tracking

Let us now highlight the main differences of the proposed tangible PSO algorithm, in which each PSO particle represents a real MAV, with the basic PSO using holonomic dimensionless particles. In the tangible PSO, we deal with the following challenges:

- Collision avoidance within the MAV swarm and between MAVs and the environment
- MAV motion constraints specified by the applied controller
- Fitness function evaluated based on measurement of smoke concentration in current position
- Relative localization constraints influencing allowed mutual positions of MAVs
- Unknown global position of MAVs, which influences knowledge of relative position of best solutions (position of MAVs) found so far

All these aspects negatively influence the performance of the PSO engine as they introduce additional constraints to the given problem. Clearly, the necessity of collision avoidance within MAV group limits the free space in which the PSO particles may search for higher smoke concentration. The collision avoidance is influenced by the size of the robots, but also by the mutual effects caused by airflow of MAV propellers.

Regarding the MAV motion constraints, we rely on trajectory tracking approach described in [6], but any available MAV control method can be used. The performance of the applied method has to be considered in the motion planning and swarm coordination to ensure that given PSO locations are reachable by the real system.

The fitness function, which is the core of the PSO technique, enables to select the best solutions found so far (the *global best*) and the *individual best*). In this application, it may be simply obtained as the gas concentration measured by onboard sensors of MAVs. Such an approach has one important drawback that has to be considered in the method design. The measurement of gas concentration by simple light-weight sensors is affected by strong uncertainties and measurement error. Beside the imprecise sensor ability of light-weight MAVs, the plume shape is dynamically changing upon to wind condition and air turbulences appearing close to the gas source that we are looking for. In addition to this dynamics of the optimization problem (the cost function changes during the optimization process), the swarm of MAVs itself significantly influences the measured plume to be tracked and therefore the PSO optimization methods influences the function being optimized. This behaviour may not be observed in standard PSO and it brings another challenging aspect of the proposed method.

The algorithm performance is most significantly affected by the issues related to the relative localization, which is employed for swarm stabilization and control (see Fig. 1 and 2 for comparison of performance of the method taking into account the constraints of relative localization and a method considering utilization of a global localization without any constraints). During the optimization, each MAV needs to be in a visual contact (in range of the onboard visual relative localization system) with at least one neighbor to ensure that its relative position may be shared within the swarm. The possibility of such a relative localization is crucial for sharing information on position of the global best location (potion of an MAV in which the best fitness function was found so far). In case the new *global best* (the highest gas concentration found so far) is obtained, the relative position of this location is propagated through the swarm via the relative localization linkages. Therefore, all swarm members have to be connected together all the time during the mission. Once the information on position of the *global best* is updated, each swarm member may guess on vector to this position from its position in future based on the dead-reckoning. Similarly, each swarm member can remember position in which its *individual best* was obtained. The dead-reckoning of MAVs (odometry) is achieved by integration of optical flow from down-looking camera via the PX4 Flow Cam Optical Flow Sensor and by data from IMU (for further details on this method and related literature see our web http://imr.felk.cvut.cz/Swarm/Swarm). Such an approach introduces an additional cumulative error of the dead reckoning, but since the individual and global best positions are usually regularly updated in the PSO process, this effect may be neglected as was observed in experiments with real MAVs.

3.1 Smoke Source Location Prediction

Using the advantage of closely cooperating swarm of multiple MAVs equipped with onboard sensors, the position of the global maximum (the location of gas source) can be predicted and used for faster convergence of the algorithm. The most straightforward approach is to employ current knowledge of gas concentration simultaneously measured by several MAVs and to compute gradient of the gas concentration, which can be added simply added to PSO rule as the $s_{estimate}$ in eq. (5). The main disadvantage of this approach is necessity to communicate the obtain measurements and also the relative positions of all team members in each PSO step.

The approach proposed here, allows us to estimate the gas source location using the stored history of global knowledge achieved during the optimization process. The proposed algorithm uses the last n values of the *global best*. It significantly increases robustness of the searching for the gas source location, which may be negatively influenced by the above mentioned dynamics of the source plume. Such an approach is not necessary if using classical PSO method with dimensionless particles that may passively search in the environment without direct influencing of the fitness function. But in the proposed tangible PSO, it enables to deal with the strong disturbances and rapidly changing shape of the gas plume, which is considered as the employed fitness function.

The vector pointing towards the estimated smoke source location, which takes into account the history of the progress of the *global best*, can be then obtained as:

$$\mathbf{s}_{estimate} = \mathbf{g}_1 + \frac{\mathbf{g}_1 - \mathbf{g}_n}{|\mathbf{g}_1 - \mathbf{g}_n|}, \tag{4}$$

where subscript 1 denotes the newest global best position. Taking into account the longer history of the global knowledge, the disturbances in gas concentration measurement may be filtered out, which results in faster convergence, as shown in the experimental part.

The PSO algorithm is then modified to contain the predicted location of the smoke source as:

$$\mathbf{v}_{i+1} = w \cdot \mathbf{v}_i + c_1 \cdot r_1 \cdot (\mathbf{p} - \mathbf{x}_i) + c_2 \cdot r_2 \cdot (\mathbf{g} - \mathbf{x}_i) + c_3 \cdot r_3 \cdot (\mathbf{s}_{estimate} - \mathbf{x}_i). \tag{5}$$

3.2 Obstacle Avoidance and Relative Localization Constraints

As mentioned above, the key aspects that may differentiate the tangible PSO with real MAVs from the classical PSO with dimensionless particles are the collision avoidance and constraints given by the visual relative localization. For simplification of the motion coordination of multi-MAV team, we suppose that only one MAV is allowed to move at the same moment. Such an approach is advantageous due to minimal communication required between the team members. In addition, only two simple procedures has to be done in each PSO step to ensure feasibility of MAV movement:

- To ensure that the new position of MAV obtained by applying the PSO rules is feasible (it is not colliding with neighbouring MAVs, it is in a safety distance from all whirlwinds caused by propellers, it does not influence other MAVs by its own propellers, it does not break the visual localization - it is still in range of the localization sensors of neighbours and it keeps the required number of neighbours in range of its own sensor of relative localization)
- To find a trajectory to the new proposed location, which is feasible for the trajectory tracking. Each point on this trajectory must respect the same constraints as the proposed new position of MAV (described in brackets in the first item of this list).

Let us now describe a basic structure of the overall PSO based algorithm proposed for cooperative plume tracking by closely cooperating MAVs. In each PSO iteration, each MAV consequently proceeds the following procedure:

1. Apply PSO updates rules, equations (5) and (3) to obtain new desired position based on current state of the particular MAV, social knowledge (position of *global best*) and its individual experience (position of *individual best*).
2. If the new position is infeasible (there is a collision or the visual relative localization is interrupted in this position), shorten the vector obtained by the velocity update rule, eq. (5), in such a way that the new position is feasible and it is as close as possible to the position proposed by the PSO rules.
3. Find a collision free trajectory to reach the new feasible position. Here, any trajectory planning approach satisfying constraints of the trajectory tracking method from [6] can be employed. For the verification experiments presented in section 4, we have employed trajectory planning originally designed by our team for control of a virtual leader of a formation of MAVs [10].
4. Follow the trajectory using the method presented in [6].
5. Regularly check the range of localization sensors and if the limit is reached stop your motion.
6. Make a measurement of the gas concentration in the new reached location.
7. If the measured concentration exceeds the value obtained in the current individual best location, remember this position as your new *individual best*.
8. If the measured concentration exceeds the value obtained in the current global best location, send a notice to all team members that a new *global best* was found.
9. Send a message to the next MAV in the ring that it may start its movement and wait for a permit to continue with the next PSO iteration. Once the permission is received, start again with point (1).

It is obvious that the necessity of moving MAVs one by one significantly increases the overall time needed for the source plume tracking. We have presented an approach that enables simultaneous swarm control, and therefore faster achievement of the desired equilibrium, in [9], but this method is hard to be decentralized and it requires more intensive communication between the swarm members.

4   Experimental Results

The main purpose of simulations presented in Fig. 1 and 2 is to verify functionality of the proposed algorithm, to show its convergence into the source smoke and to present influence of the collision avoidance ability and the constraints given by the visual relative localization on the algorithm performance. In the first basic simulations in Fig. 1, MAVs are considered as dimensionless particles that cannot collide with each other and constraints of the relative localization are not considered during the optimization. The snapshots of the simulation are taken after 1st, 12th and 18th PSO iteration. One can see that the entire swarm is located in the proximity of the gas source after the 18th PSO iteration.

The second simulation shows performance of the complete system with the collision avoidance and the constraints of visual relative localization considered in the optimization process. Although the convergence of the algorithm is significantly slower than in the previous experiment (snapshots are taken after 3rd, 8th, 29th PSO iteration), the swarm also achieved proximity of the gas source relatively fast.

The aim of the experiment presented in Fig. 3 is to verify the ability of the onboard vision system to keep the relative localization linkages between the neighboring MAVs, if following trajectories between states found by the proposed tangible PSO algorithm. In the experiment, the entire MAV group is represented by the PSO swarm with fitness function corresponding to a virtual concentration of a simulated smoke plume. The same actual map of the smoke concentration in the 3D workspace is used for planning of the movement of all MAVs. Each PSO rule is decomposed to independent motion primitives of separate helicopters in the experiment as suggested in the sketch of the method presented in section 3.2. MAVs are subsequently moved into new positions required by the PSO process. In each subsequent movement, a quadrocopter approaches into the new location, while the remaining robots keep constant pose and only their Yaw angle is changed to track the moving MAV and to realize the required relative localization. The control feedback of MAVs in this experiment is realized by the Vicon motion capture system, which is also used as a ground truth for evaluation of the performance of the relative localization system in real-flight conditions. The trajectories, obtained by the proposed PSO based method prior this experiment, satisfy constraints given by the range of the relative localization, viewing angle of the on-board cameras, mutual MAVs heading and movement constraints during the deployment of the system. Snapshots from the experiment together with pictures taken at the same moment by the onboard cameras employed for the

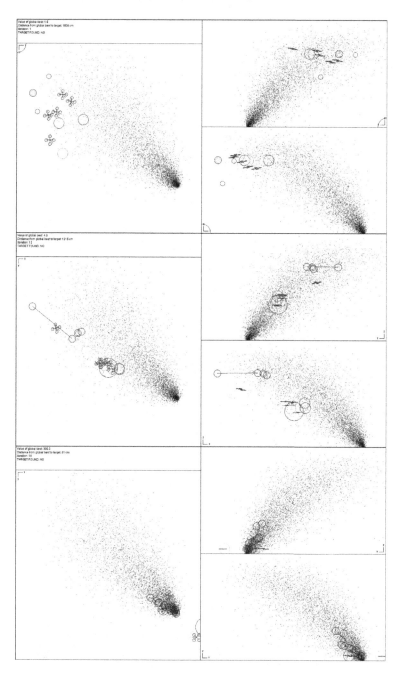

Fig. 1. Simulation of cooperative tracking of smoke plume to find its source by a closely cooperating swarm. Particles are considered as dimensionless and constraints of the relative localization are not considered. In each snapshot of the simulation, three different views are shown (x-y plane, z-y plane and z-x plane).

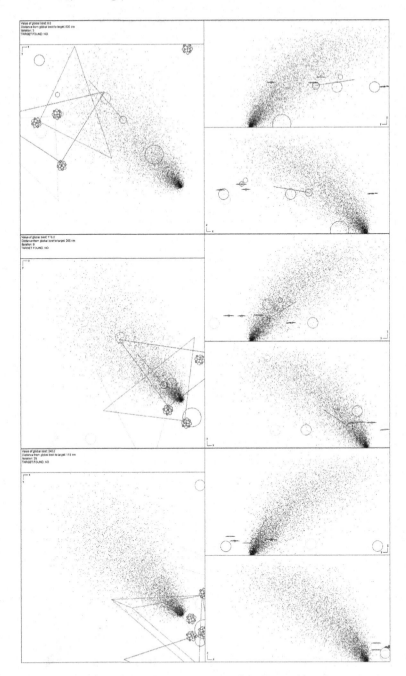

Fig. 2. The same experiment as the one presented in Fig. 1, but the constraints of the relative localization and obstacle avoidance are considered during the movement. In each snapshot of the simulation, three different views are shown (x-y plane, z-y plane and z-x plane).

(a) Initial position of the swarm

(b) Swarm after the first PSO iteration realized by the first MAV

(c) Swarm after the first PSO iteration realized by the second MAV

(d) Final position of the swarm
around simulated source of the plume

Fig. 3. 3 MAVs following trajectories obtained off-line by the proposed PSO-based
algorithm. The experiment was realized in GRASP laboratory, University of Pennsylvania thanks to kind support of professor Vijay Kumar and his team. Special thanks
go to Justin Thomas and Giuseppe Loianno.

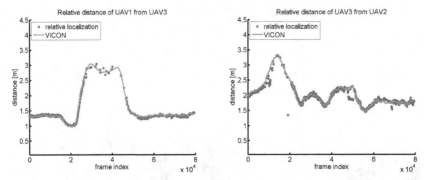

(a) Comparison of relative distances between MAVs captured by the onboard vision system and by data obtained by VICON as a ground truth

(b) Comparison of relative distances between MAVs captured by the onboard vision system and by data obtained by VICON

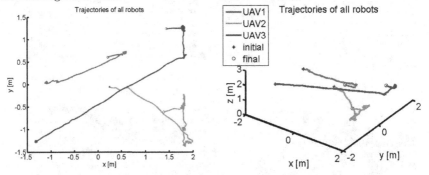

(c) Positions of MAVs captured by VICON during the experiment

(d) 3D view of positions of MAVs captured by VICON during the experiment

Fig. 4. Experimental data obtained during the experiment presented in Fig. 3.

visual relative localization are presented in Fig. 3. Fig. 4 shows that the guess of relative positions of neighbouring vehicles is continuously provided during the flight and that the given limit on the relative position between the robots of the team (3.5m) is kept. The values of PSO parameters used for these experiments were empirically set as $w = 0.4$, $c_1 = 0.4$, $c_2 = 0.55$, $c_3 = 1$ and $k = 4$.

5   Conclusions

The aim of this paper was to show possibility of using a single optimization method for control of swarm of closely cooperating micro aerial vehicles. It was verified that the cooperative deployment of the fleet of MAVs is an efficient tool for such a specific scenario as is the gas plume tracking and its source detection. The presented experiments have shown the advantage of simultaneous gas measurement by cooperatively working quadrocopters with minimal requirements on communication. In addition, a possibility of the swarm stabilization in GNSS-denied environment using only onboard sensors of relative localization was verified. In fact, the environment itself (the gradient of gas concentration) may steer the entire self-stabilized group and information on global position is not needed in this application.

References

1. Bartholmai, M., Neumann, P.: Micro-drone for gas measurement in hazardous scenarios via remote sensing. In: WSEAS International Conference on Remote Sensing (2010)
2. Caltabiano, D., Muscato, G., Orlando, A., Federico, C., Giudice, G., Guerrieri, S.: Architecture of a uav for volcanic gas sampling. In: 10th IEEE Conference on Emerging Technologies and Factory Automation (2005)
3. Ishida, H., Nakayama, G., Nakamoto, T., Moriizumi, T.: Controlling a gas/odor plume-tracking robot based on transient responses of gas sensors. In: Proceedings of IEEE Sensors (2002)
4. Ishida, H., Yoshikawa, K., Moriizumi, T.: Three-dimensional gas-plume tracking using gas sensors and ultrasonic anemometer. In: Proceedings of IEEE Sensors (2004)
5. Kennedy, J., Eberhart, R.: Particle swarm optimization. In: Proceedings IEEE International Conference on Neural Networks (1995)
6. Lee, T., Leoky, M., McClamroch, N.: Geometric tracking control of a quadrotor uav on se(3). In: 49th IEEE Conference on Decision and Control (CDC) (2010)
7. Li, J., Meng, Q., Wang, Y., Zeng, M.: Odor source localization using a mobile robot in outdoor air flow environments with a particle filter algorithm. Autonomous Robots 30(3), 281–292 (2011)
8. Marjovi, A., Marques, L.: Swarm robotic plume tracking for intermittent and time-variant odor dispersion. In: European Conference on Mobile Robots (ECMR) (2013)
9. Saska, M., Chudoba, J., Preucil, L., Thomas, J., Loianno, G., Tresnak, A., Vonasek, V., Kumar, V.: Autonomous deployment of swarms of micro-aerial vehicles in cooperative surveillance. In: ICUAS (2014)
10. Saska, M., Kasl, Z., Preucil, L.: Motion planning and control of formations of micro aerial vehicles. In: IFAC World Congress (2014)
11. Scheutz, M., Schermerhorn, P., Bauer, P.: The utility of heterogeneous swarms of simple uavs with limited sensory capacity in detection and tracking tasks. In: Proceedings 2005 IEEE Swarm Intelligence Symposium (2005)
12. Waphare, S., Gharpure, D., Shaligram, A., Botre, B.: Implementation of 3-nose strategy in odor plume-tracking algorithm. In: International Conference on Signal Acquisition and Processing, ICSAP 2010 (2010)
13. Yuli, Z., Xiaoping, M., Yanzi, M.: Localization of multiple odor sources using modified glowworm swarm optimization with collective robots. In: 30th Chinese Control Conference (CCC) (2011)

The Vision-Based Terrain Navigation Facility: A Technological Overview

Antonio Toma[1], Marcello Chiaberge[2], Mario Silvagni[1], and Gianluca Dara[2]

[1] DIMEAS, Politecnico di Torino, Turin, Italy
{antonio.toma,mario.silvagni}@polito.it
[2] DET, Politecnico di Torino, Turin, Italy
{marcello.chiaberge,gianluca.dara}@polito.it

Abstract. The VTNF (*Vision-based Terrain Navigation Facility*) is an innovative platform designed as a test bed for studying open issues related to the navigation of a planetary lander in its *Entry-Descent-Landing* (EDL) phase. The facility makes available a safe indoor flight volume, fully tracked by infrared cameras, an autonomous quadrotor equipped with a camera and a diorama representing a portion of Martian surface. The quadrotor is used to trigger pictures of the diorama from coordinates that are scaled according to a virtual mission in its EDL phase, simulated on a dedicated workstation. The pictures are then processed to provide information about the presence of particular geological features (craters, canyons, hills ...) and to estimate an hazard-free descent trajectory. This article offers an overview of the design solutions implemented in the facility, both from the hardware and from the software/control point of view.

Keywords: aerial robotics, motion capture system, quadrocopters, autonomous systems, VTNF.

1 Introduction

In the last ten years, research about micro-aerial autonomous systems has gained a great momentum. Part of this success has been triggered by the remarkable results reached by a number of research institutions and laboratories that have focused their work on the study of the dynamics of small aerial vehicles (e.g. multirotors and coaxial small helicopters) and their control. In particular, many of these results have been made possible by the development of special test beds that typically provide a large flight volume in which the exact position and attitude of one or many agents is accurately measured by an optical tracking system. The *MIT Raven* [4] test bed is commonly considered the first described in literature, with *STARMAC* by Stanford University [3], the *Flying Machine Arena* at ETHZ [7] and UPenn's *GRASP Laboratory Test Bed* [9] being other noticeable examples of this technology. The uses of these test beds range from the study of aggressive or coordinated multi-vehicles manoeuvres [8],[10], to architecture [13], construction [6] and entertainment [1]. In this paper, we present the *Vision-based Terrain Navigation Facility*. The VTNF is similar in design to the

J. Hodicky (Ed.): MESAS 2014, LNCS 8906, pp. 56–66, 2014.

already mentioned test beds, and it is explicitly designed in order to provide a simulation and validation environment in the study of vision-based routines and algorithms for space applications. By providing a scenario as similar as possible to the actual operative one, the VTNF allows a deep analysis of the *EDL* (Entry Descent and Landing) phase of a virtual Martian lander approaching Mars. In the experiments, a quadrotor with a camera attached on it facing down is used to trigger some shots on the diorama surface. The motion of the rotorcraft is dependent by the analysis of the pictures, since the quadrotor is controlled in order to reach defined waypoints in the indoor fixed flight volume, computed as a result from the image processing part. The whole system has been designed and integrated by *Thales Alenia Space Italy (TASI)* and *LIM (Mechatronics Lab)* of *Politecnico di Torino*.

2   Functional Layout

From the functional point of view, the facility is composed by three main components:

- the Tracking System;
- the Quadrotor;
- the Ground Segment.

Figure 1 depicts the main data flows exchanged between every single module.

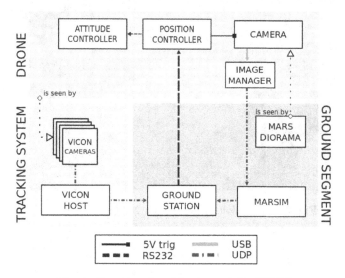

Fig. 1. Functional architecture of the VTNF

2.1 The Tracking System

The purpose of the tracking system is to measure the position and the attitude angles of the quadrotor while it flies inside the tracked volume. The tracking system used in the VTNF is based on the *Vicon Motion Capture System* [14] and is composed by 13 Vicon Bonita infrared cameras, connected together in a PoE (Power over Ethernet) network hosted by a dedicated workstation (*Vicon Host* in Fig. 1) on which the proprietary Vicon Tracker software runs. The infrared cameras are attached on a cube-shaped aluminum structure with 9 m long sides, thus providing an available fully tracked flight volume of approximately 650 m^3, not considering the volume occupied by the diorama. They acquire 0.3 Megapixel images up to 240 Hz and can track a single marker with an accuracy of 1 mm and sub-mm precision. The markers are little spheres covered with an infrared-reflective coating, attached on the body to track. In order to reconstruct without ambiguity the full pose of a rigid body, at least three markers are needed.

Fig. 2. The Vision-based Terrain Navigation Facility

2.2 The Quadrotor

Among the various solutions considered for handling the camera in the flight volume above the diorama (e.g. robotic arms, blimps, cable cameras) a quadrotor offers high maneuverability, good payload capabilities, simple mechanics and low maintenance. The model used in the VNF is shown in Fig. 3; it has a custom lightweight carbon fiber frame and can bring a payload up to 1 kg heavy with an endurance of about 15 minutes. In our setup the camera (in its gimbaled or fixed version), the position control board, the radio modem and a PC104+ single board computer constitute the payload of the vehicle; its total weight amounts to 2.5 kg.

Fig. 3. The quadrotor used in the VTNF

The intrinsic flight stability of the quadcopter is guaranteed by a *Mikrokopter* Flight Control board [15] that controls its Roll and Pitch angles in order to keep it stable while hovering in the air, or to reach the commanded angular values (attitude controller in Fig.1). The board features an Atmel ATMEGA644 microcontroller running at 20 MHz, a 3-axis accelerometer and three gyroscopes. The firmware of the Flight Control board allows the user to take external control of the UAV (i.e., bypassing the radio controller) by means of a dedicated serial protocol [16] on a UART interface; this link is used to send the *Roll, Pitch* and *Yaw* commands to the drone.

The position controller runs on an additional Arduino Mega 1280. The board runs 4 parallel PID controllers, one for each of the remaining degrees of freedom (x, y, z and *Yaw* angle). This board receives on a dedicated wireless-serial link the feedback obtained from the UDP Vicon data stream and sends the commands to the auto-pilot board. The board takes also care of triggering the camera when the MarSim requests a new picture.

A camera and a PC104+ single board computer are used to take pictures of the diorama and to deliver them to the ground segment. The computer features an Intel Atom D510 dual core 1.62 GHz CPU with 2GB RAM. It retrieves the images sent by the camera on the USB link and forwards them to the MarSim. The camera used in the project is the 1312M model by Edmund Optics. It is a CMOS gray level camera (1280x1024 resolution, 8 bits pixel depth) with a rolling shutter. This particular model has been chosen since its characteristics are comparable to the already space qualified camera based on STAR1000 sensor. It can be attached to the drone both in its fixed mount version and in a fully integrated gimbal solution.

A wireless link connects the drone to the ground segment using a couple of identical radiomodems (see Fig. 4) featuring either a standard RS232 serial interface or an IEEE 802.11a LAN wireless link. The former link is used to send every time-critical data to the position controller, i.e. the current attitude of the quadrotor, the target position and the camera-trigger signal; the latter conveys to ground the pictures coming from the camera via UDP.

Fig. 4. The Arduino board running the position controller and the on-board radiomodem attached on their carrierboard

2.3 The Ground Segment

The Ground Segment in the VTNF is composed by two software modules (the *Ground Station* and the *Marsim* in Fig. 1) and by a diorama.

The Ground Station. The Ground Station module is a simple module that accesses in real-time positions and angles of the drone, as provided by the Vicon Host on the UDP link, and adapts them to provide a continue pose feedback to the quadrotor position controller. Moreover, this module receives the target position by the MarSim and triggers a new picture when the error is less than a tunable threshold; then it acknowledges the MarSim that it is ready to compute a new target point.

The MarSim. The MarSim is a TASI proprietary module. It embeds both a complete functional and dynamical model of the extra-planetary lander and the computer-vision routines that are the object of the testing activities. The MarSim receives as inputs the pictures triggered by the drone and outputs a succession of Martian geographical coordinates, computed and updated at runtime during the experiment. These are the result of a complex chain of operations performed to simulate the behaviour of a real lander in its EDL phase (image processing, data fusing with on-board sensor, computation of the new nominal trajectory, actuation of thrusters, integration of the dynamic until the new point of interest). The coordinates are then scaled and re-projected in the diorama reference frame and passed to the quadrotor as target waypoints. Figure 5 offers an example of a hazard map generated by the simulator in this stage, starting from a picture of a portion of Martian terrain. Further details about the MarSim can be found in [5].

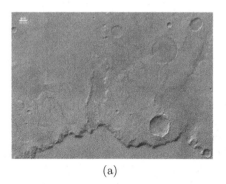
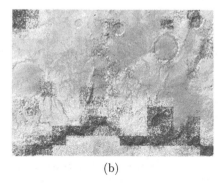

(a)   (b)

Fig. 5. A real image of Martian terrain (5a) and the output of the hazard map algorithm (5b). The dangerous areas for landing have been highlighted.

The diorama (8 m × 8 m, 1.5 m of maximum relief height) accurately reproduces four peculiar geographic details of the Mars surface in 1 : 300 scale:

- Nili Fossae
- Victoria Crater
- Xanthe Terra
- Dilly Crater

Nine mercury-vapor stage lamps provide accurate and homogeneous lighting. Figure 6 shows the good level of resemblance between two actual Martian surfaces, and their equivalent reproduction on the diorama.

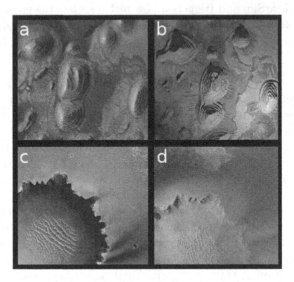

Fig. 6. A portion of Western Arabia Terra (a) and Victoria Crater (c) and the corresponding representations on the diorama (b,d)

3   System Modeling and Control

In the current application, a high dynamic response of the quadrotor does not represent a critical requirement. The drone does not have to perform aggressive maneuvers, nor has it to respect strict dynamical or trajectory constraints. Hence a very simple control architecture, featuring 4 parallel PID controllers (acting on the x, y, z and *Yaw* degrees of freedom of the quadrotor), has been designed in order to move the quadrotor on its target position.

Given the following conditions in the flight of the quadrotor:

- Small *Roll* and *Pitch* angles ($\pm 6\ °$),
- *Yaw* angle fixed at $\psi = 0\ °$,
- Low translational velocities,
- Hovering flight (i.e. constant thrust value),

the dynamical model of the vehicle can be completely linearized and the x, y, z and *Yaw* dynamics can be decoupled.

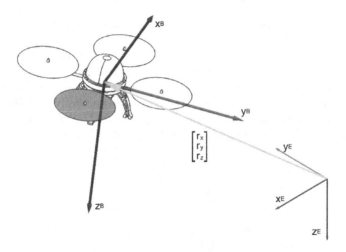

Fig. 7. Body (B) and Earth (E) reference frames

Given the global and local reference frames of Fig. 7, the following simple representation of its translational dynamics can be derived [2], [12]:

$$
\begin{bmatrix} \ddot{r}_x \\ \ddot{r}_y \\ \ddot{r}_z \end{bmatrix} = \frac{1}{m} \begin{bmatrix} 0 & \bar{T} & 0 \\ -\bar{T} & 0 & 0 \\ 0 & 0 & 1 \end{bmatrix} \begin{bmatrix} \varphi \\ \vartheta \\ T \end{bmatrix} + \begin{bmatrix} 0 \\ 0 \\ g \end{bmatrix}
\tag{1}
$$

With r_x, r_y, r_z being the coordinates of the center of mass of the drone in the earth-fixed frame, m the total mass of the quadrotor, $\bar{T}$ the hovering thrust

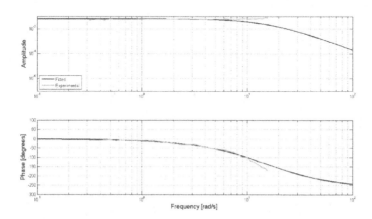

Fig. 8. Roll and Pitch frequency response. Dark grey lines represent the angular frequency response of the angular controller, identified by fitting the experimental results (light grey lines).

value; φ and ϑ respectively are the *Roll* and *Pitch* rotation around x_B and y_B axes.

However, (1) does not completely characterize the description of the dynamics since its angular dynamics is still not known. Unfortunately, Mikrokopter offers very poor documentation about the design of the attitude control loops design [11]. For this reason their dynamics have been experimentally identified.

The identified frequency response of the angular controller has been modeled with a third order transfer function described by (2) that has been experimentally found to well represent both *Pitch* and *Roll* dynamics of the system:

$$F_{\varphi\vartheta}(s) = \frac{0.063}{0.0003s^3 + 0.0133s^2 + 0.2s + 1} \tag{2}$$

its bode plot is shown in Fig. 8.

An alternative approach to model identification of Mikrokopter dynamical model in time-domain can be found in [11].

The PID controllers have been designed in order to keep the rising time in the order of 2.5 s for a 1 m step reference on x, y, z. Experimental tuning of the PID parameters have been conducted directly on the plant to further adjust the flight performance of the vehicle. Figure 9 shows the experimental results after

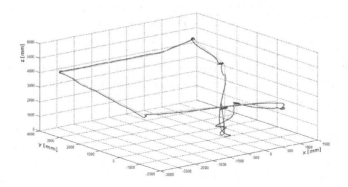

(a) *A complete flight in the tree dimensional volume*

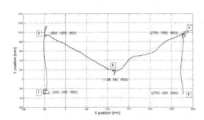

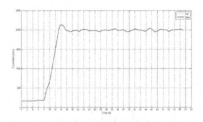

(b) *A planar flight through 5 points*   (c) *The dynamic behavior on z axis*

Fig. 9. Experimental results

some test flights. The positioning error causes the drone to hover in a circle of maximum radius 6 cm around the target point while the Z error varies within a maximum range of ± 8 cm (Figure 9a and Fig. 9b). The *Yaw* angle is kept within a precision of ± 3 °. Dedicated tests have shown that Vicon Tracking System provides, after a good calibration and with optimal camera coverage, 1 mm accurate and 0.1 mm precise position data. The maximum latency in the camera trigger signal has been measured to be 40 ms.

4   Conclusion

In this paper we have presented the Visual Terrain Navigation Facility, a test bed for studying and validating vision-based routines and algorithms to be used during planetary Entry Descent and Landing (EDL) by a lander. We have described the major technical details of the architecture and the design choices in relation with its three main functional components: the Tracking System, the Ground Segment and the Quadrotor. We have finally shown how, in our operation hypothesis, a very simple PID-based control architecture successfully stabilizes the quadrotor and allows basic autonomous navigation functionalities with good performances. The VTNF is currently used in *Thales Alenia Space*'s headquarters in Turin both for the already described purposes and in technological demonstrations. Although the VTNF has been created keeping in mind the validation of specific aerospace-derived image algorithms, it offers noticeable potentialities for a number of applications not strictly related with the original purposes of the project. Moreover our research activities in the facility are not over; experimentation with visual-aided auto-takeoff and auto-landing routines, visual odometry and new control strategies are currently carried out in the VTNF. An outdoor GPS-based version of the facility is also currently under development and will permit image analysis and EDL simulation on larger scale.

Acknowledgments. The VTNF facility has been designed and integrated with the support of the STEPS project co-funded by Regione Piemonte (Project co-financed by EC Platform: POR FESR 007/2013). The work has been carried out in collaboration with Thales Alenia Space Italy. The authors would like to thank Carlo Paccagnini and Corrado Maddaleno for the precious collaboration.

References

1. Augugliaro, F., Schoellig, A., D'Andrea, R.: Dance of the flying machines. IEEE Robotics and Automation Magazine 117 (December 2013)
2. Castillo, P., Dzul, A., Lozano, R.: Real-Time Stabilization and Tracking of a Four-Rotor Mini Rotorcraft. IEEE Transactions on Control Systems Technology 12(4), 510–516 (2004)
3. Hoffmann, G., Rajnarayan, D., Waslander, S., Dostal, D., Jang, J., Tomlin, C.: The Stanford testbed of autonomous rotorcraft for multi agent control (STAR-MAC). The 23rd Digital Avionics Systems Conference (IEEE Cat. No.04CH37576) pp. 12.E.4–121–10 (2004)

4. How, J.P., Bethke, B., Frank, A.: Real-time indoor autonomous vehicle test environment. IEEE Control Systems 28, 51–64 (2008)
5. Lanza, P., Noceti, N., Maddaleno, C., Toma, A., Zini, L., Odone, F.: A vision-based navigation facility for planetary entry descent landing. In: Fusiello, A., Murino, V., Cucchiara, R. (eds.) ECCV 2012 Ws/Demos, Part II. LNCS, vol. 7584, pp. 546–555. Springer, Heidelberg (2012)
6. Lindsey, Q., Mellinger, D., Kumar, V.: Construction with quadrotor teams. Autonomous Robots 33(3), 323–336 (2012)
7. Lupashin, S., Hehn, M., Mueller, M.: A platform for aerial robotics research and demonstration: The Flying Machine Arena. Mechatronics 24(1), 41–54 (2014)
8. Mellinger, D., Michael, N., Kumar, V.: Trajectory generation and control for precise aggressive maneuvers with quadrotors. The International Journal of Robotics Research 31(5), 664–674 (2012)
9. Michael, N., Mellinger, D., Lindsey, Q., Kumar, V.: The GRASP Multiple Micro-UAV Testbed. IEEE Robotics & Automation Magazine 17(3), 56–65 (2010)
10. Ritz, R., Müller, M.W., Hehn, M., D'Andrea, R.: Cooperative quadrocopter ball throwing and catching. In: 2012 IEEE/RSJ International Conference on Intelligent Robots and Systems, pp. 4972–4978 (October 2012)
11. Sa, I., Corke, P.: Estimation and control for an open-source quadcopter. In: Proceedings of the Australasian Conference on Robotics and Automation 2011 (2011)
12. Waslander, S.L., Hoffmann, G.M., Tomlin, C.J.: Multi-agent quadrotor testbed control design: integral sliding mode vs. reinforcement learning. In: 2005 IEEE/RSJ International Conference on Intelligent Robots and Systems, pp. 3712–3717 (2005)
13. Willmann, J., Augugliaro, F., Cadalbert, T., D'Andrea, R., Gramazio, F., Kohler, M.: Aerial robotic construction towards a new field of architectural research. International Journal of Architectural Computing 10(3), 439–460 (2012)
14. Vicon tracking system homepage, http://www.vicon.com/
15. Mikrokopter flight control 2.1 specifications, http://tinyurl.com/l86k4gf
16. Mikrokopter serial protocol specifications, http://tinyurl.com/ltabhnb

Taking Advantages of Modern Distributed Infrastructures in Modelling and Simulation

Giovanni Battista Buora, Christian Giusti, and Marco Barbina

Selex ES, Ronchi dei Legionari (GO), Italy
{giovannibattista.buora,christian.giusti,marco.barbina}@selex-es.com

Abstract. During the last years, we are experiencing the overwhelming growth of on-line services. Web applications are able to provide such services, by using cooperative, heterogeneous, decentralized and distributed infrastructures and several technologies like consolidated Service-Oriented Architectures (WSDL, WSMO, SOAP, etc.) or emerging Resource-Oriented Architectures (e.g. RESTful, etc.). When we talk about Modelling and Simulation, HLA is the de-facto standard for what concerns interoperability: such a standard, like others less used, gives different simulations the capability to interoperate together, but nothing is done for what concern the implementation or the exploitation of services in order to give added value to the already existing simulations. This paper investigates the capabilities and benefits provided by modern infrastructures currently adopted in the Web world, highlighting which kind of resources are available today online and can be accessed to enhance the quality of the simulation; then presents Selex ES approach to simulation, the SYENA synthetic environment, which by integrating the traditional HLA standard with modern Web technologies allows to realise more convincing and impressive simulations.

Keywords: Simulation techniques, interoperability, distributed architectures.

1 Introduction

During the last 30 years we assisted a paradigm shift in simulation industry: simulators, intended as stand-alone, individual and isolated special purpose systems used to train an individual in the essential skills needed to operate on the real platform, have become the building blocks of highly complex geographically distributed simulation environments. Today the architectures of simulation frameworks are focused on loosely coupled systems executing units of simulation. The simulation interconnection problem can be viewed as a computer science problem, tackled by the "modern miracles" of standards, middleware, distributed algorithms, data type coercion, and so forth[1].

On the other side, we assisted in the last years also to another revolution facing the same questions (standards, interoperation, distributed algorithms): Internet and the World-Wide-Web. Since its development in the early 1990s,

J. Hodicky (Ed.): MESAS 2014, LNCS 8906, pp. 67–76, 2014.

the Web has experienced tremendous growth and today Web applications are able to provide a full range of services, by using cooperative, heterogeneous, decentralized and distributed infrastructures and several technologies like the consolidated Service-oriented Architectures (SOAs) or emerging Resource-oriented Architectures (ROAs).

As many disciplines are re-evaluating their strategies and techniques in view of the services offered by the Internet, also Modeling and Simulation (M&S) is no less affected by this technology than any other technique, as it represents a fertile area in which to perform computer simulation research [5].

This paper aims to investigate the capabilities and benefits provided by modern infrastructures currently adopted in the Web world, highlighting which kind of resources are today available online and can be accessed to enhance the quality of the simulation. In our vision, this kind of advantage can be achieved in three steps:

- technology: adopting the technologies commonly used by Web applications (e.g. HTML, JS, WebGL, etc.);
- architecture: improving the design and achieving a higher integration with the Web in order to take advantage of tools which it offers (e.g. using architectures like SOA, ROA, etc.);
- contents: using services available on Internet which can be exploited to realize more convincing and effective simulations.

We presents Selex ES approach to simulation, the SYENA synthetic environment, which by integrating the traditional HLA standard with modern Web technologies allows to realise more convincing and impressive simulations. This approach has highly potentials, as it allows the reusing of existing applications and their integration with a wide variety of contents and services already existing on the Web.

This paper is organised as follows. Section II introduces the interoperability problem and presents the ideas and benefits of exploiting Web-based approach within M&S field. Section III introduces SYENA, Selex ES' Synthetic Environment and describes how modern Web technologies and infrastructures have been used within our framework. Section IV proposes possible extensions of the framework using on-line services. Section V provides conclusions.

2   Background and Motivation

Every time we speak about distributed systems, we must clash with the concept of *interoperability*. At a first sight, interoperability would seem to be a straightforward concept: in its most general meaning is simply the measure of the degree to which various systems and subsystems are able to operate together to achieve a common goal. When we talk about interoperability in computer systems, the definition of interoperability becomes less obvious and every little shade of the concept hides complex issues.

A reasonable definition of interoperability is proposed in [10] as the ability of a collection of communicating entities to (a) share specified information and (b) operate on that information according to a shared operational semantics in order to achieve a specified purpose in a given context. Starting from this definition and taking into account the Levels of Conceptual Interoperability Model presented in [2, 3], we can consider the problem of interoperability on three different levels:

- Syntactic level: this level deals with infrastructure and network challenges (e.g. Ethernet physical layer, Operating Systems...), with the definition of data types and structures used to exchange data (e.g. encoding, protocols, formats), and with the integrity of data exchanged. This level is relatively simple to manage, since it is required only that all the participants focus on the shape (i.e. structure) of data and respect the established conventions and rules;
- Semantic level: this level deals with the meaning of data exchanged among participants in a simulation/organisation (e.g. who is allowed to share some kind of information, how an actor must reply to a specific interaction). This is the level where we assist to the transformation of data into information: issues at this level can be more complex to manage, since all participants must share a common model and implement its meaning without ambiguities;
- Pragmatic level: this is the most complex level and concerns the use of information, the context of the application and the effects of such use. In order to achieve a complete, effective and meaningful collaboration the use of information is the most important aspect. Pragmatics deals with issues related to how the simulation is effective, how users interface with the system and are able to get what they want.

For what concerns distributed simulation and interoperability, the High-Level Architecture (HLA) is the preferred middleware standard within the M&S domain in the defence sector: HLA is a general purpose architecture for distributed computer simulation systems, which provides a flexible framework for creating simulation and interfaces to live systems. It is used to facilitate the interoperability of different models and units of simulations. There are several versions of HLA standard: just to name the most important ones, older HLA version 1.3 [14] and IEEE 1516 [11–13] with recently approved revision 1516-2010 "HLA Evolved".

Our proposal consists in integrating modern distributed infrastructures coming from Web world with HLA in order to obtain better simulations that are easy, fast and effortless.

2.1   Why Web and Simulation?

The Web-based simulation [6] or the idea of combining Simulation and Web is not new and has been growing during the past few years: first efforts are dated back in mid 1990s (as Web-front ends to simulations running as Common Gateway Interface (CGI) scripts [5]) and today the major trend is combining semantic Web, Web Service, SOA with HLA [15, 7].

The Web principles have been proven in simplifying interoperability while still providing scalability, flexibility and client simplicity [16].

Our focus is on the pragmatic level of interoperability, main goals are:

- flexibility: research of lightweight tools that allow to obtain complex scenarios starting from the simple blocks;
- velocity: "time-to-market" is a critical consideration. Being late erodes the addressable market of a product. Hence there is the need of tools that allow rapid prototyping, development and content aggregation;
- reusability: reuse is a critical strategy for all software development groups. By reusing code, it is possible to leverage existing development and research investment and lessen time to market;
- effectiveness: which means realize simulations always closer to reality by using high level details for each aspect of the scenario.

2.2 What Does the Web Offer?

In our opinion, the adoption of modern Web technologies and infrastructures meets the needs for interoperability within the M&S in three ways:

- technology: HTML5, Javascript, AJAX, CSS and WebGL are high-level, fast and reliable tools. Development time and cost can be lowered using these tools;
- infrastructures: with infrastructure we mean both flexible design and architectural patterns (e.g. SOA) and relying on existing systems to taking advantage in existing applications and systems;
- services: nowadays the Web offers a wide range of services and contents; that may become a strong point in the creation of accurate and effective simulations.

In recent years, the SOA approach and Web Services (WS) technologies have been successfully used for simplifying interoperability and providing scalability and flexibility in multiple applications. SOA requires thinking about the system in terms of Services (well-defined business functionality), Components (discrete pieces of code and data structures) and Processes (service orchestrations). WS are a powerful tool for realising SOA to achieve interoperability, but suffer of requiring heavy infrastructures and a too formal approach: data are exchanged with SOAP messages wrapped within HTTP messages while services, in addition to being implemented, must also be described and exposed in WSDL. WSDL only allows to define programming stubs, but does not teach developers how to use them, making difficult composing and mashing-up services, and constraining reuse [16]. Instead, the WWW nature has been extremely successful in providing an outsized, scalable and interoperable system that is simple and easy to understand. The Representational State Transfer (REST) provides interoperability by imitating the WWW style and principles. RESTful Web Services are gaining increased attention with the advent of Web 2.0 and the concept of mashup because of their simplicity. REST exposes services as "resources" (which are named with unique URIs similar to Web sites) and manipulated with uniform interface, usually HTTP methods. According to this vision the Web itself is just a huge database, where resources are abstractions that can be distributed in different representations like images, documents, multimedia contents and services.

Resources are the most important asset that the Web has to offer for the Simulation. Roughly we can split resources in two main categories: contents and services. With the term contents we refer to *static* assets that can be embedded in a simulation in order to create a simulation scenario. Spatial data are the best example to illustrate the idea of content. Today we can find a wide range of services providing:

- satellite images;
- elevation data;
- land cover data (drainage, vegetation, administrative boundaries, population centres, and land use);
- human impacts data (i.e. humans and the environment from a socio-economic perspective);
- ecosystems data (i.e. the natural ecosystems of the world);
- transportation data (roads, trains).

This is just a subset of the list of all spatial data available today. The usefulness and importance of this kind of information is very high for the Simulation: in CONOPs simulation, for example, the use could be able to design scenarios in any part of the world.

With the term service we indicate to *dynamic* assets. Typical examples of services exploitable in simulation are:

- meteorological data services: services providing forecasts, analyses, and observations of aviation-related weather variables, climate and historical weather data and information, real-time monitoring Meteorological, Hydrographical and Environmental data collection systems;
- transportation services: airport status, traffic control centres, real-time information on motorways and trunk roads to road users;
- general purpose GIS services: services providing spatial data entry, management, retrieval, analysis, and visualization of geographical data.

3 SYENA

SYENA (SYnthetic ENvironment Animator) is a modular Synthetic Environment framework developed to allow users to define realistic and accurate simulation scenarios and to reduce the development time of complex behavioural patterns.

SYENA is based on a brand new architecture concept where some of the founding requirements are of providing:

- high performance Computer Generated Forces (CGFs) for users that need it;
- fast exercise creation and modification with an interactive approach promoting easiness of use;

- behaviour library build-up;
- efficiency in resource usage;
- scalability beyond the limits of a single Workstation architecture.

SYENA was designed especially to be a system whose customization did not require the prerequisite knowledge of specific framework constraints. That reduces the skills and the amount of work needed every time a customer requires special features and modification of a product, so finally reducing the total operating cost. This has been achieved through the "agnostic plug-in" concept: in SYENA the behaviour of an agent is defined by means of a stack of modules (plug-ins), where each module does not necessarily need to know or understand the functions or variables used by other behaviours. Plug-ins are retrieved from a library and added to the stack of each agent of the simulation, but they can also be written by different developers without any prior knowledge of the system or of the other plug-ins constituting the behaviours stack. Even more important is that each layer is active and interacts with the others, the same way neurones do in a nervous system; this allows to realise agents whose behaviour becomes very sophisticated, while each defining layered module remains at a reasonable level of complexity.

3.1   System Architecture

SYENA has been developed following the well-accepted three-tier architectural model (Fig. 3.1) in which user interface, functional process logic and data and services access are developed and maintained as independent modules. Apart from the usual advantages of modular software with well-defined interfaces, this multi-tier architecture is intended to allow any of the tiers to be upgraded or replaced independently in response to changes in requirements or technology. Starting from the bottom to the top, the layers are organised as follows:

- data layer: this layer includes data storage mechanisms and the data access layer that encapsulates the persistence mechanisms and exposes the data. This layer provides an API to the logic layer that exposes methods of managing the stored data without exposing or creating dependencies on the data storage mechanisms;
- logic layer: this layer represents the heart of the simulation and is responsible of animating the entities and the elements of the simulation scenario;
- presentation layer: this layer represents the interface between the user and the system and is the most critical part to the application's success. If users can't interact with the system in a way that lets them perform their work in an efficient manner, then the overall success of the system will be severely impaired.

3.2   Human-Machine Interaction

SYENA's Human-Machine Interface is the part of the system whose design was most influenced by the Web-Approach philosophy. Over the past 30 years, the

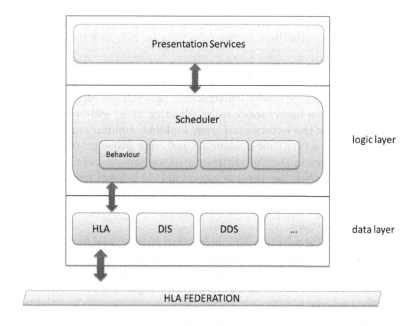

Fig. 1. SYENA architecture

mechanisms used to interact with machines and devices have changed dramatically, driven by rapidly advancing technology and by the needs of manufacturing facilities for people who use them. A number of diverse methodologies outlining techniques for human-computer interaction design have emerged. At the same time the terminology has been changing: tablets, smartphones, mobile devices are agents for that change and leading actors in augmenting existing capabilities. Nowadays HMI applications do not live on a fixed device anymore, and this presents challenges in designing HMI screens and interactions with the end user [8].

Within SYENA architecture, the HMI is not just a way to allow the user to interact with the system, but it is the main tool for managing an entire operation. An operation is a complex process which collaborates with others, and accesses critical information.

The design of HMI in SYENA is the development step more involved in adopting and using modern Web technologies and infrastructures: today the idea of building HMI based on Web technologies has become practical: HTML is no longer just a standard for presenting web content, but a viable technology for HMIs for every kind of applications. The use of HTML as an environment for delivering rich and flexible user interfaces can add functionalities and capabilities, also extending the life cycle of HMI and preparing applications for future platforms [9].

The idea exploited by SYENA is to develop also a platform-agnostic HMI, making it browsable like a Web page. As well as a Web page can be displayed

in the same way on different browsers and by different Operating Systems, so
SYENA HMI must be visualised in the same way on different devices and sub-
systems.

The main benefits of such a kind of approach are:

- ease of use: simulation model construction is a fundamentally hard problem. Simulation is a highly specialist application area, with a high degree of
  difficulty: even for the experienced user, building, running, and analysing a
  simulation can be a very time-consuming and error-prone process. One of the
  main characteristics of the Web is its ease of navigation and use and obtaining data from the Web has become second nature to most users. The idea of
  adopting such kind of ideas seems to be a good way to insulate the user from
  the intricacies involved in utilising third party models and the overheads of
  distributed simulation;
- collaboration: communication and interaction are essential factors to achieve
  a successful simulation. It is possible to develop environments with coherent Web-based support for collaborative model development, where people
  can communicate with each other from different places to develop the same
  simulation scenario;
- shorter design and development time: if the HMI must be visualised on
  different kind of devices or in different environments, HMI development in
  native C/C++ code is prohibitively expensive and too time-consuming. Web
  technologies (HTML and its ancillary technologies, like CSS3, WebGL and
  JavaScript) make design and development platform independent, and permit
  testing of the products and versions only once per release;
- cross-platform capability: HMTL allows for the ability to run an application
  on any Web browser on any operating system without compiling: this capability relieves the application developer from having to worry about a client
  configuration.
- design reuse: designs from the first stages of prototyping to final production
  can be reused. This allows designs to be changed late in the production phase,
  tested in a simulation environment, and then directly deployed. This iterative
  design process can take place with no need for modifying the underlying
  platform;
- platform agnosticism: the main goal is the platform independence and HMI
  designs can support virtually every types of embedded platforms. If the
  HMI avoids features specific to the embedded environment to make some
  a particular operation (for example, gestures to move the map), mobile and
  embedded apps share the same code base;
- versioning, customization and maintenance: using HMTL maintenance is
  minimised, since all modifications can be made through the server, enabling
  customizations and updates to be made and instantly distributed to the
  application, reducing error potential and eliminating virtually all on-site
  maintenance;
- browser based applications: the browser has probably become the most ubiquitous interface not only to any machine but to any system in the world, too.

Thanks highly graphical Web interfaces now available, it is possible to create a visual interface for the HMI entirely in HTML/JavaScript. Processing would still to be done entirely on the server, so saving the HMI from being over burdened by processing needs.

4   Future Work

One possible way of extending the proposed system is the introduction of a layer that behaves as bridge between the simulation environment SYENA and the "outside" world. The purpose of this component is to separate the simulation from the Web world: this need is driven by the following observations:

- availability: in certain kinds of simulation environments there's not the ability to interface directly with the outer world (e.g. defence industry): the bridge allows to replicate external data in a safe environment;
- reliability: if a service is not reachable, the whole simulation environment must not suffer of this limitation. In this case the bridge components acts as local copy of data;
- repeatability: a simulation must be repeatable and services can provide dynamic contents, such as meteo or air traffic data. There is the need to have a component which behaves as repository of data and information;
- dynamicity: Web is volatile by nature. Contents and information change rapidly and also new technologies grow very quickly. To be constantly aligned with current technology requires higher costs for development and maintenance of systems.

5   Conclusions

In this paper we provided a quick overview of the interoperability concept within M&S and how modern Web technologies deal with same kinds of questions. In this paper we presented SYENA, its main features and the core concept of how modelling very complex behaviours as associations of agnostic blocks. Also, we have seen how the system integrates with modern technologies and how it provides a high level of abstraction for what concerns HMI.

References

1. Page, E.H.: Theory and practice for simulation interconnection: Interoperability and composability in defense simulation. In: Handbook of Dynamic System Modeling. Chapman and Hall/CRC (2007)
2. Tolk, A., Muguira, J.A.: The levels of conceptual interoperability model. In: Proceedings of the 2003 Fall Simulation Interoperability Workshop, vol. 7 (2003)
3. Tolk, A., Diallo, S.Y., Turnitsa, C.D.: Applying the Levels of Conceptual Interoperability Model in Support of Integratability, Interoperability and Composability for System-of-Systems Engineering. Journal of Systemics, Cybernetics and Informatics (2007)

4. Wang, W., Wang, W., Zhu, Y., Li, Q.: Service-oriented simulation framework: An overview and unifying methodology. Simulation 87(3), 221–252 (2011)
5. Byrne, J., Heavey, C., Byrne, P.J.: A review of Web-based simulation and supporting tools. Simulation Modelling Practice and Theory 18(3), 253–276 (2010)
6. Fishwick, P.A.: Web-based simulation: some personal observations. In: Proceedings of the 28th Conference on Winter Simulation, pp. 772–779. IEEE Computer Society (1996)
7. Dragoicea, M., Bucur, L., Tsai, W.-T., Sarjoughian, H.: Integrating HLA and Service-Oriented Architecture in a Simulation Framework. In: Proceedings of the 2012 12th IEEE/ACM International Symposium on Cluster, Cloud and Grid Computing (CCGRID 2012), pp. 861–866. IEEE Computer Society (2012)
8. ULTRA-MOBILE PCs: Emerging technologies mobile-computing trends: lighter, faster, smarter. About Language Learning & Technology: 3 (2008)
9. Katzel, J.: Information systems: The evolution of the HMI. Control Engineering 59, 10 (2012), Reed Business Information
10. Carney, D., Fisher, D., Place, P.R.: Topics in Interoperability: System-of-Systems Evolution (2005)
11. IEEE Std 1516-2000: IEEE Standard for Modeling and Simulation (M&S) High Level Architecture (HLA) - Framework and Rules (2000)
12. IEEE Std 1516.1-2000: IEEE Standard for Modeling and Simulation (M&S) High Level Architecture (HLA) - Federate Interface Specification (2000)
13. IEEE Std 1516.2-2000: IEEE Standard for Modeling and Simulation (M&S) High Level Architecture (HLA) - Object Model Template, OMT (2000)
14. Simulation Interoperability Standards Organization Dynamic Link Compatible HLA API Product Development Group (PDG): Dynamic Link Compatible HLA API Standard for the HLA Interface Specification Version 1.3 Simulation Interoperability Standards Organization (2004)
15. Tolk, A.: What comes after the semantic web-pads implications for the dynamic web. In: Proceedings of the 20th Workshop on Principles of Advanced and Distributed Simulation, pp. 55–62. IEEE Computer Society (2006)
16. Al-Zoubi, K., Wainer, G.: Using REST web-services architecture for distributed simulation. In: Proceedings of the 2009 ACM/IEEE/SCS 23rd Workshop on Principles of Advanced and Distributed Simulation, pp. 114–121. IEEE Computer Society (2009)

A Simulation Tool for Evaluating Attack Impact in Cyber Physical Systems

Gianluca Dini[1] and Marco Tiloca[2]

[1] Dept. of Ingegneria dell'Informazione, University of Pisa, Pisa, Italy
g.dini@iet.unipi.it
[2] SICS Swedish ICT, Stockholm, Sweden
marco@sics.se

Abstract. Security is getting an ever increasingly important issue in cyber-physical systems comprising autonomous systems. However, it is not possible to defend from all possible attacks for cost and performance reasons. An attack ranking is thus necessary. We propose a simulative framework that makes it possible to rank attacks according to their impact. We also describe a case study to assert its usefulness and effectiveness.

Keywords: Security, cyber-physical systems, risk assessment, simulation.

1   Introduction

Autonomous Systems results from the convergence of communication, computing and control. They are cyber-physical systems equipped with sensing, actuating and computing capabilities, interconnected through a wireless communication network, which may operate in both isolation and cooperation.

As with many of these complex networks of systems, it is possible for adversaries to intentionally compromise their functionality or performance. As to security, autonomous systems present two peculiarities with respect to conventional complex networks such as the Internet [1]. First a security infringement may traduce into a safety infringement with possible physical consequences. Second, autonomous systems are subject to both cyber and physical attacks. They are often deployed in open, unattended, possibly hostile environments where adversaries can physically attack them as well as interfere with the sensing process.

Security in autonomous systems is quite a new research field. Security vulnerabilities and related countermeasures are increasingly being discovered and exploited. However it is well-known that perfect security cannot be achieved for both performance and cost reasons. Thus, it is vital to define a threat model and then perform a risk assessment in order to determine the extent of potential threats and identify appropriate solutions. Typically, risk assessment involves two dimensions, namely the feasibility and impact of an attack. Here, we focus on the latter.

J. Hodicky (Ed.): MESAS 2014, LNCS 8906, pp. 77–94, 2014.

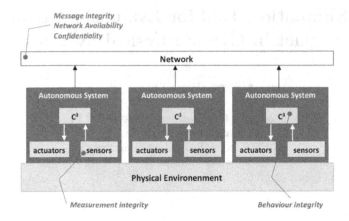

Fig. 1. Autonomous Systems

We present a simulation framework aimed at evaluating the impact of an attack in a cyber-physical system. The framework presents several advantages. First, it defines a simple *attack description language* that allows us to describe the effects of a cyber-physical attack in terms of *events* the attack generates. The language is composed of a reduced set of statements that make it possible to specify such events and thus easily describe even complex cyber-physical attacks such as a wormhole attack. Second, the simulator integrates an off-the-shelf simulator of the cyber-physical system under analysis and extends it as far as processing attack-related events is concerned. When the designer wishes to evaluate a new attack, he/she has only to provide the framework with the description of the attack. No line of code has to be re-written or part of the simular re-implemented. Third, and finally, the simulation framework makes it possible to *quantitatively* evaluate the impact of an attack, provided that appropriate security metrics have been defined. Methods and protocols for threat analysis have been defined, a recent relevant example being [5]. However, they tend tend to support a subjective analysis. This framework is a first stride towards a more objective analysis.

The paper is organizes as follows. Section 2 reports the main security requirements of autonomous systems. Section 3 provides an overall description of the simulation framework and its prototype based on Castalia [3], an off-the-shelf WSN simulator based Omnet++[7]. Section 4 discusses a case study where we apply our framework to analyze the impact of several attacks against the pollution monitoring system of an industrial plant. Finally, Section 5 reports our final conclusions.

2   Security in Autonomous Systems

With reference to Figure 1, autonomous systems result from the convergence of communication, computing and control (C3). They are cyber-physical systems equipped with sensing, actuating and computing capabilities, interconnected through a wireless communication network, and operating in isolation and/or cooperation.

From a security standpoint, autonomous systems must fulfil the usual CIA requirements, namely confidentiality, integrity, and availability.

Informally, *availability* refers to the ability of authorized entities to act and collect data in a timely way. Availability guarantees that information is accessible and usable upon demand by the legitimate entity. In brief, availability guarantees that messages are received. A violation of network availability is a *denial of service*, i.e. the prevention of authorized access to data. Denial of service attacks are mainly based on network congestion and network jamming so that the network appears to be unavailable. In the former case, the system is actually busy in serving "fake" requests. In the latter case, an adversary maliciously creates interference with the radio frequency band used by the system by exploiting the broadcast nature of the wireless medium. Recently, selective jamming, a particularly insidious form of jamming aimed at a specific node, has been considered [4,9].

Integrity refers to the confidence that actions are correct and collected data are accurate. A violation of integrity results in *deception*, a circumstance where an authorized entity receives false information about the phenomenon being monitored, and it believes it to be true (*data deception*). In addition, a deception may consist in one or more entities acting differently than specified (*actions deception*). In the most general case, an entity may be deceptive in terms of both data and actions. An integrity violation may have implications in terms of safety, loss of productivity or loss of reputation.

In computer security, the term integrity regularly refers to *message integrity*. However, this notion is limited and not sufficient to capture the integrity of the functional goal of autonomous systems. The interactions of autonomous systems with one another and with the physical world, together with the fact that the data sent by sensor nodes depends on their location, lead us to extend the notion of integrity by means of those of measurement and behaviour integrity.

Measurement integrity prevents the modification of a sensor measurement. An attack against measurement integrity succeeds when an autonomous system reports a sensed measurement that is not representative of the intended environment. A violation of the measurement integrity may derive from i) an *environment attack*, i.e. an attack affecting the environment around a sensor node by the adversary (e.g. placing a magnet on top of a magnetometer); ii) a *false position attack*, i.e. changing the location of a sensor node by the attacker, and the sensor node is unable to detect this change and report it; and iii) a *sensor spoofing attack*, i.e. sending the sensor a spoofed signal GPS spoofing [10] and ultrasound spoofing [1] are relevant instances of sensor spoofing attacks. This kind of attacks opens a new frontline that characterizes autonomous system security with respect to network security. Actually autonomous systems are designed and manufactured with certain safety measures. Once a system is manufactured and tested against natural errors, it is expected to conform to its design specifications unless accidental failures. However these safety measures are against non-malicious faults and thus usually do not consider mechanisms for adversary detection and prevention. As a consequence, the system safety may result fragile with respect to maliciously induced failures.

Behaviour integrity prevents the unauthorized modification of an autonomous system logic/behaviour. An attack against behaviour integrity succeeds when an autonomous system is compromised and does not behave as expected. The misbehaviour of a system manifests itself in reporting a fake measurement, sending a fake message, or taking a fake action. An adversary may violate the behaviour integrity of an entity by compromising it, reprogramming it in order to send incorrect data, perform wrong computations, or take wrong actions. This threat is particularly relevant in autonomous systems for several reasons. First, they are often deployed in unattended, possibly hostile environments. Second, often they are not equipped with physical protection mechanisms for cost and performance reasons. Third, autonomous systems are generally composed of several to many embedded computing units. Therefore, practical and functional reasons require a functionality of remote firmware updating. However, connecting embedded computing units over the network greatly increases the risk of attacks against behaviour integrity. Actually, if an attacker breaks into the remote firmware update channel, then he/she could compromise the security of the firmware by spoofing and counterfeiting it or even injecting a Trojan horse [6,8].

Finally, *confidentiality* refers to the confidence that no information is disclosed to unauthorised principals. Confidentiality guarantees that information provided by an entity is accessible only to legitimate users. Privacy is a special case of confidentiality when the information is personal (e.g. information collected by a camera). A successful violation of confidentiality is called *disclosure*. A disclosure not only undermines sensitive and personal information but it can provide an adversary information for more effective attacks against integrity and availability. A disclosure attacks may be thus an intermediate step of a more elaborate attack strategy.

3 A Framework for Simulation of Attack Impact

The framework is composed of three components: i) an *Attack Description Language* that makes it possible to describe the *effects* of an attack; ii) an *Attack Simulator* that simulates the effects of attacks on the system under investigation and consequently makes it possible to evaluate their impact; iii) an *Attack Description Compiler* that convert attack effects descriptions into simulator configuration files.

The user first describes the effects of an attack to be evaluated by means of the Attack Description Language—possibly, descriptions are stored for later reuse. Then, the user compiles such a description into a configuration file which is provided as input to the attack simulator. Finally, the simulator simulates executions of the system affected by the described attack.

3.1   The Attack Description Language

The Attack Description Language (ADL) allows users to describe attacks to be evaluated. It is important to notice that here we are not interested in how an attack can be actually carried out. This issue attains to the feasibility of the attack which is the other dimension of risk assessment and is not our focus. Rather, we are interested in the effects of an attack once it has been successfully played. To fix ideas, let us consider an injection attack, a kind of deception attacks. We are not interested in how the adversary can inject fake messages in the system but, rather, in what are the effects of such messages once they have been successfully injected.

From such a standpoint, we assume that the successful execution of an attack produces a sequence of *events*, which takes place atomically. ADL consists in a collection of *statements* that allow the user to specify such a sequence of events. We consider two sets of *simple* statements: i) *node statements*, that allow us to describe alterations in node behaviour and account for physical attacks; and ii) *message statements*, that allow us to describe actions on network messages—including eavesdropping, injection, and dropping—and account for cyber attacks.

The node statements are

- destroy(nodeID, t) removes node nodeId from the network at time t.
- move(nodeID, pos, t) moves node nodeID to position pos at time t.
- spoof(nodeId, sensorId, value, t) returns the spoofed value value to sensor sensorID of node nodeID at time t.

The message statements are

- drop(pkt) discards the packet pkt.
- create(pkt, fld, content) creates a new packet pkt and fill its field fld with content.
- clone(srcPkt, dstPkt) clones packet srcPkt into packet dstPkt.
- change(pkt, fld, newContent) writes newContent into field fld of packet pkt.
- retrieve(pkt, fld, var) copies the content of the field fld of packet pkt into variable var.
- put(pkt, dstNodes, TX | RX, delay) puts packet pkt either in the TX or RX buffer of all nodes in the dstNodes list after a delay delay.

ADL provides other statements that allow *delayed* and *periodical* occurrence of events. For instance

schedule time = T; nodes = <list of nodes >
  {<list of events >}

and,

schedule delay = D; nodes = <list of nodes >
  {<list of events >}

specify that the list of events takes place on the list of nodes at time T or after delay D, respectively. In contrast

schedule time = T; period = P; nodes = <list of nodes >
    {<list of events >}

and

schedule delay = D; period = P; nodes = <list of nodes >
    {<list of events >}

specify that the list of events takes place periodically, with period P, on the list of nodes since time T or a delay D, respectively.

Finally, ADL allows us to describe the *conditional* occurrence of events. For instance

schedule time = T; nodes = <list of nodes >
    if(<condition >) {<list of events >}

specifies that the list of events takes place on the list of nodes if condition evaluates to TRUE.

The ADL makes it is possible to describe complex attacks in a concise although clear way. Let us consider a *wormhole attack* starting at time 200 s, and that tunnels MAC packets sent by node 3 to a remote area of the network containing nodes 15, 17, and 18. It follows that these nodes believe that node 3 is a neighbour of theirs whereas it is actually not. This attack may have severe implications on the integrity of the network because, if the tunnel stops delivering packets, the network gets partitioned. This attack can be described as follows

dstList=15,17,18;
schedule t = 200; nodes = "*"
    if(packet.MAC.source==3 &&
      packet.MAC.type==DATA)
        put(packet,dstList,RX,0);

It is worthwhile to notice that in the boolean condition we have used the dot notation packet.layer.field in order to specify the field field of packet packet in the header of layer layer. This means that, in general, the user must be aware of the actual specific network protocols that are in use at each communication layer, for each of them the packet header structures and fields, and finally the capabilities possibly offered by the simulator. For instance, the OMNeT++ platform [7] and the WSNs simulator Castalia [3] provide a set of objects, called *descriptors*, aimed at handling packets of a given communication layer and accessing their header fields.

3.2   The Attack Simulator Architecture

With reference to Figure 2, the Attack Simulator considers every node as implemented by a *Enhanced Node* module which, in its turn, is composed of an Application Module, a Sensing Module, a Network module, and a Local Event Manager (LEM) module. All sub-modules but the LEM module can be off-the-shelf. The Application and Sensing modules may be composed of different

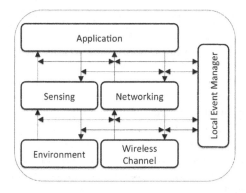

Fig. 2. Attack Simulator: the Enhanced Node module

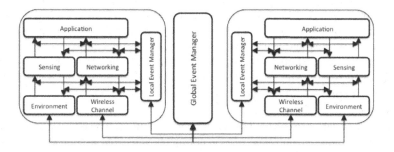

Fig. 3. Attack Simulator: the Global Event Manager

sub-modules, which model the actual node application as well as physical sensing processes. Similarly, the Network module may include an arbitrarily complex combination of communication layers, e.g. routing and MAC.

The LEM module is devoted to the management of events related to attacks. LEM operates transparently with respect to the other components of the Node module. The LEM module intercepts all sensed data as well as network packets traveling through the communication stack. LEM may inspect and alter sensor data and packets content, add new ones, or even discard them. Also, it can alter the node behavior at different layers, change the node position in space, or even remove the node from the network.

A system composed of several autonomous systems (also called nodes) is simulated by instantiating an Enhanced Node module for each node and a *Global Event Manager* (GEM) module that connects all the Enhanced Node modules. The GEM module is connected with every LEM module and allows them to communicate and synchronize in order to implement complex distributed attacks such as a wormhole attack, for example. Figure 3 shows the architecture of the simulator for a system composed of two interconnected nodes.

Reproducing Events. A node may appear as argument of a node statement. In this case we say that the event specified by the statement occurs at the node. Similarly, a node may appear in the node clause of a delayed or periodical statement. In this case we say that the events listed in the delayed/periodical statement occur at the node.

At simulation startup, the simulator receives the attack configuration file, parses the attack statements and creates an event list for each node in the system. Let el_i be the event list of node i. The list contains all the events that occur at node i sorted in cronological order. We denote by el_i^j the j-th element in the event list el_i of node i. The simulator associates a timer to each element of the list. We denote by τ_i^j the timer associated to el_i^j. A timer is responsible to schedule the associated event.

Each element in the list specifies an amount of information that depends on the type of the associated event. If a list element is associated to a node event, the element stores the event type and the related actual arguments. If a list element is associated to a delayed event, then the element specifies the scheduling time, the associated node/message event and the related actual arguments. If an element is associated to a periodical event, the element specifies the scheduling time, the scheduling period, the associated node/message event and the related actual arguments. If conditional occurrence of events is present, the condition is stored in the element as well.

Whenever, a timer expires, the simulator consumes the associated event. In doing this, the simulator takes into account the possible associated condition. The simulator evaluates the condition to determine if the event has to be consumed or not. Furthermore, if the statement specifies a periodical event, the event is rescheduled according to the period.

3.3 A Framework Prototype for WSNs

We implemented a preliminary prototype of the framework for wireless sensor networks (WSNs). With reference to Figure 2, as to the Application, Sensing and Network modules we used Castalia [3], an off-the-shelf simulator for WSNs based on the discrete-event simulation platform OMNeT++ [7]. Castalia considers the network as a collection of nodes, which sense values according to a given physical process, and communicate through a commonly shared wireless channel.

In the original architecture of Castalia, nodes are composed of different submodules. A sensor node application interacts with the physical process through a sensor manager module, and retrieves physical information from the environment. Furthermore, nodes are provided with a full communication stack, composed by a routing, a MAC, and a Radio layer. Thanks to such communication modules, the application sends/receives packets to/from the wireless channel. Also, Castalia provides the implementations of different routing and MAC layers.

In our implementation we integrated the Local Event Manager and the Global Event Manager within Castalia. With reference to Figure 4, in our preliminary implementation the Local Event Manager only intercepts incoming and outgoing packets traveling through the communication stack, between every pair of layers.

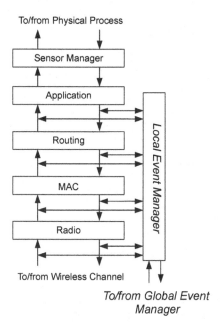

Fig. 4. A Castalia-based prototype

In other words, the Local Event Manager does not intercepts sensor data and thus the simulation framework for the moment does not support the statement spoof.

4   A Case Study: Pollution Monitoring

4.1   Application Scenario

We consider a wireless sensor network (WSN) that monitors the pollution level of an industrial plant. With reference to Figure 5, we consider a plant comprising three independent smokestacks S1, S2, and S3, that release pollutant into the air.

A WSN has been deployed in the field, in order to monitor pollution levels. The WSN is organized in three clusters, C1, C2, and C3, one for each smokestack, respectively. Each cluster is composed of three sensor nodes and one *cluster head*. We denote by CH1, CH2, and CH3, respectively, the cluster heads of the three clusters. In each cluster, every sensor node periodically senses pollution emissions of the corresponding smokestack, and sends a report to its cluster head. This node periodically computes an average pollution level, and delivers it to a *sink* node.

The sink checks whether a single report exceeds a given threshold. The sink also aggregates reports from cluster heads to detect possible infringements of

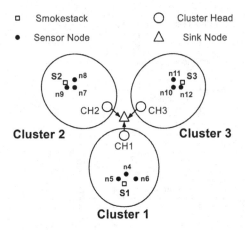

Fig. 5. The industrial plant

pollution limits at the level of the whole plant. So doing, possible anomalies, malfunctioning, or even conscious illegal deeds can be signaled to competent authorities.

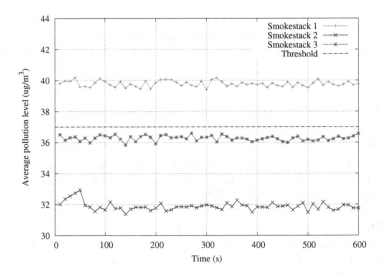

Fig. 6. Attack-free system

Figure 6 shows the behaviour of the plant in an attack-free situation. Smokestack S1 infringes the pollution level limit, that we have supposed to be fixed at $37\ \mu g/m^3$. The dashed line depicts the pollution level that smokestacks are supposed not to exceed. The other curves represent the average pollution levels over time for smokestack S1, S2, and S3. The graph shows that emissions from S1 exceeds the threshold.

Thanks to the WSN, it is possible to detect anomalies in pollutant emissions and react promptly. This of course assumes that sensor nodes and cluster head nodes work correctly, i.e. collected data are genuine and report delivery occurs regularly.

However, an adversary might have an interest to attack the WSN in order to tamper with the data collection process, alter the monitoring process, and mask the misbehavior of S1. In the next section, we discuss possible attacks against the WSN, specifically cluster C1, and evaluate their impact on the WSN overall monitoring capability.

4.2   The Threat Model

With reference to the application scenario described in Section 4.1, an adversary may compromise the monitoring service by altering reports produced by sensor nodes before being collected by cluster heads. In particular, an adversary might be interested in altering the computation of average pollution levels on cluster head CH1 in order to bring average pollution levels below the fixed threshold so that pollutant emissions from smokestack S1 would appear as regular, so concealing an actual limit infringement. In the following, we consider three possible attacks against the WSN, namely injection attack, misplace attack, and wormhole attack. The first attack is purely cyber, the second one is purely physical, whereas the third one is a cyber-physical one. Therefore, this attack selection provides the full range of attack types that can be launched against the WSN.

In an *injection attack*, the adversary creates fake report packets, and inject them into cluster C1, pretending they have been sent by a legitimate sensor node belonging to C1. Of course, fake values carried by such reports alter the computation of average pollution levels on cluster head CH1. This attack is quite hard to get detected. However, comparisons with other nodes' reports may help to contrast its effectiveness.

In a *misplacement attack*, the adversary captures one sensor node in cluster C1, and moves it from its original position to a new one. By properly choosing the new position, e.g. farther from smokestack S1 than the original, it is possible to make the sensor node measure a smaller value of the pollutant and thus alter the computation of average pollution levels on cluster head CH1. This attack is far more difficult to detect, since cluster head nodes assume that all sensor nodes' original positions remain unchanged over time.

In a *wormhole attack*, the adversary operates in two steps. First, the adversary captures one sensor node u from cluster C1, and places it in a different cluster in order to make the sensor node to measure pollutant emissions from a different but regularly emitting smokestack. Second, the adversary tampers the misplaced node u, in order to make it perform a wormhole attack. That is, node u does not send its report to the cluster head of the cluster where it has been moved to. Rather, node u forwards its report to cluster head CH1 through a dedicated low-latency channel. Therefore, as values reported by node u refer to a regular smokestack, the computation of average pollution levels of smokestack S1 by cluster head CH1 gets inevitably altered. It is well-known that wormhole attacks are particularly difficult to contrast.

4.3   Quantitative Analysis of Impact of Attacks

In this section we report on the use of our simulation framework to quantitatively evaluate the impact of the attacks described in Section 4.2. We consider a WSN where each sensor node is equipped with a CC2420 radio chipset and runs the Multipath Rings routing protocol and the the T-MAC link-level protocol. We also assume that sensor nodes collect pollution measurements every 70 ms, while cluster heads compute average pollution levels every 10 s. Report packets transmitted by sensor nodes are 39 bytes in size, and include a payload whose size is 4 bytes. Finally, we assume the pollution level threshold is set to 37 $\mu g/m^3$. The adopted pollutant propagation model is based on the *Customizable Physical Process* provided by the Castalia simulator.

Simulation results has been obtained by means of 30 simulation runs, whose length was 600 seconds each. Each attack occurs at time $t = 200$ s.

Injection Attack. In this attack, we consider an adversary injecting fake report packets into cluster C1. Specifically, the adversary creates fake report packets as follows. First, the value 4 is written in the source node ID field of each layer header. So doing, every forged packet appears originated from node $n4$ of cluster C1. Then, the report packet payload is set to 33 $\mu g/m^3$. Such a value is quite close to the average pollution level detected in cluster C2 (Figure 6) and thus results plausible from a cluster head CH1 standpoint. As a consequence, the attack is not easy detectable.

An important parameter of this attack is the adversary throughput. Of course the higher the throughput the higher the impact, but also the higher the visibility and therefore the risk of being detected. In order to evaluate the impact of the adversary throughput, we consider different *injection intervals* P_i. Figure 7 shows the effects of the injection attack for different values of P_i. As we can see, the larger the injection interval, the less effective the attack is. However, if $P_i < 50$ ms, the attack is successfully performed, and the average pollution level goes beyond the threshold. Furthermore, it is evident that the adversary has no reason to perform the attack with an injection period smaller than 35 ms. In fact, it would require a great energy expenditure by the adversary, and could even be perceived as a Denial of Service, with increased chance of being detected.

Misplacement Attack. In this attack, the adversary physically shifts $n5$ of cluster C1 away from smokestack S1. For the sake of simplicity, we assume that the node is only shifted along the y-axis only, towards cluster head CH1.

An important parameter of this attack is the displacement distance L. Figure 8 shows the impact of the attack for different values of L. As it turns out,

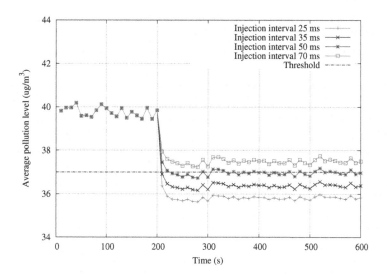

Fig. 7. Pollution level reported under injection attack

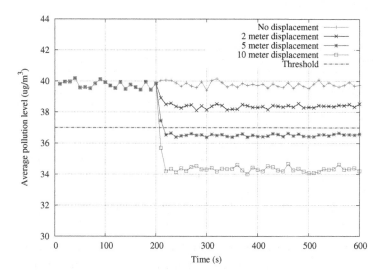

Fig. 8. Pollution level reported under misplace attack

shifting node $n5$ 2 m away from its original position is insufficient to mask over-emissions. Instead, if $L \geq 5$ meters, the adversary manages to achieve her objective. Of course, the farther sensor nodes are misplaced, the more effective the attack is.

Finally we observe that further simulative results showed us that the misplace attack is slightly less effective if it is sensor node $n4$ that gets misplaced. We omit these simulation results for the sake of brevity. However, we observe that without the simulation framework it might be difficult to estimate the attack impact by simply observing how sensor nodes are positioned in the field.

Wormhole Attack. In this attack the adversary shifts node $n5$ from cluster C1 into cluster C2, close to node $n7$. By doing so, node $n5$ measures pollutant emissions of smokestack S2 which, unlike smokestack S1, stays within an acceptable pollution level (see Figure 6). Then, sensor node $n5$ is reprogrammed in order to tunnel sensed data to cluster CH1 through a dedicated communication channel. Each sensed data is tunneled two times. Since the sample interval of $n5$ is 70 ms, and each sample is transmitted twice, we have an equivalent *wormhole period*, P_w, equal to 35 ms.

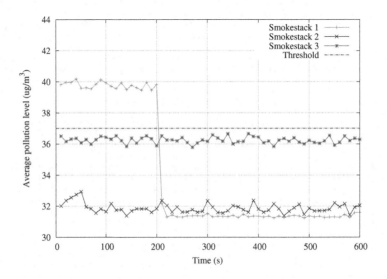

Fig. 9. Pollution level reported under wormhole attack

Figure 9 shows the effects of the wormhole attack on pollution monitoring. As we can see, the average pollution level in cluster C1 appears equal to about 31 $\mu g/m^3$, i.e. far below the threshold. This means the wormhole attack results to be even more effective than the injection attack discussed in Section 4.3. In fact, in case of injection attack with injection interval equal to 35 ms, cluster C1 displays an average pollution level comprised between 36 and 37 $\mu g/m^3$, that is closer to the threshold (see Figure 7).

4.4   Attack Ranking

In this section, we describe a possible way to rank security attacks according to their impact.

A Metric for Integrity. In this section, we define a *security metric* aimed at measuring the respective impacts of the three attacks described and analyzed in Sections 4.2 and 4.3. Since the three deception attacks are against integrity, for the sake of brevity we limit ourselves to a metric that quantifies the level of deception of an attack. In the most general case, we should define metrics also for the levels of disclosure and denial of service. However, it is worthwhile to notice that wrong data is generally worse than no data, and therefore integrity is often given more priority than availability [2].

Notice also that computing security metrics requires to collect specific information, including the number and type of packets received by recipient nodes, the expiration of real-time deadlines, and the occurrence of packet interception by compromised nodes. In the most general case, application level information only might not be sufficient to compute security metrics. In other words, we also need information related to the network behavior and the actual communication among nodes. Therefore, unless the considered system model relies on very strong, and possibly unrealistic, assumptions, we believe that network and attack simulation is a valuable and essential approach to gather essential information, and perform the attack ranking process.

Let x_A denotes the level of deception of an attack A. That is, x_A indicates how information v' in the presence of attack A differs from information v when the system is attack free. Such metric is an extension of those described by Cardenas *et al.* in [2]. Formally,

$$x_A = \frac{\sum_{i=1}^{M} r_i \cdot \left(\frac{\sum_{j=1}^{S_i} \|v_j - v'_j\|^2}{S_i} \right)}{M} \tag{1}$$

where M denotes the number of devices handling forged samples; r_i the weight of the i-th device; S_i the number of samples considered on the i-th device, and, finally, v_j and v'_j the expected and the forged j-th sample, respectively. Notice that although the adversary has no particular restrictions on the choice of v'_j, however she has to be careful that v'_j is still valid from a system standpoint.

Attack Severity Evaluation. With reference to Equation 1, for each attack A, we compute two values: i) x_A^C, which refers to the impact of the attack on cluster C1, i.e. it takes into account the average values computed by cluster head CH1; and ii) x_A^S which refers to the impact on the system as a whole, i.e. it takes into account average values computed by the sink node. In both cases, we assume $M = 1, r_1 = 1,$ and $S_1 = 60.$. As to the injection attack, we consider several injection intervals, namely, 25, 35, 50, and 70 milliseconds. As to the misplacement attack, we consider several displacement distances, namely 2, 5, and 10 meters. Finally, as to the wormhole attack, we consider several wormhole intervals, namely, 23.3, 35, and 70 milliseconds.

Table 1 and 2 report the attack rank according to the computed value of x_A^C and x_A^S, respectively. Since the adversary thwarts cluster C1 activities, the impact of each attack is more severe from a cluster standpoint rather than from

Table 1. Rank of attacks at cluster level

Position	x_A^C	Attack	Attack parameter
#1	57.203	Wormhole	$P_w = 23ms$
#2	47.159	Wormhole	$P_w = 35ms$
#3	31.655	Wormhole	$P_w = 70ms$
#4	19.735	Misplace	$L = 10m$
#5	10.493	Injection	$P_i = 25ms$
#6	7.751	Injection	$P_i = 35ms$
#7	7.048	Misplace	$L = 5m$
#8	5.297	Injection	$P_i = 50ms$
#9	3.504	Injection	$P_i = 70ms$
#10	1.332	Misplace	$L = 2m$

Table 2. Rank of attacks at system level

Position	x_A^S	Attack	Attack parameter
#1	7.056	Wormhole	$P_w = 23ms$
#2	5.906	Wormhole	$P_w = 35ms$
#3	4.168	Wormhole	$P_w = 70ms$
#4	1.135	Injection	$P_i = 25ms$
#5	0.921	Misplace	$L = 10m$
#6	0.833	Injection	$P_i = 35ms$
#7	0.564	Injection	$P_i = 50ms$
#8	0.499	Misplace	$L = 2m$
#9	0.389	Misplace	$L = 5$
#10	0.369	Injection	$P_i = 70ms$

a whole system point of view. Also, the wormhole attack always displays the most severe impact against integrity. This is because the misplaced node reports a value that is genuinely small although belonging to another cluster. Of course, the higher the wormhole transmission rate, the higher the attack impact. Finally, integrity in cluster C1 is more affected by the misplacement attack, while the injection attack results to be more effective from a whole system standpoint.

Discussion. Unfortunately space prevents us from discussing countermeasures to the above attacks. However, we would like to give at least a few intuition about how the simulation framework may help a designer to choose countermeasures that implement the best trade-off between cost and efficacy.

As to the injection attack, we can envision two possible countermeasures. The first one consists in authenticating packets. While it is highly effective against an injection attack, it has two disadvantages. First, it introduces the problem of key management. Furthermore, it requires to update the software onboard sensor nodes in order to support this security control. Second, it causes an enlargement of packets because of the attached authenticator. Such an enlargement would increase communication overhead. The other possible countermeasure consists in increasing the redundancy by deploying additional sensor nodes. Intuitively, fake packets would weight less in percentage. The advantage of this solution is that it does not require to install any software, does not require any key management, and does not cause any packet enlargement. On the other hand, by increasing the number of nodes, the overall network traffic would increase as well. The simulation framework could be used to evaluate the cost in terms of additional network traffic of each countermeasure.

Notice also that the application has a reporting period of $70ms$ whereas an injection attack has a meaningful impact at the cluster level (Table 1) if the attack injection period is comprised between 35 and $50ms$. This information could be useful to setup an intrusion detection system to suspect anomalous traffic rates that are $1.4 \div 2$. times as expected.

As to the misplacement attack, possible solutions could be secure data aggregation or secure localization. Another possible solution could be some form of physical protection of nodes, in order to physically prevent an adversary from shifting a sensor node from its established position. However, the analysis carried out by means of the simulation framework allows us to realize that it is not necessary to physically protect all the sensor nodes. As it turns out from Figure 8, physical protection is only necessary for those sensor nodes that are close to smokestack S1 (say, less than $30m$).

As to the wormhole attack we state that packet authentication would be useless. Actually, the misplaced node $n5$ would use the correct keying material to authenticate packed carrying data sensed in another cluster. Notwithstanding, increasing node redundancy would remain an option. The simulation framework would allow us to evaluate both the efficacy of this options as well as its cost in terms of traffic increment. This option should be compared to alternative options based on secure localization and/or physical protection.

5   Conclusions

Security is an important design dimension in cyber-physical systems including autonomous systems, because it is conducive of safety infringements. However, in practice it is not possible to address all possible attacks. For this reason, we need a tool that allows a designer to determine the most "important" ones. We have presented a simulation framework especially conceived to support the designer in this task. The framework allows a designer to describe and simulate attacks, quantitatively evaluate their effects, and, finally, rank them according to such effects. The framework provides a simulation description language that makes it possible to define reusable attack descriptions in a relatively simple way. Furthermore, the framework support and promotes reusing of off-the-shelf simulators. For the moment the framework has been integrated in Castalia, a WSN simulator based on Omnet++.

Acknowledgements. This work has been partially supported by the EU FP7 Project PLANET, "Platform for the Deployment and Operation of Heterogeneous Networked Cooperating Objects" (www.planet-ict.eu), and by the Italian PRIN Project TENACE, "Protecting National Critical Infrastructures From Cyber Threats" (www.dis.uniroma1.it/~tenace/).

References

1. Akdemir, K.D., Karakoyunlu, D., Padir, T., Sunar, B.: An Emerging Threat: Eve Meets a Robot. In: Chen, L., Yung, M. (eds.) INTRUST 2010. LNCS, vol. 6802, pp. 271–289. Springer, Heidelberg (2011)
2. Cardenas, A.A., Roosta, T., Sastry, S.: Rethinking security properties, threat models, and the design space in sensor networks: A case study in SCADA systems. Ad-Hoc Networks 7(8), 1434–1447 (2009)
3. National ICT Australia: Castalia, http://castalia.npc.nicta.com.au/
4. Daidone, R., Dini, G., Tiloca, M.: A solution to the GTS-based selective jamming attack on IEEE 802.15.4 networks. Wireless Networks (2013)
5. European Telecommunications Standard Institute: Telecommunications andf Internet converged Services and Protocols for Advanced Networking (TISPAN); Methods and protocols; Part 1: Method and proforma for Threat, Risk, Vulnerability Analysis, ETSI TS 102 165-1 V4.2.3 (2011-03) (2011)
6. Gorog, C.: Protect Firmware from Counterfeating (2011), http://www.embeddedintel.com/special_features.php?article=1265
7. OMNeT++ Network Simulation Framework, http://www.omnetpp.org/
8. Shade, L.K.: Implementing Secure Firmware Updates. In: Proceedings of the Embedded Systems Conference Silicon Valley (2011)
9. Tiloca, M., De Guglielmo, D., Dini, G., Anastasi, G.: SAD-SJ: a Self-Adaptive Decentralized solution against Selective Jamming attack in Wireless Sensor Networks. In: Proceedings of the IEEE International Conference on Emerging Technology & Factory Automation (ETFA 2013), Cagliari, Italy (2013)
10. Warner, J.S., Johnston, R.G.: GPS spoofing countermeasures. Homeland Security Journal (2003)
11. Wyglinski, A.M., Huang, X., Padir, T., Lai, L., Eisenbarth, T.R., Venkatasubramanian, K.: Security of Autonomous Systems Employing Embedded Computing and Sensors. IEEE Micro 33(1), 80–86 (2013)

MedALE Project: A Networked Simulation Exercise

Paolo Galati[1], Fausto Pusceddu[1], Paolo Nurra[1], Marco Pasciuto[2],
and Giovanni Riccardi[2]

[1] Alenia Aermacchi S.p.A., Torino, Italy
{paolo.galati,fausto.pusceddu,paolo.nurra}@alenia.it
[2] ENAV S.p.A., Aeroporto di Capodichino, Napoli, Italy
{marco.pasciuto,giovanni.riccardi}@sicta.it

Abstract. The recently started Mediterranean ATM Live Exercise (MedALE) project among the SESAR Integrated RPAS Demonstration Activities, has the goal to provide to a wide spectrum of European Stakeholders indications and recommendations about the validity and limits of the existing RPAS assets, practices and operational procedure, while identifying the future necessary improvements or modifications to comply with the new ATM concepts that SESAR is realizing. A combined approach will be adopted: Networked Simulation in a complex ground and flight environment with human-in-the-loop, and a Flight Demo in a real and significant operational environment. In the paper we present the Networked Simulation exercise that will be focused on a multi RPAS interaction/operation within the ATM SESAR environment, including BLOS operations in a non–segregated airspace.

Keywords: Distributed Simulation, RPAS, autonomous system, SESAR ATM.

1   Introduction

The development of Remotely Piloted Aircraft System (RPAS) has opened a promising new chapter in the history of aviation, military applications have already demonstrated their operational effectiveness and are fully operational in several services. However the new challenge will be the insertion of RPAS in the ATM. These systems are based on innovative technologies developments, offering solutions which may open new and improved civil/commercial applications, as well as improvements to the safety and efficiency of civil aviation without increase Air Traffic Control Operators (ATCOs) workload. In light of these significant benefits, the European Remotely Piloted Air Systems Steering Group (ERSG)[1] has recognised a need to identify, plan, coordinate, and subsequently monitor the activities necessary to achieve the safe integration of RPAS into a non-segregated Air Traffic Management (ATM) environment. Given that the full integration of RPAS into the European ATM System is vital and that the mission of SESAR is to create the new generation of ATM systems and operations, RPAS will need to be incorporated into future Single European Sky ATM Research Programme (SESAR) solutions. The SESAR Joint Undertaking launched a Call for Proposals[2] in order to select and co-finance a wide variety of Projects

J. Hodicky (Ed.): MESAS 2014, LNCS 8906, pp. 95–104, 2014.

offering SESAR integrated RPAS demonstration activities. The purpose of the Call was to select a number of projects or demonstration activities, including integrated pre-operational flight trials, which aim to demonstrate how to integrate RPAS into non-segregated airspace in a multi-aircraft flight environment, with the purpose of exploring the feasibility of integration within the wider aviation community by 2016. As a results of the call, 9 out of 23 RPAS Demonstration Projects were selected. MedALE is one of the 9 selected RPAS Projects: it will be developed by a Consortium made by Alenia Aermacchi (as the Project Leader), ENAV – Italian Air Navigation Service Provider), Selex ES, Thales Alenia Space-Italia, and Nimbus.

Networked Simulation Exercise will consider the capability to flight and manage, from an ATCO per-spective, a composite RPAS fleet that are dissimilar in terms of technical capability and con-figuration. Operations in Beyond Radio Line Of Sight (BRLOS) will be considered allowing to validate ad-hoc operational procedures for their management. The Real Time simulation with Human-in-the-loop will consider the interaction and cooperation among the different involved actors (ATC controllers and RPAS Operators).

2   Distributed Simulation

Simulation technologies apply throughout the entire life cycle of systems, from the definition of requirements, to development and training. Networking of simulations permits single monolithic simulations to be connected allowing the generation of complex simulation where multiple entities are able to interact in a common shared scenario. In this context MedALE simulation exercise will take advantage from the availability of different simulation platforms remotely located and from a specific defined distributed scenario in order to allow the achievements of the research specific goals. Continuous researches on distributed simulation technologies has provided the availability of different standards, main of this are High Level Architecture (HLA), Distributed Interactive Simulation (DIS), Test and Training Enabling Architecture (TENA), and others, each with its pros and cons.

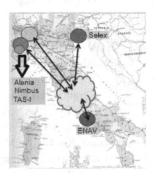

Fig. 1. MedALE Simulation Platforms

The picture below illustrates the high level architecture/topology of the Simulation Platforms that will be established in order to perform the distributed simulation Exercise, in particular it shows their physical location.

3   MedALE Concept

3.1   Simulation Exercise

The MedALE Project will be developed by two main steps that will progressively increase the level of complexity: a Networked Simulation Exercise and a Live Trial.

In this paper we present the Networked Simulation Exercise that will assess and evaluate how the ATCOs could manage the introduction of RPAS operation in a non-segregated airspace considering also the analysis of audio communication between ATCOs and RPAS Operators. Following the RPAS definition, three classes of RPAS with different performance will be involved in the simulation exer-cise: Medium Altitude Long Endurance (MALE) RPAS represented by the Alenia Aermacchi Sky-Y technological demonstrator, Light RPAS represented by the Nimbus C-Fly and Medium Altitude Medium Endurance (MAME) RPAS represented by the Selex ES Falco. A dedicated network will be used linking three simulation platforms of the three RPAS with the ENAV ATC Simulation Platform.

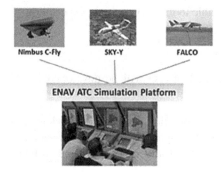

Fig. 2. MedALE Networked Simulation Exercise concept

The MedALE Networked Simulation Exercise is an important complementary step to the Live Trial (i.e. real flight) activities and will take advantage of existing National Simulation Facilities such as the Finmeccanica SimLabs network. SimLabs[3] is a scalable and reconfigurable on-demand operating network among Finmeccanica companies' simulation laboratories which has established the environment that allows "constructive" simulation systems and human operators of virtual systems to interact. Due to its complexity, Networked Simulation Exercise requires training sessions for ATC controllers in order to:

- Provide a sufficient knowledge of the RPASs domain assessed during the Exercise;
- Familiarize with the airspace settings and with the operational procedures and working methods that will be used;

- Provide a sufficient knowledge and practice of the RPAS functions and Human Machine Interface.

A proper interaction will be established to motivate a wide variety of key-Stakeholder about the validity of the existing assessed solutions and need to progress in some areas that are considered a key-priority for the success of RPAS insertion in a non-segregated airspace. The following main groups of Stakeholders have been identified:

- SESAR JU and its members demonstrating to the wider aviation community the benefits coming from the SESAR concept elements in a multi-RPAS flight environment;
- Ground and Airborne Industries;
- Airport Authorities;
- National Aviation Authorities by showing how RPAS flights can be undertaken as part of normal operations while assessing contingency events do not impact the normal flow of air traffic;
- RPAS Associations contributing to the MedALE Project communication / dissemination;
- Italian Air Force assessing ATC procedures and RPAS operations in simulated transition between Military and Civil airspace;
- NATO Modelling and Simulation Centre of Excellence by supporting the creation a virtual environment able to meet experiment expectation;

3.2 Validation Objectives

The Networked Simulation Exercise will be developed in order to demonstrate the following Objectives:

- Multi RPAS interaction/operation within the ATM environment that SESAR is defining, including BRLOS operations in non-segregated airspace (i.e. operations in BRLOS will be considered allowing to validate ad-hoc operational procedures for their proper management);
- RPAS compliance with ATCOs clearances (i.e. to assess the impact on ATCOs and RPAS Pilot workload and situational awareness, also taking into account the study of "non-nominal case(s)";
- Conflict's identification and its resolution through ATCO instructions to RPAS;
- RPAS Loss of signal (i.e. it will imply ATC procedures to ensure the safety in the area);

3.3 Simulation Platforms

The involved Simulation Platforms federated for the Simulation Exercise are described in this paragraph.

The ENAV ATC Simulation Platform provides the full set of capabilities allowing to operate in Real Time Simulations, including Flight Data Processing (FDP), Arrival Manager (AMAN), Radar Data Processing (RDP), Safety Nets (STCA, MSAW and APW), Air Traffic Generator (ATG), Data Preparation and Data Logging. It includes gateways that allow interoperability with external platforms via SVS or DIS standard.

The Unmanned Aircraft System (UAS) Full Mission Simulator is one of the main assets developed by Alenia Aermacchi S.p.A. for supporting the development of the UAS system and for the training of Operators. It is capable of simulating a complete mission of the Sky-Y Technological Demonstrator with full representative models. An essential capability is the possibility of interconnection via standard HLA/DIS allowing to share a Synthetic Scenario and to be part of a distribute Simulation Environment. The Image Generator is able to show the entities in the scenario (e.g. other UAVs or manned civil traffic). The management of the simulation session – parameters and environment set-up, failures injection, start, stop and freeze etc. – is feasible via a dedicated user interface operated by the specialists or by the instructor.

The Nimbus UAS Simulator is realized by NIMBUS and it is capable of simulating a mission of the C-Fly Light RPAS Demonstrator. Six degrees of freedom flight dynamics model is complemented by integration of two visualization programs, data registration modules, control device interface, flight data display module, landing gear damage detector and indicator, crash condition detector and monitor, wind application module, automatic flight control module and soft real-time execution module.

The Selex ES Falco Simulator is an advanced training system designed to train both RPAS Pilots and Mission Payload Operator for ISTAR missions in complex simulated scenarios. Falco Simulator pro-vides a set of advanced tools to refine the Concept of Operations (CONOPS) and to fully explore the capabilities of the Falco RPAS in a completely simulated environment. Operators' Console Assembly is the same of the real Ground Control Station and it's the simulator main subsystem.

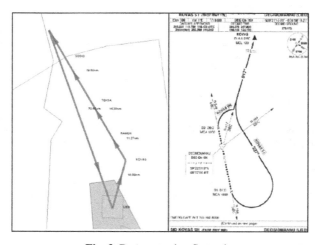

Fig. 3. Demonstration Scenario

The Thales Alenia Space Italia SATCOM Simulator will be integrated with the Alenia Aermacchi UAS Full Mission simulator in order to allow the demonstration of the MALE RPAS operations and procedures in presence of BRLOS satellite data link performances. The Satellite Communication (SATCOM) simulator will take into account several factors of the SATCOM BRLOS datalink impacting its Quality of Signal.

3.4   Demonstration Scenario

The demonstration scenario will be focused as a "round robin" during which the Real Time Simulations of Sky-Y, Nimbus and Falco RPAS will allow to analyze how the existing Operational procedures are applicable to the non-segregated airspace rules.

The Scenario will be the Decimomannu LIED airport: all the RPASs will land and take-off from this Airport following the General Air Traffic / Operational Air Traffic (GAT/OAT) procedures. The following steps will be taken into account:

- Take-off from a military airport and climb into the segregated airspace.
- Take-off from transition from segregated military airspace to the Area Of Operations (i.e. over the sea restricted area).
- Within the area of operations the RPASs will constantly interact with ATC (communication, identification, execution of instructions such as climb/descent, etc.);
- Separation minima from reserved portion of airspace (aside, below or above) will be under ATC responsibility. Non nominal case will include the case of a vicinity warning detected by ATC and issuing the instructions to re-establish navigation with proper horizontal and/or lateral separation.
- RPAS compliance with ATCOs clearances (i.e. to assess the impact on ATCOs and RPAS Pilot workload and situational awareness, also taking into account the study of "non-nominal case(s)".
- BRLOS conditions (only for MALE RPAS/Sky-Y).
- Transition again from the area of operations to segregated military airspace.
- Presence of contingency regarding for example: loss of communication, engine failure, etc.

3.5   Human Resources Involved

The following table reassumes the human resources involved in the Simulation Exercise and the related activities:

Table 1. Actors involved in Demonstration Activities

Actor	Activities
Exercise Manager	Manages the preparation process in order to ensure the execution of the exercise in line with objectives and timeline.
Exercise Technical Coordinator	Sets the Technical platform according to project requirements. Organises regular Technical and Operational Tests, according to the Project schedule.
Exercise Operational Leader	Supports the definition of the operational scenario applied. Contributes to the definition of ATCOs' working methods and operational procedures. Supports the definition and evaluation of the traffic samples. Coordinates with the ACCs the ATCOs' availability during tests and exercise. Manages the training preparation.
Scenario Set-Up	Prepares the operational scenarios for the Exercise, the traffic samples for tests, training and exercise. Implements non nominal events in the traffic samples if needed.
Human Factors Analyst	Contributes to define the organisations and the data collection methods applied. Prepares data collection materials (observation grids, scripts for debriefings, questionnaires). Contributes to define the recording specifications. Defines non nominal events to be introduced in the traffic samples. Defines experimental design, agenda of the exercise, the ATCOs seating plan according to the experimental design.
Safety Analyst	Contributes to select the data collection methods applied. Prepares data collection materials. Contributes to define the recording specifications, experimental design and agenda of the Exercise. Defines non nominal events to be introduced in the traffic samples
Other Analysts	Contribute to define the recording specifications.
RPAS Pilots	RPAS flight path definition. Contribute to the definition of the performance expectations. Interaction with the ATCOs.
Satellite Comm. Expert	Contribute to the definition of the SATCOM operational scenario (e.g. transition from LOS to BRLOS) and non-nominal events. SATCOM adaption and HMI modification based on experimentation needs. Support to SATCOM integration with MALE RPAS simulator platform and to relevant acceptance tests.

4   Current Activities

The following activities are in progress:

- Initial Demo Concept description and Assessment (i.e. Flight Demo and Networked Simulation Demo);

- Networked Simulation Requirements (i.e. RPAS simulator adaptation requirements, ATM simulator adaptation, network simulation integration);

The Demo Concept is under definition and it will detail the scope of the demonstration activities by identifying the new concept description, the operational characteristics, operational Environment and the involved actors. The Networked Simulation Requirements will define the requirements of the networked simulation addressing the adaptation of the simulation assets and the integration requirements (i.e. collection and integration of the adaptation requirements provided by the RPAS simulators involved, collection and integration of the adaptation requirements provided by the ATM simulator).

5   Results Analysis

For each simulation session execution the data will be collected by the following Collection Methods:

- Over the shoulder Observations;
- Questionnaires;
- Debriefings;
- System Data Collection;

The table below reports the used Methods and the type of assessment.

Table 2. Data Collection Methods. QUAL = Qualitative; QUAN = Quantitative; OBJ = Objective; SUBJ = Subjective.

Actor	QUAL	QUAN	OBJ	SUBJ
Over the shoulder Observations	√		√	
Questionnaires	√	√		√
Debriefings	√			√
System Data Collection		√	√	

Over the shoulder Observation techniques are based on the idea of understanding the users' behaviour in their social context. The main strength of direct observation is the possibility to capture the difference between the normative way of working and the actual one, highlighting the existence and the relevance of common practices of work, personal strategies, standard deviations from official rules, informal rules, common behaviours neither Controllers are aware of.

Questionnaires are designed to elicit user perception of the total workload required to perform the task as well as how certain characteristics of the task contributed to the overall workload and, to assess users' subjective satisfaction with specific aspects.

Debriefings allow, due to the free-form nature of the interaction, to collect unexpected viewpoints may be identified which may be otherwise overlooked if a more structured approach were adopted. Data collected though the Observations are then verified and discussed during the Debriefings, and from the other hand insights emerged during the debriefings are then used to guide the following observations.

System Data Collection will be collected by extraction from exercise platform log and it will be employed to assess the validation objectives (i.e. the analysis will provide a response about the statistical significance of the observed differences between the baseline and the different organisations as well as between organisations themselves).

6 Expected Results

The Networked Simulation Exercise will be very useful to understand how the ATCOs could be familiar with the introduction of RPAS operation in a non-segregated airspace: in particular with their performances, during main phases of flight. In addition will be very interesting the analysis on communication between Air Traffic Controller Operators (ATCOs) and RPAS Pilots. According to these concepts the following two main Key Performance Areas are investigated in the Exercise: Human Performances and Safety with particular attention to Workload as well as Situational Awareness. For this reason the identified expectations are:

- The level of Workload and/or Situational Awareness is considered acceptable in relation with the introduction of RPAS flights in non-segregated airspace;
- The perceived safety is maintained at least at the equivalent level in the ATC environment;
- No several impacts on Safety in the Real Time communication between RPAS pilots and ATCOs;
- During RPAS Departing / Arrival procedures the level of safety is maintained to an adequate level;

7 Conclusion

In this paper we have described how distributed simulations exercises involving several actors for the Mediterranean ATM Live Exercise (MedALE) would provide significant supporting experience towards the insertion of Remotely Piloted Aircraft Systems (RPASs) into non-segregated airspace. The scope of the MedALE RPAS project is to provide suggestions and recommendations useful for the new generation Air Traffic Management (ATM) environment that SESAR is defining. The Project is in the early phases of the development and the Simulator Platform's adaptation is under definition. At the end of the Networked Simulation "Campaign" the output will be included in a Final Assessment Report that will provide:

- Analysis of results;
- Suggestions and advice about validity and limits of the RPAS assets into non-segregated airspace;
- Future necessary improvements and modifications;

- Indications and Recommendations to comply with the new ATM under SESAR definition;

The output of the Networked Simulation Exercise will be considered as input for the Live Trial activities. In this way a natural evolution of the concept will be reached.

References

1. Roadmap for the integration of civil Remotely-Piloted Aircraft Systems into the European Aviation System (June 2013)
2. SESAR JU, Call Ref. SJU/LC/0087–CFP
3. Aeronautica & Difesa, pp. 60–61 (July 2013)

Integrated Simulation Facility
for Interoperability Operation

Nicola Genito, Ferdinando Montemari, Gianluca Corraro, Domenico Rispo,
Roberto Palumbo, and Pasquale Canzolino

CIRA Italian Aerospace Research Center, Capua, Italy
{n.genito,f.montemari,g.corraro,d.rispo,r.palumbo,
p.canzolino}@cira.it

Abstract. In the past years the Italian Research Aerospace Center (CIRA) has
developed several simulation facilities able to reproduce in real time the behavior of manned and unmanned aircrafts, air traffic scenario and to emulate Air
Traffic Management (ATM)/Air Traffic Control (ATC). In order to allow a simulation in which all these facilities interact among them, also including pilots
and ground control station operators in the loop, a real-time Integrated Simulation Facility (ISF) was realized. The first purpose of the ISF is to perform, in a
real-time simulation environment, the validation and verification of new ground
and onboard systems through the simulation of complex scenarios. The second
purpose of ISF is to develop, verify and optimize new procedure for the air traffic management. The paper will describe the ISF architecture, the HW/SW
component and the operating modalities.

Keywords: unmanned, aircraft, simulation, facility, real time, air traffic.

1 Introduction

Unmanned aircraft are remotely piloted aircraft, meaning that the pilot is not on board
the aircraft. An Unmanned Aircraft System (UAS) consists of one or more unmanned
aircraft, one or more control stations and the command and control links as well as
any other system elements. Until few years ago UAS were mainly used for military
missions but a non-military UAS market is rapidly emerging. UAS are considered to
be beneficial in a growing number of civil and non-military/governmental applications. In general employing UAS is considered useful for missions, where the human
being onboard becomes the limiting factor or missions putting a human pilot at risk.
Unmanned Aircraft Systems are therefore becoming increasingly important for non-
military applications, e.g. aerial photography, pipeline and power line surveillance,
fisheries and wildlife monitoring, fire-fighting, weather and climate studies, law en-
forcement, etc. A main challenge however is the integration of UAS into the existing
and future ATM proposing procedures to integrate the operation of UAS without a
significant impact on the current users of the airspace. It is predicted that air traffic
will increase to three times the current figures and this is without UAS by 2020, like it

J. Hodicky (Ed.): MESAS 2014, LNCS 8906, pp. 105–120, 2014.
© Springer International Publishing Switzerland 2014

is described in SESAR with a new dimension of European ATM (see SESAR Consortium, 2007a, ref [2]). As UAS operations cause an additional increase in the air traffic volume, it is a fundamental task to assess the feasibility of operational solutions to integrate UAS and its impact, or propose new operational solutions in order not to jeopardize the performance of the future ATM system. Both, ATM procedures and technical and operational requirements need to be taken into account for the future integration of UAS. The focus is set on a mixed traffic scenario where manned and unmanned aircraft co-exists in non-segregated airspace.

The guiding principle is that integration of UAS into non-segregated airspace must be accomplished without compromising existing aviation safety levels or increasing risk to third parties in the air or on the ground. In addition, existing "rules" that are fundamental to safe operations should not be changed (right-of-way rules, existing procedures, radio telephony, etc.) or only if required (e.g. phraseology, emergency procedures). Controllers for example should not be expected to do anything different than they would do for other aircraft under their control nor should they have to apply different rules or work to different criteria. A UAS should be able to comply with 4D Trajectory Management processes and/or ATC instructions and have equipment and capabilities applicable to the airspace within which they intend to operate. Inevitable or necessary changes of procedures shall mirror those applicable to manned aviation as much as possible. Therefore UAS operations should not be different from those performed by current manned aircraft. UAS are only accepted as another class of airspace user that, subject to conformance to appropriate regulations, are allowed to operate in non-segregated airspace when not restricting, not hazarding or otherwise unconvincing existing airspace users. The main difference is that the tasks performed by the pilot on-board the aircraft in manned aviation are now per-formed by a pilot in a control station on ground. In such a way a new concept enters into the operational scenario which is the control station. Besides certain situations may occur, because of the specific characteristics of unmanned aircraft, which are unique to UAS, e.g. loss of data link. Other situations are similar to manned aircraft but, because of the specifics of UAS, it is inevitable that they are treated differently. Therefore procedural and technological solutions have to be defined in how to deal with such situations, be it normal or abnormal operating conditions. On the other hand UAS have some unique characteristics with specific capabilities and limitations, which require adaptation to existing procedures or additional ones, e.g. due to performance limitations, flight profiles and additional abilities but basically the established operational procedures as well as those developed for manned aviation will be applied to UAS and adjusted only where required.

UAS may introduce some new technologies and capabilities which could be beneficial to manned aviation as well, specifically, due to their mission profiles most UAS already apply precision 4D trajectories and experiences may be shared. Yet UAS operations shall be compatible with the SESAR concepts of SWIM and 4D trajectories. Developments in 'sense and avoid' systems should also be faced as a significant contribution to safety while UAS voice communication to ATC will remain a special challenge given the continuing need for an immediate response to ATC instructions until replaced by data link communication. Techniques to ensure robust communications, under all conditions will require special attention and potentially special procedures. Since the airspace structure as defined by SESAR (ref. [2]) is split into managed and unmanaged airspace, it is nevertheless important to identify, define and derive a set of technical requirements for all the phases of flight of a UA flying both in managed and unmanaged airspace.

Within this framework it is a fundamental feature to be able to use a simulation facility that allows to verify technologies and procedures in a mixed traffic scenario where manned and unmanned aircraft co-exists in non-segregated airspace too and both managed and unmanaged airspace regions are simulated. In order to allow a simulation in which all agents of the Air Transport Network (Aircraft, ground control station, etc.) interact among them, also including pilots and ground control station operators in the loop, a real-time Integrated Simulation Facility (ISF) was realized by CIRA.

2   Functional Architecture

2.1   General Description

The Integrated Simulation Facility (ISF) is a HW/SW facility that allows to:

- define complex aerospace scenarios composed by interacting agents (vehicle, aircraft, UAV, UAS, meteo hazard, etc.);
- carry out real time simulations in order to validate the simulation platforms' functionalities;
- store the whole simulation data in order to perform a post-processing analysis.

The ISF functional architecture, shown in Fig. 1, is composed by a Simulation Network for the data ex-change between the simulation platforms, the Scenario Simulator and the Simulation Manager. In details, the Scenario Simulator, allows to define a complex scenario in terms of no fly zone, air traffic, ground vehicles, weather hazard, atmospheric condition, GPS satellite constellation, and area of operation which allows to define the airspace class classification, interdicted and segregated areas. Additionally, the properties of each agents can be freely set in order to get the desired behavior during the simulation session.

Whereas the *Simulation Manager* handles the platforms synchronization (initialization, start and stop of a simulation session), stores the scenario initialization files for whole the simulation platforms and record all simulation data exchanged on the network during a simulation session. Furthermore, the simulation platforms can be easily integrated on the ISF network through an *API library*. Such library allows the simulation platforms to communicate through CIRA standardized messages and to create a standalone *ISF-Like* environment in order to perform fast time simulations before integrating itself in the ISF network.

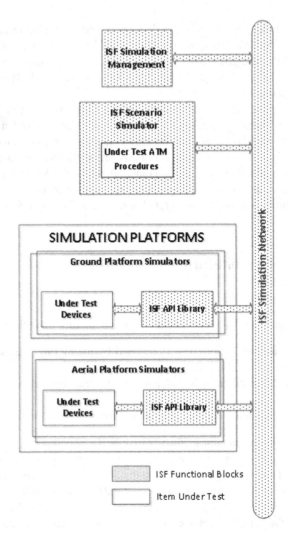

Fig. 1. Integrated Simulation Facility Functional Architecture

In summary, the ISF facility allows to carry out real time simulations for the validation in complex scenarios of:

- one or more devices or functionalities integrated in manned or unmanned aerospace aircraft;
- ATM procedures;
- Devices or functionalities belonging to Ground Platform Simulators which can deliver specific utility services for the other agents of a scenario (air traffic control station, weather stations, ground nav. aids, etc.).

2.2   Scenario Simulator

The scenario simulator has been conceived and developed in order to allow the description of an air traffic scenarios. That is, the scenario simulator enables the construction of user scenarios by mixing programming workload, and an intuitive and easy-to-use interface like a GUI in order to simulate not only an air-traffic scenario but also environmental condition like space region representing a segregated or no-fly zone areas and ATC/ATM rules and operations to be included in such a scenario.

The needs for Scenario Simulator are related to the ability to develop and simulate a relevant number of scenarios in which to recreate useful situations to test and validate the Flight Management Systems (FMS) and Health Monitoring Systems (HMS) software applications that are the main objectives of the whole ISF facility. In particular the simulation environment will allow testing of the collision avoidance and self-separation algorithms and the verification of the 4D trajectory management and of new or standard air traffic control procedures. As far as algorithms testing is concerned, the scenario simulator allows both fast-time and real-time applications.

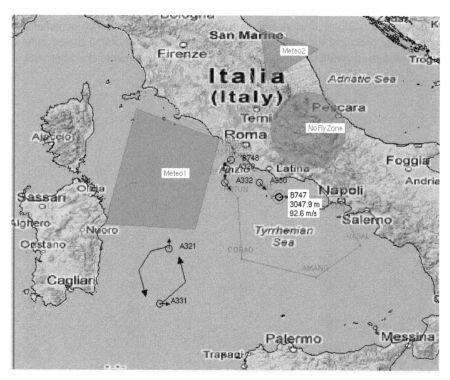

Fig. 2. Scenario Simulator, GUI layout

Specifically the scenario simulator can generate and simulate air traffic scenarios that are characterized by the following elements:

— a generic number of aircrafts occupying simultaneously a defined portion of airspace, represented by displaying a properly raster DTED map of the geographical zone where the simulation scenario is held;
— routes and/or particular trajectories that can be assigned to each aircraft and that are built by using waypoints categorized either by position or by type (according to the standard ARINC 424) and chosen from a built-in database or a database created by the user himself;
— a generic number of special space regions representing segregated or no-fly zone areas;
— space regions that could be characterized from weather conditions particularly relevant for aeronautical flight;
— a global navigation satellite system.

Therefore it is possible to include inside a scenario a generic number of aircrafts with the possibility to add or remove aircrafts from the scenario in any phase of the simulation. In other words it allows creating simple real-time sessions up to complex ones, thru the same user interface. A simple simulation can be having hundreds of dots moving on a 2D plan according to user rules to simulate crowd or behavioral models. Quite precisely the simulation environment allows to define the aircrafts of the scenario setting synthetic parameters that describe their dynamic characteristics.

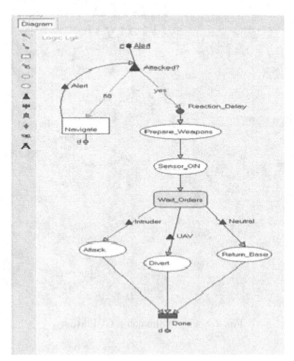

Fig. 3. Logic defined with a flow chart diagram

The dynamics of the vehicles that populate the simulation scenario can be expressed at least as position and velocity vectors as a function of time and shall be simulated either using tools embedded in the simulation environment (taking into account the characteristics of each vehicle), or through time-histories provided by the user that allow to build a specific trajectory.

Scenario simulator main paradigms are: visual components and C++ code generation for deployment. vsTasker and Visual Studio have been adopted as framework deployment for scenario simulator where vsTasker is a real-time simulation toolkit. The key point is that any object can include user C++ code in according to Object Oriented Paradigm (OOP) that will simplify development and allow integration with third party software. In such a way using state-machine descriptions or a diagrams paradigm, complex logics can be defined checked, changed, deployed.

Entry and exit points diagram are powerful triggering mechanism to start or stop a particular behavior in terms of trajectories to follow or actions to execute depending on rules that can be, in such a way, triggered according to facts, events or a user condition. Combining Logics together allows to build more complex behaviors. These behaviors can be then attached to any scenario entity with the aim to create or simulate an ATM rules or an ATC directive.

By using C++ object oriented paradigm and specifically the inheritance mechanism among classes and subclasses it is possible to define specialized component sets too, that can be used to enrich an aircraft dynamic model or to introduce new space entities like a navigation satellite constellation for instance. By combining a new space entity with a Simulink model that can be directly added into Scenario Simulator or loaded from any .mdl file, such as MATLAB functions, it is possible to simulate a new feature like a global navigation satellite constellation by encapsulating the Simulink model itself inside the simulation engine. Obviously each one of the above mentioned solutions requires to put C++ code directly into the proper objects related to the specific solutions adopted with the aim to simulate an aircraft behavior or an ATC/ATM directive in terms of combined logics.

Scenario simulators can distribute simulation using LAN socket according to UDP protocols. Several sockets have been realized to distribute data model information associated to the specific entity that can arrange a scenario: aircrafts, special space region (segregated or no-fly zone areas), meteorological phenomenon, navigation satellite constellation. In such a way it is easily possible to enable only those sockets that are necessary for the specific simulation or to modify socket synthetic parameters like frequency transmission or UDP type mode transmission (Broadcast, Multicast, Unicast) in according to the specific needs required for each entity. For instance frequency transmission required for aircrafts that are speedily crossing a certain region of aircraft-space must be much higher than that one required to spread information about a navigation satellite constellation or about a no-fly zone areas.

At the same time Scenario Simulator can receive data model information that are formatted in according to ISF protocol and are sent from an external platform by using UDP protocol transmission on WAN network. In such a way Scenario Simulator, by using a specific LAN receiver socket based on UDP protocol, can receive data model information related to an external aerial platform and retrieve the necessary information to display correctly external aerial platform on the DTED map inside the scenario simulator GUI panel. Therefore it is possible to realize a complete simulation including and distributing data model information formatted in according to ISF protocol with each external platform properly integrate in the overall simulation facility (ISF).

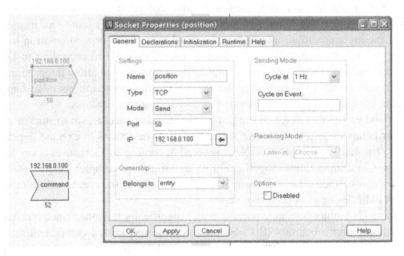

Fig. 4. Scenario Simulator, LAN socket

Finally it is worth to highlight that the scenario simulator can also take advantage of an air traffic builder tool to recreate an air traffic scenario. This tool is suitable to both build and simulate air traffic scenarios with a custom number of aircraft, assigning to each vehicle a custom flight plan. Once the simulation is started, the aircraft follow their way-points according to a motion model that is based on realistic performance parameters taken from Eurocontrol's BADA database. BADA is an aircraft performance database based on the kinetic approach to aircraft performance modeling that has been developed and maintained by the Eurocontrol Experimental Centre (EEC). The information provided in BADA is designed for use in trajectory simulation in ATM research (Ref. [4]). Therefore the air traffic simulation tool could be used either as a dynamic linked library integrated into the scenario simulator or as a separate tool with its own graphical user interface capable of communicating with the scenario simulator via UDP network connection in compliance with the network interface defined by the Interoperability Standard (ISF protocol). When used as a separate application, the air traffic simulation tool can also provide information on dangerous encounters between each couple of aircraft flying inside the simulation scenario. In fact using the statistical data provided by the European Encounter Model (EEM), the tool can calculate the probability of an encounter event (detected within the scenario) with respect to all the possible encounters observed in the European air space (according to the data contained in the EEM). This information can be very useful to analyze air traffic scenarios or assess the performance of collision avoidance devices.

2.3   Simulation Platforms

Over the past years the Italian Aerospace Research Centre (CIRA) has invested significant resources in the development of innovative algorithms, implemented into avionic software, for the guidance, navigation and control of the aircraft, aimed at increasing the autonomy of Unmanned Aerial Vehicles (UAVs) in all flight conditions, and improving the aircraft's capabilities of flight assistance for pilots of General Aviation (GA) vehicles. CIRA is also investigating avionic technologies and procedures for the integration of UAVs and Remotely Piloted Aircraft System (RPAS) within the future civil ATM system.

In order to develop and test the above mentioned algorithms, technologies and procedures, suitable analysis and verification tools should be available. Therefore the correctness of the software does not only depend on the development process of the software but also of the tools used for the development. Concerning verification, several steps are foreseen during the development cycle of new concepts. They are based on the use of functional and detailed simulation environments, for on ground tests, and on actual experimental flying facilities, for the final in flight demonstration. In particular the simulation environments allow performing fast time simulation and real-time tests with software and/or hardware and/or human in the loop. Simulation facility provides ways to emulate realistic environment to access un-measurable flight variables, to assess unforeseen human behavior, and to conduct sensitivity analysis on the performance with respect to flight and scenario parameters.

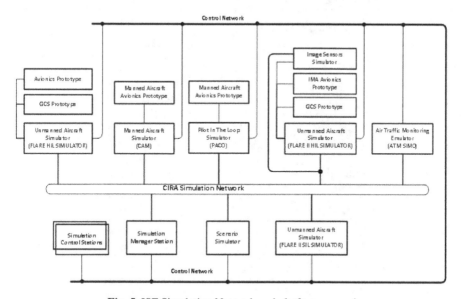

Fig. 5. ISF Simulation Network and platforms overview

In the architecture of the ISF network, a simulation platform is defined as a system, made by one or more hw machines, able to reproduce the detailed behavior of a single agent of the simulation system. The simulation platforms can be simulators of both movable actors (such as airplanes, cars, satellites, etc.) that services (as ATC, ground support stations, etc.). To support the above mentioned research activities, CIRA has developed several real-time simulation platforms. The simulation platform now available at CIRA (or that are forthcoming) are:

- FLARE, an Unmanned Aircraft System simulator;
- PACO, a Pilot-in-the-loop Avionic Cockpit simulator;
- CAM, a Manned Aircraft simulator;
- ATM, an Air Traffic Monitoring simulator.

FLARE facility is a complete fast/real-time simulation environment with Hardware-in-the-loop capabilities. This environment is used to simulate an Unmanned Aerial System and to test advanced algorithms for autonomous aircraft guidance, navigation and control (Fig. 6). PACO and CAM simulation platforms are both Hardware-in-the-loop (HIL) simulators; these platforms are mainly used to perform simulation with human pilot to test avionic SW. ATM emulate an Air Traffic Monitoring ground station.

For all the real-time simulation platforms has been applied the same development process. The simulation system and all the related algorithms for the simulation platforms are developed in a Matlab/Simulink environment.

Fig. 6. FLARE Simulator, Real Time HW

Fig. 7. FLARE Simulator, simulation control station

The entire simulation system (including simulation and controls algorithms) is implemented as a real-time application following a Rapid Control Prototyping process; in this phase automatic production code generators are used to translate the Matlab/Simulink models directly into code for ECUs/controllers in the Real-Time HW. The simulation platform is completed with a workstation with dedicate SW to use as control station during the tests (Fig. 7).

2.4   API Library

Each simulation platform is connected to the CIRA Simulation Network through the API Library. This library is a ready-to-use set of connection modules that can easily provide the correct encapsulation of all data exchanged between a Simulation Platform and all the others simulation items. For each data message, the API libraries The data encapsulation has been studied to obtain the highest efficiency in data exchange, in order to avoid any possible overload of the CIRA Network, and hence assure a data exchange with low latency and without errors or data loss. API libraries are composed of many different modules; each module is dedicated to a specific simulation platform. The creation of many different library modules was necessary given the great diversity of data exchanged between the different simulation platforms (for example, the data sent by the GPS constellation simulator are totally different from the ADS-B data exchanged between the air traffic simulator and the UAS and PACO simulation platforms). In each simulator is also possible to use simultaneously more than one API library module, so the simulator can simultaneously receive data of different types from different sources.

API libraries contain two modules for each type of message exchanged in the network ISF. The encoding module transforms the engineering data generated by the scenario simulator (or by the simulation platform) in bytes. The encoded data are sent to all simulation's stakeholders through the ISF network. The decoding module receives the bytes from the ISF network and transforms them into engineering data; these data are hence available to be used by the simulation platform receiver.

The messages actually defined are the following:

- Aircraft Message;
- GPS constellation Message
- Weather Hazards Message
- Ground Vehicle Message
- TIS-B Message

Each message exchanged over the ISF network has a structure defined by a series of data package. That structure has some fixed data packages (that are common to all the messages), and some variables data packages (which are specially designed for each message). The fixed part of each message is composed by the "ID Message" and the "Timestamp" data packages. The ID Message data package reports general information about the message, as the message type, the message length, an unique ID code related to the source platform, etc. The "Timestamp" data package contains precise information on the time at which the message was generated. The variable part of a message is typically made by many data package; for example the Aircraft message consist of four complex data packages The collection of all Aircraft messages from the airplanes that are simulated could give precise information about Air Traffic to the receiver simulation platform. For example, below is provided a brief summary table reporting the main structure of the Aircraft message as implemented in the ISF Network:

Table 1. Summary table of Aircraft Message over the ISF Network

Data Package TAG	Dimension [byte]
ID Mess	17
Timestamp	5
Actual state of Aircraft	50
Check on-board devices	1
Transponder	14
ADS-B Data	103

In addition to the modules for data encoding/decoding, API libraries provide a set of stand-alone data generators which replicate the behavior of scenario generators available in the ISF network during Real-time tests. These stand-alone generators have been designed to allow the execution of preliminary tests (fast-time) of a simulation system, prior to its inclusion in the network of real-time simulators.

3   HW Architecture

In order to guarantee an efficient data transmission also in relatively dense total traffic stream keeping the facility architecture the simplest possible, a star configuration with a UDP broadcast protocol has been chosen. Additionally, when collision occurs, namely more devices attempt to use a data channel simultaneously; the CSMA/CD (short for *Carrier Sense Multiple Access /Collision Detection*) is employed. In details, such protocol allows to identify multiple access to the data channel resulting in the detection of collisions, but do not have deterministic transmission characteristics. It follows an unknown transmission latency of the network's nodes.

In the present work, in order to assess the ISF network data budget, the following assumptions have been done:

- The Ethernet network can be considered deterministic when only the 5% of the available band is used;
- The switch delay is negligible, since its global delay is greatly lower than the maximum simulation transmission frequency of the network nodes.

In the worst case, all simulators have to transmit own messages on the network at the same time slot. So taking into account the UDP protocol message overhead and some constraints on the agents of the scenario, i.e., proportions between vehicle, aircraft, meteo hazard and nav aids of a scenario, it is possible to calculate the maximum number of aircrafts that can participate to a simulation session varying the meteo hazard and ground vehicle (see Fig. 8).

The same conclusion is achieved by using a synthetic index that defines the *CSMA/CD* efficiency in the collisions prevention [5];

$$\eta = \frac{t_{trans}}{t_{trans}+5 \cdot t_{prop}} = \frac{1}{1+5 \cdot \frac{t_{prop}}{t_{trans}}} \tag{1}$$

where t_{trans} is the transmission time of the maximum dimension ISF frame and t_{prop} is the maximum propagation time between two nodes of the network. Assuming a maximum node-switch length equal to 50 m and a propagation speed equal to the speed of light, an efficiency value next to one is obtained.

So given the constraints in Fig. 8 the star architecture with CSMA/CD protocol allows to transmit with high probability of success the messages between nodes of ISF network.

In general, the functionalities of the ISF facility can be even used by simulation platforms external to CIRA local network. In this case virtual networks mechanism could be employed (see Fig. 9).

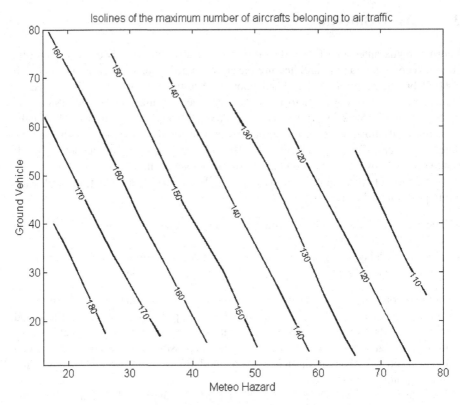

Fig. 8. Maximum number of aircrafts belonging to air traffic with respect to meteo hazard and ground vehicle agents

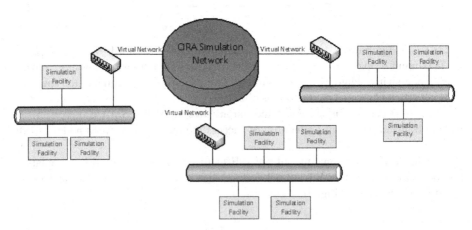

Fig. 9. Functional Architecture of ISF facility with simulation platforms external to CIRA local network

4   Preliminary Test Case

The facility was built as described in the paragraphs 2 and 3 but without the simulation manager. Then in the current ISF facility version isn't performed an exact time synchronization between simulation platforms.

Therefore the objective of the preliminary tests was only to verify the capability of the simulation platforms and scenario to operate integrated in the ISF. In details it has been verified the capability of receiving and sending data packages from and to the ISF network by the simulation platforms and scenario.

The Fig. 10 shows the comparison between the aircraft altitude simulated with PACO and the same altitude received in input by the Scenario Simulator.

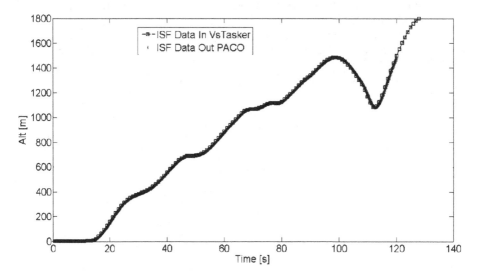

Fig. 10. Comparison between data transmitted and received in the ISF network

5   Conclusions

A real-time interoperability network facility for simulation platforms and scenario generator connection has been presented. The making of this facility has required an in-depth study of all the data types that must be exchanged between the simulation scenario and simulation platforms. Even the exchange network chosen for the ISF has required a careful study of the HW architecture characteristics, in order to meet the requirements of a real-time communication system with low delay and reduced probability of data loss. The sum of all these difficulties has made the ISF network a very challenging and exciting project.

In conclusion, the implementation of this infrastructure for the interconnection of all the main simulation facility has allowed us to increase the possibility of using all our test platforms (both simulation and scenario generation); this has increased the level of complexity and realism of the tests conducted in laboratory. This interoperability network facility has proven to be extremely useful for the research activities made at CIRA; in the future the ISF network could be expanded to include test facilities that are scheduled to be made. The next step is add the simulation manager in the facility and to verify the possibility to perform real-time tests using the HW architecture choose.

References

1. EUROCONTROL, Eurocontrol Specifications for the Use of Military Unmanned Aerial Vehicles as Operational Air Traffic outside Segregated Airspace, Brussels – EUROCONTROL-SPEC-0102 (2007)
2. SESAR Consortium: SESAR Definition Phase: Concept of Operations. Task 2.2.2 – Milestone 3. DLT-0612-222-02-00 (2007c)
3. INOUI: Annex I - Description of work (2007)
4. Eurocontrol, 2004: User Manual for the Base of Aircraft Data (BADA) Revision 3.6, EEC Note No. 10/04
5. Tanenbaum, A.S.: Reti di Calcolatori – quarta edizione (Settembre 2004)

HLA as an Experimental Backbone for Autonomous System Integration into Operational Field

Jan Hodicky

NATO Modelling and Simulation Centre of Excellence, Rome, Italy
jan.hodicky@seznam.cz

Abstract. A request for interdisciplinary project is a permanent call from all Panels working under NATO Science and Technology Organization such as System Analysis and Studies and Modelling and Simulation Group. M&S as a scientific discipline has already proved its priceless role in Concept, Development and Experimentation throughout any domain. To investigate on potential integration of Autonomous System into operational field, the only low cost solution seems to be experimentation in synthetic distributed environment. Synthetic distributed environment is based on the cooperating entities employing a data interchange mechanism. The article is focused on the current data interchange mechanisms in synthetic distributed environment from the potential Autonomous Systems implementation into the operational field point of view. High Level Architecture (HLA) is selected as suitable candidate because of its maturity and widely acceptance in military projects. Firstly, the idea of an experimental framework is explained and drawbacks are identified. Secondly, the latest version of HLA Evolved is discussed, in particular the Federation Object Model that contains the common vocabulary for the proposed experimental framework. High level ontology of Autonomous Systems is depicted to define the minimum requested set of objects represented by attributes and transactions among these object represented by parameters.

Keywords: High Level Architecture, autonomous system, operational field.

1 Introduction

Technology Organization in 1998 we were witnessing permanent calls for any collaboration among particular panels such as Modelling and Simulation Group and System Analysis and Studies. It persists till nowadays' reformed and renamed main NATO Scientific entity - NATO Science and Technology Organization. This organization is currently composed of more than 3500 Scientists and Engineers from NATO and its partners working on approximately 140 research activities. Autonomous System (AS) concept, design and implementation are covered by System Analysis and Studies panel. M&S as a scientific discipline has already proved its priceless role in NATO Concept, Development and Experimentation in any domain and is under governance of NATO M&S Group/panel. To test and evaluate, analyze and predict AS behavior and cooperation in the operational field, the M&S assets can be employed as an

J. Hodicky (Ed.): MESAS 2014, LNCS 8906, pp. 121–126, 2014.

experimental framework [1]. The general experimentation AS framework uses as a backbone distributed simulation environment. The main actors of the framework are following:

- Distribute simulation entities (Human Operator, Vehicle, C2 system, Communication node, etc.)
- Autonomous Systems
- Synthetic Environment (terrain, atmosphere, weather, etc.)

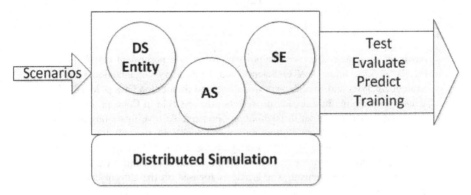

Fig. 1. General M&S Experimental Framework for Autonomous System

2   Drawbacks in M&S Experimental Frameworks for Autonomous Systems

M&S Experimental Frameworks (M&S EF) for Autonomous System are known for more than 8 years. [1] Based on the analysis the following drawbacks were identified:

- Non unique standard for data interchange mechanisms.
- Variety of Level of Details in Synthetic Environment.
- No common vocabulary for AS to be implemented into distributed synthetic environment.

Lack of single standard for data exchange mechanism is related to the current status in the distributed simulation domain. Within the 20 years history of M&S interoperability standard the Distributed Interactive Simulation (DIS), Test and Training Enabling Architecture (TENA), High Level Architecture (HLA) and Data Distribution Service (DDS) were implemented and till these days are still used [2]. Experimental framework is usually design to natively support only one of the aforementioned standards. Hand in hand with the standard selection their limitations differ mainly from the Quality of Service, Reliability and Time Synchronization points of view.

Another issue is related to the particular requirements for Level of Details (LoD) in the M&S EF. To fully integrate virtual AS into a synthetic environment, LoD requirements differ from the microscopic environment resolution for Micro Unmanned ground AS, to the very low detail resolutions, like some of the AS in the real world.

Current M&S EF are not flexible enough to incorporate this incompleteness into one solution.

The last identified drawback is non-existing common vocabulary for AS implementation into Distributed Synthetic Environment. M&S EF are based for particular projects and vocabulary that will be used interchanging mechanism is built from the scratch. It is very time consuming activity. In further part, the article focuses on this issue.

3   HLA Evolved and Modular Federation Object Model

To implement M&S EF for AS in NATO environment, the only possibility is to follow HLA standard way, because is the only distributed simulation NATO standard approved – STANAG 4603 [3]. HLA originated in 1995 in version 1.0 still shares the same principles with the latest version called HLA Evolved. HLA famous lollipop schema for AS is depicted on the Figure 2.

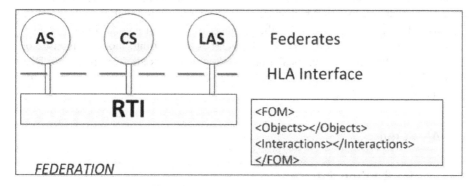

Fig. 2. HLA Lollipop schema of M&S EF for AS

FEDERATES are represented by AS, Constructive Simulation and Live AS assets. Communication among federates is carried out by Real Time Infrastructure (RTI) using the standardized API – HLA Interface. Common vocabulary interchanged inside Federation, which is collection of all previously mentioned entities, is specified in Federation Object Model (FOM).

FOM is a mutual agreement about communication among federates and is mainly composed of objects and interactions. Object is persistent long lived entity described by attributes. As an object example the AS with its parameters can be taken. Interaction is non-persistent event described by parameters. As an interaction example the event of assets detection by AS can be taken.

HLA Evolved has many improvements [4]. From the common vocabulary point of view the modularity of FOM is the most important one.

FOM can be split into independent modules that can be connected via hierarchical arrangement and therefore objects and interactions in particular module can inherit previously defined objects and interactions with hierarchically inferior module as depicted on the Figure 3.

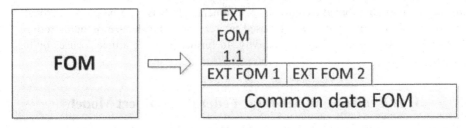

Fig. 3. HLA Evolved Modular FOM

4   A Implementation of a Common AS Vocabulary into FOM

To implement AS common vocabulary into FOM module is based on the idea to build it on the already existing FOMs that are even standardized. Simulation Interoperability Standards Organization (SISO) is the producer of the most popular Real-time Platform Reference (RPR) FOM 2.0. [5]. The FOM is divided into modules focused on the particular domain like Physical Entities, Aggregates, Radio, Logistic, etc. RPR FOM 2.0 is the best option to build AS FOM up on. Figure 4 shoves the possible implementation of AS FOM.

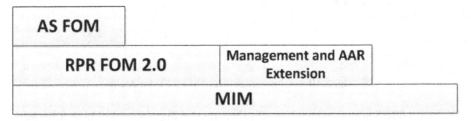

Fig. 4. AS FOM implemented on RPR FOM foundation

Therefore the AS FOM can inherit all features from lower level FOMs and it assures to not reinvent a wheel.

5   AS Common Vocabulary

To be able to implement AS FOM, the objects and interactions that can be expected in M&S EF for AS must be specified. In spite of existing AS oriented ontologies, there is no one following the idea of objects and interactions identification [6]. To create AS ontology M&S oriented the first step is to define high level AS ontology. Figure 5 depicts it.

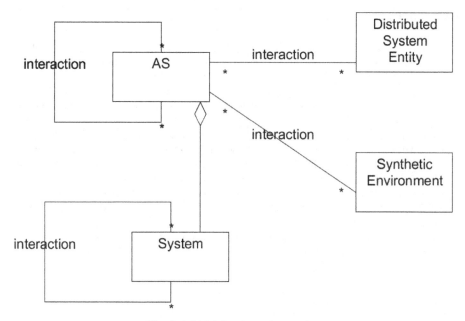

Fig. 5. AS high level ontology M&S

ASs interact among each other and can be composed of systems. Therefore AS can be understood as a system of systems. AS interacts with Distributed System Entity in M&S EF and with Synthetic Environment as well.

Next step is to define the List of potential Scenarios in M&S EF. As an example the following AS activities can be taken as examples of a scenario: Navigation, Exploration, Object Detection, Object Identification, Movement, Obstacle Avoidance, Replication of External World, Remote Control, Collaboration, etc.

Based on the scenario the Application Ontology is created and objects and interactions are identified and AS FOM is implemented.

6   Conclusion

Creation of AS common vocabulary oriented into M&S can even increase the already existing potential of EF to be used to assure the easiest and the most effective way to implement AS into the operational field. AS common vocabulary M&S oriented has a potential to become the reference for any standard in distributed simulation, not only specifically for HLA. It increases the interoperability level in all Experimental Frameworks.

References

1. Perhinschi, M.G., Napolitano, M.R., Tamayo, S.: Integrated Simulation Environment for Unmanned Autonomous Systems—Towards a Conceptual Framework. Modelling and Simulation in Engineering 2010, Article ID 736201, 12 p. (2010)
2. Loper, M.L., Turnitsa, C.: History of Combat Modeling and Distributed Simulation, in Engineering Principles of Combat Modeling and Distributed Simulation. John Wiley & Sons, Inc., Hoboken (2012)
3. STANAG 4603. Modelling and simulation architecture standards for technical interoperability: High Level Architecture (HLA). Brussels: NATO Standardization Council (2009)
4. Möller, B., Morse, K.L., Lightner, M., Little, R., Lutz, R.: HLA Evolved – A Summary of Major Technical Improvements. In: Proceedings of 2008 Spring Simulation Interoperability Workshop, 08F-SIW-064, Simulation Interoperability Standards Organization (2008)
5. SISO. Standard for Real-time Platform Reference Federation Object Model (RPR FOM). SISO-STD-001.1-2013. Version 2.0. (2013)
6. Alonso, J.B.: OASys.: Ontology for Autonomous Systems, PhD. Thesis, Universidad Politecnica De Madrid (2010)

Operational Scenarios Simulation to Support Building Design: A Hospital Design Case Study

Davide Simeone[*], Ilaria Toldo, and Stefano Cursi

Department of Civil, Construction and Environmental Engineering,
Sapienza University of Rome, Rome, Italy
{davide.simeone,stefano.cursi}@uniroma1.it,
ilaria.toldo@gmail.com

Abstract. In hospitals the configuration of the environment deeply affects the efficiency of the host organization, supporting or preventing the activities of intended users and operators. Although some simulation models have recently been introduced in architectural design, their actual application is limited to simulate people's movement in case of specific events (i.e. fire egress or crow dynamics in public stations). More effective models, able to simulate more complete building use scenarios are still missing. To overcome this lack, the research described in this paper aims at developing a model to virtually simulate use scenarios in hospital buildings, in order to provide use-related feedback to architects during the design process. The proposed model integrates two main components: 1) a formalization level, where the use scenario is represented through Business Process Modeling approach in terms of activities performed, actors involved and hosting spaces; 2) a simulation environment where the determined scenario is actually computed and executed. The resulting phenomena is visualized in a 3D virtual environment, allowing architects to observe how the building will respond to the scripted scenario in order to detect critical points and solve design errors and inconsistencies.

Keywords. Operational simulation, hospital design, Building use simulation – Virtual environment, BPMN.

1 Introduction

A hospital environment represents a complex system that requires an appropriate configuration of human and material resources in order to optimize its efficiency and effectiveness. During the design process, architects are asked to predict and evaluate future building performances according to a large number of typology and organization-based requirements. Planning and design of hospitals are largely based on functional programs and benchmarks which are interpretations of the requirements held by the organization that will occupy and use the building, namely: the main activities of future building's occupants. In the past, this interpretation process has been mainly

---

[*] Corresponding author.

J. Hodicky (Ed.): MESAS 2014, LNCS 8906, pp. 127–137, 2014.
© Springer International Publishing Switzerland 2014

supported by normative methods, regulations, general design rules and of course designer's experience following some custom practices outlined as follows:

- The clinical managers develop a descriptive models of care and functional brief developed by the clinical managers;
- Experienced hospital planners and architects consult with the managers who will be responsible for the proposed health service. The consultation may consider the patient's journey in receiving health services;
- Databases for planning and design are used to develop the design. These standards can be mandated in regulations and appointing design teams;
- The design may be tested with prototypes before documentation for construction.

Despite of its almost exclusive use, normative approaches have shown their limits due to the increasing complexity of building typology, and the intrinsic complexity of human – building interactions [1]. As a matter of fact, such instruments of abstraction are not well-suited to represent the uniqueness and context-dependence of an architectural product nor to control the internal, complex and non-linear dynamics of a hospital that require a high degree of coordination and interaction between human and material elements. Specifically, basing design decisions on a set of averaged parameters in the assumption that the building will satisfy future users' needs [2] much like "similar" buildings have done so in the past, often fails when real users, who may differ from the "average" user in many ways, finally meet the building.

Architects' ability to predict in which manner their design will be used and whether it will match the activities of its intended users, is currently only supported by architects' own expertise and imagination. Sadly, the consequences are clearly recognizable in reality: too often hospitals do not perform as expected after their construction, and sometimes they completely fail to support the activities of the organizations that will occupy them. The observation and analysis of human behaviour in built environments are usually considered the best way to understand and evaluate how a building fits the needs and support the activities of its intended users. On this basis, the Post Occupancy Evaluation (POE) paradigm proposed several approaches and techniques to assess if the project brief has been met [3]. Nevertheless, POE approaches have one major limitation: they can be applied only after the building has been realized and occupied, when it is too late or too costly to intervene in order to solve errors, critical failures and unsatisfied needs of users. In order to overcome this deficiency in the design process, we chose to investigate how to use 'virtuality' to integrate building occupancy evaluation into the design process, allowing designers to test their decisions before entering into the construction phase. In particular, the proposed model focuses on the simulation of activities in the hospital environment in order to predict how the building will match the functional needs of the organization that will occupy it.

2   Related Work

Since healthcare systems involve the coordination of interacting resources and human activities, it is natural that it can generate a range of organizational problems that it is possible to adequately address by scientific approaches of research, such as simulation modelling. The inherent flexibility of simulation models allows decision makers to implement different strategies in order to achieve the desired objectives. Consequently, the constantly evolving nature of health systems and variability in the input and output parameters can be easily accommodated. Furthermore, the simulation approach captures the variability of the input parameters and introduces constraints in the various design phases. Several studies have shown how simulation represents an effective tool for investigating complex problems such as the hospital environment, and that results can be used to enhance quality of care [4]. For example, Jones et al. [5] demonstrate how the quality of service in an emergency room can be improved by utilizing total quality management (TQM) concepts and simulation tools in the generation of feasible alternatives. With the inception of Computer Aided Architectural Design, several attempts have been made to introduce the expected users' activities in building representation models [6, 7, 8, 9]. However, in such models activities have been explicitly represented in terms of their spatial features - usually relying on the concept of "functional unit" - or implicitly inferred by using sets of functional requirements as criteria for the evaluation of the capabilities of a space [8].

Gradually, research attention in this field has turned from a 'space-based' representation of users' activities to a "process-based" representation, considering activities as entities on their own that are clearly distinct from (but connected with) spatial entities [10]. These new approaches are based on the idea of modelling processes depending on the operational workflows of the organization - or of an organization typology if specific data are not available - that will occupy the building, and then simulate their execution in the building model [11, 12, 13]. This approach has been worthily tested in buildings such as hospitals, offices and airports, where the organizational workflows and the related interactions with the built environment actually drive and heavily influence users' behaviour. Still, some criticisms has been raised of this approach in terms of its ability to realistically predict human behaviour in architectural design, since it relies on a rigid, 'functionalistic' representation of operational processes of the organization, usually completely computed before the actual simulation and not adaptable to single users' behaviours and to the overall status of the built environment (what we call 'serendipitous' or 'emergent' activities). This distortion inevitably reduces the ability of these simulative approaches to predict building response to users' needs and activities. In the last few years, Agent-Based Modelling paradigm has been introduced in this research field, aiming at simulating users' behaviour in built environments by developing a series of autonomous entities - the agents - each of whom interacting in an autonomous way with the other users and with the environment surrounding it [14, 15]. Although Agent-Based Modelling has been successfully applied to simulation of some behavioural phenomena generated by individual actors/ agents (such fire-egress and pedestrian movement), it has shown several limits in simulating agents' cooperation and collaborative activities performing.

3   The Simulation Model

3.1   The Model Conceptual Framework

The work presented in this paper aims at developing a different model to simulate users' behaviour in hospital, in which the building use representation is still based on a process-driven system, but it is more adaptable both in terms of its activities structure and of users' individual decisions and actions. In order to provide these capabilities, we intervene at two different levels of the model: in the formalization of the building use process, which we define as use scenario, and in the simulation system of the users' behaviour derived by the scenario. Operational efficiency in hospitals is strongly influenced by the physical design of the built environment. Although hospitals are relatively complex buildings, their use-pattern is relatively straight-forward, which is advantageous for our research since it provides a comprehensive and agreed-upon data set against which the model can be tested. A hospital process has a direct correspondence to the way the occupant organization works in terms of operational workflows, procedures and systems of activities [15]. Based on this assumption, we chose to rely on a modelling approach -the Building Process Modelling and Notation-already developed to represent how an organization operates and to extend it to representing the use process of a building. The BPMN level, where the use process is formalized, is connected to a 3D simulation environment (a game engine in our case), where the same process is effectively computed, simulated and visualized at the same time. In this environment, Users/Agents are provided with the abilities to autonomously adapt their behaviour within a predefined range, depending on the status of the environment model and on the reference process model. In turn, the simulated users' serendipitous actions are fed back into the process model, and can influence it. For example, in the case of a hospital, when a doctor and a nurse are scheduled to check on a patient, but the patient has chosen this particular moment to visit the bathroom, the absences of the patient is fed-back to the process model, which defines a different flow of activities for the doctor and the nurse. Likewise, if the paths taken by two agents brings them into geometric proximity, due to the geometry of the building, they may choose to stop and chat, or ignore each other and continue on their predefined missions.

The novelty of this approach lies in making the process execution more flexible and partially adaptable to serendipitous 'emergent' activities in real time during the simulation, while in current approaches the activities flow is usually compiled and fixed before stepping into the effective simulation [12]. In addition, the proposed model can represent and simulate collaborative, planned activities, such as cooperation among various users when performing their tasks. In terms of usability by architects, planners and clients, the outcome is a simulation/visualization in a 3D virtual environment of how the use process is actually carried out by the building users in the building spaces prefigured by the architect. In this way, it is possible to predict and evaluate the correspondence and the mutual influence between the building and its intended users, and rapidly compare the simulation outcomes of different design solutions and spatial configurations. To test and calibrate the model, it has been applied to simulate the functioning of two different hospital wards and its outputs has been compared with real use process phenomena.

3.2   BPMN for Hospital Processes and Scenarios

The Business Process Model and Notation (BPMN) is a modelling approach ideated for business processes that allows representation of operational processes of an organization in order to orchestrate the activities and the decisions of the different actors involved [17, 18]. Looking in particular at a hospital organization as a system whose functioning is very similar to a business process, we have chosen to extend BPMN approach to hospital processes. In fact, it provides a formalization template for processes that make explicit the activities, the actors involved and the different resources allocated, making such data machine-readable and computable by a simulation program. At the same time, its graphical representation allows different professionals to model their processes without stepping into the programming phase. This interface is particularly useful in the hospital field, because it allows also the experts in health workflows and operations (who are usually are not used to programming languages) to be involved in the design process of the building. In terms of representation of human processes, BPMN is particularly useful because it is able to describe different aspects of actors' interaction in an operational process (orchestration, collaboration, choreography, decision points), a feature we consider relevant for the purpose of our research since it allows formalization of cooperation among different building users during the performing of an activity. The BPMN formalization is based on a set of elementary entities that can be used to decompose and represent an operational process, the main ones are (fig.1):

- Activities: representation of tasks, works, or operations that have to be carried out or executed during the process;
- Connectors: links to connect an activity to another activity in order to define an operational sequence;
- Flows: other classes of connectors that allow to associate other kinds of entities to activities;
- Events: occurrences that "happen" during the process, starting, delaying, interrupting or ending a flow of activities;
- Gateways: modelling elements that control the pathways of the process, its diversions and its convergences, allowing parallel or exclusive paths.

For the purpose of our research, these classes of entities (with their subclasses) are useful but not sufficient. In order to make the BPMN system fully able to represent building use processes, we chose to rely on the ability to extend the BPMN representational approach by creating two new classes of artefacts:

- Actors: entities representing each actor involved in the hospital processes in order to connect it to the performing of the activities he/she has to carry out;

- Spaces: entities representing the spaces of the built environment and necessary in the BPMN environment in order to effectively overlap the use process to the virtual representation of built environment.

Fig. 1. Some modelling entities - activities, gateways and events- represented in the graphical template of BPMN approach (BPMN 2.0)

By adding these two modelling entities, the model provides the conceptual connection between the building use process based on the organization's operational dynamics and the building design solution provided by the architect. In this way, the activities, considered elementary units of the organization's operational workflow, are not abstract anymore, but explicitly represented in the building model, providing a representation of what is going to happen, where, and who is involved. Although the BPMN representation takes into account actors' declaration by means of "swimlanes" [17], we chose to develop a specific artefact for the actors, since in a building use process formalization each actor has to be associated to several activities and this is hard to represent with the swimlanes system (fig.2). The BPMN approach allows us to represent not only complex sequences of activities, but also their articulation in (and relation to) time: specific time-triggers or event-triggers can represent conditions for an activity to be activated, interrupted or deactivated, influencing the performing of the building use scenario. Gateways are used to formalize and control parallel or exclusive executions of multiple activities; they can be considered decision points in the flow of activities since they allow testing the model status for specific conditions and choosing which sequence of activities to perform. For instance, if we imagine a scenario where a doctor is visiting a list of patients (as the one shown in fig.2), a gateway formalizes the necessity of checking the patient presence and, in case of his/her absence, it adapts the use scenario by directing the doctor to the next patient.

The BPMN ability to encapsulate activities in sub-processes also allows us to manage complex processes and to reuse the same activities structure several times. At the same time, non-structured or intermediate activities (such as "using the restrooms", or "having a walk"), are represented by means of ad-hoc sub-processes that can be invoked during the actual simulation according to probabilistic curves. In order to make the process representation more flexible and adaptable to different systems (meant as building + activities + users), we also used BPMN messages and signals to stop and restart different sub-processes depending on specific conditions or events. The BPMN system allows us to actually export (via XML) and execute the represented building use process in external simulation environments and to use it as input for such systems. For the development of the building use scenario in the BPMN environment we chose to use Bizagi, a freeware business process modelling software [20].

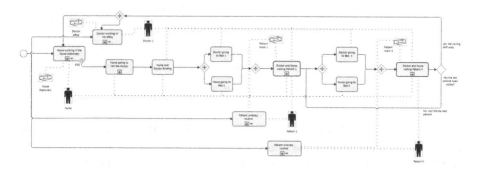

Fig. 2. A hospital workflow (in this case a visiting routine involving a doctor and a nurse) represented in Business Process Modelling and Notation

3.3   Simulating Operational Processes in 3D Virtual Environments

Although several BPMN applications embed a simulation engine to check the consistency of the process modelled, at present its potential is quite limited and not sufficient to model, manage and simulate the complexity of the hospital process in terms of actors' actions, decisions and behaviors. In order to provide architects, operational experts and hospital managers with a reliable prediction of how the building users carry out the defined activities, we chose to integrate the BPMN representation with a 3D simulation environment, where the formalized use process is simulated. In this environment (developed by means of the game engine Virtools [19]) the building use process, previously formalized in an abstract way in the BPMN system, is connected to the virtual model of the built environment where its activities are supposed to be performed. In order to compute and simulate the use scenario developed in the BPMN model, a specific script has been developed in the Virtools game engine by means of behavioural blocks -visual programming blocks that correspond to the different activities represented by them (fig.3). In Virtools' scripting environment, we chose to develop a specific programming level for the formalization and computation of the use scenario; its role is to guide and control the execution of the sequences of activities, adapting their performing to the environment and to the status of the users' involved. It also enables control and simulation of serendipitous events, triggered by the physical (actually, geometrical) proximity and location of the actors within the simulated built environment. Such chance encounters may trigger different performance paths.

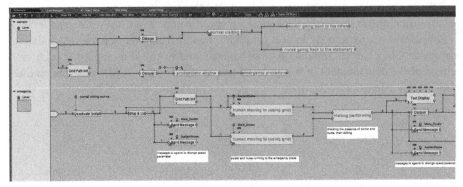

Fig. 3. A part of the hospital use scenario scripted in the programming level of the game engine *Virtools*

In addition, we chose to equip activity entities with specific scripts to simulate their performing in order to coordinate actors' actions and cooperation. This is a fundamental difference from previous agent-based models, where the activities simulation is generated by the sum of autonomous actions and decisions of the users, with several limits in terms of manageability and coherence of the output. To improve the adaptation of the scenario simulation to the built environment and its status, we chose to integrate the scenario script with some agent-based components intended to control some autonomous aspects of virtual users' behaviour (for instance, path decision, walking actions, obstacles avoidance, local interactions with other entities, such as doors or other agents). This choice has two main advantages: resemblance to the visual reality of the resulting simulated phenomenon, and improvement of the manageability of the computation system. The first consists of the possibility to reduce the rigidity of a process-driven simulation by including variations related to single actors' behaviors, actions and decisions. In that way, we can simulate serendipitous events generated by the interactions of the agents with the built environment that are not predictable in the scenario development. The ability to provide actors with some degrees of autonomy allows us to represent some aspects of users' behavior that would be difficult and time-consuming to represent and compute at the process level. For instance, the abilities of a user to compute a path in the built environment and perform the movement actions can be easily developed and controlled directly in the agent entity, while their representation and computation at the process level would be very difficult and, if iterated for each agent and activity, it would make the process representation too complex and difficult to manage. In order to test and evaluate the efficacy of the model, we chose to simulate the functioning of different hospital wards, both in routine and discrete emergency cases. These experiments, developed in collaboration with a research group at the Faculty of Architecture of the Technion Israel Institute of Technology, have been conducted after a series of data collection activities based on observations of real functioning of similar hospital departments. Reproducing the activities related to this operation in the BPNM environment and simulating it in the virtual environment was not a difficult task, because of the structured nature of the procedures involved in scheduled surgeries. Simulating the activities performed in the intensive care unit required extensive observations, long meetings with the medical staff, and still we were only able to reproduce them computationally within a high degree of abstraction [11]. During the experiments, different scenarios have been tested, changing both the environment configurations and the human resources allocated (fig.4). While in the first experiments we focused more on hospital wards, our more recent applications are related to simulation of the functioning of an acceptance and emergency department, predicting and evaluating its real capabilities in relation with extreme scenarios as disasters, structural damages and other safety issues.

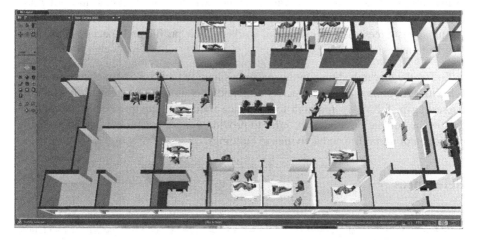

Fig. 4. A screenshot showing the Level Of Detail (LOD) of the visualization provided by the simulation

4   Conclusions

Health care needs to change in order to improve quality, productivity and job satisfaction. Major hospital building projects provide the opportunity to implement change through the planning and design phases. The building use process simulation approach can be used by architects to test the functionality of a design solution foreseeing its consequence on users' behavior it is possible to analyze processes, resources and facility requirements before buildings will actually be constructed and occupied and by clients. By integrating building use process formalization with its visual simulation in a virtual environment, architects, clients and process planners will be allowed to easily formalize a use scenario defining the activities performed, the actors involved and the spaces where such activities will take place. Elements of serendipity are given by affecting the process with the introduction of environmental constraints while the visual/geometric real time simulation of users' behavior within a defined physical environment, although limited to specific use cases and processes, provides the necessary connection of the abstract scenario to its performing in a defined physical environment. Differently from previous activity-based models where the use process is entirely computed before and then merely visualized, in the proposed model the use scenario is computed in real time during the simulation, providing a better adaptation of the sequence of activities to the built environment and its occupants and, consequently, a more coherent and reliable simulation output in routine and even in emergency situations. As result:

- More aware decisions will be made by Architects and clients by evaluating the functional performances of a design solution before it is actually built, leaving them the possibility to correct errors and solve critical points;
- Process planners, analysts and building managers will be supported in testing different workflows and operational procedures, and to test different configuration of human resources such as number of workers, their profile and specialization, their scheduling.

So far, the research shown in this paper has mainly focused on simulation of users' behaviour in terms of activities performing and operational management. It would be interesting in follow-up research to introduce social and environmental psychology data in the simulation model, in order to provide a more comprehensive and reliable prediction of users' life and activities in buildings.

References

1. Koutamanis, A., Mitossi, V.: Simulation for Analysis: Requirements from Architectural Design. In: Proceedings 6th EFA - European Full-scale Modeling Association Conference, Vienna, Austria, pp. 96–101 (1996)
2. Zimmermann, G.: Modeling the building as a system. In: Eighth International IBPSA Conference Proceedings, Eindhoven, the Netherlands, pp. 1483–1490 (2003)
3. Preiser, W.F.E., Rabinowitz, H.Z., White, E.T.: Post Occupancy Evaluation. Van Nostrand Reinhold, New York (1988)
4. Lopez-Valcarcel, B., Perez, P.: Evaluation of alternative functional design in an emergency department by means of simulation. Simulation 63(1), 20–28 (1994)
5. Jones, A., Ridener, A., Smith, K.: Preparing for change: emergency department queuing theory and computer simulation. Topics in Emergency Medicine 19(2), 40–46 (1997)
6. Eastman, C., Siabiris, A.: A generic building product model incorporating building type information. Automation in Construction 4(4), 283–304 (1995)
7. Carrara, G., Kalay, Y., Novembri, G.: KAAD - Knowledge- Based Assistance for Architectural Design. In: Teaching and Research Experience with CAAD – Proceedings of the 4th eCAADe Conference, Rome, Italy, pp. 202–212 (1986)
8. Ekholm, A., Fridqvist, S.: Modelling of user organizations, buildings and spaces for the design process. In: Construction on the Information Highway, Proceedings of the CIB W78 Workshop, Bled, Slovenia (1996)
9. Simeone, D., Kalay, Y.E.: An Event-Based Model to simulate human behaviour in built environments. In: Digital Physicality– Proceedings of the 30th eCAADe Conference, Czech Technical University in Prague, Faculty of Architecture (Czech Republic), September 12-14, vol. 1, pp. 525–532 (2012)

10. Archer, B.: Activity Data Method: A method for recording user requirements. Ministry of Public Buildings and Works, London (1966)
11. Simeone, D., Kalay, Y.E., Schaumann, D.: Modelling and Simulating Use Processes in Buildings. In: Computation and Performance–Proceedings of the 31st eCAADe Conference, Faculty of Architecture, Delft University of Technology, Delft, The Netherlands, September 18-20, vol. 2, pp. 59–67 (2013)
12. Wurzer, G.: Schematic Systems – Constraining Functions Through Processes (and Vice Versa). International Journal of Architectural Computing 8(2), 197–214 (2010)
13. Goldstein, R., Tessier, A., Khan, A.: Space Layout in Occupant Behavior Simulation. In: Conference Proceedings of the IBPSA-AIRAH Building Simulation Conference, Sydney, Australia, pp. 1073–1080 (2011)
14. Macal, C., North, M.: Agent-based modeling and simulation: ABMS examples. In: Proceedings of the 40th Conference on Winter Simulation, pp. 101–112 (2007)
15. Simeone, D., Fioravanti, A.: An ontology-based system to support agent-based simulation of building use. ITcon (Journal of Information Technology in Construction). Special Issue CAAD and Innovation 17, 258–270 (2012), http://www.itcon.org/2012/16 ISSN 1874-4753
16. Ekholm, A.: Modelling of User Activities in Building Design', Architectural Information Management. In: Proceedings of the 19th eCAADe Conference, Helsinki, Finland, pp. 67–72 (2001)
17. White, S.: Introduction to BPMN. IBM Corporation (2006)
18. Lam, V.: A Precise Execution Semantics for BPMN. IAENG International Journal of Computer Science 39(1), 20–33 (2012)
19. Bizagi Modeller, http://www.bizagi.com
20. 3DVIA Virtools, http://www.3ds.com/products/3dvia/3dvia-virtools

Use of HLA Federation for the Evaluation of Naval Operations in Ship Design

Davide Tozzi, Federica Valdenazzi, and Aldo Zini

CETENA S.p.A., Genova, Italy
{divide.tozzi,Federica.valdenazzi,aldo.zini}@cetena.it

Abstract. Simulation, physic based analysis, computational calculations has been largely used since long time in ship design process but an exhaustive evaluation of ship's performances and capabilities is unlikely to be done in the early design phase. In this sense a proper simulation tool can be a valuable solution, giving the possibility to test and validate a wide range of naval operations' procedures in different environmental conditions. Usually these operations involve more entities than the single ship, so it becomes important to arrange a synthetic environment in which different simulators and simulations can cooperate for demonstrating complex operations. Besides this, the "system of systems" approach finds its applicability in the naval field where a warship can be represented as the cooperation of several subsystems. HLA distributed simulations represent a good solution for creating and simulating complex scenarios, allowing several simulators and partners to work together just exchanging inputs and outputs, but keeping safe intellectual properties rights. Experiences in using this framework either in a single company or with multiple companies scenario are presented. CETENA's experience in using its HLA based simulator for the development of complex interactive man-in-the-loop federations to evaluate operations like Replenishment At Sea, Landing Craft maneuverability, Vertical Take Off and Landing, Small Craft Launch and Recovery, is presented in this paper.

Keywords: High Level Architecture, ship design, naval operations.

1 Introduction

The ship is a very complex system of systems and interacts with an even more complex environment which influence and is influenced by the ship behavior.

Large ships are usually stand alone constructions. Even twin ships are usually slighting different among them. This means that usually the ship is the only prototype of herself. It is quite difficult and very expensive to modify the ship when built.

All these assumptions are the reasons why simulation, physic based analysis, computational calculations has been largely used since long time in ship design process.

The point is that all these tools and methods are usually used separately, in different ways and by different expert people.

J. Hodicky (Ed.): MESAS 2014, LNCS 8906, pp. 138–151, 2014.
© Springer International Publishing Switzerland 2014

Moreover, the final user is rarely involved in the process since interactions are usually among experts and not final users.

These are only some of the reasons for improving the use of simulation in a Virtual Reality environment in order to produce an interactive synthetic environment as much realistic as possible.

2   Virtual Prototyping as a Tool for Decision Making

A prototype is any preliminary working implementation of a product, component or system. It is often more abstract or less detailed than the final version. Two main classes of prototypes are used in design processes: physical prototypes and virtual prototypes.

A physical prototype is a physical model of a product, component or system. Physical prototypes are characterized by fabrication time that typically requires weeks-to-months and by modification procedures that require days-or-weeks.

A virtual prototype is a computer simulation model of a final product, component or system. A virtual prototype can be used in a design process specifically for : exploring design alternatives, demonstrating design concepts, testing for requirements satisfaction and/or correctness [1].

To be useful in a system design, a virtual prototype must comprise three elements:

- Visualization: virtual reality can be used for navigating inside the model. The user can walk through the complex project viewing exactly how the product will look like. Since the environment in which he is moving is all virtual and controlled by the computer, the user can easily query physical, topological and geometrical characteristics to any system or component.
- Simulation: a static 3D view or a flythrough can be insufficient to point out problems deriving from the movement of objects on deck or interaction between correlated components. Virtual reality can help in keeping together simulation results and real time photo-realistic visualization in synthetic environments.
- Interactivity: the capability to consider the human interaction with the object we are designing may represent a considerable step forward in the ergonomic field or in stressing operational efficiency during design time. The "man in the loop" represents an important design aspect rarely or difficulty taken into account in standard design processes.

Virtual prototyping is a good way to synthesis and visualize all design efforts either for the designer than for the client who can be more directly involved in strategic decisions from the very beginning since they can view and choose between different solutions [2,3].

Opposed to a physical prototype, which requires detailed hardware and software design, a virtual prototype can be configured more quickly and cost-effectively, can be more abstract and can be invoked earlier in the design process. Comparatively, virtual prototypes introduce some risks due to the possibility of modeling inaccuracy or incorrectness.

Moreover a single simulator can improve its capabilities and usefulness if included in a common environment where more simulators interoperate each other to reproduce the behavior of a more complex system.

Great effort is necessary to combine design expectation (simplicity, integration, etc.) with physical and mathematical modeling and simulation. Some interaction effects which are automatically accounted for in physical models need to be consciously accounted for in numerical modeling. E.g. a problem that we frequently face during our simulations is the "hull to hull" interaction which involves interactions between two or more ships and hence ship motion models. Few numerical codes are able to completely model the interaction between two ships, while reality accounts for interactions automatically.

Validation, verification and accreditation of simulation will be the next important step for virtual prototyping credibility and interoperability.

2.1   A Laboratory for Virtual Prototyping

Starting from this perspective, CETENA has developed during the years, tools, SW, competence in Virtual Prototyping for Ship design. In its Virtual Integrated Ship Laboratory (VISLab) experts from different ship design fields and IT experts created a technology architecture devoted to incorporate and reuse all available software tools (commercial or developed in-house) normally used for different purposes with the objective of building a common environment for studying, use and operate virtual prototypes of existing and under design ships [4].

The underlying approach is HLA (High Level Architecture – IEE1516) which let the development of complex distributed simulations [5].

Being the ship an intrinsic system of systems, the HLA approach results well suited for modeling and building federations which are able to have different levels of details in the implementations of complex behaviors.

In particular the approach let us create simulation systems which can easily updated inserting new or more detailed physic effects and new interacting entities in the synthetic environment.

2.2   SAND: CETENA's Ship Simulator

First step in the development of the VISLab has been the implementation of the interactive ship simulator system called SAND.

SAND is the simulation system used for manoeuvring simulation and training. It is compliant with the HLA 1516 architecture and it includes a ship console and high quality visualization system (Fig. 1). A dedicated computing station is used to set the simulation conditions, in terms of scenario, environmental conditions, ship characteristics; the controls on the console can be easily set up through reconfigurable LCD touch panels in order to reproduce those of the simulated ship. During each simulation, all relevant data are stored for subsequent debriefing sessions.

Fig. 1. SAND and 3D visualization system

In the tack of reusing all existing tools and competences and thanks to more than twenty years of R&D in ship design and consultancy for harbor designers and Port Authorities, SAND has rapidly reached a very high level of confidence in the representation of the ship behavior.

The CETENA's ship mathematical model included in SAND is based on a Maneuverability and Seakeeping model integration, that allows to calculate the six degrees of freedom (Surge, Sway, Heave, Roll, Pitch, Yaw) and has been validated during the years either from the use and sensitiveness of the Port pilots who used it during the port assessment activities and, moreover, from the huge real data coming from the experiment activities CETENA performs onboard ships.

The simulation model is designed to be "open" and configurable for all type of ship (cruise, bulk carrier, petrol, LNG, container ship) and for all environmental scenarios (map, sea state, wind, sea current, time of day).

Different type of vessels can be easily configured using wide range of characteristics like:

- hull data
- engine type (diesel, diesel-electrical, turbine, or every combination of them)
- propulsion (azimuth, fixed/controllable pitch propeller, POD, water-jet)
- thruster
- rudder (simple type, compound butt, under hung deep horn, shallow horn, spade)

The physical model is completely modular allowing the implementation of add-ons to take into accounts new or more detailed environmental and interaction effects.

The user can choose the environmental condition through a set of sea state, wind intensity and sea current and the software compute the interactive ship behavior for very accurate and realistic vessel simulation taking into account several aspects like:

- shallow water effects
- navigation in narrow channel

- collisions
- anchors and chains

SAND can be used either as a stand-alone system or as a federate, therefore as part of a more complex HLA federation. This can be useful when other simulation entities has to be considered as actors in the same simulation environment. For this reason a basic standard HLA federation (Fig. 2) was designed and developed within the VIS-Lab and it is structured as follows:

- *Execution Manager federate* is used to set up the whole federation and to specify all the initial parameters.
- *Data Logger* records all the data send through the RTI, in order to be able to replay the federation in offline mode.
- *3D Visualization federate* visualize the simulation scenario in a 3D environment.
- *Environment federate* sets all the parameters concerning the marine and atmosphere conditions, as sea state, current, wind.

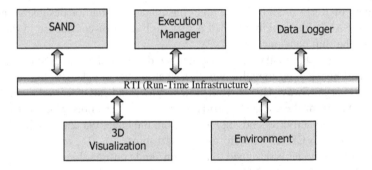

Fig. 2. CETENA's basic standard HLA Federation

Fig. 3. Portable SAND

In order to be compliant with HLA distributed simulations standards, the above mentioned federation was developed using the VS-FOM (Virtual Ship – Federation Object Model) [9], deriving from the RPR-FOM (Real-Time Platform Reference – FOM).

Multiple entities of SAND can be run in a federation allowing different ships interact in the same synthetic environment.

A portable version of the SAND simulator (see Fig. 3) was recently developed in order to easily transport the simulation system into possible partners' facilities and to participate to any other HLA based federation.

3   Experiences in Evaluating Naval Operations

As previously stated, the driving idea in the VISLab activity is that interactive real-time simulation can be used for investigate complex ship operations for verifying performances and receiving feedback for the design phase.

The implemented architecture and the open structure of the SAND "federate" are the basic ingredients for implementing complex distributed federation simulating operations involving multiple ships or multiple other entities.

All these with high attention to the physic representation of the involved effects rather than the visual aspects which are surely important but are not the primarily focus of the investigation.

In all the following presented experiences, many of the engineering and physical aspects simulated comes from experiences, tools and studies previously performed but, probably, with the focus on particular effects and scenarios but not interactive and not composed each other in a more complex and "realistic" scenario.

From a strict engineering point of view, traditional approach is sufficient and expert people are able to take decisions but non expert people, operative people, the final user, usually are not involved in these decisions and can't bring their experience in the design loop. The Virtual Prototyping approach can facilitate this man in the loop approach. The Virtual Ship can be tested by the final user before cutting metal.

Moreover Virtual ships can be efficiently used to verify contractual requisites and also extreme conditions scenarios which may be dangerous to verify in reality.

3.1   Replenishment at Sea (RAS) Operation

Replenishment At Sea is one of the more complex operations performed by modern navies. The operation is executed in three main phases:

- The vessels approach each other and sail alongside.
- The transfer system is established between the vessels using a cable system and the fuel is transferred.
- The transfer system is removed and the ships depart (breakaway).

In all these phases there is a risk of ship collision, especially in high sea states, and when small receiving vessels are involved. A simulation of the RAS operation will allow safe operating conditions to be determined and may influence the design of the supply ship, receiving ship and transfer rigs.

Primary goals of the simulation scenario are:

- to simulate Replenishment operations in open seas with different meteorological conditions;
- to verify operation constraints (ship speed, distance, etc.);
- to analyse different RAS devices in term of position, operative behaviour and efficiency;
- to study refuelling operation (no solid objects transfer).

Basically the operation is focused on the capability of the two ships to navigate parallel for a enough long period of time avoiding collisions and early breakaway. Studies of port manoeuvrability or approaching operations also in open seas are similar to RAS operations and the implemented federation reused all these experience improving the mathematical model of interactions between the two ships.

The two ships are interactively manoeuvrable and the systems reacts in real-time to any change in speed and direction of each ship. In particular the federation can take into account problems deriving from a malfunction in the manoeuvring devices (rudder, propeller…) of one of the two ships in order to accordingly evaluate the capability of the other ship to avoid collision and to continue in the parallel course. This may be very interesting in the design assessment of either the supply and the receiving ships.

From the implementation point of view, two SAND federates were involved in the federation in order to simulate both the supply and the receiving ships. In addition to the standard CETENA's federation two federates were developed and inserted in the federation: a RAS equipment federate and an Interaction federate.

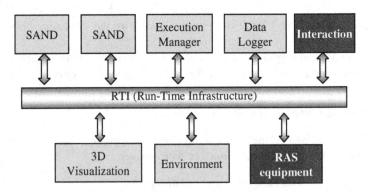

Fig. 4. RAS federation

RAS equipment federate was design for the calculation of the forces applied to the cables used for the fuel transferring operation. In case the RAS cables were subjected to a tension exceeding the maximum allowed, federate is able to give a warning representing the unsuccessfully result of the operation.

Interaction federate was designed in order to simulate the forces due to the side by side shipping; it was developed using mathematical models deriving from towing tank tests and it can be configured to simulate this specific behaviour for different kind of ships.

Fig. 5. Screenshot of the RAS simulation

The implemented simulation system is completely configurable and parameterized so that it can be used to simulate ship-to-ship transfer of liquids for:

- Any pair of ships
- Any sea state
- Any type of transfer rig
- Any type of liquid
- Any flow rate of liquids transfer.

The used architecture allows the reuse of each federate in other federation and the improvement of the mathematical model for any of the effects to take into account. This evolutive approach let us maintain and upgrade the developed software for future purposes.

Nowadays some of the federates will be used in an international project having the purpose of validating the simulation results with sea trials data and other towing tanks tests results.

We are now implementing the heavy load transfer between the two ships simulating the cable and the transfer mechanism adding in this way another functionality to the already existing RAS federation.

3.2   Landing Craft Unit Operations Inside Amphibious Ship

Another example of complex operation involving multiple interactive but independent entities is the federation we designed an built for reproducing the manoeuvrability of a landing craft (LCU) inside the wet dock of an amphibious ship (LPD) and the transfer of a tank from the Landing Craft to the dock of ship.

As in previous case, the development of the federation takes inspiration and reuse all the already available competences, expertise and software using in the past for studying similar scenarios [8]. In particular stand alone simulation for collision detection of the landing craft with the interior (bottom and sides) of the dock was reused in the new federation.

All the entities in the scenario are completely manoeuvrable interactively: the ship, the landing craft and the tank. This last one was simulated in a very simplified but enough realistic way while the ship and the boat are modelled in details and their behaviour is accurate. Again, the ship is implemented using the SAND federate while the Landing Craft Unit is a completely new mathematical model due to the particular type of hull and propulsion and moreover due to the shallow water effect inside the dock.

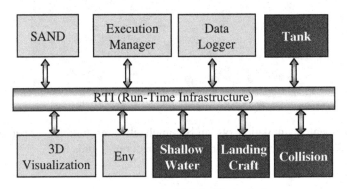

Fig. 6. Federation for LPD-LCU simulation

Four additional federates were developed in order to simulate the following entities:

- The Landing Craft maneuverability: this model was developed using Physx SDK, an open source physics simulator [10]. With Physx it is possible to simulate the dynamics of one or more objects with different geometries and characteristics. Moreover, Physx allows to interact with the simulated objects by applying to them some forces and moments.
- The Shallow Water effect: the hydrodynamic forces due to the shallow water inside the dock were applied to the Landing Craft. The Tank: when the Landing Craft approaches to the dock and it is stable, the tank can be moved from the landing craft itself to the LPD dock.
- The Collision Detection: when the Landing Craft is inside the LPD dock it is important to monitor the clearance among the craft and the dock. At the end of the simulation the federate can produce a report with the list of collisions detected during the running.

Particular attention has been put in the sloshing effect which is very complicate due to the fact that it is generated by the LPD Ship and is characterized by the volume of the water in the wet dock. Experimental test have been performed to tune the mathematical model.

Fig. 7. Sloshing experimental tests

The implemented federation has been used during the design of a possible LPD ship and one of the asked question was to determine which was the optimal trim for the internal wet deck in order to have enough ware to avoid collisions with the bottom of the LCU during movements inside and especially loading and unloading operation of the tank.

During the development also the external approach phase of the LCU has been simulated with a very simplified but effective mathematical model. Even if the main purpose is for inside operations, also external behavior of the ship and the LCU are simulated

Fig. 8. Screenshot of the Landing Craft simulation

Now the work is going on and the federation will be updated with a more sophisticated physic model of the behavior of the LCU behind the Ship. The LCU travels in a wave field that is the superposition of the LPD's stern wave and the sea waves modified by the presence of the LPD.

Hydrodynamic motion and forces due to the wave actions are now accurately predicted in frequency domain and time domain module accounting for complete wave actions is under development.

All these development will be included as supporting effect to the main SAND engine and will be reused in future federations requiring them.

3.3   Vertical Take Off and Landing (VTOL)

Take-off and landing operations involves different issues related to the interaction between the ship and the air vehicle.

One of the problems is related to the forces during touch down: the ship moves and air vehicle approaches her choosing the best moment for touching the deck. The forces involved are the ones coming from the ship motions and the ones coming from the drop of the vehicle. Especially in heavy sea state the sum of the forces can be very high and can damage the air vehicle landing devices [6].

This effect has been studied in one of the first federation developed inside an international group studying the best landing period for an helicopter to land on a frigate [7].

Besides this impact effect, another important aspect to take care of is the turbulence generated by superstructure in the surrounding of the landing spots. This aspect involves an heavy interaction between fluid dynamic calculations (CFD) for simulating the flows around the structures (Air Wake) and the relative position of the two moving entities: the helicopter and the ship. As in other experiences, these two separated effects were already studied in CETENA and we have the competences and codes for simulation the two effects separately.

Fig. 9. CFD results for VTOL simulation

Again, reusing these knowledge and making the relative tools interoperable, has brought to the design and implementation of a federation simulate the interactive scenario of an helicopter landing on a ship dynamically taking into account in real-time of the air-wake effect and the relative movements and forces between the two moving entities.

The developed system was composed by the standard basic federation for the ship with the addition of some new federates: the helicopter and the airwake.

The helicopter federate is in reality a ultra simplified federate which simulate a point in the space and collect information from the flows deriving from the airwake and the distance from the ship.

The airwake federate is basically a sophisticated interpolator of pre calculated values coming from offline CFD processing. Depending on the relative position from the ship, the speed, the wind direction and other physical parameters, the federate determine the flow pressure and speed in a certain point.

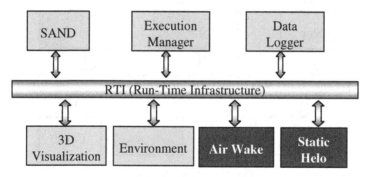

Fig. 10. VTOL federation

Fig. 11. Screenshot of the VTOL simulation

As a matter of fact, since the federation was developed in compliance with both the VS-FOM and the RPR-FOM, a whatever Helicopter federate compliant with the above mentioned FOMs can be easily integrated

3.4   Small Craft Launch and Recovery

CETENA, as a member of CRS (Cooperative Research Ships) group, participated to a Simulation Group focused on the design and implementation of a HLA federation to be used to simulate Small Craft Launch and Recovery (SCLaR) operations.

Also in this context many of the expertises and algorithms developed in previous studies has been reused and integrated in the complete federation.

In particular, in the international project, CETENA provided its VISLab laboratory to integrate the whole federation structured as described in Fig. 12 where the "blue" federates were developed by CETENA and the "yellow" ones were developed by other partners.

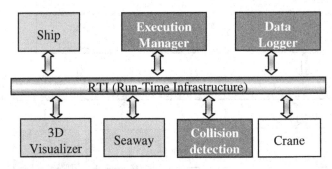

Fig. 12. SCLaR Federation

Primary scopes of this application were the following:

- To share with CRS-SIM group members the knowledge in the development of distributed simulations.
- To set up a common framework able to be improved with detailed simulation models, for the following purposes:
  - To test the winch system in different weather conditions
  - To monitor the waves contact on the small craft during the launching phase
  - To measure the time spent to perform the whole Launch/Recovery operation.

Many of the software and solutions identified in the development of the project have been reused in other applications during the years.

4   Conclusions

New technologies, higher computational resources and a new cultural way in the relationship with the computer (especially derived by video games) have foster the idea that something new could be done to face the above mentioned distortions.

Tools, systems and standards are growing. Now it is our turn to put all these staff together and build the Virtual Ship. Two major obstacles on the horizon: costs and culture.

The first one is mainly evident when simulation is seen only as a tool for design purposes and no "reuse" is foreseen. In this case, yes, simulation is a cost and the return of the investment is very small. Making simulations and simulator reusable for other purposes and for other project is a solution to overcome the problem. In this perspective if most of the models and algorithms developed in the design phase can be reused for instance in a training environment, the ROI is shifted in this second phase which can start before the ship is built and can be a benefit for the customer who can train the crew in advance but also for the shipbuilder who has the chance to expand its business also in the post sale area of the ship and can build an even more strong relationship with the ship-owner.

The cultural obstacle is more complicated. Why I need to enhance the way I'm doing my job? What's the benefit to make things more sophisticated? Why using a realistic visualization, may be also in real time? People who usually play computer games have become accustomed to certain visual and interactive performance and recognize the effectiveness. Unfortunately usually these people are not the decision makers of today but they will be the ones of tomorrow.

If visualization and interactivity are important features, what distinguish a Virtual Ship from a ship in a video game is the realism and the reliability of the behavior which should be deeply physic based and comparable with actual one. In other words is important that the actual expert becomes confident in the behavior of the Virtual Ship as he is now in the results of the detailed analysis tools he is using.

A effective and accredited validation of the simulation is one of the most important challenges in Virtual Ship implementation.

These and other issues are driving the creation and re-use of new technologies, standards and methodologies will bring us closer to realizing the dream of the virtual ship.

References

1. Andert Jr., E.P., Morgan, D.: Collaborative Virtual Prototyping and Test. Naval Engineers Journal, 17–23 (November 1998)
2. Nilsson, P.-O.: The digital product model – a valuable tool for shipbuilders and ship-owners. Scandinavian Yearbook of Maritime Technology, pp. 37–38 (2000)
3. Kanerva, M.: Virtual Reality – 4D Product Modelling Tool for Efficient Shipbuilding Process
4. Tozzi, D., Zini, A., Necrisi, R., Lommi, A., Perra, F., Guagnano, A.: Distributed Simulation in Total Ship Design for Naval Vessels, SIW (2004)
5. Department of Defense, High Level Architecture (1988)
6. Ferrier, B., Le Bihan, O.: The use of simulation tools in the calculation of aircraft-ship interface optional limits. In: 20th Congress on the International Council of the Aeronautical Sciences, Italy (1996)
7. Budde, E.: The Multi-National HLA Federation Development Supporting Simulation Based Acquisition. In: International Conference on HLA Simulation Methodology and Applications (2005)
8. Zini, A., Rocca, A., Raffa, M., Costa, R.: Building a Virtual Ship, HMS (2000)
9. NATO STANAG 4684 Virtual Ship
10. Physx, see NVIDIA website

ASCARI: A Component Based Simulator for Distributed Mobile Robot Systems

Mirko Ferrati*, Alessandro Settimi, and Lucia Pallottino

Centro di Ricerca "E.Piaggio", Dipartimento di Ingegneria dell'Informazione,
Università di Pisa, Italy
{mirko.ferrati,l.pallottino}@centropiaggio.unipi.it
alessandro.settimi@for.unipi.it

Abstract. *ASCARI* is a simulator dedicated to distributed and cooperative mobile robotics systems, designed as a framework for implementing and testing multi-agent collaborative algorithms, especially suited to evaluate algorithms performances with a non-perfect communication channel (e.g. delayed, limited bandwidth, limited range). Compared to state-of-art simulators, *ASCARI* meets a complex new requirement: inter-agent communication has to be integrated in the simulation loop.

The project core is a simulation server with a dynamic engine, a synchronization facility and a set of simulated communications providing the characteristics of the communication channel. Different channel requirements can be added by users.

Inter-agent communication is provided in a transparent way to the user by template communication classes. Simulated communications and filters are handled automatically. The simulator is completed by a 2D-3D viewer and a simple GUI.

In this paper we describe *ASCARI* and validate it on a distributed traffic control and a task assignment algorithm.

Keywords: Multi Agent, Simulation, Communication Channel, Distributed Algorithms.

1 Introduction

Simulations are widely used in multi-robot systems as a validation method, yet most of the software simulators are usually developed to target a specific application/algorithm, thus they lack the capabilities to become a general and stardardized tool for researchers in this field. While, for generic robotics applications, there exist some simulators that are recognized as standard tools, these softwares are not very suited to multi-robot systems. Here we will briefly examine the features of some of the most known robotic simulators from the point of view of multi-agent applications. Specifically, our aim is to build a system that allows easy testing of communication-based distributed algorithms, where the communication channel and equipment can be specified by the user. The most inspiring

---

* Corresponding author.

J. Hodicky (Ed.): MESAS 2014, LNCS 8906, pp. 152–163, 2014.

simulator for our work was Stage, from the project Player/Stage/Gazebo. The Player/Stage (P/S) [1] project is an open-source software for rapid development of robot control code. Player [3,2] is based on a set of simple interfaces for communicating and controlling sensors and actuators, while Stage is a 2D simulator for multiple robots that includes a simple physical simulations. Stage uses a set of simulated devices that are compatible with standard Player interfaces. Thus the interface that is presented to the user by Player can be used unchanged from simulation to real hardware.

For example, a program that drives a simulated laser-equipped robot in Stage will also drive a real laser-equipped robot, with no changes to the control code.

Stage software architecture was designed with multi-robot systems in mind, the resulting software is capable of handling thousands of mobile agents with simple dynamics and an arbitrary control code. The main limitation of P/S is the communication between robots: it was not designed for simulating a communication, and the Wifi interface has been only declared as a possible sensor, but it was not implemented.

We believe that not taking into account the capability of simulating communications among agents during the design of Stage makes it very hard to add that feature now. Anyway, the project is no longer developed since some years, maybe due to the focus of open source robotics community on Gazebo. Gazebo has recently evolved as a standalone project integrated with ROS, and lost its old Player interface coupling. The main difference between Gazebo and Stage is the quality and the precision of the dynamic integration: Gazebo is a 3D environment with accurate body collisions and joint simulations, focused on a single robot hardly interacting with the environment. Since one year Gazebo provides an 802 wireless simulated sensor with Hata-Okumara propagation model. This sensor can be used as a starting point for developing other type of wireless communication sensors. Gazebo is not suited for thousands of robots because of the computational complexity of the simulation: simulating thousands of robots in Gazebo would require too much time and usually researchers in distributed control algorithms for multi-robot systems are more interested in fast approximated simulations than in realistic ones. The same considerations stand for similar simulators such as V-rep [9], USARSim [8] and Microsoft Robotics Studio [7].

MatSim [4] uses a totally different approach to multi-agent simulations: by ignoring agent dynamics it is capable of simulating more than 1 millions of agents in the same environment. It is a grown and stable software easy to use, but as such, it appears complex to understand and edit in its simulating capabilities.

Webots [5] is a commercial closed-source 3D mobile robot simulator. The robot controllers can be programmed with the built-in IDE (Integrated Development Environment) or with third party development environments. The robot behavior can be tested in physically realistic worlds. The controller programs can optionally be transferred to commercially available real robots. A simulated wifi-communication module is implemented inside the simulator but, since Webots is not expandable by the user, the communication model cannot be changed or improved.

Argos [6] was inspired by Stage. The main differences can be found in the simulation speed (Argos is faster) and in the decoupling of the physics engine from the simulated world. Argos suffers the same design problem of Stage related to the possibility of simulating communication channels. The user cannot influence the simulator side, meaning that he/she can't write a communication module integrated with the simulated world. As in Stage, the wifi sensor exists but it has an empty behavior, meaning that it was not implemented.

Mason [10] is a multi-agent simulation suite written in Java to be portable on different operating systems. It was not built as a complete simulator, but as something to be easily adapted by other researchers into a custom simulator. Mason is focused on agents in a wider sense, so it does not provide any mobile robotics facility such as communications, sensors or a realistic dynamic.

It is worth noting Swarm [11], which is probably one of the oldest multi-agent simulators and served as inspiration for Mason, Argos and Stage.

Finally, two new simulators have been growing in the last years: RoboRobo! [12] and Morse [13]. They are both inspired by the need of new fast simulators dedicated to multi-agent research and developed with state-of-the-art technologies. Roborobo! can be pretty useful as a base for developing a custom simulator for a particular application (e.g. a specific swarm mobile robotics environment and simulation), but not as simulator capable of providing a platform for testing many different algorithms. Morse is built with interoperability as a priority: it supports most known middlewares (ROS, YARP) and uses a script to set up simulations. Robot models inside Morse are controlled through interprocess communication, new models can be added by writing sensors and actuators simulation code as python scripts. At the moment of writing, there are no simulated communication sensors in the simulator sensor library.

Although the state of art of simulators is mature and fulfills almost every research requirements, we believe that a generic communication system integrated in the simulation loop is a missing feature. We will propose a design capable of providing this new feature while keeping the best practices from state of art simulators. We believe that our communication system design can successfully be added to newborn simulators such as RoboRobo and Morse.

Our work aims to have a completely application–independent simulator suited for distributed mobile robotics with simulated communication network, which can be used together with simulated robots and real ones, see figure 1.

This paper is organized as follows. In section 2 we describe the requirements which our simulator was designed for. The global software architecture is addressed in section 3, here the communication facilities are introduced, a more detailed description is in section 4. The hardware integration is addressed in section 5. We describe two application that use our simulator in section 6.

2   Design Requirements

ASCARI has been developed with a set of requirements that were identified as main features from state of art simulators. In fact, we believe that building a

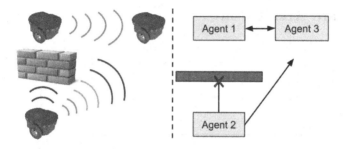

Fig. 1. The *ASCARI* simulated communication

simulator primarily around novel features would lead to a custom non-generic software, our target is instead to set a new standard for multi–robot systems simulations (as Stage did in 2008).

One of the major features of modern simulators is the possibility to use the same code for both simulated and real agents. The only changes required should be the input/output drivers, not the control law or its implementation.

A difference between custom simulators and the widespread ones is their modular and expandable design. A simulator should never have hardcoded assumptions on the system that will be simulated, new modules with new features should be easily integrated into the simulator, even core features should be built as modules. Argos and Gazebo fully represents this approach by using interfaces and plugins.

Usually, simulators support multi–process systems where each robot controller runs in its own process or computer, while the simulation handles dynamic integration and model collisions. This approach is a limitation when simulating thousands of robots, and the solution is the capability of integrating the robot controllers directly into the same simulation process, as Stage does. Designing *ASCARI*, we chose a mixed approach where controllers can be wrapped in a standalone process or run in a different thread of the simulator process itself. In the next section we will show how this capability emerged naturally from *ASCARI* software architecture design.

Following the Gazebo plugin approach, *ASCARI* supports any kind of dynamic law required by the user. Dynamic laws can be expressed directly as code or as a set of equations: $\dot{x} = f(x, u)$ where $x \in \mathbb{R}^n$ is the state of the agent, $u \in \mathbb{R}^m$ is the controller output and f is, in general, a non-linear function.

Finally, our main target is the design of a communication system integrated in both the simulation loop and the real robots. The implementation of the communication between agents is based on communication primitives. Such primitives manage any kind of message data and hide the simulator to the user providing the same API for real and simulated agents. The communication module inside the simulator has been designed as a plugin that may be changed to model various communication channels with different characteristics such as ranges, signal noises and visibility.

3   Software Architecture

In this section we describe some of the main *ASCARI* software components, focusing in particular on the design choices related to the communication facilities. From an high level point of view, *ASCARI* has a server that acts as a world simulator, a set of clients (simulated agents) and a simple 2D/3D visualizer.

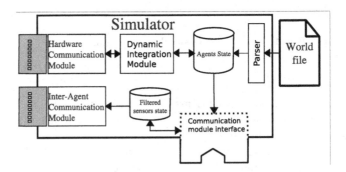

Fig. 2. The *ASCARI* server architecture

The important server sub-modules are shown in figure 2. The server parses a configuration file where the world and the agents are described. A database with each agent state is then created and updated by a dynamic integration module at each simulation step after receiving commands from clients. A user code is loaded as a communication module, it has reading access to the agent state database, and updates an agent communication filter database, which is used to allow or block inter-agent communications. At the moment, two dynamic modules are available, a simple fixed step forward integration (default) and an external robot state receiver, which can receive updated states from any external dynamic integration system or real hardware sensors, allowing hardware in the loop simulations (see details in section 5). The server basic loop flowchart is shown in figure 3.

It sends the updated state to each agent, receives new actuator controls from them, integrates the dynamic, executes the communication module update function, forwards all the inter-agent communications, based on the agent communication filter database, and starts again.

The agent structure is represented in figure 4. As already said, *ASCARI* is based on many little building blocks, so many client sub-modules are similar to their respective ones in the server. Hardware and inter–agent communication module are connected to the server modules. The configuration file is read by the parser and it is used to provide initialization parameters to the agent control loop.

The control loop handles sensors and actuators, providing the data to the custom control loop as it was local and not remotely simulated. The custom loop interface is where user code is running. It has access to the agent state

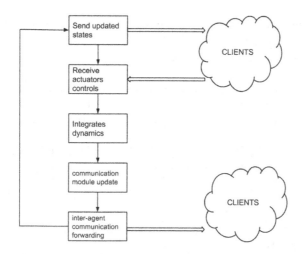

Fig. 3. The *ASCARI* server flowchart

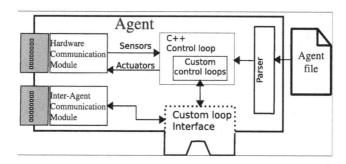

Fig. 4. The *ASCARI* client architecture

and to the inter-agent communication primitives that allows the user to create distributed algorithms. The parser results are given also to the custom loop, so that user can specify additional parameters in the same agent configuration file. The client basic loop flowchart is shown in figure 5.

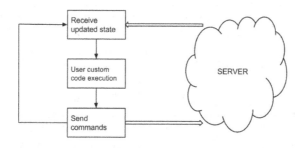

Fig. 5. The *ASCARI* client flowchart

It receives the updated state from the server, executes the user custom code, and sends the resulting commands to the simulator.

Configuration File Structure and Options. An example of a configuration file is reported. The structure is the classic one of the yaml files. The user can use the provided parser to get the information from the file in his/hers custom code.

Inside the tag *WORLD* (where we can define additional variables) there are the two main tags: *BEHAVIORS* and *AGENTS*.

```
- WORLD:

  BEHAVIORS:
  - name: unicycle
    states: [x,y,theta]
    control_commands: [v,w]
    DYNAMIC_MAP:
    - x: 'v*cos(theta)'
      y: 'v*sin(theta)'
      theta: 'w'

  AGENTS:
  - agent: Agent1
    COMMUNICATION_AREA:    circle(50)
    INITIAL:
    - x: '3'
      y: '3'
      theta: '0'
    BEHAVIOR: unicycle
    SIMULATED: 1
```

Inside the *BEHAVIORS* tag the user can define many agent types with different states and dynamics.

Inside the *AGENTS* tag the user can define as many desired agents with their own parameters and behaviours. In the example, the variable *COMMUNICA-TION_AREA* is used by a communication filter module to filter all the messages outside a circle centered in the robot and with a radius of 50 meters. The *SIM-ULATED* tag allows to use the same configuration file for real and simulated agents, which can also be mixed together to obtain an hardware in the loop simulation.

Finally, a 2D/3D visualizer and a simple GUI to start both the server and all the agents specified in a configuration file complete the *ASCARI* software architecture. The visualizer reads the network traffic generated between the server and the clients in a transparent way, so that zero or many viewers can be attached to the same simulation.

4   Communication Facility

The core of our system is a set of communication modules and interfaces organized as generic basic building blocks, usually a sender and a receiver. Both the communication between clients and server and inter-agent communication modules are implemented using these blocks. Messages are strongly typed and can be any complex c++ structure, including any STL container. Receiver and sender are c++ classes template–ized on the type of message they work with, they are initialized with an IP address, as 1-to-1 or 1-to-N connections, and they can have an optional topic name similar to ROS topics used to filter messages. Usually a developer uses both classes and creates a transceiver made with a pair of receiver/sender. The agent code can use the transceiver to communicate with other agents without caring about the presence of a simulator. In fact, if a simulation is running, communications are automatically synchronized with the simulation loop among all the agents, while in the case of real agents, the same transceiver creates direct inter–agent connections, thus the agent code does not require any changes in the communication part when switching from simulated to real hardware. The only changes required are inside the configuration file, by editing the *SIMULATED* tag.

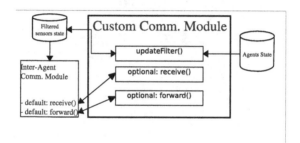

Fig. 6. The *ASCARI* custom Communication Module

From the simulator point of view, the user needs to inherit a simple *filter-Module* that represents a communication channel and to create a custom communication module (figure 6). We chose to give the user maximum freedom on the channel behaviour but, in its simpler form, the inherited class has just to implement an *updateFilter(...)* method. The *updateFilter* inputs are the simulation states of all the agents, defined as states variables (e.g. planar coordinates of agents). This method updates a filtering table that tells the simulator if two agents are able to communicate to each other at each simulation step. If the user wants more control, he can also override the *receive(...)* and *forward(...)* methods. These two methods are the ones used by the server in order to receive and transmit inter–agent messages by acting as a gateway. If they are reimplemented, advanced behavior such as delays on the channel, random packets drop, bandwidth limitations and so on can be obtained. Note that *receive* and *forward* methods have access to the messages content, while the *updateFilter* has, as input, only the agents state.

5   Hardware Integration

All the code written in *ASCARI* can be reused on the real hardware thanks to the communication facility. During the execution, if in the configuration file an agent has been declared as not simulated, instead of sending the commands to the simulator, these are sent via serial communication directly to the hardware through a serial communication block that fully complies with the standard messages that the client/server exchanges during the simulation. Basically instead of using the actuation commands to simulate the dynamics of the robot, these are used to move the real robot. With this configuration the only thing a user, that want to pass to the hardware, has to care about is to have something that can receive via serial bus the actuation commands and execute them. The commands for the robots currently used are *linear acceleration* and *angular acceleration*.

An example of the hardware we used is shown in figure 7.

Fig. 7. A mobile robot, equipped with a *Raspberry Pi* and an *Arduino Uno*

In this robot there is a *Raspberry Pi*, which is the core of the robot. On board there are a wireless key to communicate with the other agents and a Linux system on which the various algorithms run. Plugged to it via serial bus there is an *Arduino Uno* which receive the actuation commands from the Raspberry and send them to the motors via a shield board (wires have been omitted for the sake of clarity).

One advantage to have this architecture is that we can work with real and simulated robot as well just defining the type of the robots in the configuration file. For example we can run a collision avoidance algorithm on two real robot and a simulated one. In the real scenario we will see the real robots steering 'near' the simulated one, even if there is nothing in front of them.

6   Applications

Many applications have been developed thanks to *ASCARI*, both on the software and on the hardware side. These applications concern for example: collision avoidance, agents localization using webcams and markers and classical distributed robotics algorithm such as rendez-vous and distributed consensus.

Two of the most interesting applications are a distributed task assignment algorithm and a distributed traffic control one.

In the task assignment application a subgradient method based algorithm allows to assign various tasks to heterogeneous robots optimally, [15]. Concerning *ASCARI*, it has been used to simulated the various robots' dynamics and to coordinate them during the scenario evolution. Thanks to the communication facility the agents exchange through the network their local subgradient, allowing the other robots to compute the total subgradient until the algorithm converges. In the simulated scenario, the simulator takes into account the dynamicity of the tasks, making them appearing, evolving and expiring during time. The tasks' state is sent through the network by the simulator, so the various agents can know if a task is already taken, or expired, or if some new tasks are available. In the real scenario the tasks are the classical industrial ones, such as putting material on a conveyor belt, or move pallets across a warehouse. In this application the robot recharging is seen has a high priority task, depending on the amount of charge of the robot, which appears if the amount of a robot's charge goes below a certain value. In Figure 8 a frame of a simulation of the algorithm in an industrial scenario is depicted.

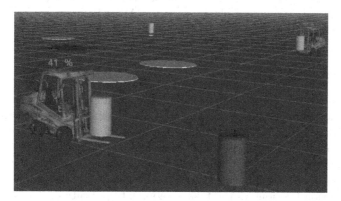

Fig. 8. Distributed task assignment algorithm in *ASCARI*

In [14], a distributed traffic control protocol has been proposed. The algorithm uses communication to foresee and avoid agents collisions on a topological map represented with a graph (see Figure 9). The messages exchanged by agents are a set of future nodes and arcs that each agent would like to cross, a resource locking algorithm ensures that agents will not try to cross the same node in the same future time and hence ensure the safety of the system. The algorithm was tested with different communication ranges and with random packets drop to assess its robustness. In the single-process version of *ASCARI* 30 agents with a simple unicycle dynamics were simulated at around 50x real time with an integration step of 0.001 s.

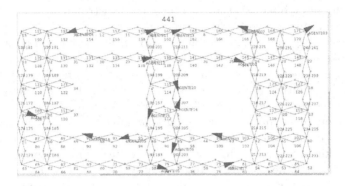

Fig. 9. Distributed traffic control algorithm in *ASCARI*

Notice that *ASCARI* can be used to implement and test any robot control algorithm, but it is especially suited for multi–agent collaborative algorithms also with a non–perfect communication channel. A user must define the agents' control law and a dedicated communicator if particular data exchange between the agents (or between the agents and the simulator) is needed.

To view the original videos please go to the ASCARISimulator channel on: http://www.youtube.com/user/ASCARIsimulator.

7   Conclusions

In this paper the *ASCARI* distributed mobile robotics simulator with simulated communication network has been presented. The simulator is suited to develop many applications, and in particular it has been designed to be scalable and hence it is able to handle many robots. The hardware integration is straightforward and the user can use real robots and simulated ones as well. Future works include: export the communication facilities to Argos and RoboRobo! and real object simulation (as done in the task assignment application).

References

1. Vaughan, R.: Massively multi-robot simulation in stage. Swarm Intelligence 2(2-4), 189–208 (2008)
2. Vaughan, R.T., Gerkey, B.P., Howard, A.: On device abstractions for portable, reusable robot code. In: Proceedings of 2003 IEEE/RSJ International Conference on Intelligent Robots and Systems (IROS 2003), vol. 3. IEEE (2003)

3. Gerkey, B., Vaughan, R.T., Howard, A.: The player/stage project: Tools for multi-robot and distributed sensor systems. In: Proceedings of the 11th International Conference on Advanced Robotics, vol. 1 (2003)
4. Balmer, M., et al.: MATSim-T: Architecture and simulation times. In: Multi-agent Systems for Traffic and Transportation Engineering, pp. 57–78 (2009)
5. Michel, O.: Webots: Symbiosis between virtual and real mobile robots. In: Heudin, J.-C. (ed.) VW 1998. LNCS (LNAI), vol. 1434, pp. 254–263. Springer, Heidelberg (1998)
6. Pinciroli, C., et al.: ARGoS: a modular, parallel, multi-engine simulator for multi-robot systems. Swarm Intelligence 6(4), 271–295 (2012)
7. Jackson, J.: Microsoft robotics studio: A technical introduction. IEEE Robotics & Automation Magazine 14(4), 82–87 (2007)
8. Carpin, S., et al.: USARSim: a robot simulator for research and education. In: 2007 IEEE International Conference on Robotics and Automation. IEEE (2007)
9. Freese, M., Singh, S., Ozaki, F., Matsuhira, N.: Virtual robot experimentation platform V-REP: A versatile 3D robot simulator. In: Ando, N., Balakirsky, S., Hemker, T., Reggiani, M., von Stryk, O. (eds.) SIMPAR 2010. LNCS, vol. 6472, pp. 51–62. Springer, Heidelberg (2010)
10. Luke, S., et al.: MASON: A Java multi-agent simulation library. In: Proceedings of Agent 2003 Conference on Challenges in Social Simulation, vol. 9 (2003)
11. Minar, N., et al.: The swarm simulation system: a toolkit for building multi-agent systems. Santa Fe NM: Santa Fe Institute Working Paper (1996): 96-06
12. Bredeche, N., et al.: Roborobo! a fast robot simulator for swarm and collective robotics. arXiv preprint arXiv:1304.2888 (2013)
13. Echeverria, G., et al.: Modular open robots simulation engine: Morse. In: 2011 IEEE International Conference on Robotics and Automation (ICRA). IEEE (2011)
14. Ferrati, M., Pallottino, L.: A time expanded network based algorithm for safe and efficient distributed multi-agent coordination. In: IEEE Conference on Decision and Control, Florence, Italy, pp. 2805–2810 (2013)
15. Settimi, A., Pallottino, L.: A Subgradient Based Algorithm for Distributed Task Assignment for Heterogeneous Mobile Robots. In: IEEE Conference on Decision and Control, Florence, Italy, pp. 3665–3670 (2013)

Simulation System for Teleoperated Mobile Robots

Tomáš Kot, Václav Krys, and Petr Novak

VŠB - Technical University of Ostrava, Department or Robotics, Ostrava, Czech Republic
{tomas.kot,vaclav.krys,petr.novak}@vsb.cz

Abstract. The paper presents a mobile robot simulator designed primarily for teleoperated mobile robots, to aid in the prototyping phase of development or as a training tool for existing robots. The simulator uses virtual reality with realistic 3D graphics to simulate complex behaviour of a mobile robot in various conditions and with different properties. The system can be used to discover or verify driving and manipulation abilities of a mobile robot defined by its kinematics structure and dimensions, and also to simulate navigation using the camera subsystem containing one or more cameras.

Keywords: mobile robot, simulation, teleoperation, navigation, virtual reality.

1 Introduction

The area of service robotics has rapidly developed lately especially in terms of the scope of applications. Mobile service robots are relatively often used not only for operations associated with safety engineering such as firefighting, chemical accidents, terrorist attacks, disposing of explosives, surveying of hazardous and cramped areas, searching for earthquake victims, but also in the commercial and science sectors, e.g. checking and maintenance of piping, exploration of planets, etc. Also military applications cannot be neglected.

Vast majority of the above applications use mobile robots remotely controlled by a human operator. Compared to autonomous robots, this is still the cheaper and above all more reliable solution. Algorithms of robot artificial intelligence and sensory systems still have not reached the level when it would be possible to use a robot for tasks when human lives are at stake.

Owing to the immense range of possible applications, the mobile robotics field is subject to continuous development and innovation. The development process of a new mobile robot requires a lot of time and funds, and therefore it is convenient to use virtual prototyping – in an ideal case the resulting first physical prototype developed would meet all requirements and no additional modifications would be required. As for the mechanical construction of a robot, the existing CAD/CAM systems may be used. However, these systems usually do not allow complex simulation of behaviour of the whole mobile robot in the conditions similar to reality. So a situation may occur when a physical prototype would be fully operational in terms of its mechanical aspects but due to an unsuitable concept, the mobile robot would be difficult to control

J. Hodicky (Ed.): MESAS 2014, LNCS 8906, pp. 164–172, 2014.

in the required conditions, the camera subsystem would not provide the operator with sufficiently clear images, and suchlike.

The possibility to carry out extensive testing on a virtual prototype of a whole robot in a simulated real environment may make the whole development process much faster, much more efficient, and especially cheaper. The virtual model may be further used even when the robot is physically manufactured, fully tuned, and used in practice – the virtual model may be used for training of operators without the necessity to use the actual robot.

2   Basic Structure and Properties of the Simulator

There is a great number of simulation systems available, for example [1-7]. However, most of them focus on testing of various algorithms of autonomous behaviour, and therefore they offer advanced possibilities of programming of robot control systems. However, creation of a programme code is also necessary even for basic tasks, unless one of the ready-made mobile robots based on actual commercial robots is used. It is quite difficult to install and commission the systems, which is given particularly by their composition of various more or less independent modules and libraries. The primary view of the 3D simulated scene is from top, but there usually is a possibility to define virtual robot cameras and use them to monitor the scene. The graphic output is average, created using basic principles and simple shadowing is usually the most advanced effect.

RoboSim simulation system described in this article tries to excel compared to the competition of the already existing systems particularly in the following areas:

- Short time needed to start working with the system, application with ease of use even for designers and other professionals not skilled in programming.
- Possibility of quick verification of the concept and kinematics of the mobile robots plus easy modifications.
- Advanced simulation of virtual cameras, superior virtual presentation for more realistic feel for operators when controlling virtual robots.
- Specialization in verification of the ease of operator control and navigation in an unknown or complex environment.

Simulation requirements may be divided into two large groups:

- **Movement physics** (driving properties, handling in various terrains, stability, ability to avoid various obstacles, turning radius and manoeuvrability in general, speed, power, etc.).
- **Navigation** (ability of the operator to control the robot using only the feedback from the cameras and sensory subsystem, verification of the required quantity, placement and the type of cameras, benefits of stereovision, etc.).

The application is based on our own application core and is programmed in Visual C++. The Direct3D application programming interface (API) is used for graphics [8] and the Havok engine for rigid objects physics simulation [9].

Fig. 1. Six-wheeled mobile robot displayed in the simulator

The rendered virtual scene consists of a greater number of separate entities (these are usually separate bodies), where each of them has its visual and physical properties [10,11]. Various relations and dependencies may be defined between the entities. Rendering of entities is optimized for maximum speed and therefore suitable filtering is applied according to visibility and the rendered objects are also ordered for more efficient calling of Direct3D functions. Hardware acceleration of rendering is a matter of course. Therefore, a graphic chip supporting at least Shader Model 3.0 (DirectX 9.0c) is required to run the application.

3   Kinematics and Dynamics of Movement

Comprehensive simulation of Newton physics of a mobile robot is achieved through proper use of the above-mentioned Havok engine. The mobile robot is divided into individual parts (entities) with suitably adjusted physical properties. The enti-ties are then connected by appropriate physical links and action parts (e.g. driven wheels) are complemented with physical actions (drives). When the mobile robot defined this way is placed in a virtual environment also containing entities with a physical component (at least a floor or ground), complex simulation of robot behaviour is secured.

The current version of the simulator uses only rigid body dynamics from the Havok library, and therefore it is impossible to simulate e.g. flexible wheel tyres. However, simulation of springs for sprung wheel suspension is possible. Each rigid body (entity) has particularly the following properties:

- weight, centre of gravity position, inertia moments,
- shape for detection of collisions,

- restitution (degree of energy loss upon collision),
- friction,
- linear and angular damping (degree of energy loss when moving without effect of external forces).

Body shape is used for detection of collision with other objects and calculation of correct reaction to these collisions. Calculation of collisions is an operation whose complexity rises significantly with the complexity of body shapes. Therefore, it is desirable to define the collision shape of the body as simple as possible while preserving sufficiently accurate behaviour. Therefore, in most cases a different shape is used for visual representation of an object (rendered triangular mesh with many details) and for collisions (Fig. 2). Examples of some shapes ordered starting with the least demanding: sphere, capsule, box, cylinder, general convex body, general concave body.

Fig. 2. Comparison of detailed visual representation and simplified collision

Restriction of movement of two bodies against each other may be achieved by links. Havok allows definition of new arbitrarily complex links but it also contains ready-made links of which the following are the most suitable for undercarriages, handling superstructures or other parts of mobile robots: *hinge* – axial rotation, *limited hinge* – restricted rotation, *wheel* – rotation round one axis, optional rotation round another axis (steering) and optional translation along a third axis including a spring and dampening (wheel suspension) and *prismatic* (translation).

Behaviour of objects in a certain way is affected by *actions*. Analogous to links, new actions also may be easily defined according to actual needs. Rotational and translation motors in particular belong to the prearranged actions. A new link was created for the needs of RoboSim, simulating behaviour of a DC motor including characteristic dependence of torque on speed.

4   Simulation of Camera and Sensoric Subsystems

With regard to the primary designation of the simulator for testing of operator controlled robots particularly when using a feedback from a camera subsystem, great attention was paid to correct simulation of cameras.

The simulation system allows fitting of the robot with an arbitrary number of virtual cameras, which may be used for monitoring of the robot surroundings. These cameras may be visually rendered as a 3D model (Fig. 3).

Fig. 3. Virtual mobile robot with 2 stereovision cameras and one rear camera

Each camera needs to have specified the basic optical properties – viewing angle, resolution in pixels, or even for example parameters of barrel distortion of the image.

The actual optics of cameras usually does not have sufficient depth of field to cover large distance range of viewed objects, and therefore focusing is implemented. The objects outside the focused depth of field then appear to be blurry. This effect may substantially affect operator's ability to navigate in a complex environment using only the cameras and therefore RoboSim includes simulation of depth of field (Fig. 4). When rendering a scene, this visual effect is achieved using a special *pixel shader*. It is not an exact physical simulation of this optical phenomenon but only its rough and simplified approximation.

When using *stereovision* it is necessary to specify a pair of cameras with suitable mutual position and identical optical parameters (Figure 3). Stereovision may then be viewed in the following ways:

- *Anaglyph* – encoding images for individual eyes to different colours and subsequent filtration using simple passive spectacles with coloured glasses through which the monitor is viewed [12].
- *Head-mounted display (HMD)* – various types of active displaying devices placed directly on user's head [13]. Two general methods of displaying are supported – interlacing and image alternating.
- *Oculus Rift* – new HMD with exceptional properties and very low price. This device requires a specific way of rendering when the images for both eyes are placed

next to each other and software barrel distortion is applied to them to eliminate the opposite distortion created subsequently in the device optics [14].

Fig. 4. Depth of field effect

Simulation of sensors is only simple in the current version of *RoboSim*. There are three types of sensors available – *linear* (measuring linear distance to one point of an obstacle, simulation of IR and suchlike sensors), *conical* (measuring distances in a cone and returning the smallest value, simulation of ultrasound sensors etc.) and *planar* (measuring distances in a fan pattern on a plane and providing a set of measured values, simulation of laser scanners). All sensors are sending imaginary mathematical beams and detect intersections with object in the scene. In order to prevent unrealistic absolute accuracy, it is possible to add random noise.

5   Realistic Testing Environments

Besides the possibility to define completely new environments, RoboSim also of-fers three predefined scenes covering various conditions of possible applications of robots – a family house (complex interior with narrow spaces and a large number of obstacles, Fig. 5), an outdoor scene (open space, uneven terrain with various slop-ing, Fig. 1, 4) and a special testing laboratory (various exactly defined sizes of corridors, door openings, obstacles, stairs, inclined planes, ramps, etc., Fig. 2, 3, 6).

In order to provide the most authentic feel of the view available from the mobile robot cameras, the testing environments are created with emphasis placed on the visual quality and details using some advanced methods to achieve realistic 3D graphics. Common graphics applied in CAD systems and in most of the existing simulation systems uses only simple dynamic lighting and possibly textures. The resulting uniform colour surfaces and repeating textures do not provide the operator with sufficiently authentic image when testing navigation using the camera subsystem and the result may be biased due to this fact – it is much more difficult for the operator to find his/her way in the virtual environment than in reality.

Fig. 5. One of the rooms in the family house testing environment

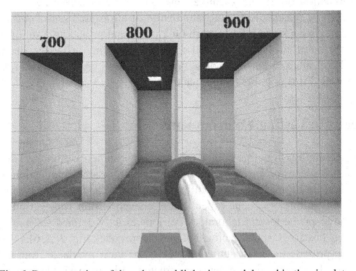

Fig. 6. Demonstration of the advanced lightning model used in the simulator

The advanced techniques used in RoboSim include for example:

- *Shadows* – very important for understanding the mutual spatial relations between objects. The used technique is shadow mapping including an optional degree of smoothing (Fig. 1).
- *Lightmapping* – replacement of real-time dynamic lighting by much more accurate pre-calculated model simulating even reflected light (walls on Fig. 6).
- *Environment mapping* – simplified simulation of highly reflective materials (robot arm on Fig. 6).
- *Normal and specular mapping* – simulation of uneven and diverse surface using a suitable lighting calculation without the necessity to create a very complex 3D model (Fig. 1).
- *Multitexturing, texture layers* – alleviating of undesirable effect of repetition of texture patterns, adding of imperfection, impurities, etc.

6   Conclusion

To compare simulation with reality, virtual models of several actual robots were created and their behaviour was tested (Fig. 7). Although the simulation of dynamics in real time implemented by Havok system is quite realistic, it is not fully physically accurate, which is given by the necessary simplifications in order to allow sufficient calculation speed.

The basic simplification directly concerning wheeled mobile robots is the replacement of simulation of soft rubber of wheels (or even air filled tyres) with ideally rigid

Fig. 7. Mobile robot on an obstacle course in reality and in the simulator

objects. Neither is it possible to simulate accurately the tyre tread and so the possible shape contact of the wheel with an obstacle is replaced by mere friction of a cylinder against an obstacle. Despite that, the behaviour of robots in the simulation is depicted relatively accurately in particular in terms of manoeuvrability and ease of control.

The strongest point of *RoboSim* – simulation of camera subsystem – brought several interesting findings even during the development of the simulator. It was successfully used for optimization of camera position on a developed mobile robot and this SW was also used for testing of stereovision and particularly its usability for navigation.

The application is currently being extended by a more convenient and fully graph-ical editor of mobile robots and testing scenes and adding of simulation of tracked chassis would be also desirable. There is also a plan for the possibility to control the virtual robot in the simulator using the operator's station for the actual robot, which instead of the real robot would establish connection with the PC with the running simulation.

Acknowledgment. This article has been elaborated in the framework of the project Opportunity for young researchers, reg. no. CZ.1.07/2.3.00/30.0016, supported by Operational Pro-gramme Education for Competitiveness and co-financed by the European Social Fund and the state budget of the Czech Republic.

References

1. Microsoft MSDN. Microsoft Robotics Developer Studio, `http://msdn.microsoft.com/en-us/library/bb905420.aspx`
2. The Player Project. Gazebo, `http://playerstage.sourceforge.net/wiki/Gazebo`
3. CyberRobotics Webots 6, `http://www.cyberbotics.com/`
4. Universität Leipzig. Research Network for Self-Organization or Robot Behavior, `http://robot.informatik.uni-leipzig.de/`
5. Virtual Robot Experimentation Platform, `http://www.v-rep.eu/`
6. OpenSim, `http://opensimulator.sourceforge.net/`
7. Simbad Project Home, `http://simbad.sourceforge.net/`
8. Microsoft. Direct3D 9 Graphics <Literal>http://msdn.microsoft.com/ cs-cz/library/bb219837(en-us,VS.85).aspx</Literal>
9. Havok, `http://www.havok.com/`
10. Eberly, D.H.: 3D Game Engine Design: A Practical Approach to Real-time Computer Graphics, 561p. Morgan Kaufmann Publishers (2000) ISBN 978-1558605930
11. Gregory, J.: Game Engine Architecture, p. 860. AK Peters, Ltd., Massachusetts (2009) ISBN 978-1-56881-413-1
12. Wikipedia. Anaglyph image, `http://en.wikipedia.org/wiki/Anaglyph_image`
13. Wikipedia. Head-mounted display, `http://en.wikipedia.org/wiki/Head-mounted_display`
14. Oculus VR. Oculus Rift, `http://www.oculusvr.com/rift/`
15. Kot, T., Mostýn, V., Novák, P.: Application of Virtual Reality for Verification of Charac-teristics of Mobile Robots. In: Proceedings of the ICMT 09 - International Conference on Military Technologies, pp. s.517–s.524. University of Defence, Brno (2009) ISBN 978-80-7231-649-6

Simulation-Based Goal-Selection
for Autonomous Exploration

Miroslav Kulich, Vojtěch Vonásek, and Libor Přeučil

Department of Cybernetics
Faculty Electrical Engineering
Czech Technical University in Prague
Technická 2, 166 27 Prahue 6, Czech Republic
{kulich,vonasek,preucil}@labe.felk.cvut.cz
http://cyber.felk.cvut.cz

Abstract. High-level planning can be defined as the process of selection of an appropriate solution from a set of possible candidates. This process typically evaluates each candidate according to some reward function consisting of (1) cost, i.e., effort needed to accomplish the candidate and (2) the utility of accomplishing it and then selects the best one according to this evaluation. The key problem lies in the fact that the reward function can be rarely evaluated precisely. At the example of the problem of exploration of an unknown environment by a modular robot we show that precise simulation-based estimation of the cost function leads to better decisions of high-level planning and thus improves exploration process performance. State-of-the-art techniques compute the cost function in goal-selection as a length of the path from the current robot position to a goal-candidate. This is sufficient for robots with simple kinematics for which time to reach a candidate highly correlates with a path length. As this does not hold for complex (modular) robots, we introduce the approach that generates a feasible trajectory to each goal-candidate (taking into account kinematic constrains of the robot) and determines the cost function as time needed to perform this trajectory in a simulator. The experimental results with a robot consisting of eight modules operating in several environments show that the proposed simulation-based solution outperforms standard solutions.

Keywords: exploration, modular robot, simulations, goal-selection.

1   Introduction

Modular robots consist of many small interconnected robotic modules. Depending on hardware architecture, the modules can be equipped with various actuators to achieve a motion, basic sensors, communication bus and a simple processing unit; we refer to [17] for a comprehensive survey of existing modular platforms. In comparison to conventional fixed-shapes robots, which are usually built for performing a specific job, the modular robots are more flexible as they can be reconfigured to various shapes according to a target application. It may bring additional abilities in applications like space exploration [26], search & rescue missions [25,3] or object manipulation [12].

J. Hodicky (Ed.): MESAS 2014, LNCS 8906, pp. 173–183, 2014.

For example, a quadruped modular robot can be used for efficient motion over a complex terrain. When the robot needs to pass a narrow space, it can reconfigure to a snake-like robot. Beside the ability to form robots of various shapes, the advantage of modular robots stands in the possibility of changing failed modules by simple reconnection for the organism.

The aforementioned properties predetermine modular robots for search and rescue missions. A typical task in these missions is exploration, which is the process of autonomous navigation of a robot in an unknown environment in order to build a model (map) of the environment. A natural condition is to perform the exploration with a minimal usage of resources, e.g. trajectory length, time of exploration, or energy consumption.

The key component of the exploration algorithm is determination of a next goal in each exploration step, which can be made in two stages: candidates for the next goal are found first and the most appropriate one is selected then. Two main streams for goal candidates generation were developed and widely used in the robotic community. Yamauchi [23] introduced a frontier-based approach, where candidates are placed at a border between the space detected as free and an unexplored area (frontiers). Gonzalez-Banos and Latombe [7] generate candidates in the free space and within the visibility range of frontiers (free curves in their terminology).

Many techniques evaluating the goal candidates were studied in the last fifteen years. They are based only on estimation of the effort needed to reach the goal (e.g. distance cost) [23,11] or they combine a distance cost with other criteria. In [7], a measure $A(q)$ of an unexplored region of the environment, which is potentially visible from the candidate q, is combined with the distance cost $L(q)$ to get the overall utility of q:

$$g(q) = A(q)e^{-\lambda L(q)},$$

where λ is a positive constant. A utility of the next action as the weighted sum of the distance cost and expected information gain computed as a change of entropy after performing the action is presented in [19]. Another strategy taking into account the distance cost and the information gathered (based on the relative entropy) is introduced in [1] together with solid mathematical foundations. Moreover, the localization utility can be integrated into the overall utility to prefer places traveling to them improves information about the robot pose [16]. Criteria forming the overall utility are not typically independent. General approach that reflects dependency among the criteria based on multi-criteria decision making is used in [2].

An exploration framework for a modular robot is presented in this paper with a special attention to a distance cost definition. Contrary to the aforementioned approaches that evaluate the distance cost simply as the length of the path from the current robot position to the next goal position produced by a standard graph-based planners (Dijkstra, A*) or potential fields, we use the estimation of robot's real trajectory based on RRT (Rapidly-Exploring Random Tree) planner and a physical model of the robot. We show that realistic estimation of robot's effort needed to reach the goal can improve performance of the whole exploration process.

In order to focus on studying distance cost influence, several simplifications are made. First, a robot operates on a flat, smooth, and uniform terrain and it is equipped with a 2D range-finder (e.g. laser) that is always oriented parallel to the terrain. More-over, the workspace is static and obstacles are detectable by the range-finder. Finally, we assume a fixed configuration of the modular robot, i.e. the robot can not change its structure (for example, it can not split into individual parts).

The rest of the paper is organized as follows. In Section 2 the exploration problem is defined, while Section 4 deals with RRT planning for a modular robot. A comparative study of distance is presented in Section 5 and concluding remarks in Section 6.

2   Problem Definition

Exploration is the process in which a robot autonomously operates in an unknown en-vironment with the aim to create a map of it. The map is built incrementally as actual sensor measurements are gathered and it serves as a model of the environment for fur-ther exploration steps.

The exploration algorithm consists of several steps that are repeated until some un-explored area remain. The process starts with reading actual sensor information. After some data processing, the existing map is updated with this information. New goal can-didates are then determined and the next goal for the robot is assigned using a defined cost function. This assignment is called exploration strategy and can be formalized as follows.

Let the current n goal candidates be located at positions $G = \{g_1, \ldots, g_n\}$. The problem is to determine a goal $g \in G$ that will minimize the total required time (or the maximal traveled distance) needed to explore the whole environment.

Having assigned the goal, the shortest path from the robot's current position to the goal is found. Finally, the robot is navigated along the path. The whole exploration process is summarized in Algorithm 1.

Algorithm 1. The exploration algorithm

---

while *unexplored areas exist* **do**
 read current sensor information;
 update map with the obtained data;
 determine new goal candidates;
 determine the next goal;
 plan paths to determined goal;
 move the robot towards the goals;

---

3   Exploration Framework

In this paper, we follow Yamauchi's frontier based approach [24], which is based on occupancy grids, i.e. the working space is divided into small cells, where each cell stores information about the corresponding piece of the environment in the form of a probabilistic estimate of its state. Moreover, it assumes that the next best view (goal) lies on the border between free and unexplored areas (this border is called *frontier*).

We present two strategies for goal-candidates determination. The first one (denoted *"all-frontiers"*) is widely used; it takes all frontiers cells, while the second one (*"representatives"*) is more sophisticated. It filters frontier cells in order to get a set of representatives approximating the frontier cells such that each frontier cell is detectable by the robot sensor from at least one representative. This is done by k-means clustering for each compact set each of frontier cells, where the representative of each cluster is the closest frontier cell to the cluster's mean. The number of clusters/representatives in a frontier is defined similarly to [4] as

$$n_f = 1 + \left\lfloor \frac{N_f}{1.8\rho} + 0.5 \right\rfloor,$$

where N_f is the number of cells forming the frontier and ρ is the sensor range. This guaranties that all frontier cells will be explored (i.e. it will be detected whether the frontier contains the searched object or not) after visiting all representatives. Moreover, reduction of goal candidates dramatically decreases computational burden of more sophisticated and time-consuming goal-selection strategies and therefore allows their usage for non-trivial environments.

The key to effective exploration is selection of the most appropriate goal candidate as the next goal according to the defined criterion. The proposed method generates a trajectory from the current robot position to each goal-candidate (taking into account kinematics constrains of the robot) as described in the next section and selects the frontier to which the trajectory is shortest.

4   Planning for a Modular Robot

To move a modular robot towards a desired frontier, suitable locomotion of the robot needs to be generated. The problem of locomotion generation is well studied in the modular robotics. Usually, the Central Pattern Generators (CPG) [9] providing rhythmic control signals are utilized. By choosing suitable parameters of the CPGs, various locomotions like walking, crawling of even swimming can be achieved.

In the exploration task, the robot typically operates in a environment with obstacles, where more types of locomotion need to be utilized and a switching mechanism is required. In this paper, we utilize a motion planner equipped with the CPGs to find a feasible plan to reach the goal position.

While the motion planning can be solved using grid-based A* planner, Visibility graphs or Voronoi diagrams in the case of mobile robots [14], these methods cannot be used in the case of modular robots due to many DOFs. To solve the motion planning for a complex many-DOF system, sampling-based methods like Probabilistic Roadmaps [10] or Rapidly Exploring Random Trees [13] and their variants can be used. As these methods work in the configuration space, whose dimension equal to the number of DOF of the system, the sampling-based methods are suitable especially for systems with many DOFs. The methods has been utilized in many applications [8,15,5] including modular robotics [27,22,21].

To reduce the complexity of the planning problem for modular robots, one can employ a predefined set of motion primitives. Motion primitive provides a short-term control strategy for the robot, like 'go-forward' or 'turn-left'. In the case of modular robots, these motion primitives can be realized using the CPGs. In this paper, the motion planning problem for the modular robots is solved using the RRT-MP (RRT with Motion Primitives) [22] method.

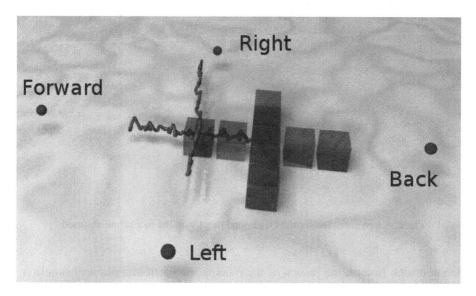

Fig. 1. Four motion primitives for the Quadropod robot. The primitives are depicted as trajectory of the pivot module.

Configuration of a modular robot with n modules is described as $q = (x, y, z, \alpha, \beta, \gamma, a_1, \ldots, a_{n-1})$, where (x, y, z) and (α, β, γ) denotes position and orientation of the pivot modules resp., and a_i are the angles between the connected modules. The set of all possible configuration is the configuration space $\mathcal{C}$ and the set of feasible configurations is the $\mathcal{C}_{free} \subseteq \mathcal{C}$. The robots is controlled by a control signal $u(t) = (a_1(t), \ldots, a_{n-1}(t))$, where $a_i(t)$ are desired angles of joints connecting two neighbor modules. In the RRT-MP approach, the control signals $u_i(t), i = 1, \ldots, m$ are modeled using m CPGs. The details about finding a suitable CPGs can be found in [22].

The RRT-MP planner iteratively builds a tree of feasible configurations rooted at the initial configuration q_{init}. In each iteration, a random configuration $q_{rand} \in \mathcal{C}$ is generated and a nearest node in the tree q_{near} is found. Then, the tree is expanded from the q_{near} using the motion primitives to obtain a set of new reachable configurations R. From this set, the nearest configuration towards q_{rand} is selected and added to the tree. The algorithm terminates, if the tree approaches the goal configuration q_{goal} to a predefined distance ϱ_g. The details of the RRT-MP as well as the preparation of the motion primitives can be found in [22]. The example of the four motion primitives for the Quadropod robot is depicted on Fig 1 and a tree generated with these motion primitives is on Fig. 2.

As the response of a modular robot to a control signal depends both on its kinematics as well as on the shape of underneath terrain, it is not easy to derive a closed-form

Fig. 2. A tree generated for the Quadropod robot with the four primitives used

motion model. Instead, the motion of the robot is simulated in a physical simulator. Therefore, to obtain a response of the robot to a control signal $u(t)$ defined by a motion primitive being examined, the simulated robot is placed to position q_{near} and controlled by the control signals $u(t), t = (0, T_{mp})$, where T_{mp} denote the duration of each motion primitive. The resulting configuration of the robot is then added to the set R if it is feasible and the robot does not hit any obstacle or moved over an unknown area during execution of the primitive.

For the purpose of exploration task, the motion planner needs to be extended. First, more desired goal position may be presented to the planner. Therefore, the RRT-MP planner is terminated when all goals are reached by the tree to a distance less than radius ϱ_g. To speed up the motion planner, the principle of the goal-bias [14] can be used. The random sample q_{rand} is set to q_{goal} with probability p_g, otherwise it is generated from the C with probability $1 - p_g$. When more than one goal is presented to the planner, the probability of selecting q_{goal_i} instead of the q_{rand} is determined by its distance d_i to the tree:

$$p_{g_i} = \begin{cases} \frac{d_i}{\sum_{j=0}^{G} d_j} & d_i > \varrho_g \\ 0 & otherwise \end{cases} \tag{1}$$

This ensures, that the closest goals are preferred until they are reached by the tree. This is important when the number of allowed iterations of the RRT-MP is limited, because this increases the probability, that a trajectory will be found to at least one goal.

5   Experiments

The performance of the above presented exploration framework has been experimentally verified in the Player/Stage framework [6]. All experiments were performed on the Intel P4@2.0 GHz with 4 GB of RAM under FreeBSD 8.2. To obtain the motion model of the Quadropod modular robot (depicted on Fig 1), ODE physical engine has been utilized [18] with 10 ms physical time step. The size of each module is 0.01 m and its weight is 1 kg. The robot was equipped with four motion primitives: 'go-x', where $x \in \{left, right, forward, back\}$). The duration of each primitive is $T_{mp} = 5$ s. The primitives are modeled using simple sinus-based CPG, where $a_i(t) = A_i \sin(\omega_i t + \varphi_i) + B_i$. We refer to [22] for details about searching of suitable parameters of these CPGs. The laser sensor is placed in the middle of the robot. To allow scanning of the environment parrallely to the ground, a 0.5 s decline phase is added to the end of each motion primitive. Therefore, the inputs $a_i(t) = 0$ for $t = (T_{mp} - 0.5, T_{mp})$.

Free space   ● Frontier   ● Approached goal
representative

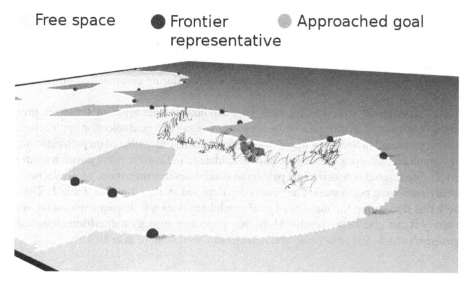

Fig. 3. An example of a plan generated during the exploration

The algorithms have been implemented in C++ as client programs for the Player/Stage in version 3.0.2 and compiled by the GCC 4.3.5 with -O2 optimization flag.

The experiments were conducted in two environments both representing an empty space without obstacles. The first environment (*small*) is scaled so it represents an area of 8×12 m, while the second one (*empty*) is scaled to 24×21 m. To gather information about the environment, a sensor with 360° field of view with 3 m range and 0.5° resolution was used, while the occupancy grid with cell size 0.05×0.05 m was chosen to represent the working environment.

Table 1. Comparison of lengths of a path traversed during the exploration in form: mean-value (deviation). The column *p-value* is the p-value of the Wilcoxon test between mean values of the *trajectory* and *nearest* strategies. The last column highlights in the mean lengths of *trajectory* or *nearest* strategies is same (=) or if the *trajectory* approach provides significantly shorter paths (+) at 0.05 significance level.

Map	Frontiers	Nearest	Trajectory	p-value	
Empty	represent.	212.9 (11.57)	189.6 (13.23)	8.10^{-6}	+
	all-frontiers	208.6 (13.34)	199.6 (15.63)	0.261	+
Small	represent.	46.39 (3.83)	43.45 (5.06)	0.0265	+
	all-frontiers	46.18 (4.79)	45.0 (4.61)	0.08	=

As the current implementation of the motion planning algorithm is slow, the exploration iteration (i.e. the body of the loop in Algorithm 1) was run whenever the robot reached the previous goal, and the robot was stopped during computation of the new goal.

The experiments were run for both goal-candidates determination strategies presented in Section 3: *all-frontiers* and *representatives* and two goal selection approaches: the one presented in Section 3 *trajectory* and a standard strategy based on path planning on a graph and selecting the nearest goal-candidate to the current robot position (*nearest*). For each setup consisting of a pair ⟨goal-candidates determination, goal-selection⟩ twenty runs were performed. The results are depicted in Fig. 4 and in Table 1. They show that decreasing the number of goal candidates does not worsen exploration, on contrary it can give better results. Moreover, *trajectory* strategy outperforms standard *nearest* approach. For *empty* map and *representatives* it is more than 10%.

Table 2. Comparison of all methods on empty/small maps. Here, '+' denotes, that the method in column provides longer path than the method in the row at 0.05 significance level; '=' indicates, that mean values of the path lengths are same.

		Nearest	
		Representation	All-frontiers
Trajectory	Representation	+/+	+/=
	All-frontiers	+/=	=/=

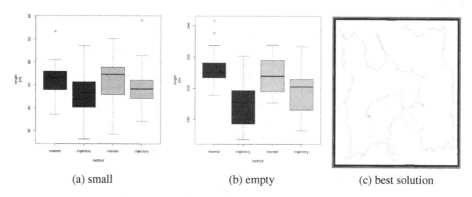

| (a) small | (b) empty | (c) best solution |

Fig. 4. Statistics for (a) *small* and (b) *empty* environment. *representatives* goal-candidates determination strategy is in blue, *all-frontiers* in green. (c) The best solution found for the *empty* environment.

6   Conclusion

In this paper an autonomous exploration of an unknown environment by a modular robot is presented. The results show that more precise estimation of the distance cost based on trajectory length determined by motion planning taking kinematics constrains into account leads to better performance of exploration, i.e. paths needed to explore the whole environment are significantly shorter than for standard approaches.

Probabilistic nature of the standard RRT makes it inappropriate for fast replanning as trajectories generated in two consecutive exploration iterations are typically different, which leads to undesirable oscillations of robot movement. Therefore, to use the presented approach for frequency-based decisions [20] (i.e. exploration iterations are run at some fixed frequency, without need to reach the current goal), RRT have to be derandomized. This can be for example done by using a pruned tree grown in the previous iteration for the current iteration.

The proposed motion planning algorithm is slow so it is not feasible to run the exploration real-time. In the future work, the planning methods will be improved to provide real-time planning. The number of goal-candidates will be decreased by preselecting most promising ones, which should also speed-up the planning process. Of course, experiments in more complex environments and with real robots are necessary to confirm the presented results.

Acknowledgments. This work has been supported by the Technology Agency of the Czech Republic under the project no. TE01020197 "Centre for Applied Cybernetics".

References

1. Amigoni, F., Caglioti, V.: An information-based exploration strategy for environment mapping with mobile robots. Robotics and Autonomous Systems 58(5), 684–699 (2010)
2. Basilico, N., Amigoni, F.: Exploration strategies based on multi-criteria decision making for an autonomous mobile robot. In: Proc. of the Fourth European Conference on Mobile Robots, pp. 259–264. KoREMA (2009)
3. Erkmen, I., Erkmen, A., Matsuno, F., Chatterjee, R., Kamegawa, T.: Snake robots to the rescue! IEEE Robotics Automation Magazine 9(3), 17–25 (2002)
4. Faigl, J., Kulich, M., Preucil, L.: Goal assignment using distance cost in multi-robot exploration. In: 2012 IEEE/RSJ International Conference on Intelligent Robots and Systems (IROS), pp. 3741–3746 (October 2012)
5. Gayle, R., Redon, S., Sud, A., Lin, M., Manocha, D.: Efficient motion planning of highly articulated chains using physics-based sampling. In: ICRA 2007 (2007)
6. Gerkey, B.P., Vaughan, R.T., Howard, A.: The Player/Stage project: Tools for multi-robot and distributed sensor systems. In: Proc. of the 11th Int. Conf. on Advanced Robotics, pp. 317–323 (2003)
7. Gonzalez-Banos, H.H., Latombe, J.C.: Navigation strategies for exploring indoor environments. The International Journal of Robotics Research 21(10-11), 829–848 (2002)
8. Guibas, L., Holleman, C., Kavraki, L.: A probabilistic roadmap planner for flexible objects with a workspace medial-axis-based sampling approach. In: IROS 1999 (1999)
9. Ijspeert, A.J.: Central pattern generators for locomotion control in animals and robots: A review. Neural Networks 21(4), 642–653 (2008)
10. Kavraki, L.E., Svestka, P., Claude Latombe, J., Overmars, M.H.: Probabilistic roadmaps for path planning in high-dimensional configuration spaces. IEEE Transactions on Robotics and Automation 12, 566–580 (1996)
11. Kulich, M., Faigl, J., Preucil, L.: On distance utility in the exploration task. In: 2011 IEEE International Conference on Robotics and Automation (ICRA), pp. 4455–4460 (2011)
12. Lau, H., Ko, A., Lau, T.: A decentralized control framework for modular robots. In: IROS 2004 (2004)
13. LaValle, S.M.: Rapidly-exploring random trees: A new tool for path planning (1998), tR 98-11
14. LaValle, S.M.: Planning Algorithms. Cambridge University Press, Cambridge (2006), http://planning.cs.uiuc.edu/
15. LaValle, S., Yakey, J., Kavraki, L.: A probabilistic roadmap approach for systems with closed kinematic chains. In: ICRA 1999 (1999)
16. Makarenko, A.A., Williams, S.B., Bourgault, F., Durrant-Whyte, H.F.: An experiment in integrated exploration. In: IEEE/RSJ Int. Conf. on Intelligent Robots and System, pp. 534–539. IEEE (2002)
17. Moubarak, P., Ben-Tzvi, P.: Modular and reconfigurable mobile robotics. Robotics and Autonomous Systems 60(12), 1648–1663 (2012)
18. Open source library: ODE — Open Dynamics Engine, http://www.ode.org/
19. Stachniss, C., Grisetti, G., Burgard, W.: Information gain-based exploration using Rao-Blackwellized particle filters. In: Proc. of Robotics: Science and Systems, Cambridge, MA, USA (2005)
20. Valtazanos, A., Ramamoorthy, S.: Evaluating the effects of limited perception on interactive decisions in mixed robotic domains. In: Proceedings of the 8th ACM/IEEE International Conference on Human-Robot Interaction, HRI 2013, pp. 9–16. IEEE Press, Piscataway (2013)

21. Vonásek, V., Košnar, K., Přeučil, L.: Motion planning of self-reconfigurable modular robots using rapidly exploring random trees. In: Herrmann, G., Studley, M., Pearson, M., Conn, A., Melhuish, C., Witkowski, M., Kim, J.-H., Vadakkepat, P. (eds.) TAROS-FIRA 2012. LNCS, vol. 7429, pp. 279–290. Springer, Heidelberg (2012)

22. Vonasek, V., Saska, M., Kosnar, K., Preucil, L.: Global motion planning for modular robots with local motion primitives. In: International Conference of Robotics and Automation (ICRA), Karlsruhe, Germany (2013)

23. Yamauchi, B.: A frontier-based approach for autonomous exploration. In: Proc. of IEEE Int. Symposium on Computational Intelligence in Robotics and Automation, pp. 146–151. IEEE Comput. Soc. Press (1997)

24. Yamauchi, B.: Frontier-based exploration using multiple robots. In: Proc. of the Second International Conference on Autonomous Agents, pp. 47–53 (1998)

25. Yim, M., Duff, D.G., Roufas, K.: Modular reconfigurable robots, an approach to urban search and rescue. In: 1st International Workshop on Human-friendly Welfare Robotics Systems (January 2000)

26. Yim, M., Roufas, K., Duff, D., Zhang, Y., Eldershaw, C., Homans, S.: Modular reconfigurable robots in space applications. Auton. Robots 14(2-3), 225–237 (2003)

27. Yoshida, E., Kurokawa, H., Kamimura, A., Tomita, K., Kokaji, S., Murata, S.: Planning behaviors of a modular robot: an approach applying a randomized planner to coherent structure. In: Proceedings of 2004 IEEE/RSJ International Conference on Intelligent Robots and Systems (IROS 2004), September 30-October 2, vol. 2, pp. 2056–2061 (2004)

Integration Scheme for Modular Snake Robot Software Components

Kamilo Melo, Jose Monsalve, Alvaro Di Zeo, Juan Leon,
Andres Trujillo, Wilson Perdomo, Diego Roa, and Laura Paez

KM-RoBoTa s.a.s., Bogota D.C., Colombia
kamilo.melo@km-robota.com
http://km-robota.com

Abstract. Research and development in Modular and Snake robots, has become an important area of study among the robotics community, due to the potential real applications in the field that these systems feature. Particular efforts in the locomotion analysis of these machines, along with better hardware design, created in our lab the need for adopting a robot architecture that integrate all the software components specifically developed. Robustness and modularity to add/remove components suited for specific applications or future enhancements, are the prime objective in the integration scheme shown in this paper. The systems that this architecture integrate, range from the front-end graphic user interfaces, a physics simulator, a visualization tool, to the low level robot controller. We have tested such architecture in the design and operation of multi-locomotion capabilities of modular snake robots, towards improvement of their performance and solution of tasks in real scenarios.

Keywords: Modular Snake Robot, Robot Architecture, Simulator.

1 Introduction

Related to tasks that involve locomotion, the modular and snake robot community has been proving the increasing functionality and versatility of these robotic systems [1,2]. A variety of locomotion strategies, according to the type of modular or snake robot used, have been developed to understand their motion. The selection of the control strategies has been improved by studying the snake robot's biological counterpart [3,4]. However, in most of the cases, these studies match with the use of planar robotic mechanisms. The complex spatial locomotion of some of these robots [5,6] adds new challenges to model and capture the locomotion output results. On the other hand, several applications as de-mining [7], pipe inspection [9], rough agricultural terrain inspection and disaster victim rescuing, among others, requires the locomotion of this robotic technology to be precisely determined and modeled.

We have been working on the locomotion of a particular type of modular robot (Fig 1.) which presents a series of n 1-DoF modules connected to each other, with a twist shift of $90°$ in their rotating axes. A sequence of configurations (entirely

J. Hodicky (Ed.): MESAS 2014, LNCS 8906, pp. 184–191, 2014.

Fig. 1. Modular Snake Robot Lola-OP^{TM}[10]

defined by the n joint angles) in some cases correspond to gaits. Two motion schemes arise, named if the joint angles are obtained by means of a cyclic function or, with previously defined joint angles changing the robot's configuration step by step. In the case of gaits generated by cyclic functions, two sinusoidal functions are used to generate those angles (one for the odd numbered modules and another one for the even ones). Parameters in those equations correspond to offsets, amplitudes, wavelengths, frequencies and a phase shift between the functions. Thus, a reduced set of parameters define a gait. Further details about motion generation in these robots are reported in [8].

Given the complex interaction of this kind of robot with the environment and its high number of DoF, proposed locomotion strategies must be proven experimentally. However, due to the prototype stages of the robot and the complexity of the measures, carrying out experiments is time consuming. Hence, a simulator is proposed as an alternative to test motion controllers. By using a simulator to emulate system dynamics and the robot-environment interaction, time reduction can be achieved as well as rich data collection. Additionally data analysis by means of plotting tools is required to effectively compare models proposed and results of both simulations and experiments. Consequently, a software architecture was designed to allow the collaborative development of software tools, the use of existent ones and the capability to include future components that might be created as the result of new needs.

2 Software Architecture

The software architecture proposed here is not intended to be the final software released with the robot. Instead, it responds to the needs of a research and development stage. It must allow the use, test and reconfiguration of interconnected software components with specific tasks, such as the graphic user interface or simulator mentioned previously. Messages between components and file formats are defined so new modules can be implemented and new features can be added to the robot, for example new sensors or similar robots provided by the snake robots community.

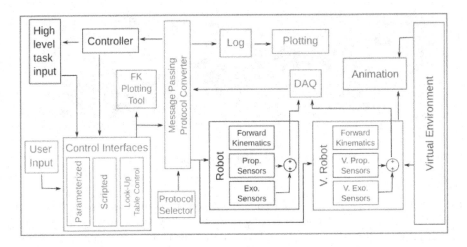

Fig. 2. Modular Snake Robot Software Architecture

Figure 2 shows a block diagram of the robot architecture designed [10]. Its structure corresponds to a *Model-View-Controller* software architecture. Names in the diagram, are used to indicate each one of the constituting parts of the system. Following subsections describe each of the components of the designed framework.

2.1 Control Interfaces

The control front-end, shown in figure 2, consists of two graphical user interfaces. The *scripted* interface allows the user to specify each joint angle and test the configuration in the real robot or the simulated one. Once the robot reaches the configuration, the user can save the current joint angles to a file if the result is successful, otherwise he can discard that configuration and return to the previous one to test another configuration, and so on. This way, the user can complete motion sequences that can be loaded from the file in the future.

The *parametrized* interface allows the user to specify the values for the generation of parametrized gaits and then create a file with the joint angles, just as with the *scripted* interface [10]. In this case the duration of the gait must be defined by the user. An additional feature of the *parametrized* interface is the existence of check boxes for each module of the robot. The check boxes determine whether its corresponding module will be enabled to move or not. Finally the capability to launch predefined parametrized gaits has proven useful to perform gait transitions.

Finally the file containing the joint angles can be generated by any means the user prefers. High level controllers, shown in 2, can take advantage of such feature to perform real time changes on the gait generation according to the state of the robot. System feedback will be discussed in 3.

2.2   The Robot

The intention of this software architecture is to be used with different types of modular and snake robot platforms. So far, the robot Lola-OP^{TM}, developed by KM-RoBoTa s.a.s. has been used as a development and experimental prototype to test the different capabilities of the architecture.

Lola-OP^{TM} is constructed by a series of interconnected single actuator modules, twisted 90° [5]. This offers mechanical simplicity, versatility and at the same time, it simplifies the control. Each robot uses 16 modules as depicted on figure 1. The modules are constructed with Dynamixel AX-12+/18 servomotors, as actuators, and high strength plastic frame brackets for the links. Each module is covered by foam pads to protect the wiring and to add extra friction features.

Instructions to actuators are sent serially through a shared connector on all modules. Data frames are fully described on the ax-12+/18 user manual. In order to simplify the operation, Robotis Inc. (the actuator manufacturer) has provided a C/C++ SDK to build the mentioned data frames. Each actuator has a built-in micro-controller that manages the motion control and the communication. There are registers defined for each controllable variable in the micro-controller. In order to change the actuator position, the desired position must be written in the corresponding register. Confirmation messages from the actuator can be turned on and off. Finally, feedback signals of current position, speed and load are available by built-in sensors and retrieved using a simple status call instruction. The previous description belongs to our most simplified version of robot, however the range of the architecture covers the inclusion of new devices attached to the robot as sensors.

2.3   Physics Simulator

Given the complexity of this kind of robots (i.e. high number of DoF), the formulation of a mathematical model that captures the robot's dynamics is not trivial [9,6]. As mentioned above a physics simulator was proposed as an alternative. A physics engine and a graphics library together perform a similar experience for the user, such that of a real robot experiment. Furthermore, carrying out a simulation generates a large amount of useful data. Taking advantage of the data, the simulation can be complemented by adding slow-motion playback of the output (both in backward and forward mode), augmented reality features such as highlighted robot-environment contact points or module tracking, and additional measures like relative displacement of each module or average speed of the center of mass (see Fig. 3).

The structure of the simulator, shown in figure 2, is organized in a process architecture fashion. The *Simulator Control* class acts as the pipeline controller. There are two containers, one for the snake (the *Snake Container*) and one for the environment (the *Environment Container*). The *Snake Container* consists of: a collection of bodies for the collision detection, hinge restrictions to represent the snake body, and engine models. The *Environment Container* consist of a height-field to represent the ground and a collection of bodies to represent objects on it,

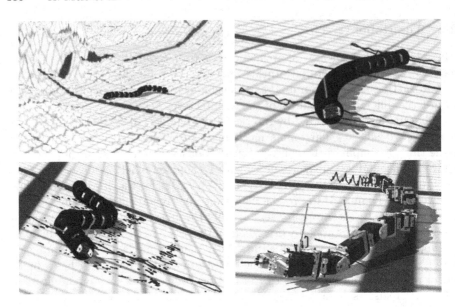

Fig. 3. Features of the Modular Snake Simulator: from top left to bottom right: terrain modeled out of a height-field, lateral rolling gait with module center of mass trajectories, side-winding gait with ground contact points and a linear progression gait showing module frames of reference

such as pipes or boxes. In order to perform the rigid body dynamic interaction and collision detection a *Physics co-processor* is used. In a similar manner, a *Graphics co-processor* is used to manage the visual output. Finally there is a *Data co-processor* which serves as the communication's port for the system and a *timing control* to manage real time communications and graphical output synchronization.

2.4 Plotting Tools

While carrying out experiments with the robot, data is collected from the sensors on board or emulated sensors on the simulation. All retrieved data is saved in log files to be discussed in section 3. Visualizing such data for analysis is achieved by means of the open source application KST. This application allows multiple data to be plotted both real-time and off-line.

Additionally there is a forward kinematics plotting tool [10], conceived to calculate homogeneous matrix transformations, this GNU-octave script allows the visualization of the robot configuration in a determined time step (see Fig. 4). Recent research results, such as *floating body frame of reference* formulation and a velocity estimation model, allow the visualization of the robot's configuration through time on this script (see Fig. 5).

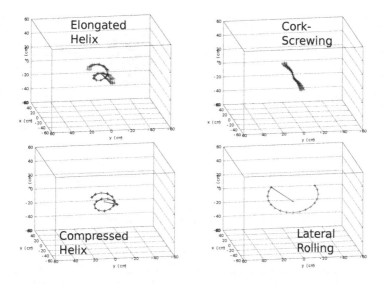

Fig. 4. Floating body frame of reference result for various rolling gaits on a virtual pipe

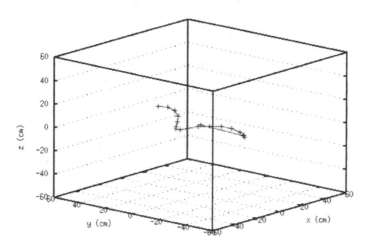

Fig. 5. Floating body frame of reference result for a side-winding gait on a virtual flat terrain

3 Integration

Control of the robot can be completed in one of the following manners. By connecting directly a serial communication's port to the actuators, and then using the Dynamixel SDK to send the instruction, or by using the computer on-board. Computer on-board consists currently of a OpenCM-9.04 board, developed by Robotis Inc., connected to the actuators by a RS-232 link and to the master

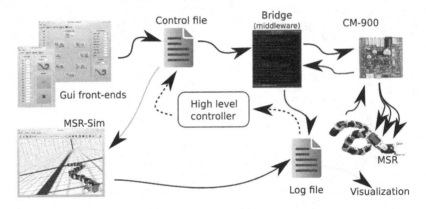

Fig. 6. Software integration scheme for Modular Snake Robots

PC by an USB connection which emulates a serial port. The micro-controller on-board takes high level instructions and translates them into actuator instructions, allowing the interchange of the master PC, so in the future, an embedded PC can be used. Communication among framework modules is achieved by two means: the use of files and the use of a serial communication port. In the first case there are two kinds of files, control files and log files.

Control files include, in the first line, the number of modules and the writing baudrate, while the remaining lines are joint angles for each step, with the complete configuration in a single line. New parameters can be added to each line after the joint angles, in case stiffness is wanted to be controlled, for instance. Control files are written by any of the three control interfaces described above and are read later to be sent to the robot. The piece of software that performs such lecture can either use the Dynamixel SDK to send instructions directly to the robot actuators, use the developed on-board program and send angles through a serial port, or use the protocol that the snake under test works with.

Log files on the other hand, are filled while carrying out experiments or performing simulations. Data is retrieved by the same piece of software which sends instructions to the actuators, in the scenario where they are connected directly, otherwise they are read from the serial port (see Fig. 6).

4   Conclusions

The software architecture for controlling and simulating a modular snake robot during the research and development stage was described. The architecture corresponds to a *Model-View-Controller* software architecture. The software architecture design responds to research needs. It allows collaboration and lets researches focus on their investigation rather than on developing middle-ware. This robot software architecture offers the flexibility to add new components to the framework, enhancing its robustness, and allowing improvements in the hardware robot implementations, like the addition of new sensors and communication channels, with minimum software changes.

It is worth to mention that besides the fact that only one robotic platform has been used, the whole architecture was designed with robotic platform interchangeability in mind. In the future, researchers in other laboratories can test their simulation-based controller designs and results with this framework. They will be able to execute experiments with a real robot connected remotely by means of an Internet channel to enter data to the robot from distant places, by simply adjusting the corresponding communication protocol.

References

1. Yim, M., Eldershaw, C., Zhang, Y., Duff, D.: Limbless Conforming Gaits with Modular Robots. In: Ang, M., Khatib, O. (eds.) Experimental Robotics IX. STAR, vol. 21, pp. 459–468. Springer, Heidelberg (2006)
2. Liljebäck, P., Pettersen, K., Stavdahl, O., Gravdahl, J.: Snake Robots, Modelling, Mechatronics, and Control. Advances in Industrial Control. Springer, London (2013)
3. Hirose, S.: Biologically Inspired Robots: Snake-like Locomotors and Manipulators. Oxford University Press (1993)
4. Toyoshima, S., Matsuno, F.: A study on sinus-lifting motion of a snake robot with energetic efficiency. In: 2012 IEEE International Conference on Robotics and Automation (ICRA), pp. 2673–2678 (May 2012)
5. Melo, K., Paez, L., Parra, C.: Indoor and outdoor parametrized gait execution with modular snake robots. In: 2012 IEEE International Conference on Robotics and Automation (ICRA), pp. 3525–3526 (May 2012)
6. Enner, F., Rollinson, D., Choset, H.: Simplified motion modeling for snake robots. In: 2012 IEEE International Conference on Robotics and Automation (ICRA), pp. 4216–4221 (May 2012)
7. Melo, K., Paez, L., Hernandez, M., Velasco, A., Calderon, F., Parra, C.: Preliminary studies on modular snake robots applied on de-mining tasks. In: Robotics Symposium, IEEE IX Latin American and IEEE Colombian Conference on Automatic Control and Industry Applications (LARC), pp. 1–6 (October 2011)
8. Melo, K., Paez, L.: Experimental Determination of Control Parameter Intervals for Repeatable Gaits in Modular Snake Robots. In: IEEE Int. Symp. Safety, Security, and Rescue Robotics (October 2014)
9. Melo, K., Paez, L.: Modular Snake Robots on Horizontal Pipes. In: 2012 IEEE/RSJ International Conference on Intelligent Robots and Systems (IROS) (October 2012)
10. Melo, K., Leon, J., Monsalve, J., Fernandez, V., Gonzalez, D.: Simulation and Control Integrated Framework for Modular Snake Robots Locomotion Research. In: 2012 IEEE/SICE International Symposium on System Integration (SII) (December 2012)

A Modular Approach for Remote Operation of Humanoid Robots in Search and Rescue Scenarios

Alessandro Settimi[1,2]*, Corrado Pavan[2], Valerio Varricchio[1,2], Mirko Ferrati[2], Enrico Mingo Hoffman[1], Alessio Rocchi[1], Kamilo Melo[2], Nikos G. Tsagarakis[1], and Antonio Bicchi[1,2]

[1] Department of Advanced Robotics, Istituto Italiano di Tecnologia, Genova, Italy
{enrico.mingo,alessio.rocchi,nikos.tsagarakis}@iit.it
[2] Centro di Ricerca "E.Piaggio", Dipartimento di Ingegneria dell'Informazione, Università di Pisa, Italy
{mirko.ferrati,antonio.bicchi}@centropiaggio.unipi.it
{alessandro.settimi,valerio.varricchio}@for.unipi.it
corrado.pavan@unipi.it, kamilo.melo@km-robota.com

Abstract. In this work we present a modular, robust and user-friendly Pilot Interface meant to control humanoid robots in rescue scenarios during dangerous missions.

YARP is used to communicate to low-level hardware components and to interconnect control modules (receive the status and request actions). ROS is used to retrieve many sensors data and to display the robot status. The operator is immersed into a 3D reconstruction of the environment and can manipulate 3D virtual objects.

The operator can control the robot at three different levels. The high-level control deals with human-like actions which involve the whole robot's actuation and perception. The mid-level control generates tasks in cartesian space w.r.t. a reference frame on the robot. Finally the low level control operates in joint space.

Keywords: Robot Tele-operation, Humanoid Robotics, Software Integration.

1 Introduction

A number of recent calamities, such as the Deepwater Horizon oil spill and the Fukushima Dai-ichi nuclear disaster, have highlighted the enormous potential of robots capable to perform hazardous activities in future disaster response operations[1], thus producing a growing interest in Urban Search And Rescue (USAR) robotic research worldwide. In this context, initiatives such as the DARPA

---

* Corresponding author.

[1] http://spectrum.ieee.org/automaton/robotics/industrial-robots/fukushima-robot-operator-diaries

J. Hodicky (Ed.): MESAS 2014, LNCS 8906, pp. 192–205, 2014.
© Springer International Publishing Switzerland 2014

Robotics Challenge (DRC) introduced the idea of using humanoids to manage disaster situations. Although several robot typologies (e.g. wheeled [1] or snake robots [2]) have been considered to cope with USAR missions, humanoid robots can take advantage of a natively superior suitability to deal with environments and tools designed for humans.

On the one hand, despite the increasing low-level capabilities of humanoid robots, teleoperation is still essential to exploit the human competence in terms of decision making, strategic thinking, perception capabilities and overall awareness of a task [3].

On the other hand, telecommunication problems like intermittent availability, low-bandwidth and latency of the connection can occur in disaster scenarios and make the need for a certain degree of autonomy undeniable. The mentioned remarks enforce the ever increasing trend towards a *semi-autonomous* or *supervisory* control [3].

We hereby present ideas to build a semi-autonomous framework for the control of a humanoid robot in disaster scenarios and describe features of our teleoperation Pilot Interface. Among the main desirable functionalities recognized, we require that the human operator is able to issue symbolic commands to the robot, select the level of autonomy with which the robot performs each task and receive visual and status information feedback. In addition, the interface is designed to be modular and reconfigurable based on the peculiar needs for the task or the environment conditions and is thought to be general in order to be used by different kinds of robots performing in disaster scenarios.

This paper is organized as follows. We introduce the main concepts related to robot autonomy in section 2. In section 3 we address our Pilot Interface software architecture, while a few implementation details are provided in section 4. The main GUI components are depicted in section 5. Finally in section 6 some applications are shown.

2   The Need for Semi-autonomy

Due to the relatively low autonomous capabilities of state-of-the-art humanoid robotics, teleoperation still turns out among the most popular control solutions. In fact, literature includes examples of fully-teloperated robots able to perform complex tasks like driving lift trucks [4] with *ad-hoc* cockpits. At the forefront of this field, NASA's Robonaut humanoid can be reliably piloted to perform Extravehicular Activities [5] through haptic interfaces, predictive displays and telepresence devices, while in recent works motion capture technology substitutes master-slave systems for whole-body motions [6] and power tools manipulation [7].

However, despite the practical effectiveness of such methods, they embrace the paradigm of direct control, which neglects telecommunication problems and is not feasible to deal with disaster scenarios addressed in this work.

In order to tackle communication problems, literature proposes examples of semi-autonomous control architectures. The semi-autonomous control is a scheme which effectively integrates teleoperation with the increasing low-level robot autonomy. It allows a robot to focus on low-level tasks (e.g. terrain traversing), while leaving the human operator in charge of high-level control and supervisory tasks such as specifying the direction of motion or a point to be reached [8]. Basically, in semi-autonomous control "the remote is given an instruction that it can safely do on its own [9]".

In particular, adjustable autonomy allows the operator to choose the level of autonomy of the robot on the fly and according to the task, thus letting the operator continuously and transparently adjust it in order to meet the imposed performance expectations. Additionally, this approach can significantly reduce the amount of bandwidth needed [10].

In humanoid robotics, examples of semi-autonomous controllers have been presented recently to reduce the high-DOF humanoid control problem to the command space of a three axis joystick exploiting the improved low-level capabilities of robots. This approach is followed in [11], where an intelligent joystick for biped gait control is proposed, while a single joystick teleoperation system for whole body control is described in [12]. Both works refer to the HRP-2 robot.

A significant step towards the reduction of control complexity is found in [13]. In this work, symbolic command interfaces through mouse or keyboard are exploited - among other applications - to let the operator indicate a target object to be grasped on a graphic interface, whereupon the approach-grasp operation is autonomously carried out by the robot.

In a recent survey [3], Goodrich offered an overall view of Teleoperation for Humanoid Robotics, stressing particularly on the challenges that make teleoperation still essential for humanoids:

- object recognition,
- interpretaion and understanding of scenes and semantic spatial reasoning,
- prediction and planning.

In a recent survey on Urban Search And Rescue (USAR) robotics [8], various examples of semi-autonomous controllers are presented as trade-off solutions to combine the recent improvements on low-level robot autonomy and the necessity to include a human-in-the-loop in the control systems, showing better performances in terms of area coverage, number of victims identified, number of collision and decreasing the workload of the operator.

As mentioned in [14], in a well performing teleoperation system, the Human-Robot Interaction (HRI) must be as efficient and capable as possible, and "maximize the information transfer while minimizing cognitive and sensorimotor workload of the operator". It should be noted that "the importance of the operator interface does not diminish as the level of autonomy increases". In a supervisory control context, as the robot becomes more autonomous, the interface must "provide a mechanism for the operator and the robot to exchange information at different levels of details or abstraction", moving toward a supervising interface. In [15], Yanco defined the design guidelines for an effective HRI interface, based on a multi-year study during USAR Competitions:

- Use of a single monitor for the interface with large video windows,
- Include a third-person view of the robot,
- Use a map of the reconstructed environment using sensor fusion,
- Use graphical representation of information rather than textual or numerical,
- Reduce cognitive fatigue, context switching and negative effect of neglect and at the same time improve situational awareness,
- Design of the interface based on the intended user rather than the developer.

2.1 Motion Description Languages

The problem of connecting the implementation of autonomy in tele-operated robotics and behavior-based, hybrid control methods emerged in [16]. One solution to this problem was provided by Roger Brockett, who first introduced the MDL approach in [17]. MDL is a formal language used to abstract different types of control into a simple set of basic control laws (*atoms*) that can be chained together in order to obtain *behaviors*. MDLe (extended MDL) [18], enriches the approach introducing the concept of a reactive behavior using triggers.

In humanoid robotics the attempt of simplifying the control problem and composing parallel whole-body primitives has been tackled with the operational-space or task-function approach, introduced in [19]. In this framework, the whole-body motion control problem of a humanoid robot is simplified considering the cartesian space instead of the state space of the robot. This solution eases the design of control laws, making it more intuitive, with the additional possibility to use the sensor space, thus closing the control loop in a more robust and accurate way.

A task in the task-function approach can be seen as an atom in the MDL, consisting in the lower level motion primitive of the robot behavior; tasks can be combined sequentially or simultaneously, thus defining behaviors in the MDL framework. Examples of this approach are the whole-body control introduced by Sentis [20] and the stack of tasks presented by Mansard in [21].

2.2 Semi-autonomy via MDLs

By means of a library of *parameterized* motion primitives (atoms) and behaviors based on the MDL framework, we implemented an adjustable semi-autonomous control with three different levels of autonomy, according to the classification proposed in [3]:

- *Traded Control,*
- *Shared Control,*
- *Direct Control.*

Every control level acts in a particular level of the MDL hierarchy. This gives to these levels a new meaning oriented to MDL: the operator can issue in the highest level of the control MDL plans, while in the middle level, atomic actions or behaviors. Finally, in the lowest level, the operator controls the robot at the joint level. Figure 1 depicts how the different levels of operation work. In *Direct*

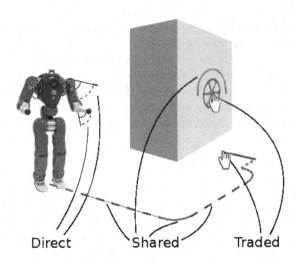

Fig. 1. Graphical representation of control levels

control, the operator regulates the joint displacement, in *Shared* control he can issue atoms or behaviors (depicted as segments), in *Traded* control he selects a point in the environment requesting a plan (on a wheel valve or a point in the ground).

3 Software Architecture

We developed a pilot control interface consistent with the three different levels of possible controls. The high-level (*Traded*) control deals with the computation and execution of plans composed by primitives. *Shared* control is constituted by a set of 3D Interactive Markers that represents body parts of the robot or objects of interest to be positioned in the cartesian space. The operator can thus issue associated primitives or standalone primitives. Finally, we used *RobotMotorGui* (by YARP) to access each joint in *Direct* control.

As the control level gets lower, the robot loses autonomy but acquires more safety. It is reasonable that the operator could seamlessly switch between the levels of autonomy, depending on the task and on the environment condition.

The Pilot Interface is designed to provide both visual feedback to the user for validation purposes (or confirmation if needed) in a high level of autonomy, e.g. the planner shows the planned path before execution, and as a display control apparatus in the middle level, e.g. the operator can adjust the position of a 3d model of an object superimposing it onto a point cloud.

Our Pilot Interface is used to control IIT's *COmpliant huMANoid* (COMAN) [22], which is a torque controlled robot with 31-DOFs equipped with two Pisa/IIT - SoftHands[2]. The robot will have a Carnegie Robotics MultiSense S7 sensor[3] mounted as a head, but we are currently using a RGB-D camera (Asus Xtion Pro Live) mounted above the torso.

Modularity in complex systems is needed for robustness and reconfiguration. In our overall architecture many control modules have been developed using *YARP* as a middleware. These modules perform manipulation, locomotion, planning, perception and whole-body loco-manipulation tasks.

Each module is a standalone process that runs on the robot and interacts through messages with the Pilot Interface, from which it can receive a start/stop message and custom commands.

Due to the large number of different tasks that a *USAR* robot might perform, a modular and reconfigurable Pilot Interface is needed. Since each robot control module is an independent process, we want its respective operator widget to be an independent UI as well. With our approach we can run each individual control module widget as a standalone GUI, so that it can be tested or used without starting the whole Pilot Interface.

Our architecture (figure 2) easily allows the addition and removal of single graphic components into the main GUI window, and each component can be enabled or disabled from the Pilot Interface main control bar.

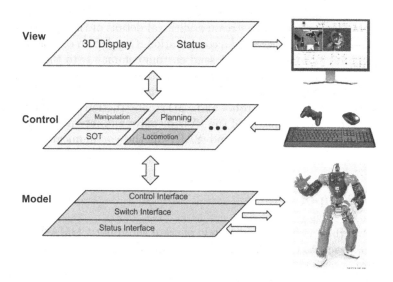

Fig. 2. Architecture

---

[2] http://softhands.eu
[3] http://carnegierobotics.com/multisense-s7/

4   Implementation

Similarly to most of our software, the Pilot Interface uses *YARP* as a communication facility. Nevertheless, while most of the control modules rely on *YARP* mainly to command the robot boards (or the simulated ones) through the low level library *Robolli*, the Pilot Interface uses *YARP* to send commands to the modules and receive feedback of their statuses.

As an implementation priority, we enforce into the modules some behaviours and structures specifically designed to ensure consistency, robustness and continuous monitoring of the software execution. Therefore, the communication between our Pilot Interface and the modules is wrapped into a number of standard interfaces shared by all the software components. Namely, we use a *switch*, a *status* and a *command* interface.

The *switch* interface makes it possible to *start, pause, resume* and *stop* modules.

A practical advantage offered by a switch interface is the capability to recover the robot control in unforeseen situations. For instance, if the robot gets stuck in some position while performing a manipulation task, the operator can *stop* the manipulation module (such that actuators do not receive instructions), perform a reset procedure through a dedicated module and then *restart* the manipulation module.

The *status* interface is used to receive the module statuses at a constant rate. This offers the ability to visually check through the pilot interface that each module is running and possibly stream additional details of the operation being performed (e.g. percent progress of a computation, time left to complete a task).

The *command* interface is used to send custom commands to the modules.

In addition, the popular *Robotic Operative System* (ROS) framework is heavily relied on both as a bridge with perception hardware (e.g. the 3D Camera sensor) and to visualize the state of the robot and a 3D reconstruction of the environment in the Pilot Interface, by means of the RViz displays and interaction utilities.

In figure 3 some uses of ROS and YARP in the communication layer are shown.

5   GUI Components

Our Pilot Interface is being used to tele-operate the robot COMAN to execute a number of practical tasks that can be encountered in disaster scenarios, some of which are described in the sequel.

One of the most basic tasks of a humanoid is *walking* on a flat ground. The currently implemented flat walking skills of our robot encompass four parametric motion primitives: *forward, backward and side walk*, specified with a distance parameter and *turn in place*, which comes with an angle amplitude parameter (figure 4).

Coherently with the need for multiple control levels, walking can be performed through the pilot interface with two levels of autonomy. In the *Shared* control

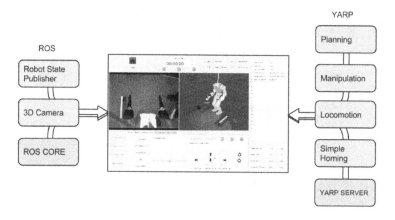

Fig. 3. The usage of YARP and ROS in the communication layer

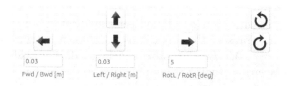

Fig. 4. Walking widget

mode, the pilot can manually choose among walking primitives and navigate the robot through the environment by sending elementary commands one by one. In the *Traded* control mode, shown in the figure 5, the pilot selects a destination pose (green arrow) on a sensed 2D map of the environment, thus delegating the generation and online correction of an obstacle-free control sequence of walking primitives to a *flat walk planner*.

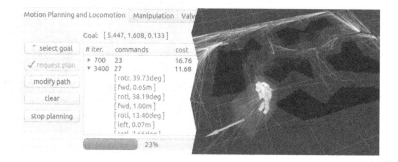

Fig. 5. Planning widget and display

Fig. 6. Valve Turning control widget

We developed a dedicated widget for a valve turning behaviour (section 6).

Every single pre-computed action can be triggered by clicking the related button (see figure 6).

The main rViz feature we use is 3D object visualization and interaction. We use a 3D display to represent the robot status as shown in figure 7(b).

rViz 3D Interactive Markers are also widely used. The widget depicted in figure 8(b) collects various tools to manipulate 3D objects (e.g. a valve, in figure 8(a)) or elements of the robot (e.g. hands, feet, COM, head, ...).

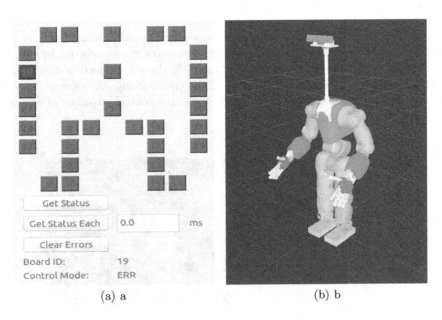

(a) a   (b) b

Fig. 7. (a) Control Boards Status widget, (b) Robot 3D Visualization

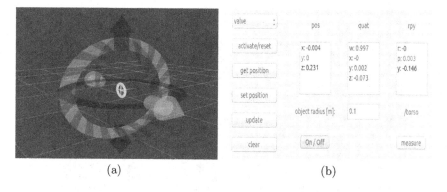

(a)   (b)

Fig. 8. (a) Valve 3D object, (b) Object manipulation widget

Simple Homing	Start	Stop
Manipulation	Start	Stop
Locomotion	Start	Stop
Locomotion Planning	Start	Stop
SOT	Start	Stop

Fig. 9. Module Manager widget

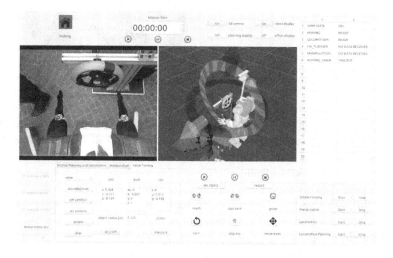

Fig. 10. The Valve Turning

A significant issue we encountered on our robot *COMAN* is that when an overcurrent happens, the board related to the actuator that caused it will stop the control on the motor.

Fig. 11. The Valve Task

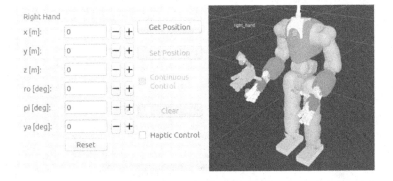

Fig. 12. The Stask Of Tasks

To reset the boards singularly and remotely we developed the widget shown in figure 7(a) that gives us the various information of the boards periodically or by request. The 'clear errors' button resets the state of the boards so that the standard work-flow can continue.

As mentioned in section 4, we can use the *switch* interface for single control modules through the Pilot Interface. In figure 9, we show the widget used to send the *start* and the *stop* commands to the various control modules.

We decided to separate the *start/stop* commands from the *pause/resume* ones because the first ones are more 'dangerous', since they can actually stop the thread related to the control module.

6   Applications

The first practical task addressed has been the capability to *turn a valve*. In this task the robot is required to reach, grasp and turn a few valves of various sizes and orientations.

The current approach for this task is to first walk the robot towards a location close to the valve. Once a suitable proximity location is reached, the operator performs an estimation of the valve radius and pose by visually superimposing a 3D model of the valve on the point cloud. This operation is performed by moving and scaling a rViz 3D *interactive marker*. Eventually, a first guess of this estimation will be provided by a fully autonomous vision algorithm and confirmed or fine-tuned by the pilot. Once validated, the valve data is sent the manipulation module, which then computes suitable end-effector and joint trajectories. Finally, the operator can execute the computed task related commands, namely: *reach, approach, grasp, turn, ungrasp, move away*.

In the snapshots in figure 11 we display all the different steps of a *valve-turning* task.

Our team developed a *Stack of Tasks* (SOT) application to perform cartesian trajectories minimizing some loss function (to not work near joints limits for example).

As shown in figure 12 we use 3D rViz Interactive Markers to move a hand as said in section 5. The pilot can choose wether the command should be sent continuously or upon request. Furthermore, we can use the SOT to control the COM and a foot in a static equilibrium configuration.

7   Conclusions

In this paper, the design of a Pilot Interface for humanoid robots in USAR scenarios has been presented. We described the most relevant capabilities of our current implementation and showed its effectiveness during a demonstration based on the DRC valve-turning task. This task was fulfilled by sole means of a semi-autonomous *Shared* control level.

As a part of our future work, we plan to improve the capabilities of our robot by developing increasingly complex behaviors to address tasks that can be encountered in disaster scenarios. Our aim is to simplify the interface while reducing the pilot's cognitive fatigue and gradually move towards a more autonomous framework.

In addition, while the Pilot Interface can be seamlessly used to control the real and a simulated robot thanks to the *Gazebo-Yarp Plugins* [23] developed by our team, it appears desirable to embed simulation capabilities into the pilot interface, thus allowing a safe validation of planned actions prior to the execution on the real platform.

Acknowledgments. Research leading to these results has received funding from the European Union Seventh Framework Programme [FP7-ICT-2013-10] under grant agreements n.611832 WALKMAN.

References

1. Kohlbrecher, S., Meyer, J., Graber, T., Petersen, K., von Stryk, O., Klingauf, U.: Robocuprescue 2014 - robot league team hector darmstadt (germany). tech. rep., Technische Universität Darmstadt (2014)
2. Melo, K., Leon, J., di Zeo, A., Rueda, V., Roa, D., Parraga, M., Gonzalez, D., Paez, L.: The modular snake robot open project: Turning animal functions into engineering tools. In: 2013 IEEE International Symposium on Safety, Security, and Rescue Robotics (SSRR), pp. 1–6 (October 2013)
3. Goodrich, M.A., Crandall, J.W., Barakova, E.: Teleoperation and beyond for assistive humanoid robots. Reviews of Human Factors and Ergonomics 9(1), 175–226 (2013)
4. Hasunuma, H., Kobayashi, M., Moriyama, H., Itoko, T., Yanagihara, Y., Ueno, T., Ohya, K., Yokoi, K.: A tele-operated humanoid robot drives a lift truck. In: Proceedings of IEEE International Conference on Robotics and Automation, ICRA 2002, vol. 3, pp. 2246–2252. IEEE (2002)
5. Hambuchen, K., Bluethmann, W., Goza, M., Ambrose, R., Rabe, K., Allan, M.: Supervising remote humanoids across intermediate time delay. In: 2006 6th IEEE-RAS International Conference on Humanoid Robots, pp. 246–251. IEEE (2006)
6. Stanton, C., Bogdanovych, A., Ratanasena, E.: Teleoperation of a humanoid robot using full-body motion capture, example movements, and machine learning. In: Proc. Australasian Conference on Robotics and Automation (2012)
7. O'Flaherty, R., Vieira, P., Grey, M., Oh, P., Bobick, A., Egerstedt, M., Stilman, M.: Humanoid robot teleoperation for tasks with power tools. In: 2013 IEEE International Conference on Technologies for Practical Robot Applications (TePRA), pp. 1–6 (April 2013)
8. Liu, Y., Nejat, G.: Robotic urban search and rescue: A survey from the control perspective. Journal of Intelligent & Robotic Systems 72(2), 147–165 (2013)
9. Murphy, R.: An introduction to AI robotics. The MIT press (2000)
10. Bradshaw, J.M., Feltovich, P.J., Jung, H., Kulkarni, S., Taysom, W., Uszok, A.: Dimensions of adjustable autonomy and mixed-initiative interaction. In: Nickles, M., Rovatsos, M., Weiss, G. (eds.) AUTONOMY 2003. LNCS (LNAI), vol. 2969, pp. 17–39. Springer, Heidelberg (2004)
11. Chestnutt, J., Michel, P., Nishiwaki, K., Kuffner, J., Kagami, S.: An intelligent joystick for biped control. In: Proceedings of the IEEE International Conference on Robotics and Automation, pp. 860–865 (May 2006)
12. Stilman, M., Nishiwaki, K., Kagami, S.: Humanoid teleoperation for whole body manipulation. In: IEEE International Conference on Robotics and Automation, ICRA 2008, pp. 3175–3180. IEEE (2008)
13. Sian, N., Yoki, K., Kawai, Y., Muruyama, K.: Operating humanoid robots in human environments. In: Proceedings of the Robotics, Science & Systems Workshop on Manipulation for Human Environments, Philadelphia, Pennsylvania. Citeseer (2006)
14. Fong, T., Thorpe, C.: Vehicle teleoperation interfaces. Autonomous Robots 11(1), 9–18 (2001)
15. Yanco, H.A., Drury, J.L.: Rescuing interfaces: A multi-year study of human-robot interaction at the aaai robot rescue competition. Autonomous Robots 22(4), 333–352 (2007)
16. Goodrich, M.A., Schultz, A.C.: Human-robot interaction: a survey. Foundations and Trends in Human-Computer Interaction 1(3), 203–275 (2007)

17. Brockett, R.W.: Formal languages for motion description and map making. Robotics 41, 181–191 (1990)
18. Manikonda, V., Krishnaprasad, P.S., Hendler, J.: Languages, behaviors, hybrid architectures, and motion control. Springer (1999)
19. Khatib, O.: A unified approach for motion and force control of robot manipulators: The operational space formulation. IEEE Journal of Robotics and Automation 3(1), 43–53 (1987)
20. Sentis, L.: Synthesis and control of whole-body behaviors in humanoid systems. PhD thesis, Citeseer (2007)
21. Saab, L., Ramos, O.E., Keith, F., Mansard, N., Soueres, P., Fourquet, J.: Dynamic whole-body motion generation under rigid contacts and other unilateral constraints. IEEE Transactions on Robotics 29(2), 346–362 (2013)
22. Tsagarakis, N.G., Cerda, G.M., Li, Z., Caldwell, D.G.: Compliant humanoid coman: Optimal joint stiffness tuning for modal frequency control. In: ICRA, pp. 665–670 (2013)
23. Hoffmann, E.M., Traversaro, S., Rocchi, A., Ferrati, M., Settimi, A., Natale, L., Bicchi, A., Nori, F., Tsagarakis, N.G.: A yarp based plugin for gazebo simulator. In: MESAS (2014)

A Light-Weight Robot Simulator
for Modular Robotics*

Vojtěch Vonásek, Daniel Fišer, Karel Košnar, and Libor Přeučil

CTU in Prague, Faculty of electrical engineering,
Technicka 2, Prague, 166 27, Czech Republic
{vonasek,danfis,kosnar,preucil}@labe.felk.cvut.cz

Abstract. Physical simulation are frequently used in robotics for evaluation of control strategies or planning techniques. In this paper, a novel, light-weight open-source robotic simulator is introduced. It provides both physical and sensor simulation and it was designed to be run in a headless mode, i.e., without any visualization, which makes it suitable for computational grids. Despite this fact, the progress of the simulation can be later visualized using external tools like Blender 3D. This brings advantage in comparison to more general and powerful simulators that cannot be easily run on such machines. The paper briefly introduces architecture of the simulator with description of its utilization in evolutionary modular robotics.

Keywords: robotic simulation, modular robotics, evolutionary robots.

1 Introduction

Robot simulators are frequently used in robotics as they allow researches to develop control strategies for robots without the necessity to deal with physical robots. Simulations are faster and usually less effort is required to prepare complex setups comparing to hardware experiments. Simulated robots cannot be damaged, their operation time is not limited and one can easily re-run an experiment with same initial conditions later to verify the results or to study influence of individual parameters of algorithms being studied.

These properties are important especially in evolutionary robotics, where robot behaviors and controllers are developed using evolutionary computation. The evolutionary robotics has been studied behaviors of many systems like mobile, legged, flying and swimming robots, as well as groups or even swarms of robotic entities. Another area utilizing simulators is modular robotics. Modular robots consist of several robotic modules connected together. Depending on the

---

* The work in this paper was supported by TACR grant No. TE01020197, Access to computing and storage facilities owned by parties and projects contributing to the National Grid Infrastructure MetaCentrum, provided under the programme "Projects of Large Infrastructure for Research, Development, and Innovations" (LM2010005), is greatly appreciated.

J. Hodicky (Ed.): MESAS 2014, LNCS 8906, pp. 206–216, 2014.

facilities of the modules, the motion of a robotic organism can be reached by various types of locomotion (e.g. by changing relative angles of the connected modules) or using reconfiguration. Many modular platforms have been developed in last two decades; we refer to [26] for a comprehensive survey. Typical tasks studied in modular robotics include locomotion generation, motion planning and reconfiguration. All these tasks require precise physical simulation.

In this paper, we describe a novel light-weight robotic simulator called *Sim*. The simulator is focused on the simulation of the modular robots, nevertheless it can be used for general types of robots. The simulator was developed within the EU project Symbrion [22] that was focused on development of evolutionary and bio-inspired techniques to explore biological concepts with robot populations.

2 Related Work

Many simulators have been developed in robotics including simulators of robotics manipulators, mobile robots and modular robots. The early simulators, like Player/Stage [14] or Gazebo, provide simulation of sensors and robots in 2D environment. As only wheeled robots are presented in Stage, and the robots are simulated without dynamics, the motion of a robot in a flat 2D environment is described by simple motion equations, which can be simulated very fast. These simulators are suitable especially for mobile robots. Sensors simulated in 2D environments are usually distance sensors (IR-based, sonars and laser range-finders) or position sensors (odometry, GPS).

Nowadays, more advanced robotic platforms are being developed (e.g. legged robots, humanoids, modular robots) which requires advanced simulations. The interaction between robots and a working environment became crucial and it needs to be simulated using realistic models of environments and sensors. Moreover, the dynamics of the robots is important and it cannot be computed analytically with a set of simple equations.

The simulation of robot's dynamics as well as simulation of robots in 3D workspace is provided by Gazebo simulator [20], which uses ODE physical engine for physics simulation. Gazebo (similarly to aforementioned Stage simulator) can be controlled using the Player API and from Robot Operating System (ROS).

Simulation of urban search & rescue scenarios is provided by the USAR-Sim [11] simulator. The USARSim is based on the commercial Unreal game engine (UT2004) [3] for physics simulation and visualization. The simulator was initially focused on wheeled robots, but it was later improved to provide simulation of underwater vehicles, legged robots and humanoid robots [32]. In addition to research applications, USARSim is the basis for the RoboCup rescue virtual robot competition (RoboCup) as well as the IEEE Virtual Manufacturing Automation Competition (VMAC).

The OpenHRP3 (Open Architecture Human-centered Robotics Platform) [19] platform focuses on simulations of humanoid robots. Nowadays, there is no sensor simulation, but it is planned for future.

Webots [30,25] is a commercial general robot simulator. Webots can simulate any wheeled, legged robot or even flying robots, and it provides also a sensor simulation. The code can be transferred to real platforms like Aibo, Lego-Mindstorm, Khepera or Koala. The physical simulation is realized using the ODE physical engine. Beside the basic functions, it allows to simulate multi-agent systems with local and global communication facilities. The simulator can be run on Windows, Linux and Mac OS X. Another general-purpose simulator is V-REP [7]. The simulator employs either ODE or Bullet physical engine, it provides interface for several programming languages, ROS interface, and it can be controlled using Integrated Development Environment (IDE). It supports surface cutting, simulation of various communication channels and dynamic particles. Moreover, it provides modules for collision detection, distance calculation and path planning.

The XPERSim [10] simulator focuses on realistic visualization and sensor simulation. This is achieved by using OGRE library for rendering the scene. For physics simulation, ODE is employed.

Delta3D [2] is an open source simulation framework. The framework can be interfaced with several physical engines through the Physical Abstraction Layer (PAL). It provides sensor simulation and advanced techniques for environment modeling like simulation of fog or lighting. The Delta3D has been used in several applications including Robot3D simulator [31].

The requirements on the simulators for modular robots are little different than in the general robot case. The sensor simulation is not so important, because not all available modular robotic platforms are equipped with sensors. On the other side, the physical simulation needs to be precise as the operation like docking or reconfiguration of the organisms are simulated. To allow easy transfer of the controllers developed using the simulation to real robots, the software interface should be same for both simulated and real robots. Therefore, specialized simulators for specific modular robots are available. The Molecubes [33] simulator was developed for Molecubes modular robots. It is based on NVidia PhysX and the visualization is implemented using the OGRE library. The real modules can be controlled with the code developed within the simulator. Another simulator for modular robots called Swarmbot3D was developed in the S-Bot project [6]. Here, the physical simulation is based on the commercial Vortex engine [8] and the Swarmbot3D simulator is tailored for the S-bot robots solely.

The selected properties of the aforementioned simulators are summed up in Tab. 1. As can be seen, many simulators depend on several external libraries, which can limit their portability to machines, where these libraries cannot be installed. For example, some graphic libraries require access to a graphic card, which could be problematic on computational grids or in cloud environments. Absence of the visualization allows to speed up the simulation and to run multiple instances of he simulator in the grid computing facilities [12]. Running a GUI application on a grid can be complicated and sometimes prohibited at all.

Table 1. Properties of the selected robotics simulators. (*): sensor simulation is not possible in headless mode.

Name API	Middle-wares	External libraries	Headless mode	Physical engine
Stage C/C++	player,ros	freeglut3, fltk1.1, gtk2.0, ltdl7, png12-0	Y	
Gazebo C/C++	player, ros	bullet, tinyxmltbb, xml2qt4, protoc, freeimage, protobuf, protobuf-compiler, boost, freeglut3, ogre, cegui	Y*	ODE/Bullet
Usarsim C/C++	player, moast, pyro, ros	Unreal tournament 2004	N	UT2004
Morse Python, C	moos, ros, pocolibs, yarp	blender, python	N	Blender GE
Webots C, C++, Java, Python, Matlab, URBI	ros, urbi	libjpeg62, mencoder	N	ODE
Delta3D C++, Python	-	gdal, osgcal, cal3d12, cegui-mk2, ceguiogre, fltk1.1, python, bopenal, alut, gdal1, uuid, xerces28, gnet, boost, boost-python, opensg-glut	N	ODE/Bullet
V-Rep C/C++, Python, Java, Matlab, lua, Urbi	ros	QT, QtOpenGL, aavcodec, avformat, aveutil, lua5.1, qscitilla2, swscale, vvcl	N	Bullet/ODE
Sim C/C++	-	ODE / Bullet, opensg	Y	ODE/Bullet

3   Sim: A New Robotic Simulator

The simulator Sim was developed in the EU project Symbrion, that was aimed at the development of a modular robotic system to study principles of evolution applied to robotics. The simulator can support development of evolutionary-based control strategies and motion planning techniques.

3.1   System Description

The simulation Sim is written in C++ and it is published as open source [13]. For the physical simulation, Open Dynamics Engine (ODE) [4] or Bullet engine [1] can be used, similarly to other robotic simulators. The visualization part of the simulation is implemented using the Open Scene Graph [5] library. The visualization system can be turned off, which is important when the simulator needs to be run on a non-GUI machines, like computation grid [12]. Its robustness and precision depends on the quality of used 3D/physical models and therefore can be compared to other simulators.

The simulation runs in two threads; one for the physical simulation, and another one for the visualization. Therefore, the visualization part can be completely turned off without affecting the physical simulation.

The simulation loop (depicted on Fig. 1) works as follows. The simulation starts with an initialization of objects and components. Here, the components control other objects in the simulation. After initialization, the main loop is started, in which physical simulation provided by either Bullet or ODE is called. To control the simulated objects, the components are called using callback functions. These callback function can be called before of after the physical step. The messages are delivered to the components before the physical engine is called.

The core of the simulator consists of four main parts:

1. **Bodies.** The bodies represent physical properties of the robots. The position of the bodies is calculated in the physical simulation. The bodies can be connected with several types of joints. This allows to create various hinges or even a steerable wheel. The user control the bodies usually by applying forces or moments to the object using a component. Each body has physical properties such as size, weight or mass density.

2. **Visualization Bodies.** Not all objects need to participate in the physical simulation. Typical examples of these objects are visualization geometries, that can be more detailed than physical bodies used to compute collisions in the physical simulation. The utilization of both Bodies and more detailed Visualization bodies allows us to achieve robust physical simulation.

3. **Messages.** The communication between various components in the simulation is done using messages. The messages can have assigned priorities. In the case of modular robots, messages are important to synchronize control strategies distributed among the individual modules.

4. **Components.** The components are used to control other objects in the simulation. Each component has several callback methods, which are periodically called from the simulator. The users implements robot controller using the components. Moreover, the components can send and receive messages.

3.2 Robots

In the Sim simulator, the robot models are created as C++ classes. The robot models define physical and visual properties of the robots and also a set of functions to control them. The robot is then controlled from a component using

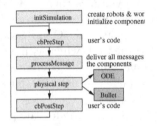

Fig. 1. The main loop of the simulator

these functions. The implementation of basic robot classes for mobile as well as modular robots is provided. This allows to understand how new robot should be created in the simulator and how to control them with a component. These predefined robot classes are:

- **MMP5.** This class represents a simple four-wheel mobile robot [23]. Example of such simplified model is depicted on Fig. 2. The MMP5 robot is controlled using left and right wheel velocities.
- **Scout.** In this class, the model of the Scout robot developed in the Symbrion [22] project is implemented. The Scout robot is a robotic module equipped with two tracks and a main hinge, which allows to change angle between two connected modules. The connection of the modules is done on request when the two modules to be connected are close enough. The Scout modules are depicted on Fig. 3.
- **Syrotek.** The Syrotek is a two-wheeled mobile robotic platform intended for education purposes developed at Czech Technical University in Prague. The details about the platform can be found in [21]; the robot is depicted on Fig. 2.

To provide fast simulation, one can simplify models of the robots. For example, the tracks of the Scout robot can be turned off. This is useful when more modules are connected to a larger organism, that moves using the movable hinges. Another way to achieve a fast simulation is to use simplified geometries. Example of such simplification of Scout robot can be seen on Fig. 3.

Fig. 2. The MMP5 mobile robot (left) and the Syrotek robot (right)

3.3   Components

The components are used to control robots or other objects in the simulation. To control the objects, callback functions are used. The callback functions are registered in the simulator's core on the beginning of the simulation. During initialization of the components, one should provide the components references to the objects, that need to be controlled by the component, e.g. references to a robot model. To control a robot, one needs only to create the callback and program the controller within the callback. This architecture allows to control the same robot (or its parts) by different controllers as well as to control more

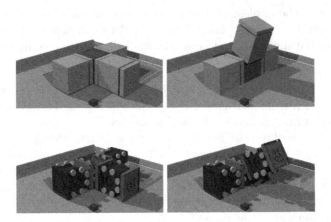

Fig. 3. Example of four Scout modules connected to a simple organism. The top row shows the simplified geometry, the detailed version of the robot is shown bottom.

robots by the same controller. Moreover, the simulator's internal methods are hidden for the programmers, which facilitate later porting of the controllers to the real platform.

The simulation is equipped with basic components allowing to control the robots. For example, the MMP5 component is available for the MMP5 robot. Although simulations can be run in the headless mode, one may require to visualize the results of the simulation later. For this purpose, two visualization components are provided.

- **Povray.** The task of the Povray component is to save positions of all objects in the simulation to a text files. From these files, pictures or even a video sequence can be rendered.
- **Blender.** This component creates a script for the Blender animation tool to visualize results of the experiment. Currently, the Blender 2.49 is supported. The objects and trajectories are loaded into the Blender using its internal Python API.

4   Use-Case: Locomotion Generation

One of the most studied problems in modular robotics is the locomotion generation, where the task is to generate control signals for the actuators to move the robot in a desired direction or to achieve a desired behavior. Due to many actuators presented in such a system, the locomotion generation is a challenging task. One approach to achieve a locomotion, is to utilize evolutionary approaches, like genetic programming or genetic algorithms, as these allow to efficiently search the high-dimensional search-space. Crucial part of the evolutionary principles is

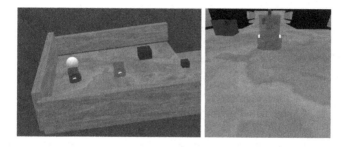

Fig. 4. Example of camera sensor mounted on the blue robot. The right picture shows the scene from the blue's robot camera.

the evaluation of fitness function, which describes quality of a candidate solution. As the fitness function needs to be computed many times, conducting of such an experiment with real robots would be time consuming. Instead, a robot simulator can be employed to evaluate the fitness function. This allows to find a set of solutions, that can be later examined on real robots.

The usage of the proposed simulator to generate locomotion using genetic programming is described in [18]. Another approach can be based on Central Pattern Generator (CPG). The CPGs produce periodic signals for the actuators. This is inspired by nature evidence, that motions are generated by a coupled neuro-oscillators providing a rhythmic signals [27]. CPGs are widely used in modular robotics [15] as they are able to generate various type of locomotion like crawling, walking or even swimming.

The CPGs can be modeled using non-linear coupled oscillators. For example, the oscillator [16] can be described as:

$$\dot{\varphi}_i = 2\pi v_i + \sum_j r_j w_{ij} \sin(\varphi_j - \varphi_i - \phi_{ij})$$

$$\ddot{r}_i = a_i(\frac{a_i}{4}(R_i - r_i) - \dot{r}_i)$$

$$y_i = r_i(1 + \cos\varphi_i),$$

where φ_i and r_i are state variables representing amplitude and phase of i-th oscillator. The parameters R_i and v_i represents the intrinsic amplitude and frequency and $a_i > 0$ control the response to change of R_i. The oscillators are coupled with weight w_{ij} and phase biases ϕ_{ij}. The output signal y_i is then used to control the joints of the modules.

This CPG can produce various gaits, that is controlled by changing parameters $x = (R_i, v_i, a_i, \phi_{ij}, w_{ij})$, $i, j = 1, \ldots, N$, where N is the number of oscillators. The number of oscillators is the same as the number of the actuators in the system. To generate a desired locomotion, the parameters x have to be optimize [24,28,17].

In this paper, we briefly describe how to find the parameters x using Particle Swarm Optimization (PSO) [9]. In this evolutionary approach, the problem is

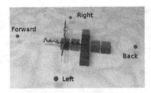

Fig. 5. Example of four virtual goals. iThe resulting gaits are visualized as the trajectory of the robot's head.

Fig. 6. Visualization of the motion of a modular robot approaching the virtual goal (depicted as sphere)

solved using a swarm of particles, where each particle x_i represents the parameter vector. The movement of a particle is influenced by its best solution found so far as well as by the best solution obtained among all other particles. The motion of the particle i can be then described as:

$$v_i = av_i + 2r_p(x_{local} - x_i) + 2r_g(x_{global} - x_i)$$
$$x_i = x_i + v_i, \tag{1}$$

where v_i is the particle's velocity, x_{local} denotes the best position of the particle in the past and x_{global} denotes the best particle among all particles. The parameter a controls the inertia of the particles. The r_p and r_g are random numbers from uniform distribution $U(0,1)$. In each step of the PSO algorithm, the positions of the particles are updated according to the Eq. 1. The particles are mainly attracted by both best positions (x_{local} and x_{global}). The random numbers r_p and r_g add variability, which allows the particles to explore the search space. Quality of each particle is evaluated using a fitness function.

The fitness function needs to be defined according to a desired locomotion. In our case, where the task is to find a straight motion, the fitness function is computed as the distance between the robot's head and a virtual goal. The virtual goal is placed in the desired direction of the motion. When the virtual goal is placed far enough, it ensures, that fast motions will be preferred. An example of four virtual goals to find four motions (forward, left, right, back) is depicted on Fig. 5.

Here, the simulator is used to evaluate the fitness function. During the simulation, which is run over the time T, the actuators of the simulated robots are controlled with the signals generated by the CPGs defined in the particle being evaluated. After the simulation terminates, the fitness function is computed.

5 Conclusion

This paper introduced a novel robotic simulation called Sim. Besides physical simulation of rigid bodies, robots and robotic organisms, sensor simulation is also possible. The simulator was designed especially for purpose of evolutionary modular robotics, but it can be used as a general robotic simulator.

The proposed simulator Sim has been used for locomotion generation of modular robots in several projects [18,29]. To facilitate creation of robot models as well as post-simulation work, the import of models from other tool (Webots or Blender) will be implemented. While the C++ language is commonly used in robotics, the researches involved in evolutionary computation may prefer other languages. Therefore, in the future work, the API for high-level languages like Python or Java will be provided. As the simulator is being used in several research activities, it will be continuously extended with new robot models.

References

1. Bullet physics engine, http://bulletphysics.org/
2. Delta3d, http://www.delta3d.org
3. Epic games, http://www.epicgames.com
4. Open dynamics engine, http://www.ode.org/
5. Open scene graph, http://www.openscenegraph.org/projects/osg
6. Swarm-bots: Swarms of self-assembling artifacts, http://www.swarm-bots.org/
7. V-rep, virtual robot experimentation platform, http://www.coppeliarobotics.com/
8. Vortex physical engine, http://www.vxsim.com/en/simulators
9. Particle swarm optimization. In: Proceedings of IEEE International Conference on Neural Networks, vol. 4, pp. 1942–1948 (November/December 1995)
10. Awaad, I., León, B.: XPERSim: A simulator for robot learning by experimentation. In: Carpin, S., Noda, I., Pagello, E., Reggiani, M., von Stryk, O. (eds.) SIMPAR 2008. LNCS (LNAI), vol. 5325, pp. 5–16. Springer, Heidelberg (2008)
11. Carpin, S., Lewis, M., Wang, J., Balakirsky, S., Scrapper, C.: Usarsim: a robot simulator for research and education. In: 2007 IEEE International Conference on Robotics and Automation, pp. 1400–1405 (April 2007)
12. CESNET. Metacentrum grid infrastructure, http://www.metacentrum.cz/
13. Fišer, D., Vonásek, V.: Simulator sim, http://imr.felk.cvut.cz/Research/Simulator
14. Gerkey, B.P., Vaughan, R.T., Howard, A.: The player/stage project: Tools for multi-robot and distributed sensor systems. In: Proceedings of the 11th International Conference on Advanced Robotics, pp. 317–323 (2003)
15. Ijspeert, A.J.: Central pattern generators for locomotion control in animals and robots: A review. Neural Networks 21(4), 642–653 (2008)
16. Ijspeert, A.J., Crespi, A., Ryczko, D., Cabelguen, J.-M.: From swimming to walking with a salamander robot driven by a spinal cord model. Science 315(5817), 1416–1420 (2007)

17. Ijspeert, A.J., Hallam, J., Willshaw, D.: Evolving swimming controllers for a simulated lamprey with inspiration from neurobiology. Adaptive Behavior 7(2), 151–172 (1999)
18. Cerny, J., Kubalik, J.: Co-evolutionary approach to design of robotic gait. In: Proceedings of the EvoStar 2013 (2013)
19. Kanehiro, F., Hirukawa, H., Kajita, S.: Openhrp: Open architecture humanoid robotics platform. I. J. Robotic Res. 23(2), 155–165 (2004)
20. Koenig, N., Howard, A.: Design and use paradigms for gazebo, an open-source multi-robot simulator. In: Proceedings of 2004 IEEE/RSJ International Conference on Intelligent Robots and Systems (IROS 2004), September 30-October 2, vol. 3, pp. 2149–2154 (2004)
21. Kulich, M., Chudoba, J., Kosnar, K., Krajnik, T., Faigl, J., Preucil, L.: Syrotek — distance teaching of mobile robotics. IEEE Transactions on Education 56(1), 18–23 (February)
22. Levi, P., Kernbach, S. (eds.): Symbiotic Multi-Robot Organisms: Reliability, Adaptability, Evolution. Springer (2010)
23. The MachineLab. Mmp-5 mobile robot platform, http://www.themachinelab.com/MMP-5.html
24. Marbach, D., Ijspeert, A.J.: Online optimization of modular robot locomotion. In: Proceedings of the IEEE International Conference on Mechatronics and Automation (ICMA 2005), pp. 248–253 (2005)
25. Michel, O.: Webots: Professional mobile robot simulation. Journal of Advanced Robotics Systems 1(1), 39–42 (2004)
26. Moubarak, P., Ben-Tzvi, P.: Modular and reconfigurable mobile robotics. Robotics and Autonomous Systems 60(12), 1648–1663 (2012)
27. Mulder, T., Van De Crommert Hw Duysens, J.: Neural control of locomotion: sensory control of the central pattern generator and its relation to treadmill training. Gait & Posture 7(3), 251–263 (1998)
28. Taga, G., Yamaguchi, Y., Shimizu, H.: Self-organized control of bipedal locomotion by neural oscillators in unpredictable environment. Biological Cybernetics 65(3), 147–159 (1991)
29. Vonásek, V., Kulich, M., Krajník, T., Saska, M., Fišer, D., Petřík, V., Přeučil, L.: Techniques for Modeling Simulation Environments for Modular Robotics. In: Proccedings of International Conference on Mathematical Modelling, pp. 1–6. Vienna University of Technology, Vienna (2012)
30. Webots. Commercial Mobile Robot Simulation Software, http://www.cyberbotics.com
31. Winkler, L., Vonasek, V., Worn, H., Preucil, L.: Robot3d—a simulator for mobile modular self-reconfigurable robots. In: 2012 IEEE Conference on Multisensor Fusion and Integration for Intelligent Systems (MFI), pp. 464–469 (September 2012)
32. Zaratti, M., Fratarcangeli, M., Iocchi, L.: A 3D Simulator of Multiple Legged Robots Based on USARSim. In: Lakemeyer, G., Sklar, E., Sorrenti, D.G., Takahashi, T. (eds.) RoboCup 2006: Robot Soccer World Cup X. LNCS (LNAI), vol. 4434, pp. 13–24. Springer, Heidelberg (2007)
33. Zykov, V., Chan, A., Lipson, H.: Molecubes: An open-source modular robotics kit

Guided Motion Planning for Modular Robots*

Vojtěch Vonásek[1], Ondřej Penc[2], and Libor Přeučil[1]

[1] CTU in Prague, Faculty of electrical engineering,
Technicka 2, Prague, 166 27, Czech Republic
{vonasek,preucil}@labe.felk.cvut.cz
[2] Faculty of Nuclear Sciences and Physical Eng. Brehova 7,
Prague, 115 19,
Czech Republic
penc.ondrej@gmail.com

Abstract. Modular robots consist of many modules that can be connected into various structures. This allows modular robots to adapt their shape according to a given task and environment. To visit a desired place in an environment, motion planning is required. To generate feasible plans for these robots with many degrees of freedom and many kinematic and dynamic constraints, a physical simulation is required to precisely model motion of the robots. As the physical simulation can be time consuming, motion planners need to be extended to decrease the number of simulation queries. In this paper, we propose a novel motion planning for modular robots based on guided sampling of configuration space. The guided sampling utilizes a precomputed simple path in the environment, along which the configuration space of the robot is sampled with higher probability. This approach significantly decreases the number of calls of physical simulations which increases the speed of the planning process.

Keywords: motion planning, physical simulation, modular robots, Rapidly Exploring Random Tree.

1   Introduction

Modular robots are composed of many robotic modules, that can be connected together to form robots of various shapes [17]. This allows the robots to adapt for unstructured environments, which may bring advantages in comparison to fixed-shape robots. As the modular robots have many degrees of freedom, they can perform various gaits which further increases their ability to move and adapt in the environment.

---

* The work in this paper was supported by TACR grant No. TE01020197, Access to computing and storage facilities owned by parties and projects contributing to the National Grid Infrastructure MetaCentrum, provided under the programme "Projects of Large Infrastructure for Research, Development, and Innovations" (LM2010005), is greatly appreciated.

J. Hodicky (Ed.): MESAS 2014, LNCS 8906, pp. 217–230, 2014.

The core problem in modular robotics is the motion planning and navigation. Low-level motions, i.e., basic gaits, can be achieved using locomotion generators. Widely used approach for locomotion generation is based on the concept of Central Pattern Generators (CPGs) that provide periodic control signals for the actuators. This is inspired by nature, where motions of complex organisms are generated as a combination of simple motions. Although CPGs can realize various gaits like crawling or walking, pure locomotion generation cannot ensure avoiding of obstacles and reaching of arbitrary places in complex environments. To avoid obstacles, multiple locomotion generators should be utilized and switched by a high-level motion planner.

Motion planning for such complex systems with many degrees of freedom is a challenging task. To decrease the complexity of the planning problem, the idea of motion primitives has been proposed [23]. In this paper, we propose an efficient approach to further speed up the planning algorithm. The proposed approach utilizes a guiding path leading from the initial to the goal place. The guiding path, that is represented as a simple 3D path, can be found very fast using classing graph-based search methods. To find a feasible motion plan for a modular robot, the sampling is restricted to the vicinity of the guiding path.

2   Related Work

Depending on the architecture of modular robots, three basic approaches can be utilized to achieve motion of the robots: a) reconfiguration, b) joint-control locomotion, and c) locomotion using dedicated actuators like wheels, belts or even screw-drives [15]. The motion through reconfiguration is achieved by repeated disconnection/reconnection of the modules. The joint-control motion, which is considered in this paper, is achieved by controlling joints between the connected modules.

The joint-control motion can be achieved using Central Pattern Generators (CPGs) [5] that produce periodic control signals for the actuators. By changing parameters and coupling of the CPGs, various gaits like caterpillar-like motion, walking or even swimming can be produced. The advantage of the CPGs is that the desired gait can be realized efficiently and smoothly. To cope with altering environments, sensory feedback can be introduced [2,5]. This allows a robot to change or adapt its gaits to an environment. To further increase robustness of the gaits, these can be adapted on-line [18,16]. However, a global situation in the environment is not considered in the CPGs. Therefore, CPGs cannot ensure reaching of a far goal in complex environments with obstacles.

The overall situation in the environment can be considered in motion planning methods. The task of the motion planning is to find a feasible trajectory between two given places or configurations of a robot. Motion planning for the modular robots with many degrees of freedom and with many kinematic constraints can be solved using sampling-based methods like Rapidly Exploring Random Tree (RRT) [12]. The sampling-based methods create a roadmap of free configurations by randomly sampling the configuration space $\mathcal{C}$ of the robot. The configuration space is space of all possible configurations and its dimension is equal to the number of DOFs of the robot. As the number of all configurations grows exponentially with the number of DOFs (and therefore with the number of modules in a robot), the configuration space $\mathcal{C}$ cannot be searched by classic state-space search methods. Instead, a roadmap of free configurations $q \in \mathcal{C}_{\text{free}}$, where $\mathcal{C}_{\text{free}} \subseteq \mathcal{C}$, is created by random sampling of the configuration space $\mathcal{C}$. Each sample is classified as free or non-free using collision detection and by checking if all kinematic constraints are satisfied. Then, the free samples stored in the roadmap are connected using a local planning. The resulting trajectory can be found in the roadmap using graph-search methods. The sampling-based methods can generate motion for systems with many DOFs [14,3] and they can cope with dynamic and kinematic constraints [13]. Sampling-based planners have been used in many applications including modular robots [24,22,20].

To speed up the motion planning of modular robots and to improve quality of the resulting motions, the locomotion generators and motion planning techniques can be combined by the concept of motion primitives [23,10]. The motion primitives represent a set of basic motion skills and these are modeled using CPGs. The motion primitives are considered as atomic actions in a motion planner. The concept of motion planning with motion primitives utilizes advantages of both approaches: the motions are efficiently modeled using CPGs, while the global situation in the environment is considered by the planning method.

The most time consuming part of the motion planning for modular robots is the physical simulation, that is used to model motions of the robots. To speed up the planning process, the number of simulation queries should be minimized. In this paper, we propose a guiding sampling schema to suppress unnecessary sampling of the configuration space and therefore, to decrease number of simulation queries. The idea of the guided sampling is to find a simple path leading from the initial to the goal configuration. Then, the configuration space is sampled with a higher probability around the path. Our approach thus utilizes two state-of-the-art concepts to speed-up the motion planner: the growth of the tree is biased by the knowledge about the environment [11,4], while the low-level motions are realized via motion primitives. This allows us to generate feasible motion plans for modular robots of various morphology in complex environments.

3   Preliminaries

We assume a modular robot without loops, with one robot dedicated as a pivot. The pivot is used to determine the configuration of the whole robot. Let $q = (x, y, z, \alpha, \beta, \gamma, a_1, \ldots, a_n) \in \mathcal{C}$ denote the configuration of a modular robot with n joints, where (x, y, z) and (α, β, γ) denote the 3D position and orientation of the pivot module respectively, and a_i denotes the angles of the joints. Let $\mathcal{C}$ denote the configuration space of the robot and let $\mathcal{C}_{\text{free}} \subseteq \mathcal{C}$ denote a space of free configurations, where the robot does not collide with an obstacle and the modules do not collide with each other.

In the joint control approach, a robot moves by changing angles between the consecutive modules. The joint signals $a_i(t), 0 \leq t \leq \tau^p$ are produced using a CPG with a parameters x^p, where p is the motion primitive and τ^p is its duration. For example, sine-based control $a_i(t) = A_i \sin(\omega_i t + \varphi_i) + B_i$ is described by parameters $x^p = (A_i, B_i, \omega_i, \varphi_i), i = 1, \ldots, n$. In the first step of the robot control using motion primitive p, the settings x^p are retrieved from a look-up table and the joint signals $a_i(t)$ are generated. These signals are then distributed to individual modules.

4   Basic Motion Planning

The pure locomotion generation provide efficient low-level motion primitives (e.g. walking or other repeating motions). To allow the robot motion in an environment with obstacles, multiple gaits are needed and a plan to switch is required. The task of the motion planning is to find a feasible trajectory from the initial configuration $q_{\text{init}} \in \mathcal{C}_{\text{free}}$ to the goal configuration $q_{\text{goal}} \in \mathcal{C}_{\text{free}}$, which is solved using the RRT method in this paper. The RRT incrementally builds a tree $\mathcal{T}$ of free configurations that is rooted in the initial configuration q_{init}. In each iteration, a random sample $q_{\text{rand}} \in \mathcal{C}$ is generated and its nearest neighbor $q_{\text{near}} \in \mathcal{T}$ is found in the tree. The configuration q_{near} is expanded by applying control inputs $\mathcal{U}$ to the motion model of the robot. The closest configuration q_{new} towards q_{rand} is selected from the expanded configurations and it is added to the tree. The algorithm terminates if the tree approaches the goal configuration q_{goal} to a predefined distance d_{goal} or if the maximum number of allowed iterations k is exceeded. The algorithm is listed in Alg. 1 and its expansion procedure is listed in Alg. 2. To compute new position of the robot after a motion primitive is applied, physical simulation is used. The simulation can evaluate motions of robots of various complexity and it allows to model different environments [22].

To enable expansion of the node q_{near}, the set of control inputs $\mathcal{U}$ needs to be defined. It can be generated as a combination of discretized control inputs in the case of robots with few control inputs (such as differential drive mobile robots). As the number of these combinations grows exponentially with the number of inputs (and therefore with the number of modules in an organism), this approach is not suitable for modular robots. Another approach is to generate the set $\mathcal{U}$ randomly, either before the planning process or in each iteration of the RRT. Due to exponential growth of the possible combinations of control inputs, the probability of choosing a good control input rapidly decreases with the increasing number of modules. Therefore, similarly to the previous approach, generating $\mathcal{U}$ randomly is suitable only for small robots with few modules. The third approach to generate $\mathcal{U}$ is to utilize a locomotion generator. In this case, the number of possible expansions is given only by the number of motion primitives, not by the number of actuators or modules as in the previous cases. This significantly reduces the complexity of motion planning, as motion in an environment can be achieved using only few primitives [23]. The result of the planning process is then a sequence of motion primitives, as is depicted in Fig. 1.

RRT quickly explores the configuration space, because the boundary nodes of the tree are more likely selected for the expansion. The probability that a node

Algorithm 1. RRT algorithm

Input: initial configuration q_{init}, goal configuration q_{goal}, goal region d_{goal},
  maximum number of iterations k
Output: path to the goal configuration or failure
$\mathcal{T}$.add(q_{init});
for *iteration* $= 1 \dots k$ **do**
 | q_{rand} = generate random sample in $\mathcal{C}$;
 | q_{near} = nearestConfiguration($\mathcal{T}$,q_{rand});
 | q_{new} = expandConfiguration(q_{near},q_{rand},$\mathcal{U}$);
 | **if** $R \neq failure$ **then**
  | $\mathcal{T}$.addNode(q_{new});
  | $\mathcal{T}$.addEdge(q_{near},q_{new});
  | **if** $\rho(q_{\text{new}}, q_{\text{goal}}) < d_{goal}$ **then**
   | return path in the tree from q_{init} to q_{goal};
  | **end**
 | **end**
end
return failure; // q_{goal} is not approached in k iterations

---

will be selected for the expansion is given by the area of its Voronoi cell. The nodes located on the boundary of the tree have larger Voronoi cells, hence they are chosen for the expansion more frequently than the nodes located inside the tree [12]. This Voronoi bias may however cause a slow growth of the tree towards the goal configuration, especially if the robots move in large environments. To speed up the growth towards the goal states, the random sample q_{rand} can be replaced by q_{goal} with a probability p_{goal}. Utilization of goal-bias can be however counter-productive in environment with obstacles, because the pure goal-bias attracts the tree without considering the obstacles. For example, if the tree is too close to an obstacle and the q_{goal} lying behind the obstacle is frequently used to select a node for expansion, the tree will not be expanded. Therefore, a different goal-bias principle has to be used in an environment with obstacles, which is described in the following section.

The distance between configurations is measured by a metric ϱ. The metric also influences the speed of the RRT algorithm [1] and it has to be defined with respect to solved task. In this paper, the task is to generate global plans for a modular robot moving in a large environment. The metric should therefore consider mainly by the position of the robot, which can be realized using 3D Euclidean metric.

5   RRT–Path: Guided Sampling for Motion Planning

The most time consuming part of the motion planning for modular robots is the physical simulation used to evaluate motion model of the robot. The number of evaluations depend on the number of expansions of the tree. Therefore, unnecessary expansions should be avoided. Unnecessary expansions can

---

Algorithm 2. expandConfiguration()

Input: configuration to be expanded q_{near}, random configuration q_{rand}, set of $\mathcal{U}$
    of possible control inputs
Output: resulting configuration or failure
$R = \emptyset$;
foreach $u \in \mathcal{U}$ **do**
    $q = $ physicalSimulation(q_{near},u, Δt);
    $R = R \cup \{q\}$;
end
if $R \neq \emptyset$ **then**
    $q_{new} = $ closest configuration to q_{rand} from R;
    return q_{new};
end
return failure; // no expansion

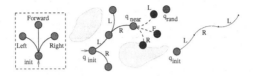

Fig. 1. Example of the expansion procedure for a robot equipped with three motion primitives (Move-Left,Move-Right and Move-Forward). The resulting trajectory is a sequence of motion primitives.

be suppressed by decreasing growth of the tree into the whole environment and boosting the sampling of certain areas. These areas can be set around a simple path in the environment, that will guide the tree growth. The guiding path $P = (p_1 = q_{init}, p_2, \ldots, p_{N-1}, p_N = q_{goal})$ consists of N waypoints $p_i \in \mathcal{C}_{free}$ leading from q_{init} to q_{goal}. Let v denote an index of a point on the guiding path P. This point p_v is denoted as virtual goal in the rest of the paper.

To boost growth of the tree along the guiding path, the probability of sampling around the path has to be increased. However, this cannot be done without considering actual state of the tree, especially in environments with obstacles. Instead, the virtual goal move in the guiding path. If the tree approaches the virtual goal, the goal is moved towards on the guiding path towards the goal configuration. The RRT-Path is listed in Alg. 3. The random samples q_{rand} are generated with probability p_{path} around the virtual goal p_t from $N(p_t, \sigma_v^2)$. The variance σ_v^2 of the Gaussian distribution should be chosen according to the speed of the robot. In our experiments, σ_v^2 is set to a distance, that the robot can travel by the slowest motion primitive. The idea of the guiding is simple: when the guiding path is approached close enough, the virtual goal is moved forward. To set a new virtual goal, a point $p_r \in P$, $r > v$ approached by the tree to distance d_{path} with the highest index r is found and the new virtual goal is set to $v = r + 1$. Setting the virtual goal to a reached point with the highest index on the guiding path is shown in the Fig. 2.

Algorithm 3. RRT–Path

Input: Configurations q_{init}, q_{goal}, the maximum number of iterations K, the
temporal goal bias p_g, the number of the temporal goal neighbors w,
a guiding path $P = \{p_1, \ldots, p_n\}$
Output: A trajectory between q_{init} and q_{goal} or failure

---

$T.add(q_{init})$;
$v = 1$;   // index of the temporal goal point ;
for $iteration = 1 \ldots k$ **do**
    for $r = N \ldots t$ **do**
        $q_n = \text{nearestNeighbor}(T, p_r)$;
        if $\text{distance}(q_n, p_r) < d_{path}$ **then**
            $v = r + 1$; // new temporal goal
            break;
        end
    end
    if $\text{rand}(0, 1) < p_{path}$ **then**
        $q_{rand} = $ random point from $N(q_v, \sigma_v^2)$;
    else
        $q_{rand} = $ random configuration in $\mathcal{C}$;
    end
    $q_{near} = \text{nearestConfiguration}(\mathcal{T}, q_{rand})$;
    $q_{new} = \text{expandConfiguration}(q_{near}, q_{rand}, \mathcal{U})$;
    if $R \neq failure$ **then**
        $\mathcal{T}.\text{addNode}(q_{new})$;
        $\mathcal{T}.\text{addEdge}(q_{near}, q_{new})$;
        if $\rho(q_{new}, q_{goal}) < d_{goal}$ **then**
            return path in the tree from q_{init} to q_{goal};
        end
    end
end
return failure; // q_{goal} is not approached in k iterations

---

The balance between path following and exploration of $\mathcal{C}$ depends on the
variance σ_v^2 and by the distance between the consecutive points on the guiding
path. High variance σ_v^2 and high distance between the guiding points cause that
the tree will rather explore the whole $\mathcal{C}$ instead of following the guiding path.
Contrary, small distance between consecutive guiding points and small σ_v^2 will
attract the tree more closer towards the guiding path. Too close following of
the path may prevent the robot from moving, especially in environments with
obstacles. To overcome these situations, the distance between consecutive sample
points on the guiding path should be similar to the distance traveled by the robot
with the slowest motion primitive.

As the tree grows in the configuration space, the path P should be constructed also in this space. However, this leads to the full motion planning between q_{init} and q_{goal}. To generate the guiding path fast, it can be computed
in the workspace and then extended to the configuration space. In the case of

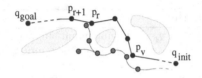

Fig. 2. Example of setting a new virtual goal. The actual goal is p_v and the tree approaches also p_r. Therefore, new virtual goal is set to p_{r+1}.

modular robots moving on a terrain represented by a 3D mesh, the path P can be computed using a graph-search algorithm on a graph constructed from the nodes and edges of the mesh.

It should be noted, that a pure geometric path may not help if the robot is not equipped with sufficient motion primitives. For example, a pure geometric path computed using Voronoi diagram cannot be followed by a robot equipped with 'move-forward-30' and 'move-forward-60' primitives, where the number denotes change of the orientation of the robot in degrees. Obviously, such motion primitives move the robots only forward with simultaneous rotation, that prevents to follow a straight path. In such a case, the guiding path has to be found by a different approach, e.g. using iterative refining [21].

6   Experimental Verification

The efficiency of the RRT–Path was measured and compared to basic RRT in a set of simulated experiments. Three modular robots with different topology were utilized: snake robot with six modules, Dog with 14 modules and Spider with 9 modules. The robots are depicted in Fig. 4. The experiments were performed using physical simulation based on ODE physical engine. The models of the robots are based on HW platform CoSMO [7], examples of real robots are shown in Fig. 3. The modules are cubes of side length 10 cm and weight ~1 kg equipped with actuators for both 2D and 3D locomotion, four docking mechanisms, camera, IR receivers/transmitters, accelerometers and a small PC with μClinux.

Each robot was equipped with three locomotion generators: a) nonlinear oscillator [6]; b) neural oscillator [8]; and c) harmonic oscillator. The harmonic oscillator provides control signal $a_i(t)$ of each hinge as $a_i(t) = A_i \sin(2\pi f_i t + \varphi_i)$, where (A_i, f_i, φ_i) are parameters, $i = 1, \ldots, n$. The number of parameters to be optimized is: a) $3n + 2c$; b) $2n + 1c$; and c) $3n$, where n is the number of modules in the organism and c is the number of the links. The links are depicted as arrows in Fig. 4. We refer to [19] for detailed description of the utilized generators and their implementation for modular robots.

The above described locomotion generators were used to model motion primitives. The Spider and Dog robots were equipped with 'move-forward', 'move-left', 'move-right' and 'move-back' primitives. The Snake robot can move only in two directions, hence it was equipped only with 'move-forward' and 'move-back' primitives. The parameters of the generators were optimized using Particle

Fig. 3. Example of three modular robots made of CoSMO modules. The modules were developed at IPR/KIT Karlsruhe, Germany, within Symbrion/Replicator projects.

Swarm Optimization (PSO) [9] technique with 20 particles and 200 iterations. In the PSO, each particle x represents a candidate solution (parameters of a CPG) and its quality is evaluated using a fitness function describing ability to move in a desired direction. The fitness function is $f(x) = dist(q(T_{sim}), q_p) + a|\beta|$, where the first term describes the distance between a desired place q_p and the point reached by the robot after $T_{sim} = 30$ s of motion (Fig. 4). The second term penalizes possible rotation β of the robot during the motion. The point q_p was placed in the distance 30 cm in the desired direction of motion. The achieved values of 'move-forward' primitive are given in Tab. 1.

Table 1. Values of the fitness function of the 'move-forward' motion primitives achieved by the optimization process

CPG	Snake	Spider	Dog
Non-linear	0	26	26
Neural	25	28	23
Harmonic	25	29	28

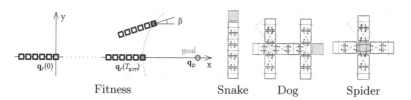

Fitness   Snake   Dog   Spider

Fig. 4. Example of fitness evaluation for a snake-like robot (left) and configurations of robots. The arrows denote coupling for the Nonlinear and Neural CPGs. The filled rectangles denote pivot modules used to compute the distance between configurations.

6.1 Planar Environment

In the first experiment, the task was to generate trajectory between two locations in an planar environment with circular obstacles. The size of the environment is 200 by 200 map units, size of each module is 0.5 map units. Therefore, the length of tested robots is approximately 3 map units. The maximum number of iterations was set to $k = 5000$ for both algorithms. The goal-bias in RRT was $p_{goal} = 0.05$, and the biased sampling around path in RRT–Path was $p_{path} = 0.9$.

Examples of found solutions are depicted in Fig. 5. The pictures clearly show the difference between both methods. While the configuration trees generated by RRT are more spread in the environment, the trees generated by RRT–Path follow the guiding path.

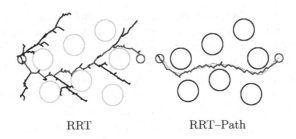

RRT   RRT–Path

Fig. 5. Examples of configuration trees generated for Dog robot. The tree generated by RRT grows more into the configuration space than the tree generated by RRT–Path.

The runtimes of the planners are depicted as boxplots in Fig. 7 for an environment without obstacles and in Fig. 8 for an environment with obstacles. The RRT–Path provided solutions significantly faster than RRT in the case of Spider and Dog robots in both environments. Moreover, the runtimes have significantly smaller variance, which is caused by the sampling restricted to the vicinity of the guiding path. The efficiency of the RRT–Path over RRT can be observed with all employed locomotion generators. The difference between runtimes of RRT-Path method for one robot and different generators is caused by the efficiency of the motion primitives, as they move the robot with different speed and rotation.

The results significantly differ in the case of Snake robot. In this case, the goal configuration q_{goal} was placed in front of the robot, which allows the robot to reach it even with only the 'move-back' or 'move-forward' primitives. The goal was reached only with the motion primitives realized using Harmonic generators (runtimes of both planners are in order of tens of seconds), but no solution was found with motion primitives realized by the Non-linear and Neural oscillators, which is indicated by runtimes around 2000 s. As both Non-linear and Neural oscillators provided motion primitives (according to fitness in Tab. 1), one can expect, that the planners will find a solution. However, during the forward motion realized by Neural or Non-linear generator, the robot slightly changes its heading towards one side. Therefore, the Snake robot cannot reach a goal placed in front of the robot. The second motion primitive (move backward) does not help here, as it moves the robot in the opposite direction. Therefore, the planning methods cannot grow the tree close enough to the goal place, which is depicted on Fig. 6. Similar experiments with other robots can be found in [19].

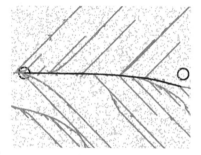

Fig. 6. Example of a configuration tree generated by RRT for the Snake robot driven by Non-linear motion primitives. The robot can move only forward with a slight rotation, or backward. The goal (red circle) thus cannot be approached by the robot. The straight lines in the tree show how the robot changes its orientation during the 'move-forward' and 'move-back' primitives. The blue points represent the random samples, which where drawn from the whole configuration space.

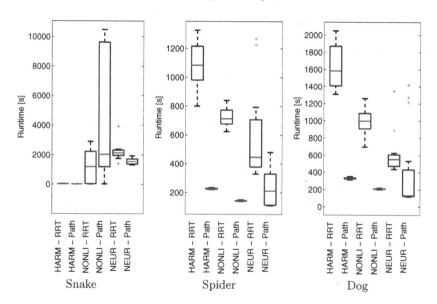

Fig. 7. Runtimes of RRT and RRT–Path in planar environment without obstacles

6.2 Surface Scenario

In the second scenario, the task of the robots was to move on a surface modeled with a 3D triangular mesh. The surface of size 200×200 map units contained small hills with maximum height of 10 map units. The guiding path was found as a sequence of nodes of the mesh using Dijkstra algorithm. For each combination of the tested algorithms (RRT and RRT–Path) and motion control approach ('angles' or 'primitives'), 50 trials were run. In the 'angles' motion control approach, the CPGs are replaced by direct control of the actuators [22,23].

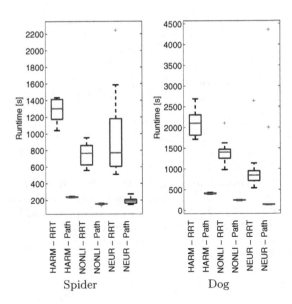

Fig. 8. Runtimes of RRT and RRT–Path in planar environment with obstacles

Table 2. Runtimes of the planners in the Surface scenario.

| | | Dog | | Spider | |
		Mean (Std. dev)	Success-ratio	Mean (Std. dev)	Success-ratio
angles	RRT	832.74 (0.00)	100.00	156.17 (85.70)	100.00
	RRT–Path	188.22 (104.27)	100.00	56.07 (23.02)	100.00
primitives	RRT	664.85 (36.53)	6.00	307.59 (59.62)	6.00
	RRT–Path	342.93 (149.38)	100.00	215.17 (172.37)	86.00

The maximum number of iterations of the planners (parameter k in Alg. 1 and 3) was set to $k = 500$.

Examples of the configuration trees are depicted in Fig. 9. The runtimes of the planners are shown in the Tab. 2. Besides the overall runtimes of the planners, the success ratios are shown. The success ratio is computed as the ratio of trials, where the planner approached goal configuration to a distance less than a size of two modules over number of all trials. For the robots controlled by the 'angles' approach, the success ratio is 100 % and the runtimes of the RRT–Path are significantly shorter than the runtimes of the basic RRT planner.

The results differ if the robots are controlled by the motion primitives. In this case, the success ratio of the original RRT is only 6 percent for both robots, while it is 100 % for the RRT–Path. It is caused by the fact, that the arena is very large comparing to the size of the robots. Therefore, the original RRT is quickly spread into this area without being attracted by the goal configuration. Contrary, the sampling in the RRT–Path is more attracted by the guiding path leading towards the goal configuration.

The results of this scenario have shown, that the guided sampling significantly increases the speed of the planner as well as its success ratio. Moreover, the superior performance was observed under two different approaches for motion generation.

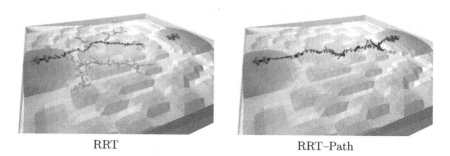

RRT   RRT–Path

Fig. 9. Examples of solutions found by RRT and RRT–Path for Dog robot

7   Conclusion

Motion of modular robots has to be effectively planned considering the presence of obstacles. In this paper, we proposed a simple and efficient RRT–Path method for the guided sampling. The idea of the guided sampling is to employ a simple path, that attracts the growth of the configuration tree in the configuration space. This allows the planner to reach the goal configuration in less iterations and thus with less simulation queries. Consequently, this speeds up the planning process. As has been shown in the experimental section, the guiding principle allows us to find motion plans in significantly shorter time comparing to a non-guided sampling-based planner.

References

1. Cheng, P., LaValle, S.: Reducing metric sensitivity in randomized trajectory design. In: IEEE/RSJ IROS (2001)
2. Chiel, H.J., Ting, L.H., Ekeberg, O., Hartmann, M.Z.: The brain in its body: motor control and sensing in a biomechanical context. Journal of Neuroscience 29(41), 12807–12814 (2009)
3. Gayle, R., Redon, S., Sud, A., Lin, M.C., Manocha, D.: Efficient motion planning of highly articulated chains using physics-based sampling. In: ICRA (2007)
4. Hsu, D., Latombe, J.-C., Kurniawati, H.: On the probabilistic foundations of probabilistic roadmap planning. International Journal of Robotics Research 25(7), 627–643 (2006)
5. Ijspeert, A.J.: Central pattern generators for locomotion control in animals and robots: A review. Neural Networks 21(4), 642–653 (2008)

6. Ijspeert, A.J., Crespi, A., Ryczko, D., Cabelguen, J.-M.: From swimming to walking with a salamander robot driven by a spinal cord model. Science 315(5817), 1416–1420 (2007)
7. Liedke, J., Matthias, R., Winkler, L., Wörn, H.: The Collective Self-Reconfigurable Modular Organism (CoSMO). In: IEEE/ASME International Conference on Advanced Intelligent Mechatronics (AIM) (2013)
8. Kamimura, A., Kurokawa, H., Toshida, E., Tomita, K., Murata, S., Kokaji, S.: Automatic locomotion pattern generation for modular robots. In: IEEE ICRA (2003)
9. Kennedy, J., Eberhart, R.: Particle swarm optimization. In: IEEE International Conference on Neural Networks (1995)
10. Kuffner, J., Nishiwaki, K., Kagami, S., Inaba, M., Inoue, H.: Motion planning for humanoid robots. In: ISRR (2003)
11. Kurniawati, H., Hsu, D.: Workspace importance sampling for probabilistic roadmap planning. In: IROS (September 2004)
12. LaValle, S.M.: Rapidly-exploring random trees: A new tool for path planning, TR 98-11 (1998)
13. LaValle, S.M., Kuffner Jr., J.J.: Randomized kinodynamic planning (1999)
14. LaValle, S.M., Yakey, J.H., Kavraki, L.E.: A probabilistic roadmap approach for systems with closed kinematic chains. In: IEEE ICRA (1999)
15. Liedke, J., Winkler, L., Worn, H.: An alternative locomotion unit for mobile modular self-reconfigurable robots based on archimedes screws. In: International Symposium on Mechatronics and its Applications (ISMA) (2013)
16. Matthey, L., Righetti, L., Ijspeert, A.J.: Experimental study of limit cycle and chaotic controllers for the locomotion of centipede robots. In: IEEE/RSJ IROS (2008)
17. Moubarak, P., Ben-Tzvi, P.: Modular and reconfigurable mobile robotics. Robotics and Autonomous Systems 60(12), 1648–1663 (2012)
18. Nassour, J., Hénaff, P., Ben Ouezdou, F., Cheng, G.: A study of adaptive locomotive behaviors of a biped robot: Patterns generation and classification. In: Doncieux, S., Girard, B., Guillot, A., Hallam, J., Meyer, J.-A., Mouret, J.-B. (eds.) SAB 2010. LNCS, vol. 6226, pp. 313–324. Springer, Heidelberg (2010)
19. Penc, O.: Motion planning for modular robots, Master's thesis. Czech Technical University in Prague, FEE, Dept. of cybernetics (2013),
http://cyber.felk.cvut.cz/research/theses/detail.phtml?id=362
20. Sucan, I.A., Kruse, J.F., Yim, M., Kavraki, L.E.: Reconfiguration for modular robots using kinodynamic motion planning. In: ASME – Dynamic Systems and Control, Ann Arbor, Michigan, USA (2008)
21. Vonásek, V., Faigl, J., Krajník, T., Přeučil, L.: A Sampling Schema for Rapidly Exploring Random Trees Using a Guiding Path. In: Proceedings of the 5th European Conference on Mobile Robots. AASS Research Centre (2011)
22. Vonásek, V., Košnar, K., Přeučil, L.: Motion planning of self-reconfigurable modular robots using rapidly exploring random trees. In: Herrmann, G., Studley, M., Pearson, M., Conn, A., Melhuish, C., Witkowski, M., Kim, J.-H., Vadakkepat, P. (eds.) TAROS-FIRA 2012. LNCS, vol. 7429, pp. 279–290. Springer, Heidelberg (2012)
23. Vonásek, V., Saska, M., Košnar, K., Přeučil, L.: Global motion planning for modular robots with local motion primitives. In: ICRA (2013)
24. Yoshida, E., Kurokawa, H., Kamimura, A., Tomita, K., Kokaji, S., Murata, S.: Planning behaviors of a modular robot: an approach applying a randomized planner to coherent structure. In: IEEE/RSJ IROS (2004)

Accepted Autonomy for Search and Rescue Robotics

Petr Zuzánek[1], Karel Zimmermann[1,2], and Václav Hlaváč[1,2]

[1]Czech Institute of Informatics, Robotics and Cybernetics,
Czech Technical University in Prague,
Zikova 4, 166 36 Praha 6, Czech Republic
{zuzanp1,zimmerk,hlavac}@cmp.felk.cvut.cz
http://cmp.felk.cvut.cz
[2]Center for Machine Perception, Dept. of Cybernetics,
Faculty of Electrical Engineering, Czech Technical University in Prague,
Karlovo namesti 13, 121 35 Prague 2, Czech Republic
http://ciirc.cvut.cz

Abstract. Since exploration of unknown disaster areas during Search and Rescue missions is often dangerous, teleoperated robotic platforms are usually used as a suitable replacement for a human rescuer. Advanced robotic platforms have usually many degrees of freedom to be controlled, e.g. speed, azimuth, camera view or articulated sub-tracks angles. Manual control of all available degrees of freedom often leads to unwanted cognitive overload of the operator whose attention should be mainly focused on reaching the mission goals. On the other hand, there are fully autonomous systems requiring minimal attention but allowing almost no interaction which is usually not acceptable for the operator. Operator-accepted level of autonomy is usually a trade-off between fully teleoperated and completely autonomous robots.

The main contribution of our paper is extensive survey on accepted autonomy solutions for Search and Rescue robots with special focus on traversing unstructured terrain, however brief summary of our system is also provided.

Since, integral part of any Search and Rescue robot is the ability to traverse a complex terrain, we describe a system for teleoperated skid-steer robot with articulated sub-tracks (flippers), in which the operator controls robot speed and azimuth, while flipper posture and stiffness are controlled autonomously. The system for autonomous flipper control is trained from semi-autonomously collected training samples to maximize the platform stability and motion smoothness on challenging obstacles.

Keywords: Urban Search And Rescue, Ground Robots, Robot-Terrain Interaction, Autonomy, Traversability.

1 Introduction

Ground robotics systems offer huge potential for utilization in Urban Search And Rescue (USAR) missions. USAR robots may be used as suitable replacement for

J. Hodicky (Ed.): MESAS 2014, LNCS 8906, pp. 231–240, 2014.

Fig. 1. Search and Rescue mission: NIFTi UGV operating in a simulated deployment. Earthquake disaster training field, Vigili del Fuoco Prato, Italy.

rescuers during investigation of poorly accessible locations or dangerous areas, and reduce the risk of injuries in target environments. Fig. 1 gives an example of NIFTi UGV deployment in USAR mission. Advanced robotic platforms have many degrees of freedom (DoF) that have to be controlled in time either manually or autonomously.

While the teleoperated platforms allow their full control, many DoF in such system might lead to unwanted cognitive overload of the operator. It is even more crucial in USAR scenarios. During the missions, the rescuers operate under extreme cognitive load and stress as a consequent of a dangerous environment they are deployed in, and their attention should not be primarily paid for controlling the robot, but reaching the mission goals—such as victim search and rescue or analyzing a risk of secondary disaster. This brings up the question: *How can we decrease the operator's cognitive load when driving the robot?* The answer lies in autonomous behaviors of the robot. Of course, an ideal scenario is to use full autonomy and let robots follow only high level commands, such that: *"Robot, search for the victim!"*, and robot performs all necessary steps for reaching the goal by itself. Artificial intelligence has focused on developing completely autonomous solutions, though systems based on human-robot interaction seem more productive (Murphy [16]).

The amount of interaction and task-sharing can vary depending on the scenario as well as platform construction and capability. If such human-robot cooperation should be productive, it is necessary to find an accepted level of autonomy which will be suitable for the USAR. It is a trade-off between teleoperation and full autonomy.

The aim of this paper is to: (i) summarize related solutions in motion control suitable for Urban Search And Rescue missions and (ii) briefly introduce our solution to operator-accepted autonomy designed for skid-steer NIFTi UGV platform with articulated flippers.

Rest of the paper is organized as follows: Sec. 2 provides survey on motion control and consists of both: (i) survey on related works—see Sec. 2.1 and (ii) our solution to motion control—outlined in Sec. 2. We conclude this work in Sec. 3.

2   Survey on Motion Control

Over the last few years, there were published several motion control approaches whose solutions varied significantly depending on the application (target environment, autonomy level), platform capabilities, on-board computation power, etc. Instead of focusing on comparison of methods outcomes (which is nonsense due to above described differences), we provide comparison of motion control approaches on design level based on the framework depicted in Fig. 2.

Generally, the aim is to find a mapping (policy) between robot state described by sensory measurements and optimal motion control action. Since finding direct mapping might be difficult, it is common to decompose the problem into two parts. While the first part computes the Robot-Terrain Interaction (RTI) based

Table 1. Overview (sorted by alphabetical order of the authors) of the related work on motion control including our solution of AT. Table corresponds to the motion control design framework depicted in Fig. 2. The system outputs are summarized also.

Approach	RTI model	Evaluating	Output
Brunner et al. [1]	KM⊕TM	motion graph	robot conf., heading
Caforo et al. [3]	KM⊕TM	traversability graph	4× flipper angle, heading, velocity
Colas et al. [4]	KM⊕TM	motion graph	4× flipper angle, heading, velocity
Dornhege and Kleiner [5]	KM⊕TM⊕ML	behavior maps	heading, skill
Dube [6]	KM⊕TM	stability index	manipulator and 2×flipper angle.
Ho et al. [8,9]	KM⊕TM⊕ML	traversability map	attitude,chassis conf.
Iagnemma and Dubowsky [10]	KM	traction, power consumption	wheel velocities
Kolter et al. [12]	KM⊕TM	motion graph	desired contact points
Lee et al. [13]	KM⊕TM	potential field	leg movement
Mathur and Pandian[14]	ML	navigability	heading
Nagatani et al.[17,18]	KM⊕TM	NESM stability	4xflipper angle
Ohno et al. [19]	KM	control rules	4xflipper angle., 4xflipper ang. vel., moving velocity
Okada et al.[20,21]	KM⊕TM	NESM stability	4×flipper angle
Papadakis and Pirri [22]	KM⊕TM	ground clearance, robot orientation, angle stability	attitude, 4×flipper angle
Sheh [23]	ML⊕TM	decision trees	atomic action
Zimmermann et.al [26]	ML⊕TM	action-state values	4×flipper angle, 4×flipper stiffness

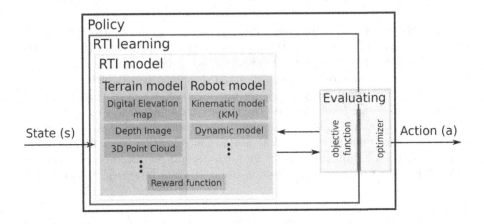

Fig. 2. General wrapped up design of motion control approaches: The mapping between robot *state* coming as input and optimal *action* can be done in several ways: (i) learning direct state-action association—*Policy* (ii) evaluating computed action-state RTI quality and choosing optimal one for control or (iii) using machine learning techniques that predict (sometimes approximated) action-state qualities without explicit RTI computation—*RTI-learning*.

on the current state and candidate action, the second part evaluates every action-state solution and, based on the defined objective function, chooses the most suitable action.

Since that retrieving the real RTI is not feasible due to terrain and/or platform complexity, approximative models of interacting objects are used as a suitable replacement. Their choice depends on both (i) computational power of the platform and (ii) sensor suite.

To overcome the complexity of RTI modeling, terrain models—such as Digital Elevation Map (DEM), depth image, $3D$ point map, etc.—and robot models (kinematic/dynamic) are often used. In this framework, reward function of RL is a joint RTI measure of both terrain and robot—see. Fig. 2.

Tab. 1 do the categorization based on Fig. 2 including the description of expected motion control outcome for given task. The rest of this section is focused on detailed description of approaches given in Tab. 1. First, related work is described in Sec. 2.1. Second, our solution (Zimmermann et al. [26]) is described in Sec. 2.2.

2.1 Related Work

Dube [6] modeled flipper-ground contact points using kinematic robot description and terrain slope to estimate flippers and manipulator poses of PackBot robot in order to enhance its stability in complex terrain. Ohno et al. [19]

aimed at development of a semi-autonomous active control system for the rescue crawler Aladdin. The reasoning about suitable control is made using judgment based rules designed in advance by experience. Such judgment considers flipper-ground contact points determined reactively using both KM and proprioceptive measurements.

Nagatani et al.[18] and Okada et al. [20] focused on development of active flipper control for their tracked robots Kenaf and its second generation Quince. These works resulted in development of shared autonomy system [21] which already had real deployment [17]. RTI is described by means of kinematic model and local terrain shape along the main tracks. Kinematic model and terrain properties are used for initial robot posture computation and then, flipper angles are determined to touch the ground. The optimal control is based on NESM stability criteria [7], which implies minimization of the risk of rolling over.

Papadakis and Pirri [22] introduced RTI model for quantifying the static 3D traversability cost for tracked robot NIFTi in known terrain map. The motion quality is expressed as combination of intrinsic robot characteristics and articulating capabilities (robot orientation and angle stability), in combination with the terrain surface (ground clearance). The approach is limited by the necessity to have the terrain map in prior. But, it is is not often possible from different reasons (i) large scale maps are not available because the environment is unknown, (ii) local maps are not complete due to either limited sensor capabilities or object occlusions.

The latter issue tackled Ho et al. [9] who proposed solution for predicting the complete configuration map from incomplete terrain map for Mawson rover using Gaussian Process Regression (GPR). RTI is modeled by kinematic model in visible areas and then, RTI is interpolated using GPR in occluded parts of the map. Even more not only the rigid terrain assumption, but also with considering deformation caused by robot movement over deformable terrain [8]. Despite of the traversability has been assigned through the estimated robot configuration, it is not further discussed how to turn out complete configuration map into motion control plans.

Kolter et al. [12] used experience based database for assigning the terrain characteristics in the missing regions and used complete RTI description (using kinematic model and terrain shape) for creating the cost map and appropriate motion plan for the quadruped robot LittleDog whose joints are PD controlled.

Limited capabilities of the sensors (not uniform sample distribution) overcame Colas et al. [4] by using distance filter and tensor voting procedure [15] for robust terrain representation that is further used by path planner for NiftiBot. Novel map representation, able to deal with unknown structure (assume earthquake scenario) were introduced by Caforo et al. [3]. The map is build inductively from raw 3D point cloud and at the end provides information about the traversable regions. These are used for generating the motion plan of Nifti UGV robot.

Brunner et al. [1], in order to overcome the exhaustive search in full configuration space of 4 tracked robot, divided terrain map into difficult and easy to traverse regions. Whereas motion planning within easy regions considers partial robot configuration, planning through the difficult areas reflects complete robot configuration. The robot configurations are, in this case, gained through simulation.

Dornhege and Kleiner [5] expressed the traversability by concept of Behavior maps where terrain properties are directly mapped to specific robot skill using Fuzzy rules (considering kinematic constraints on robot climbing capabilities) and Markov Random Field classification. The paths found in Behavior maps can be turned into robot motion plans directly.

Sheh [23] with a four wheel robot Emu used high dimensional terrain description for designing a controller by learning RTI response (posterior probability $p(action|state)$) using decision tree. According to maximum posterior prob., one of eight atomic actions (forward-left-turn, straight- forward-move, etc.) was used for control.

Iagnemma and Dubowsky [10] presented a control methodology based on wheel-ground contact angle (computed from kinematic model and proprioceptive data) for improved traction (on uneven terrain) or reduced power consumption (on relatively flat terrain) for wheeled mobile robot on Mars-like soil.

Mathur and Pandian[14] classified terrain using textural analysis of visual imagery into Navigable and Not navigable regions and used them for planning through the assessed terrain.

Lee et al. [13] learned quadruped robot to negotiate obstacles using hierarchical reinforcement learning. Low level controller used policy search for finding the parameters of potential field serving for moving a certain leg into a goal position while the remaining legs are stationary. In high level controller, learned sum of discounted rewards were used as cost-to-go functions for planning the sequence of foot positions. The reward function used here gave (i) positive rewards for movement towards the goal, (ii) small punishment for the excessive time it took to execute the movement and (iii) very large punishment when the command execution failed.

2.2 Our Approach to Motion Control

We aimed in development of semi-autonomous motion control system for NIFTi UGV skid-steer robot[1] (technical specifications provide Sec. 2.2) whose purpose is to control the flipper configuration (angle and stiffness) autonomously while the motion speed and trajectory will be controlled manually by the operator.

Methodology and Design. Reinforcement learning (RL) technique (survey on RL in robotics provided Kober et al. [11]) was used to learn long-term RTI response, expressed as a (discounted) sum of rewards the robot can get when behaves optimally from the current state onward.

The rewards, for every action-state pair, are expressed as a summation of: (i) too-low pitch and roll reward, (ii) smoothness reward (iii) moving-forward

---

[1] Developed within NIFTi and TRADR projects—see
http://www.tradr-project.eu

Fig. 3. NIFTi UGV climbing capability: Articulated flippers and passive differential increase the platform stability on uneven terrain and enlarge its operability space

reward (iv) user denoted reward (penalty) indicating the success (failure) of the particular maneuver.

We choose to learn action-state value $Q(\mathbf{a}, \mathbf{s})$ representing sum of discounted rewards when taking action $\mathbf{a}$ at state $\mathbf{s}$ and behaving optimally onwards. Then, the optimal control in current state $\mathbf{s}$ can be described as:

$$\mathbf{a}^* = \arg\max_{\mathbf{a}} Q(\mathbf{a}, \mathbf{s}) . \tag{1}$$

The state is described by proprioceptive measurements (torques in flippers, speed, attitude) and by local terrain model created from the data in a robot's neighborhood. Since no global map is required, our approach can be used in USAR missions during the exploration of unknown environments or may support map creation—of course, precise localization is still required [24].

Since handling all possible Q values covering real high dimensional action-state space is not feasible, we adopted following simplifications: (i) finite number of possible morphological adjustments—each configures angle and stiffness per flipper, and (ii) Q values approximation (least-squares fitted Q-iteration with parametric approximation algorithm [2]) caused by high dimensional state $\mathbf{s}$ representation.

As experimentally shown in the challenging outdoor forest environment (see Fig. 4), proposed concept outperformed the manual control in terms of time and smoothness of traversal, which might be seen as a quantitative measure of operator's cognitive load.

Robot Specification. NIFTi UGV (see Fig. 1, 3, 4) consists of two main tracks, equipped with passive differential, and four articulated subtracks (so called flippers). Although such construction has many DoF and accepted autonomy has to be considered, the design has following reasons: (i) increased platform stability on rough or unstructured terrain and (ii) enlarged operability space (climbing up/down the obstacles)—both situations are depicted in Fig. 3. Platform is equipped with SICK LMS-151 range finder, Ladybug 3 omnicam and Xsens MTi-G IMU.

Fig. 4. Autonomous flipper control in challenging outdoor forest environment: The sequence goes from left to right, from top to bottom. In the upper parts of the images, there are real scenes captured by external camera, in the bottom parts there are visualization of digital map used by the robot.

3   Conclusion

In this paper, we provided survey on motion control approaches with focus on robot-terrain representation which helps to reveal advantages or limitations of individual solutions.

Methods based on robot models, often considering only its kinematics, are able to achieve satisfactory good performance using robot-terrain contact properties. Some of them use just proprioceptive data [10], [19], others do combination with exteroceptive data resulting in simple terrain representation [6], [17], [18], [20], [21]. Such autonomy is accepted in an unknown complex terrain or running on platforms suited with poor exteroceptive sensors.

Once the environment is explored, more autonomy is accepted since there is no threat of failure caused by incomplete information and thus motion planning [1], [3], [4], [12], [22] can be executed. Such approaches are more demanding, require reliable suite of sensors, enough computation power onboard, they are more complex which might go against its generalization and robustness.

Since there are a lot of difficulties to model, not only in such a complex USAR scenarios, several simplifications are considered. To overcome these imperfection in modeling, machine learning technique are used to replace the description by the knowledge, as for example [5], [8], [9], [14].

Machine learning can also replace classical feedback control loop design and instead of modeling system dynamics by differential equations, which is difficult in case of nonlinear system, learn the mapping between states and actions from the collected training samples [23], [26]. Widely used is Reinforcement learning [25], since it guarantee optimal behavior from any state onwards [11].

Acknowledgements. The authors were supported as follows: Petr Zuzanek by the project EU-FP7-ICT-609763 TRADR, Karel Zimmermann by the project SGS13/142/OHK3/2T/13 of Czech Technical University in Prague, Vaclav Hlavac by the project TE01020197 of Technology Agency of the Czech Republic.

References

1. Brunner, M., Bruggemann, B., Schulz, D.: Towards autonomously traversing complex obstacles with mobile robots with adjustable chassis. In: 2012 13th International Carpathian Control Conference (ICCC), pp. 63–68 (May 2012)
2. Busoniu, L., Babuska, R., Schutter, B.D., Ernst, D.: Reinforcement Learning and Dynamic Programming Using Function Approximators, 1st edn. CRC Press, Inc., Boca Raton (2010), http://rlbook.busoniu.net/#download
3. Cafaro, B., Gianni, M., Pirri, F., Ruiz, M., Sinha, A.: Terrain traversability in rescue environments. In: 2013 IEEE International Symposium on Safety, Security, and Rescue Robotics (SSRR), pp. 1–8 (October 2013)
4. Colas, F., Mahesh, S., Pomerleau, F., Liu, M., Siegwart, R.: 3d path planning and execution for search and rescue ground robots. In: 2013 IEEE/RSJ International Conference on Intelligent Robots and Systems (IROS), pp. 722–727 (November 2013)
5. Dornhege, C., Kleiner, A.: Behavior maps for online planning of obstacle negotiation and climbing on rough terrain. In: IEEE/RSJ International Conference on Intelligent Robots and Systems, IROS 2007, October 29 - November 2, pp. 3005–3011 (2007)
6. Dube, C.: Modeling the manipulator and flipper pose effects on tip over stability of a tracked mobile manipulator. In: Robotics and Mechatronics Conference (2011)
7. Garcia, E., Estremera, J., de Santos, P.G.: A comparative study of stability margins for walking machines. Robotica 20, 595–606 (2002), http://journals.cambridge.org/article_S0263574702004502
8. Ho, K., Peynot, T., Sukkarieh, S.: A near-to-far non-parametric learning approach for estimating traversability in deformable terrain. In: 2013 IEEE/RSJ International Conference on Intelligent Robots and Systems (IROS), pp. 2827–2833 (November 2013)
9. Ho, K., Peynot, T., Sukkarich, S.: Traversability estimation for a planetary rover via experimental kernel learning in a gaussian process framework. In: Internation Conference on Robotics and Automation (ICRA) (2013)
10. Iagnemma, K., Dubowsky, S.M.: Mobile robot rough-terrain control (rtc) for planetary exploration. In: Proceedings of the 26th ASME Biennial Mechanisms and Robotics Conference, DETC, Baltimore, Maryland, USA, pp. 10–13 (September 2000)
11. Kober, J., Bagnell, A.J., Peters, J.: Reinforcement learning in robotics: A survey. International Journal of Robotics Research (IJRR) 32, 1238–1274 (2013), http://www.ias.tu-darmstadt.de/uploads/Publications/Kober_IJRR_2013.pdf
12. Kolter, J., Youngjun, K., Ng, A.: Stereo vision and terrain modeling for quadruped robots. In: IEEE International Conference on Robotics and Automation, ICRA 2009, pp. 1557–1564 (2009)

13. Lee, H., Shen, Y., Han Yu, C., Singh, G., Ng, A.Y.: Quadruped robot obstacle negotiation via reinforcement learning. In: Proceedings of the IEEE International Conference on Robotics and Automation (ICRA) (2006)

14. Mathur, P., Pandian, K.S.: Terrain classification for traversability analysis for autonomous robot navigation in unknown natural terrain. International Journal of Engineering Science and Technology (IJEST) 4, 38–49 (2012)

15. Medioni, G., Tang, C.K., Lee, M.S.: Tensor voting: Theory and applications. In: Proceedings of RFIA (2000)

16. Murphy, R.R.: Disaster Robotics. MIT Press, Cambridge (2014), http://books.google.cz/books?id=Q9HMAgAAQBAJ

17. Nagatani, K., Kiribayashi, S., Okada, Y., Otake, K., Yoshida, K., Tadokoro, S., Nishimura, T., Yoshida, T., Koyanagi, E., Fukushima, M., Kawatsuma, S.: Emergency response to the nuclear accident at the fukushima daiichi nuclear power plants using mobile rescue robots. Journal of Field Robotics 30(1), 44–63 (2013), http://dx.doi.org/10.1002/rob.21439

18. Nagatani, K., Yamasaki, A., Yoshida, K., Yoshida, T., Koyanagi, E.: Semiautonomous traversal on uneven terrain for a tracked vehicle using autonomous control of active flippers. In: IEEE/RSJ International Conference on Intelligent Robots and Systems, IROS 2008, pp. 2667–2672 (September 2008)

19. Ohno, K., Morimura, S., Tadokoro, S., Koyanagi, E., Yoshida, T.: Semi-autonomous control system of rescue crawler robot having flippers for getting over unknown-steps. In: IEEE/RSJ International Conference on Intelligent Robots and Systems, IROS 2007, October 29 - November 2, vol. 2, pp. 3012–3018 (2007)

20. Okada, Y., Nagatani, K., Yoshida, K.: Semi-autonomous operation of tracked vehicles on rough terrain using autonomous control of active flippers. In: IEEE/RSJ International Conference on Intelligent Robots and Systems, IROS 2009, pp. 2815–2820 (2009)

21. Okada, Y., Nagatani, K., Yoshida, K., Tadokoro, S., Yoshida, T., Koyanagi, E.: Shared autonomy system for tracked vehicles on rough terrain based on continuous three-dimensional terrain scanning. Journal of Field Robotics 28(6), 875–893 (2011), http://dx.doi.org/10.1002/rob.20416

22. Papadakis, P., Pirri, F.: 3d mobility learning and regression of articulated, tracked robotic vehicles by physics-based optimization. In: Workshop on Virtual Reality Interaction and Physical Simulation (VRIPHYS), pp. 147–156 (2012)

23. Sheh, R., Hengst, B., Sammut, C.: Behavioural cloning for driving robots over rough terrain. In: 2011 IEEE/RSJ International Conference on Intelligent Robots and Systems (IROS), pp. 732–737 (September 2011)

24. Simanek, J., Reinstein, M., Kubelka, V.: Evaluation of the ekf-based estimation architectures for data fusion in mobile robots. IEEE/ASME Transactions on Mechatronics PP(99), 1–6 (2014)

25. Sutton, R.S., Barto, A.G.: Introduction to Reinforcement Learning, 1st edn. MIT Press, Cambridge (1998), http://webdocs.cs.ualberta.ca/~sutton/book/ebook/the-book.html

26. Zimmermann, K., Zuzanek, P., Reinstein, M., Hlavac, V.: Adaptive traversability of unknown complex terrain with obstacles for mobile robots. In: International Conference on Robotics and Automation (ICRA) (to appear, 2014)

Harbour Protection Strategies with Multiple Autonomous Marine Vehicles

Gianluca Antonelli[1], Filippo Arrichiello[1,*], Giuseppe Casalino[2],
Stefano Chiaverini[1], Alessandro Marino[3], Enrico Simetti[2], and Sandro Torelli[2]

[1] University of Cassino and Southern Lazio, Cassino, Italy
f.arrichiello@unicas.it
[2] University of Genova, Genova, Italy
[3] University of Salerno, Salerno, Italy

Abstract. This paper presents the ongoing research activities of the Italian Interuniversity Center of Integrated Systems for the Marine Environment, ISME, in the field of harbour protection with autonomous marine vehicles. In particular, two different strategies have been developed in the recent years and have been extensively tested both in numerical simulations and in scale experiments. In the first case, a set of vehicles is positioned around an asset to be protected on the base of an optimization process of two cost functions, namely, the maximization of minimum interception distance and the minimization of maximum interception time. When an intruder is detected, an on-line optimization process selects, among the different vehicles, the one that exhibits the lowest estimated time to the menace. A motion planning algorithm with real-time obstacle avoidance is then used to drive the vehicle toward the intruder. In the second case, a team of vehicles is required to dynamically patrol a certain region by means of a decentralized control approach. The proposed solution is based on the merging of two concepts, the Voronoi tessellations and the Gaussian processes, and it allows robustness with respect to events as temporary communication or vehicle losses. It also exhibits characteristics of flexibility/scalability with respect to the number of team-mates.

Keywords: Autonomous marine vehicles, multi-vehicles system, coordinated control, harbour patrolling.

1 Introduction

The problem of maintaining civilian harbours safeguarded against terroristic attacks, coming from the so-called "blue border" (i.e. the sea-side), is receiving an increasing interest in the recent years. In this context, the use of a team of "protecting" autonomous marine vehicles certainly represents a promising solution for reducing the harbour vulnerability. Indeed, under normal conditions, the vehicles can perform patrolling surveys of the more crucial waterways; instead,

---

* Corresponding author.

J. Hodicky (Ed.): MESAS 2014, LNCS 8906, pp. 241–261, 2014.

whenever a possible "menace" (i.e. an unauthorized vessel or a vessel moving in a suspect way) is detected, one vehicle can be used for "intercepting" the menace, allowing to determine whether the suspect vessel is "hostile" or "friend" without exposing humans directly to threats.

The Italian Interuniversity Center of Integrated Systems for the Marine Environment (ISME) is actively doing research, since more than 15 years, in the field of marine technologies and oceanic engineering. Among the different research interests, harbour protection by mean of multiple autonomous surface and underwater vehicles has recently taken an important role. Two different approaches to solve the latter problem have been developed and will be summarized in this paper.

In a first case, a set of vehicles is *silently* positioned around an asset to be protected. The positioning of the vehicles is obtained as the result of an optimization algorithm. The *optimal* vehicle is then selected in case of detection of an intruder and a real-time motion planning, capable of avoiding obstacles and current traffic, finally drives the vehicle toward the intruder ([16,18]).

In the second case, a team of vehicles is required to patrol a certain region, i.e., to move *around* while properly collecting information. Patrolling is achieved with a sub-optimal solution satisfying the severe constraints we face in such a mission. Surface ([4], [13]) as well as underwater scenario ([12]) have been considered.

The above algorithms have been achieved in the framework of European FP7 projects such as Co3AUVs ([5]) and they have been tested via extensive numerical simulation as well as via experiments with marine vehicles.

2   Interception of Suspect Vessels with ASVs

Experiments with Autonomous Surface Vehicles (ASVs) are usually performed in open sea or in waterways in the absence of other unknown moving vessels. When dealing with harbour protection, however, the scenario is far different from those above and several crucial issues arise: the ship traffic is intense and the operations of tourist or merchant ships cannot be delayed or affected anyway by the security vehicles. Therefore the manoeuvres of ASVs must not perturb at all the normal harbour activities. Furthermore, there is a concrete risk of collision with other vessels, with consequent risks of personal injuries and property damages. Thus, the ASVs have to be provided with good path-following capabilities, since they need to follow a reference path with a certain accuracy. Moreover, they need reliable emergency sensory devices enabling a prompt detection of any incipient obstacle, and suitable techniques for implementing reactive obstacle avoidance capabilities, in case an unforeseen obstacle is actually detected.

In this perspective, DIST (University of Genova, Italy) and Selex Sistemi Integrati (a Finmeccanica Company, Italy), one of the international leading players in providing large systems for security and defence, are cooperating within an on-going joint research project, on the realization of the so-called Swarm Management Unit (SMU), a tool conceived for supervising the operations of a team

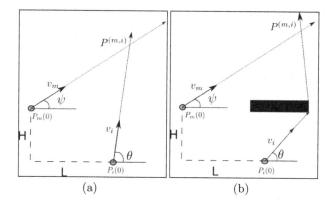

Fig. 1. The interception problem: (a) without obstacles (b) with an obstacle

of ASVs performing (semi-)autonomous surveillance activities within civilian harbours. Details on the SMU project are provided in [6,17], together with a description of the levels of interaction between the SMU and the operator in charge of monitoring the ASVs activities.

Here we focuses on the problem of intercepting a detected menace before it could reach a particular "asset" (i.e. a crucial site to be maintained safeguarded) and of how to determine a-priori the better nominal positioning of the "interceptors" ASVs in order to increase their chances of success.

2.1 On-line Selection of the Interceptor

Once a menace is detected, the key factor for a prompt reaction is time. Therefore the better ASV for the interception is the one which is predicted to reach the menace in the shortest possible time. In the considered harbour scenario, all the other vessels in the area represent fixed or moving obstacles which have to be avoided by the interceptor ASV; as a consequence, for every ASV, the computation of its predicted time of interception is strictly related with the identification of its minimum-time path to reach the menace, which in turn depends on the contingent traffic situation.

A detailed description of the motion planner has been presented in [6,17] and only its basic results are here reported for the reader's convenience. At first, the simplified problem depicted in Fig. 1 is first considered; i.e., given a single ASV, say the i-th, moving at its maximum speed v_i, find (if any) the ASV heading angle θ enabling the interception of a menace m, starting from a generic position $P_m = (-L, H)$ w.r.t. the ASV and moving at a constant speed v_m with a constant heading angle ψ.

By defining the motion of the i-th ASV as:

$$P_i(t) \triangleq \begin{bmatrix} x_i(t) \\ y_i(t) \end{bmatrix} = \begin{bmatrix} v_i cos(\theta)t \\ v_i sin(\theta)t \end{bmatrix} \tag{1}$$

and the motion of the menace as

$$P_m(t) \triangleq \begin{bmatrix} x_m(t) \\ y_m(t) \end{bmatrix} = \begin{bmatrix} v_m cos(\psi)t - L \\ v_m sin(\psi)t + H \end{bmatrix} \tag{2}$$

if no obstacles are located between the menace and the ASV (Fig. 1.a), the angle θ can be calculated as:

$$\theta = asin\left(\frac{v_m}{v_i} sin(\psi + \phi)\right) - \phi \tag{3}$$

clearly subject to

$$-1 \leq \frac{v_m}{v_i} sin(\psi + \phi) \leq 1 \tag{4}$$

where $\phi \triangleq arctan(-H/-L)$.

In case solution (3) exists, given the angle θ, the time needed for the interception can be calculated as:

$$t^{(m,i)} = \frac{-L}{v_i cos(\theta) - v_m cos(\psi)}, \quad L \neq 0 \tag{5}$$

while the point of the interception is obtained as:

$$P^{(m,i)} \triangleq \begin{bmatrix} P_x^{(m,i)} \\ P_y^{(m,i)} \end{bmatrix} = \begin{bmatrix} v_i cos(\theta)t^{(m,i)} \\ v_i sin(\theta)t^{(m,i)} \end{bmatrix} \tag{6}$$

where the notation $(\cdot)^{(m,i)}$ means that the quantity $(\cdot)$ refers to the i-th vehicle intercepting the menace m.

The more realistic situation where at least one obstacle (be it a static or a moving one) prevents the ASV from moving on a straight line is sketched in Fig. 1.b.

By now moving back the attention to the original problem of on-line selecting the better interceptor, consider Fig. 2, representing a situation where a menace is discovered at point P_m and is moving towards an asset, located at point $P_a = (x_a, y_a)$. A given number of vehicles $i = 1, \cdots, N$ are located in their respective positions P_i. As soon as the menace is detected, for every ASV, the predicted point of interception $P^{(m,i)}$ and related instant of interception $t^{(m,i)}$ is first of all calculated by the motion planner, as explained before. The problem of selecting the most suitable vehicle can then be simply stated as the following minimization problem:

$$\arg\min_i t^{(m,i)} \tag{7}$$

which can be easily on-line solved, given the availability of all the $t^{(m,i)}$ terms.

2.2   Off-line Optimization of the ASVs Position

The problem of better positioning the ASVs for achieving adequate levels of protection can be considered as a special instance of the so-called spatial resource-allocation problem, which has been studied for many years and has registered

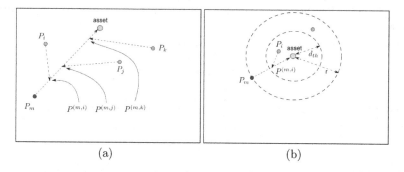

(a)   (b)

Fig. 2. (a) Schema of the intercept problem (b) with a minimum distance of interception required

interesting results in particular in the field of fixed or mobile sensing networks (see, among the others, [9], [7] and references therein indicated). The proposed solution is based on the following two criteria. First of all, the ASVs must be in the condition of *always* intercepting *any* menace before it can reach a certain security distance from the asset. As shown in the following, the adoption of such a primary criterion, other than reducing the chances of the menace to harm the asset, provides, as a by-product, an indication on the minimum number of "asset-protector" ASVs. All the (eventually available) other ASVs can then be employed for the secondary criterion, here stated in terms of reducing the maximum interception time.

Preventing Menaces from Getting Too Close to the Asset. The problem of guaranteeing that *any* menace can be *always* intercepted, before it gets too close to the asset, can be translated into a worst-case-scenario optimization problem. Indeed it has to be granted that, even if the menace is detected in the closest possible position to the asset (i.e. at a distance r), the ASVs are always in the condition of intercepting it on time (i.e. before the menace reaches a given security distance $d_{th} < r$, see Fig. 2b).

Let $P \triangleq \{P_1, \cdots, P_N\}$ denote the set of initial positions of a team of N ASVs, while be P_m the initial position of a detected menace m. For any given set of initial conditions (P_m, P), the distance between the interception point related to the i-th ASV and the asset can be easily computed as follows:

$$d_i(P_m, P) \triangleq \| P^{(m,i)} - P_a \| \tag{8}$$

It then follows that, for any given (P_m, P), the most suitable ASV for the interception is selected as:

$$i^o = \arg \max_{i | P_m, P} d_i(P_m, P) \tag{9}$$

whose corresponding distance between the interception point and the asset is

$$D(P_m, P) \triangleq \max_{i | P_m, P} d_i(P_m, P) \tag{10}$$

By now solving the above problem for any possible P_m (while still maintaining fixed the set P), the worst-case-scenario, i.e. the point P_m leading to the closest to the asset interception point, can be calculated as:

$$D_w(P) \triangleq \min_{P_m|P} D(P_m, P) \tag{11}$$

By finally letting the optimization variable P vary, the optimal positions of the ASVs are obtained as:

$$P^o \triangleq \arg\max_P D_w(P) \tag{12}$$

By combining all the above relationships, the following formulation of the original optimization problem is obtained:

$$P^o = \arg\max_P \left\{ \min_{P_m} \left[\max_i \left(\| P^{(m,i)} - P_a \| \right) \right] \right\} \tag{13}$$

whose corresponding distance from the interception point and the asset in the worst-case-scenario is clearly:

$$D^o = \max_P \left\{ \min_{P_m} \left[\max_i \left(\| P^{(m,i)} - P_a \| \right) \right] \right\} \tag{14}$$

In case D^o results lower than d_{th}, it means that the considered amount of ASVs is not sufficient to always guarantee the fulfillment of the security threshold distance, and a simple algorithm for determining the minimum number of ASVs required for protecting the asset can be applied solving the problem (14) for an increasing number of vehicles k.

Minimizing the Maximum Interception Time. In case the number of available vehicles N is greater than the number k of vehicles necessary to meet the required minimum distance of interception from the asset, the remaining $N - k$ ASVs can be exploited to solve another kind of optimization problem: minimizing the maximum interception time.

To better approach the problem, it is convenient to split the set of ASVs into two subsets: the first k vehicles with a fixed optimal positioning, as determined by the previous problem; and the remaining $N - k$ ones, whose set of positions $\hat{P} \triangleq \{P_{k+1}, \cdots, P_N\}$ is the subject of the here considered secondary optimization problem.

With these premises, for any given initial conditions (P_m, P), the most suitable ASV for the interception is now the one with the lowest interception time, that is:

$$i^o \triangleq \arg\min_{i|P_m,P} t^{(m,i)} \tag{15}$$

whose corresponding interception time is

$$T(P_m, P) \triangleq \min_{i|P_m,P} t^{(m,i)} \tag{16}$$

Then, by again considering the menace in all the allowed positions, the worst-case-scenario can be found as:

$$T_w(P) \triangleq \max_{P_m|P} T(P_m, P) \qquad (17)$$

Therefore the optimal positions of the extra-ASVs can be found by minimizing the time of interception in the worst-case-scenario; that is:

$$\hat{P}^o \triangleq \arg\min_{\hat{P}} T_w(P) \qquad (18)$$

Finally note that, since problem (17) considers all the possible P_m points, the extra ASVs are spread out, the farther away from the asset, the bigger the considered area is. The following more convenient formulation of problem (17) can therefore be made, by introducing a proper weighting function $0 \le W(P_m) \le 1$ expressing the "probability of detection" of a menace in any particular point:

$$T_w(P) \triangleq \max_{P_m|P} W(P_m) T(P_m, P) \qquad (19)$$

In this way the points at the boundaries of the considered area could have a very low weight, as those inside the circle of radius r should have a zero weight.

By also considering the weighting function, the final formulation of the secondary optimization problem becomes:

$$\hat{P}^o = \arg\min_{\hat{P}} \left\{ \max_{P_m} \left[W(P_m) \min_i t^{(m,i)} \right] \right\} \qquad (20)$$

2.3   Simulative Results

Here we presents the results obtained when the scenario of Fig. 3 is used as area of operation. In the following pictures, the dark dot represents the asset to protect, the squares with black frame represent the position of the ASVs, while the smaller dots instead indicate that if a menace appears in such position.Moreover, the smaller circumference around the asset is a graphical representation of the minimum safety distance d_{th}, while the bigger one represent the minimum distance of detection r. Figures 4a and 4b show the paths of the ASVs when intercepting the candidate menace, which is represented with a circle.

The first simulation is depicted in Fig. 5. Between the two cases, only the detection distance r has been changed. When r is increased, the position of the ASVs can be further away from the asset, as r guarantees that the first detection of the menace cannot occur at ranges closer than it. Moreover, as it can be clearly seen, the ASVs are chosen to guard the entry points to the inner harbour area, as these points are choke points, where a surface menace must pass through if it wants to reach the asset.

The second simulation, presented through Fig. 6, shows what happens if the minimum required interception distance is increased. This increase in the required performance of the system imposes that two vehicles are now necessary to satisfy the first optimization problem. Such change will obviously decrease the performance of the system w.r.t. the secondary optimization problem.

Fig. 3. Dark star: asset; Squares: ASV; Smaller circle: d_{th}; Bigger circle: r

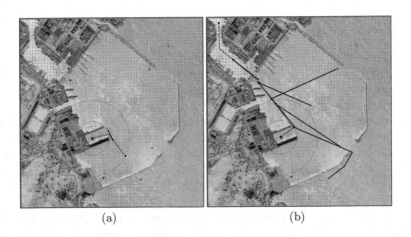

(a)   (b)

Fig. 4. Different computed paths for the intercepting vehicles. (a) as the menace is detected just at the minimum distance r, the selected vehicle intercepts it before the minimum required distance d_{th}. (b) menace is detected far away (top left corner) and thus multiple vehicles can intercept it.

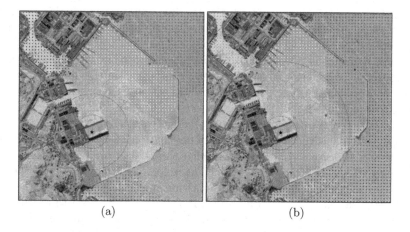

(a)   (b)

Fig. 5. Comparison by changing the detection distance r (a) $r = 400$, $d_{worst} = 214$, $t_{worst} = 22.93$, (b) $r = 750$, $d_{worst} = 373$, $t_{worst} = 22.62$

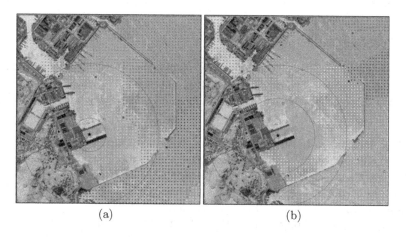

(a)   (b)

Fig. 6. Comparison by changing the minimum required interception distance d_{th} (a) $d_{th} = 178$, $d_{worst} = 374$, $t_{worst} = 20.64$, (b) $d_{th} = 400$, $d_{worst} = 460$, $t_{worst} = 20$

3   Dynamic Patrolling

This section deals with the problem of dynamic patrolling with a team of marine vehicles. The patrolling task consists in traveling around an area, at regular intervals, in order to protect or supervise it [1]. Patrolling, thus, involves repeatedly visiting key locations within the working area, to assess environmental state with respect the presence of eventual intruders or any unexpected event. Despite of the fact that the patrolling tasks have been widely faced in literature from a theoretical point of view, only a few experiments have been carried out, especially in marine environment, without simplistic assumptions due to the existing technical problems. Indeed, the marine environment exhibits an additional challenge due to the extremely harsh conditions in which the vehicles need to operate.

For this reason, the problem at hand as been afforded at DIEI (University of Cassino, Italy) considering a list of realistic constraints in the development of a motion control solution for a team of autonomous vehicle that will be detailed in the following.

To the purpose, the developed strategy merges together two useful mathematical tools: Gaussian Processes and Voronoi tessellations. Given acquired samples, the Gaussian Processes [15] allow to predict the field at unknown location and to compute the uncertainty involved in that prediction [10]. Gaussian Processes allow us to address in the proposed algorithm in an elegant fashion the time and space variability, i.e., both a forgetting factor and the need to patrol more often certain regions. The Voronoi tessellations represents a subdivision of a set given a finite number of points [8,14]. One of their main feature is that they can be calculated in a distributed way. Each vehicle, thus, is able to compute its Voronoi cell relying only on its exteroceptive sensors and/or communication capabilities.

3.1   Problem Description

The problem at hand is characterized by challenging theoretical as well as implementation issues. Strongly motivated by the need to perform experimental validation of the derived algorithm, the follwing constraints have been considered:

- Coordination. Robotic missions such as the one addressed in this paper are more efficient by means of a coordinated, multi-robot strategy;
- Decentralization. One central computational unit represents a weak point for a multi-robot algorithm. This is particularly significant when a security application, such as patrolling, is considered;
- Robustness. When robots move around in the real world, they are necessarily confronted with a number of unexpected events that may seriously jeopardize the success of their missions. It is not realistic to design a multi-robot algorithm that is not *robust*, in a wide sense, with respect to the possibility that one or more robots simply stop functioning, or hold in place, or that the communication among them may experience temporary black outs;
- Scalability. As a scalability constrain we want that the computational burden associated to each robot does not change with the number of robots;
- Communications. Different communication technologies (e.g. for surface or underwater communication) come with different bandwidths and ranges that directly impact on the performance achievable with multiple vehicle patrolling algorithms. A reliable algorithm must be customizable with respect to the available communication bandwidth;
- Real-time. Each robot needs to take *decision* in real-time, thus preventing the use of off-line planning algorithms;

– In view of practical implementation, additional features such as, for example, obstacle avoidance policies, need to be considered.

These constraints are fundamental for experiments in a real scenario and, differently form other solutions, are naturally taken into account by the designed solution.

We now describe the patrolling problem addressed in this paper: consider a region $\mathcal{A} \in \mathbb{R}^l$, $l = 2, 3$ and a function $y = f(\boldsymbol{x}, t)$, $\boldsymbol{x} \in \mathcal{A}$, with $f : \mathbb{R}^l \times [0, \infty) \to \mathbb{R}_{0+}$, where f is application dependent. For example, in the case of patrolling/security applications y represents the level of safety of the environment at point $\boldsymbol{x}$ and at time t.

The function f exhibits a spatial correlation that is mainly affected by the nature of the underlying phenomenon under study and/or the sensor suite used. It is also important to stress that the function may be time-varying, at a scale that once again is determined by the phenomenon under investigation.

Our main goal is to develop a strategy to estimate the function f by taking appropriate measurements using robots equipped with sensor suites. In what follows, we let N_r denote the number of robots and $x_{r,i}(t) \in \mathbb{R}^l$, $i = 1, 2, \ldots, Nr$ the position of robot i at time t. In addition, each robot is assumed to be able to sense or receive the position of some neighbors, where the term neighbor indicates a robot $\boldsymbol{x}_{r,j}$ that is close to $\boldsymbol{x}_{r,i}$ with respect to a certain metric (for example the Euclidean distance).

The patrolling task shares several aspects with sampling. In particular, at given instant the knowledge about the safety status of a location in the area depends on the team configuration and, therefore, on the robots' positions $\boldsymbol{x}_{r,i}$, $\forall i = 1, 2, \ldots, N_r$. Thus, given a robot with position $\boldsymbol{x}_{r,i}$, it is possible to state whether this position is safe or not based on the value of function f at this point; it can be argued that this information can be used to infer the status at other locations in the neighbourhood (*spatial* dependence). An example is represented by an intruder or a toxic substance spill at location $x_{r,i}$. Finally, it can be also argued that in a dynamic scenario, a location that has been marked as safe (because it was visited in the past) but has not been visited by any of the patrolling robots for a certain amount of time should no longer be considered as safe; instead, a high uncertainty should be associated to its status. Thus, high uncertainty must be associated not only to those cells that have remained unvisited but also to the cells that were visited but long back in time (*time* dependence). An example is represented by a moving intruder, a moving oil spill, or a changing temperature field. The aim is, therefore, to estimate the map function $f(\boldsymbol{x}, t)$ by reducing the uncertainty in its knowledge; namely, by bringing the robots toward those locations characterized by a high degree of uncertainty. It is assumed that a robot will be able to measure the degree of safety, f, of a location by means of some sensor as, for example, a vision sensor. Moreover, it should be clear that the developed strategy is suitable both for patrolling and sampling as shown in [4]. In addition, the use of multi-robot systems requires a coordination mechanism among robots. Specifically a Voronoi tessellation is used for both distributing the calculus of the function f and coordinating the motion of robots. A Gaussian process strategy is, instead, used to predict function f.

3.2   The Voronoi Partition

Voronoi partitions (or diagrams) are subdivisions of a set $\mathcal{D}$ characterized by a metric with respect to a finite number of seed points belonging to that set.

Assuming that at the current time t the seed points are the robots' positions $\{\boldsymbol{x}_{r,1}, \boldsymbol{x}_{r,2}, \ldots, \boldsymbol{x}_{r,N_r}\}$, the corresponding N_r Voronoi cells, $Vor(\boldsymbol{x}_{r,i})$, $i = 1, 2, \ldots, N_r$ are given by

$$Vor(\boldsymbol{x}_{r,i}) = \{\boldsymbol{x} \in \mathcal{D} \quad | \quad \|\boldsymbol{x} - \boldsymbol{x}_{r,i}\| \leq \|\boldsymbol{x} - \boldsymbol{x}_{r,j}\|, \, \forall j\}.$$

The union of the Voronoi cells gives back the entire set and the intersection of two cells is always empty. The most important property of the Voroni tool for the use on decentralized robotics is that each robot can compute its own cell by applying a *local* algorithm, i.e., by simply knowing its position and the *neighbors'* positions, either by direct sensing or by communication. An example is reported in Figure 7 where the Voronoi tessellation of a three-dimensional set has been generated according to three randomly generated seed points. Further details on the Voronoi-based theory and its applications can be found in [8] or [14].

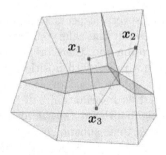

Fig. 7. Example of a Voronoi partition for 3 points in a 3D set

3.3   The Gaussian Processes

A Gaussian process is a collection of random variables, any finite number of which have a joint Gaussian distribution. One of the key features of Gaussian Processes is their potential to yield methods to predict the value of a function at any location, given a set of previously collected observations (either in space or in time), with an explicit representation of the uncertainty of that prediction. For this reason, they will be used as a means to estimate the field f. What relates one observation to another in such cases is just the covariance function. In what follows we summarize the key facts about Gaussian Processes needed to understand the method that we propose. A comprehensive exposition of the theory can be found in [15].

We view at function $f(\boldsymbol{x}, t)$ as a zero-mean spatio-temporal Gaussian Process

$$f(\boldsymbol{x}) \sim \mathcal{GP}(0, \mathcal{K}(\boldsymbol{x}_1, t_1; \boldsymbol{x}_2, t_2) \tag{21}$$

where $\mathcal{K}(\boldsymbol{x}_1, t_1; \boldsymbol{x}_2, t_2)$ is the covariance function. We will assume that the covariance function $\mathcal{K}$ is generically defined as

$$\mathcal{K}(\boldsymbol{x}_1, t_1; \boldsymbol{x}_2, t_2) = C(\|\boldsymbol{x}_2 - \boldsymbol{x}_1\|, |t_2 - t_1|) \tag{22}$$

with $C : \mathbb{R}_0^+ \times \mathbb{R}_0^+ \to \mathbb{R}^+$. Notice that both space and time are taken into account to handle also the non stationary case. For the sake of simplicity, in equation (22) we assume that the process is homogeneous, second order stationary and isotropic, which basically implies that the covariance only depends on the distance between two generic points $\boldsymbol{x}_1$ and $\boldsymbol{x}_2$ and on the absolute value of the time difference $t_2 - t_1$.

Given the set $S = \{(\boldsymbol{x}_1, t_1), (\boldsymbol{x}_2, t_2), \dots, (\boldsymbol{x}_n, t_n)\}$ made of pair of locations $\boldsymbol{x}_i \in \mathcal{A}$ and instants of time t_i and the corresponding vector of observation $\boldsymbol{y} \in \mathbb{R}^n$, the symbol $\Sigma_S \in \mathbb{R}^{n \times n}$ represents the symmetric non-negative covariance matrix whose elements (i, j) is $\mathcal{K}(\boldsymbol{x}_i, t_i; \boldsymbol{x}_j, t_j)$.

Moreover, given a single element $(\boldsymbol{x}^*, t)$ and the set S, $\boldsymbol{\sigma}_{Sx}(\boldsymbol{x}^*, t) \in \mathbb{R}^n$ is a column vector whose i-th element is $\mathcal{K}(\boldsymbol{x}^*, t; \boldsymbol{x}_j, t_j)$.

The objective is to predict $y^* = f(\boldsymbol{x}^*, t)$ at the generic location $\boldsymbol{x}^*$ and at the current time instant t based on the vector of observations $\boldsymbol{y}$. In the case of a multivariate normal distribution over a set S of random variables associated with n pairs of positions and time instants, the posterior distribution of y^* is characterized by a normal distribution $y^* | \boldsymbol{y} \sim \mathcal{N}(\hat{\mu}, \hat{\Sigma})$ with [15]:

$$\hat{\mu} = \boldsymbol{\sigma}_{Sx}(\boldsymbol{x}, t)^{\mathrm{T}} \boldsymbol{\Sigma}_S^{-1} \boldsymbol{y} \tag{23}$$

$$\hat{\Sigma} = \mathcal{K}(\boldsymbol{x}^*, t; \boldsymbol{x}^*, t) - \boldsymbol{\sigma}_{Sx}(\boldsymbol{x}^*, t)^{\mathrm{T}} \boldsymbol{\Sigma}_S^{-1} \boldsymbol{\sigma}_{Sx}(\boldsymbol{x}^*, t). \tag{24}$$

The best estimate of y^* is given by (23) and the uncertainty of the estimation is captured by its variance, described in (24). Thus, while the predicted value is useful for establishing the most likely appearance of the function f based on the available sensor data, it can also be misleading if considered in isolation. One of the key advantages of Gaussian Processes is, therefore, the possibility to compute the variance of each prediction.

In the considered problem, the ith robot measures the status of location $\boldsymbol{x}$ using dedicated sensors. We assume that the measurement made by robot i at position $\boldsymbol{x}$ and time t is given by

$$y = f(\boldsymbol{x}, t) + w_i,$$

where $w_i \sim \mathcal{N}(0, \sigma_i)$ is a white noise Gaussian Process with zero mean and standard deviation σ_i. For simplicity, we assume that $w_i = w \sim \mathcal{N}(0, \sigma)$, i.e., the robots are equipped with identical sensors. In this case, equation (23) becomes

$$\hat{\mu} = \boldsymbol{\Sigma}_{Sx}^{\mathrm{T}} \left(\boldsymbol{\Sigma}_S + \sigma^2 \boldsymbol{I} \right)^{-1} \boldsymbol{y} \tag{25a}$$

$$\hat{\Sigma} = \mathcal{K}(\boldsymbol{x}, t; \boldsymbol{x}, t) - \boldsymbol{\sigma}_{Sx}(\boldsymbol{x}, t)^{\mathrm{T}} \left(\boldsymbol{\Sigma}_S + \sigma^2 \boldsymbol{I}\right)^{-1} \boldsymbol{\sigma}_{Sx}, \tag{25b}$$

where $\boldsymbol{I}$ is the identity matrix of proper dimensions.

In the above equations, the matrices $\boldsymbol{\Sigma}_S$ and $\boldsymbol{\sigma}_{Sx}$ are completely defined once the function C in equation (22) has been specified. According to [15] and [19], one possible choice for this function is the Square Exponential Covariance Function:

$$C(\|\boldsymbol{x}_2 - \boldsymbol{x}_1\|, |t_2 - t_1|) = \phi^2 e^{-\dfrac{\|\boldsymbol{x}_2 - \boldsymbol{x}_1\|^2}{2\tau_s^2} - \dfrac{(t_2 - t_1)^2}{2\tau_t^2}}, \tag{26}$$

where ϕ is a weighting scalar parameter that will be selected to be unitary and the parameters τ_s and τ_t are positive scalars used to affect the space and time scales, respectively. In addition, it is worth noticing that the choice in equation (26) refers to isotropic domains and known constant τ_s and τ_t.

3.4   Application to the Patrolling Mission

From equation (24), the variance of the estimation at position $\boldsymbol{x}$ given the already acquired samples and the current time t takes the form

$$\hat{\Sigma}(\boldsymbol{x}) = C(0, 0) - \boldsymbol{\sigma}_{Sx}^{\mathrm{T}} \boldsymbol{\Sigma}_S^{-1} \boldsymbol{\sigma}_{Sx}. \tag{27}$$

It turns out that minimizing the uncertainty, which corresponds to minimizing the positive definite right-hand side of equation (27), is the same as maximizing (given the available degrees of freedom) the function

$$\xi_S(\boldsymbol{x}) = \boldsymbol{\sigma}_{Sx}^{\mathrm{T}} \boldsymbol{\Sigma}_S^{-1} \boldsymbol{\sigma}_{Sx}. \tag{28}$$

Note also that due to the time dependency of the covariance function in (26), a point that has been visited too far in the past (with respect to the time parameter τ_t) is candidate to be visited again. This feature is exploited by assigning proper time constants according to the applications.

It is interesting to reproduce graphically equation (28) for some case studies. In the simple case we consider, the region of interest is a planar square with unitary length. Three location have been visited, $S = \{(\boldsymbol{x}_1, t_1), (\boldsymbol{x}_2, t_2), (\boldsymbol{x}_3, t_3)\}$, with $\boldsymbol{x}_1 = \begin{bmatrix} 0 & 0 \end{bmatrix}^{\mathrm{T}}$, $\boldsymbol{x}_2 = \begin{bmatrix} 1 & 0 \end{bmatrix}^{\mathrm{T}}$, and $\boldsymbol{x}_3 = \begin{bmatrix} 0.5 & 1 \end{bmatrix}^{\mathrm{T}}$ at time t_1, t_2 and t_3, respectively.

- First example (Figure 8 (top left)): $t_1 = t_2 = t_3 = 0$, current time $t = 0$, $\tau_s = 0.5$, $\tau_t = 8$.
- Second example (Figure 8 (top right)): $t_1 = t_2 = t_3 = 0$, current time $t = 0$, $\tau_s = 0.2$, $\tau_t = 8$.
- Third example (Figure 8 (bottom)): $t_1 = 0$, $t_2 = 7$, $t_3 = 10$, current time $t = 10$, $\tau_s = 0.5$, $\tau_t = 8$.

In the classical sampling task as in [11,19,20] the field to sample is related to a physical variable such as temperature, salinity, etc.; the *hyper-parameters*, ϕ, τ_s, τ_t, are usually identified or learned by training. On the other hand, in the

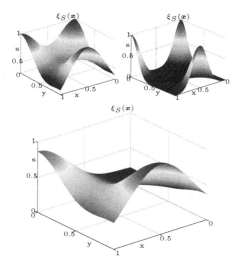

Fig. 8. Graph of the function (28). Top left: first example. Top right: second example. Bottom: third example.

case of patrolling a different point of view can be used: the hyper-parameters, in particular the constant τ_s and τ_t, are not related to any physical phenomenon. On the contrary, they are decided by the user and, then, known beforehand by the robots. Their value may be chosen so as to confer to the system specific behaviors. As examples of the above concept, let us consider the following cases:

- a low value of the the the parameter τ_s in equation (26) implies low *space* correlation between different locations. On the contrary, a larger value implies high correlation between even far locations. Such a feature may be used to take into account the range of robot' sensors. In addition, τ_s can be function of the location (i.e., $\tau_s = \tau_s(\boldsymbol{x})$); such a feature can be useful, e.g., for modeling different visibility conditions;
- a low value of the parameter τ_t in equation (26) implies low *time* correlation between cells. This means that the patrolling team needs to visit each position more frequently. Also in this case, the τ_t can be functions of the location (i.e., $\tau_t = \tau_t(\boldsymbol{x})$), in order to take into account the case of environments where some locations are more exposed to unexpected events than others (eg., in an harbor patrolling scenario it may be required to visit more frequently the harbour entry).
- by setting $\tau_t = \infty$ a static field is obtained as in the case of a coverage mission.

3.5 Proposed Coordination Strategy

Figure 9 illustrates the proposed control architecture for a single robot. At the top level, the planner is in charge of deciding the robot trajectory. At the lower level, the Null-Space-based-Behavioral (NSB) control approach allows following reference trajectory provided by the upper level, while properly handling unexpected events such as the presence of obstacles. The NSB has been widely used by some of the authors and its description will not be given here to avoid repetion; the interested reader will find in [2], [3], the details of this strategy and its properties.

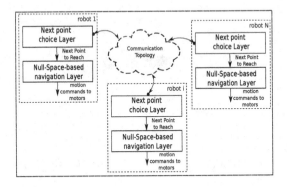

Fig. 9. Control architecture

3.6   The Top Level: Algorithm Description

The top layer in Figure 9 represents the *core* of the proposed algorithm, i.e., the block in charge of computing the next point to be visited by each robot. As described in the previous Sections, our objective is the maximization of the function $\xi_S(x)$ expressed by equation (28). To this effect, a partition of the area $\mathcal{A}$ according to the Voronoi tessellations is computed, and each robot performs such a maximization in its own cell. The strategy designed for each robot is given as: **Algorithm**
loop

1. exchange data with the neighbors
2. build its own cell: $Vor(x_{r,i})$
3. select next point $\overline{x}_i$ in its own Voronoi cell, and move to that point
4. send $\overline{x}_i$ to the NSB layer

end loop
   To select the next point to, we propose the following strategy. Let $x = h(s) = x_{r,i} + (x_u - x_{r,i})s$ be a parametrization of the line segment joining the actual position $x_{r,i}$ of the robot and a generic point $x_u \in S_u$, with $s \in [0, 1]$; the next target in S_u is determined by

$$\overline{x}_i = \min_{x_u \in S_u} \frac{\int_0^1 \xi_S(h(s))ds}{\|x_{r,i} - x_u\|}. \tag{29}$$

The heuristics behind the strategy (29) is that, among the unvisited points in the set S_u, the one characterized by the most unvisited path (normalized by the path length) is chosen. Another possible strategy would be to simply drive the robot toward the point of global minimum of $\xi_S(x)$ inside its Voronoi cell, that is, compute

$$\overline{x}_i = \min_{x \in Vor(x_{r,i})} \xi_S(x). \tag{30}$$

As an example, Figure 10 shows a comparison between the strategy in (29) and (30) in a $50\,\text{m} \times 100\,\text{m}$ rectangular environment with three vehicles. The space (τ_s) and time (τ_t) constants in equation (26) are $4.7\,\text{m}$ and $400\,\text{s}$, respectively. In particular, the performance index adopted is represented by the integral of $\xi_S(x)$ over the environment normalized by its area. It is worth noticing that, as $\xi_S(x) \in [0, 1]$, the considered index belongs to the same interval. Because of the meaning of function $\xi_S(x)$,

- a performance index equal to 1 means that the field is completely known;
- a performance index equal to 0 means that the field is completely unknown;
- a performance index equal to 1 can be asymptotically reached only in the case of static fields;
- lower values of the time constant τ_t imply lower values of the index at steady-state.

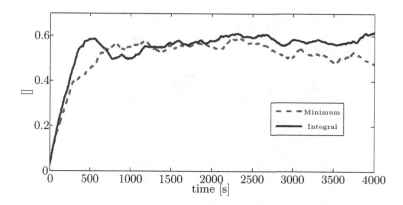

Fig. 10. Normalized integral of function $\xi_S(x)$ in a comparison between strategy in equation (29) (continuous line) and equation (30) (dashed line)

3.7 Experimental Results

Due to lack of space, only the surface experiments will be briefly reported, the underwater implementation is described in [12]. Video of the underwater as well as the surface experiments can be downloaded from
`webuser.unicas.it/lai/robotica/video.html`.

Fig. 11. The three Medusa surface robots setup (the red, black and yellow robots).

The *surface* experiments were performed in July 2011 at the Parque Expo site, Lisbon, PT, using three Medusa autonomous surface robots designed and built by the marine robotics team of IST/ISR (Instituto Superior Técnico/Institute for Systems and Robotics) and shown in Figure 11 (red, black, and yellow robots).

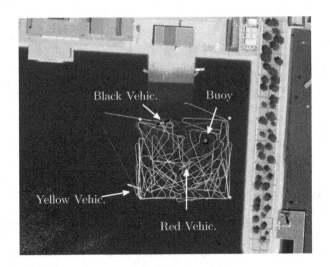

Fig. 12. The map of the Parque Expo site in Lisbon with the paths described by the robots in a typical experiment. The robots (red, black and yellow) are restricted to move in a 60 m×70 m rectangular environment.

Figure 12 shows the map of the site, with the robots moving in a 60 m×70 m rectangular map. An obstacle consisting of a buoy is placed inside the patrolling region (the dot in Figure 12). The position of the buoy is fixed and known in advance by the robots. The maximum robots speed was limited to 0.7 m/s. In what follows, we summarize the results of an experiment that run for approximately 1 hour.

The robots exchanged information via WI-FI network. The τ_s and τ_t parameters were set to 3.7 m and 200 s, respectively; the constant θ in Section 3.6 was set to 0.5.

In Figure 13, the sequence of steps performed by the robots is shown. In each frame, on the left are shown the Voronoi cells with the robots and the current targets (big bullets), while, on the right, the plot of function (28) is shown. The red color is representative of higher values of the function while the blue color of lower ones. Focusing the attention on the black robot, the following steps are shown:

1. the robot moves toward the current target as generated by the algorithm described in Section 3.5,
2. the robot reaches the current target,
3. the robot chooses the next target inside its own Voronoi cell,
4. the robot moves toward the new target.

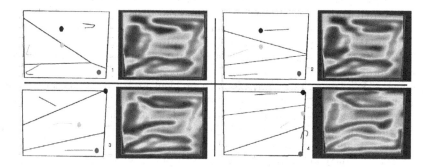

Fig. 13. Frames of the experiments. In each frame, on the left are shown the Voronoi cells with the robots and the current targets (big bullets) while, on the right, the plot function $\xi_S(\boldsymbol{x})$ in equation (28) is shown (red color is representative of high values of the function, blue color of low values)

4   Conclusions

In this paper we presented the latest research of the Italian Interuniversity Center ISME in the field of harbour protection using autonomous marine vehicles. Specifically, we at first presented a solution for the displacement of a fleet of vehicles by optimizing either the interception distance or the interception time to a menace. Then, we presented a decentralized control approach, based on Voronoi tessellations and Gaussian processes, to make a fleet of vehicles dynamically patrol a given area. The approaches have been validated via numerical simulations and experiment with autonomous surface vessels.

References

1. Almeida, A., Ramalho, G., Santana, H., Tedesco, P., Menezes, T., Corruble, V.: Recent advances on multi-agent patrolling. In: Bazzan, A.L.C., Labidi, S. (eds.) SBIA 2004. LNCS (LNAI), vol. 3171, pp. 474–483. Springer, Heidelberg (2004)
2. Antonelli, G.: Stability analysis for prioritized closed-loop inverse kinematic algorithms for redundant robotic systems. IEEE Transactions on Robotics 25(5), 985–994 (2009)
3. Antonelli, G., Arrichiello, F., Chiaverini, S.: The Null-Space-based Behavioral control for autonomous robotic systems. Journal of Intelligent Service Robotics 1(1), 27–39 (2008)
4. Antonelli, G., Chiaverini, S., Marino, A.: A coordination strategy for multi-robot sampling of dynamic fields. In: Proceedings 2012 IEEE International Conference on Robotics and Automation, St Paul, MN, pp. 1113–1118 (May 2012)
5. Birk, A., Pascoal, A., Antonelli, G., Caiti, A., Casalino, G., Caffaz, A.: Cooperative cognitive control for autonomous underwater vehicles (CO3AUVs): overview and progresses in the 3rd project year. In: IFAC Workshop on Navigation, Guidance and Control of Underwater Vehicles, NGCUV 2012, Porto, PT (2012)
6. Casalino, G., Turetta, A., Simetti, E.: A three-layered architecture for real time path planning and obstacle avoidance for surveillance USVs operating in harbour fields. In: OCEANS 2009, Bremen, Germany (May 2009)
7. Cortés, J., Martínez, S., Karatas, T., Bullo, F.: Coverage control for mobile sensing networks. IEEE Transactions on Robotics an Automation 20(2), 243–255 (2004)
8. Du, Q., Faber, V., Gunzburger, M.: Centroidal Voronoi tessellations: applications and algorithms. SIAM Review 41(4), 637–676 (1999)
9. Huang, C.F., Tseng, Y.C.: The coverage problem in a wireless sensor network. Mobile Networks and Applications 10, 519–528 (2005)
10. Krause, A., Gestrin, C., Gupta, A., Kleinberg, J.: Near-optimal sensor placements: Maximizing information while minimizing communication cost. In: IPSN 2006, Nashville, Tennessee, USA, April 19-21 (2006)
11. Krause, A., Guestrin, C.: Nonmyopic active learning of Gaussian processes: An exploration-exploitation approach. In: International Conference on Machine Learning, pp. 449–456 (2007)
12. Marino, A., Antonelli, G.: Experimental results of coordinated coverage by autonomous underwater vehicles. In: Proceedings 2013 IEEE International Conference on Robotics and Automation, pp. 4126–4131. Karlsruhe, D (May 2013)
13. Marino, A., Antonelli, G., Aguiar, A., Pascoal, A.: Multi-robot harbor patrolling: a probabilistic approach. In: 2012 IEEE/RSJ International Conference on Intelligent Robots and Systems, Vilamoura, PT (October 2012)
14. Okabe, A., Boots, B., Sugihara, K.: Spatial tessellations: Concepts and applications of Voronoi diagrams. John Wiley & Sons (1992)
15. Rasmussen, C.E., Williams, C.: Gaussian processes for machine learning. MIT Press (2006)
16. Simetti, E., Turetta, A., Casalino, G.: USV-based security system for civilian harbors. Sea Technology 51(11), 41–43 (2010)
17. Simetti, E., Turetta, A., Casalino, G., Storti, E., Cresta, M.: Towards the use of a team of USVs for civilian harbour protection: Real time path planning with avoidance of multiple moving obstacles. In: IEEE IROS09 3rd Workshop on Planning, Perception and Navigation for Intelligent Vehicles, St. Louis, MO, US (October 2009)

18. Simetti, E., Turetta, A., Torelli, S., Casalino, G.: Civilian harbour protection: Interception of suspect vessels with unmanned surface vehicles. In: 9th IFAC Conference on Manoeuvring and Control of Marine Craft (MCMC 2012) (September 2012)

19. Xu, Y., Choi, J.: Mobile sensor networks for learning anisotropic Gaussian processes. In: American Control Conference, St. Louis, MO, USA, June 10-12 (2009)

20. Xu, Y., Choi, J.: Adaptive sampling for learning Gaussian processes using mobile sensor networks. Sensors 11(3), 3051–3066 (2011)

An Effect of Sandy Soils on the Movement in the Terrain

Dana Kristalova

University of Defence, Brno, Czech Republic
`dana.kristalova@unob.cz`

Abstract. An analysis of geographic factors is the primary and necessary step for the preparation of military operations on the territory. Relief, hydrology, soil conditions, vegetation and other factors greatly affect the pass ability of an area and the movement of vehicles in the terrain. Sandy soils are the majority of the soil type in the areas of the current fighting conflicts in which NATO troops operate. These areas are characterized by a significant reduction in the speed and capabilities of overcoming the sloping terrain from roads or stable surfaces. Simulation of the influence of sandy soils in laboratory conditions is difficult. Testing and simulation of the movement of vehicles outside of communication can be used not only by military units, but also ambulatory vehicles or vehicles of integrated emergency systems in times of natural disasters such as floods, fires etc.

Keywords: geographical factors, movement of vehicles, pass ability of an area, cross-country movement, sandy soils, movement in terrain, reduction of speed, overcoming the sloping terrain.

1   Introduction

Geographic conditions significantly influence the activities of military units. One of the important factors is the mobility [1, 2, 3, 4 and 5]. The primary impact on the mobility is given mainly by soils. Secondary factors are the slope of the terrain, the elements of micro-relief and other objects [6, 7 and 8].

The sandy soils are not typical for the Czech Republic, yet the Czech troops are confronted with this type of soil on foreign missions. This issue is therefore re-searched by the Department of Military management and tactics and the Department of Military Geography and Meteorology, University of Defence. Just knowledge of mobility vehicles in sandy soils is a factor supporting the preparedness of drivers in real situations. Since these soils occur in the Czech Republic only sporadically the Cross-Country Movement which is contingent on a sandy soil was the subject of test-ing in a very attractive location in Slovakia. The routes were measured by geodetic methods and subsequently they were used to simulate the movement of unmanned vehicles.

Field tests took place in a geographically unique environment of the Military Training Area "Záhorie" (Slovak Republic).The Environment and the field conditions are rare in Central Europe. During the testing driving characteristics of military

J. Hodicky (Ed.): MESAS 2014, LNCS 8906, pp. 262–273, 2014.

vehicles, the ability to overcome the slope, the influence of micro-relief and vegetation were determined. Different measurement methods and different types of data have been used for testing and evaluation of experiments [9, 10].

Similar tests were held in other types of terrain and other locations and the results of the tests and simulations are described in these articles [11, 12 and 13].

Results will be used to create a methodology of determining cross country movement in sandy areas. Currently there are two publications (The Methodology of the Evaluation of the Micro-relief and the Terrain Obstacles on the Movement of the Military Wheeled Vehicles and The Methodology of the Determination of the Effect of the Terrain Cover on the Movement of the Military Wheeled Vehicles) where the provisional results of research are [14, 15]. This new methodology will be usable for the optimization of routes in the sandy terrain.

All of these experiments would be suitable to verify for using by unmanned ground vehicles (UGV) to human influence was excluded [6], [16, 17].

2   The Selection of a Suitable Area and the Preparation of the Experiment

Military training area Záhorie in the territory of the SR was selected as a suitable terrain based on an analysis of the availability of the appropriate territory and analysis of the capabilities to perform individual measurements, including the verification of properties of military equipment directly in the field.

Field measurements and tests with military technology took place after a number of planning processes. In the context of testing these vehicles were available: T-72M, BVP-1, medium truck AKTIS 4 4.1 R and personal off-road vehicle SANTANA PS10. They are not identical to the vehicles, which were used for the previous measurement and testing in the Czech Republic, but such vehicles are similar to their tactical-technical data and properties previously used BVP 2, T 810, LR 110 and UAZ 469).

Fig. 1. The geography characteristic terrain in the tested area in Zahorie in Slovakia

The selected location is unique for its nature on the territory of Central Europe. The layer of the wind-blown sands reaches thickness of tens of meters and is located throughout the territory of the military area. This is largely covered with artificially introduced pine (possibly Oak) trees. Still, enough free sandy and grassy areas found within the military area. The area of the wind-blown sands is situated on the Czech-Slovak border in the vicinity of the river Morava.

Several suitable spaces for our own measurements, to meet their basic requirements on the geography characteristic terrain (see Figure 1), was selected in cooperation with local experts on the territory of the training area.

All the measurements were focused to the problems associated with identifying of cross-country movement in sandy areas. The most important issues were:

- determination of the traffic capacity of the sandy terrain of one or more vehicles;
- evaluation of the influence of micro-relief shapes on movement speed in the sandy terrain;
- restrictions on mobility of vehicles on sandy subsoil due to the slopes;
- the ability to overcome sparse mature vegetation (trees) in the axis of the movement;
- The measurement of the dynamo-metric characteristics of the tested vehicles on sandy substrates.

3   The Field Measurement and the Verification of Pass Ability of the Terrain

3.1   The Methodology of the Measurement

The selected locations (on which the measurements took place) have been targeted using GPS technology and soil samples for the implementation of subsequent laboratory analysis have been removed.

Position location has been made, in particular for the possibility of future repetitions of the experiments for different meteorological conditions and for any additions to the recorded values.

Already processed methodologies [3], [14, 15] was used to measure the pass ability of the terrain. The first methodology describes the method of determining the cross-country movement of the wheeled vehicles in a variety of terrain and geographic conditions under the influence of the terrain surface. In particular, relief, micro-relief, soil and soil cover belongs to the elements of the ground surface. The methodology is based on the field manual FMS-33, the model determines the index of the mobility (TMI) of vehicles according to STANAG 4307/TMI AVTP-1 01-80, from the technical documentation of the wheeled vehicles and tests in the field. These methodologies resolve issues of the cross-country movement in a comprehensive concept.

For the part concerning the issue of soil the methodologies are based on the use of the measurement by standard cone penetration-meter (introduced in the armies of NATO), the distribution of soil based on the united soil classification (standardized within NATO) and on the assessment of the measurement of FM 5-430-00-1 (Planning and Design of Roads, Airfields, and Heliports in the Theatre of Operation –Road Design).

3.2   The Calculation of the Influence of Different Geographical Factors on the Pass Ability of the Territory - Generally

The calculation is based on an estimate of time slowing down a certain type of vehicles passing terrain, where it operates the geographical factors, compared to ideal conditions where the vehicle can move at maximum speed. It is necessary to talk about "estimate" a slowdown, because so far, thanks to a small number of practical and theoretical analyses, we are able to accurately capture complex dependencies between geographical elements of the terrain and the degree of pass ability. And geographic elements are closely related to each other, which is also hard to be quantifiable (e.g. the joint influence of the weather, the soil cover, slope, etc.).

The value of the coefficient of the slowdown (C_i, $C_i \in \langle 0, 1 \rangle$ or ($C_i \in \langle 100\%, 0\% \rangle$)) is assigned to each geographical factor F_i, which is located in the section of the ground, and that affects the speed of the vehicle. The value of this coefficient indicates how many times (how much percent) the factor slows down the vehicle. The coefficients of the slowdown (according to the table 1) define the degree of Cross-Country Movement.

Table 1. Determination of the levels of Cross-Country Movement (Pass Ability of Terrain)

Pass ability of the section	C_i
NO GO section	0
SLOW GO section	0,5
GO section	1
Section without information	1

The resulting effect of all the geographic factors on the deceleration of the vehicle in a given section of track shall be expressed by the following formula:

$$v_j = v_{max} * \prod_i^n C_i , \qquad i=1...n, \qquad j=1...k \qquad (1)$$

where: v_j [km/h] ... is the speed of the vehicle in the j-th section of track vehicles;
v_{max} [km/h] ... is the maximum speed of the vehicle for communication;
C_i ... is the i-th coefficient of a slowdown;
n ... is the number of geographic factors operating in the given section of the terrain;
k ... is the number of sections of the vehicle on the track.

The next step is the calculation of the resulting impact of all geographical factors on the deceleration of the vehicle along the track in the terrain, which is expressed by:

$$v = \frac{1}{\sum_{j=1}^{k} w_j} \sum_{j=1}^{k} w_j v_j, \quad j=1..k, \qquad w_j = \frac{s_j}{\sum_{j=1}^{k} s_j} \qquad (2)$$

where: v [km/h] ... is the speed of the vehicle along the whole track in the field,

  w_j ... is the weight assigned to the value of the v_j, depending on the length of the section of the s_j,

  s_j [km] ... is the length of the j-th segment,

  k ... is the number of sections of the vehicle on the track.

3.3   The Calculation of the Influence of the Soil Condition and Other Factors on the Pass Ability of the Territory

The Coefficient of Slowdown. Penetration capacity of the terrain is possible to express as a function of a resistance of the soil before a skid. This is the default value for the limit state of the interaction of vehicle and some soil. It is a dimensionless number used to indicate the number of vehicles of a certain weight and type to pass safely diagnosed in the same terrain and the same track. It is dependent on the mechanical-physical properties of the surface of the terrain, the characteristics of the vehicle and the current geological, hydrological, climatic, weather and other conditions.

  The capacity of the terrain for a military technique, which is measured by using the cone penetration-meter, is determined by the mutual interactions between the load characteristics of the terrain (it is expressed as a **Rating Cone Index - RCI**) and the effects of a passing vehicle on a terrain (it is expressed as a **Vehicle Cone Index - VCI**). The RCI is a dimensionless number that is expressed as the product of a **load capacity of the terrain** (it is expressed as a **Cone Index – CI**) in the critical layer and a **Remolding Index – RI** [14]. The RI expressed the power that corresponds to the changes of compaction of the soil after the passages of the vehicle. The VCI represents a dimensionless number expressing the effects of vehicles on the ground. This is a value that is either fixed to the vehicle, or assigned on the basis of the calculation of mobility vehicle (**a Mobility Index - MI**). This value is based on the pressure characteristics of the touch of the vehicle tires, vehicle weight, axle load and clearance of the vehicle.

  The value of penetrate soil resistance before and after the passage of the particular types of vehicles have been (on the individual sections) measured by using the cone penetration-meter.

  The index value of the RCI is determined from these measurements. Due to the value of the RCI the capacity can be determined in a given location for each vehicle-depending on the type of soils, natural moisture and soil compaction. The times required to overcome the individual sections were measured for all transits of vehicles after test runways. The speed of movement of vehicles in the sandy terrain was determined from the measured times, lengths of sections, and for different types of terrain. In addition to the measure of the length of the section also the survey of profiles of measured sections using electronic total station Leica 1500 was carried out.

  The coefficient of the slowdown (C) on the leg (which is dependent on the characteristics of the terrain) is possible to determine from the measured values:

$$C_j = \prod_i C_i \quad , \qquad i=1,3,4,8, \qquad j = 1...k. \qquad (3)$$

where C_i ... is equation that expresses the coefficients of a slowdown due to the maximum (design) speed of the vehicle,

C_1... the coefficient of a slowdown due to the relief and micro-relief shapes;

C_3 ... the coefficient of a slowdown due to the soil conditions;

C_4... the coefficient of a slowdown due to meteorological conditions;

C_8... the coefficient of a slowdown due to the driver's experience.

The resulting speed of the vehicle in the sandy terrain will be according to [3], [14,
and 15] expressed as follows:

$$v_j = v_{max} * \prod_i^n C_i , \qquad i=1,3,4,8, \qquad j = 1...k. \qquad (4)$$

Fig. 2. Collecting of the input data. There are the cone penetration-meter for obtaining of the
soil samples (on the left) and the electronic total station Leica 1500 for the measurement of the
terrain profiles (on the right).

The Dynamo-metric Characteristics. In addition to the described measurements and
experiments also the measurement of dynamo-metric characteristics of the tested
vehicles on different sandy substrates was carried out.

These characteristics are used to determine the traction vehicle and the possibility
of establishing curves ability of the vehicle to transfer engine power to the surface on
which the vehicle is moving.

The universal multichannel measuring unit Spider 8 (company Hottinger) was used
for static and dynamic measurement of the dynamo-metric characteristics and for measuring of the stroke (in tonnes) for medium and heavy wheeled or tracked vehicles
(T-810, KBVP, BVP 1). The force sensor LPC was used for the measurement of the
coupling strength (in Newtons) for the Land Rover and UAZ. For the measurement of the
coupling strength can be used to set some parameters (time step, measurement, etc.).

The values of the adhesive forces were measured on sandy paths without vegetation and on grassy meadows at a time when the adhesion of the vehicles occurred.
These values have been graphically processed and also the overall table of all so far
carried out dynamo-metric measurements was created.

The formula for determining the coefficients of adhesion of φ are as follows:

$$\varphi = \frac{F_{adh}}{G_{adh}} \tag{5}$$

$$G_{adh} = m * g * \cos\alpha \tag{6}$$

where: φ... coefficient of adhesion;

F_{adh} ... adhesive force;

G_{adh} ... adhesive gravity;

m ... weight;

g ... Earth's gravity;

α ... angle of climbing up.

Fig. 3. The measurement of dynamo-metric characteristics of tested vehicles on sandy and grassy surface (on the left) and electronic total station Leica 1500 for the measurement of the terrain profiles (on the right)

3.4   Next Experiments

The last two additional experiments served to validate the actual traffic properties of wheel and tracked vehicles when they are overcoming the various slopes (table 2 and figure 3) and self-growing trees.

To determine the mobility of vehicles on the slopes on certain gradients a few rides was carried out, see figure 4. Slope was measured using a clinometer throughout the length of the slope for each track of the vehicle. In case of unsuccessful attempt the value of the slope was measured only in the highest places, where the vehicle was reached.

The second test was focused on the possibility of overcoming the tall tree in the path of the movement. In most cases, it would be of course possible to drive around the tree. But thanks to the natural, or combat activities resulting from conditions a situation can occur when a narrow area (in which is the grown tree located) is the only gauge. The thickness of the stem, which limits the ability of selected vehicles to overcome the tree either debunked or breakage, was tested.

Table 2. Final values of climbing up the slope of tested vehicles

Type of vehicle	Max. angle of climb up the slope - on the tough surface	Tested angle of climb up the slope - on the incoherent surface	Result
Santana PS 10	40°	17°	Yes
		24°	ne
		24° ***	Yes
AKTIS 4*4.1R	27°	14°	Yes
		17°	With difficulty
		24°	No
		24° ***	With difficulty
T-72M	30°	14°	With difficulty
		24°	No
BVP 1	35°	14°	With difficulty
		24°	No

*** down from the slope

Fig. 4. The evaluation of the mobility of vehicles on the slopes on certain gradients on sandy surface

4   The Simulations of a Movement of Unmanned Ground Vehicles

4.1   Possible Approaches

Lots of approaches to the evaluation of the effect of the terrain surface on a movement of vehicles should be used [6].

The two best of them are these: the evaluation of the simulate rides on the real surface in software ADAMS as a first and the evaluation of the effect of surface on a movement by program language C^{++} in vector data format as a second.

The Evaluation of Simulate Rides on the Real Surface in Software ADAMS. The models of vehicle transits after real terrain have been compiled in the ADAMS, see web sites: http://www.mscsoftware.com/Products/CAE-Tools/Adams.aspx.

The aim of the model was to evaluate the mobility of vehicles at certain speeds. The vehicles pass through different (constant) speed after the terrain profiles, which were aimed by the method of terrestrial laser scanning or by total station Leica. The coordinates of the centers of the wheels were recorded and the speed and acceleration of these wheels were counted as input parameters to the next model.

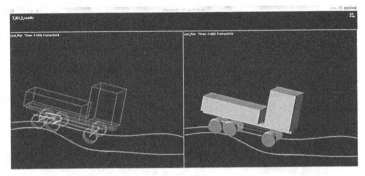

Fig. 5. The simulation of a real ride of Tatra T-810 on the real surface measured by Leica 1500. The left and right track may be different. These vehicles run at a constant speed. Touch the wheels of the vehicle to the surface at certain speeds was examined.

The Evaluation of the Effect of Surface on a Movement by Program Language C^{++} in Vector Data Format. Model simulating the ride vehicles in the field has been created in the programming language C^{++}.

Input data defining the profile field curve were obtained by two methods – by terrestrial laser scanning (measurement of the coordinates of the profile was targeted with step 10 cm) and by total station Leica (characteristic fracture points of terrain shapes in the same profile were targeted on the basis of a subjective selection of meters). Length and height coordinates were used.

Several algorithms have been built. Their purpose was: to retrieve data, to display the off-road curve, refining the methodology of the rolling wheel after the terrain and the final output was the determination of the value of the time needed to complete the profile.

Other input data were maximum vehicle speed, wheel diameter, the maximum speed of the vibrations the wheels – always relevant to a given type of vehicle.

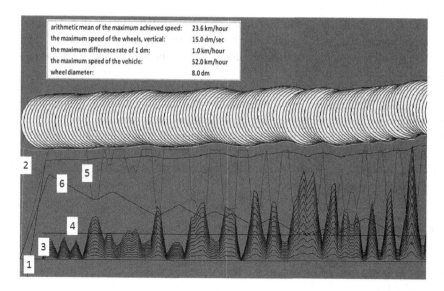

arithmetic mean of the maximum achieved speed:	23.6 km/hour
the maximum speed of the wheels, vertical:	15.0 dm/sec
the maximum difference rate of 1 dm:	1.0 km/hour
the maximum speed of the vehicle:	52.0 km/hour
wheel diameter:	8.0 dm

Fig. 6. Sample of an estimate of a calculation of time moving in the model in a programming language C++. In the picture the issue of the rolling wheel on real terrain (curve Nr. 1 under the wheel) and on the substitute terrain (the curve Nr. 2 under the wheel) is illustrate. The results of the calculation algorithms for actual speed are the red curve (Nr. 3), the maximum speed of oscillation wheels as the dark blue curve (Nr. 4), the maximum actually speed (Nr. 5) and the maximum possible speed profile limited convolucion filter is rendered as the curve Nr.6 (it is a pyramid-shaped).

5   Conclusions

Some partial conclusions can be drawn already at this early stage of the project and on the basis of measurements and partly processed results. They are not yet complete, the completion of additional analyses and complete evaluation of measurements and tests is assumed. The following evaluation of the impact of sandy soils can be noted from the information already obtained: Despite the fact that the sands have a granular, hard consistency and their compaction crimps vehicles should be minimal, it occurs. This occurs in particular in the case of rainfall, which changes the character of the surface. This compaction has a significant impact on the cohesion of the subsoil and therefore on the multiple transit of military equipment by the place. So a higher speed is achieved on the compacted soil. Penetration measurements made clearly confirm this fact.

Any (also rare) vegetation has a positive influence on the movement of vehicles along the sandy surface. Vegetation greatly increases the ability to transit the territory, in particular for wheel vehicles. The influence of the vegetation is shackled and reduced to the zero value in the case of rapid changes in the direction of motion and when driving to the slopes. At that moment the entrainment of the upper soil layer occurs and moving vehicles will gradually get stuck (up to the maximum light height). Getting stuck of vehicles moving in the rear part of the column should be due to this fact. From the drives to the slopes it can be tentatively say that the ability to overcome the slope on the sand compared to other surfaces is reduced by approximately 40-50% in relation to the indicated values of the TTD or detected during tests on clay soil and hard surfaces.

Correct Assembly of computing algorithms and choosing the appropriate methods for obtaining input data is very important for the virtual simulation of vehicle. Both models used meet expectations and provide nutrition-results corresponding to the drive in real terrain. It still will be needed to perform many tests to improve these models. It will be needed to perform additional drive in the field, in particular for the different meteorological conditions, since the change of weather conditions is the most difficulty determined factor.

References

1. Kristalova, D., Mazal, J., Neubauer, J.: The Effect of Geographical Environmental on Speed and Safety of Movement on Vehicles. The Conference Paper, 8 p. The Czech Republic (2012)
2. Kristalova, D., Rybanský, M.: The Methods Used for Creating a New System of Cross-Country Movement and Determination of Possible Movements in the terrain. The Conference Paper, 8 p. Romenia (2012)
3. Rybanský, M.: Cross-Country Movement, The Impact and Evaluation of Geograpfical Factors, 114 p. The Czech Republic, Brno (2009)
4. [4] Cibulová, K., Sobotková, Š: Průjezdnost vozidel terénem, (The Trafficability of Vehicles in the Terrain). The Conference Paper, 4 p. (in Czech). Slovakia, Žilinská univerzita (2006)
5. Zelinková, D.: Analýza získávání a využitelnosti informací pro vyhodnocení průchodnosti území (The Analyse of collecting and applicability of information for the Cross-Country Movement), The Diploma Thesis (in Czech), 118 p. The Czech Republic, Brno: VA Brno (2002)
6. Kristalova, D.: Vliv povrchu terénu na pohyb vojenských vozidel (The Effect of the Terrain Cover on the Movement of Military Vehicles), The Ph.D. Thesis (in Czech), 318 pp. The Czech Republic, Brno: The Univerzity of Defence (2013)
7. Rybanský, M., Mazal, J., Zelinková, D.: Vliv mikroreliéfu na průchodnost terénu. (The Evaluation of Microrelief Shapes on the Mobility of Vehicles) The Study (in Czech). The Czech Republic, Brno: VA Brno (2002)
8. Rybanský, M., Vala, M.: Modeling of the Relief Impact to Cross-Country Movement. The Conference Paper, 5 p. Egypt, Cairo (2010)
9. Kristalova, D.: The overview of existing digital data and GIS used in the Army of the Czech Republic and their possible use in tactical-geographic analysis. The Conference Paper, 8 p. MMK 2011. The Czech Republic (2011)
10. Křišťálová, D.: Nové datové trendy pro stanovení průchodnosti území (The New Data Trends for the Determination of the Levels of Cross-Country Movemnt), (in Czech). The Conference Paper, 8p., Conference Taktika. The Czech Republic (2012)
11. Křišťálová, D.: Optimalizace délek tras přepravních prostředků v terénu (The Lenht Optimalization of the Routes of the Vehicles in the Terrain) (in Czech). The Conference Paper, 8 p. The Czech Republic, Conference MMK 2010 (2010)

12. Kristalova, D.: The Contribution of the methods of terrestrial laser scanning to evaluation of the impact on movement of military vehicles.The Conference Paper, 8 p. IDEB Bratislava (2012)
13. Kristalova, D.: An evaluation of methods of optimization of movement routes according to tactical aspects of the combat operation planning process. The Conference Paper, 8 p. The Czech Republic, ICMT 2011, Brno (2011)
14. Rybansky, M., Zikmund, J., Kristalova, D., Rydel, M.: Metodika vyhodnocování vlivu mikroreliéfu a terénních překážek na průchodnost vojenských vozidel – kolová vozidla (The Metodologhy of the Evaluation of the Micro-relief and the Terrain Obstacles on the Movement of the Military Wheeled Vehicles), (in Czech), 30 p. The Czech Republic, Vyškov (2010)
15. Rybansky, M., Zikmund, J., Kristalova, D. Metodika určování vlivu povrchu terénu na pohyb vojenských kolových vozidel dle AVTP-1 / 01-80 a FMS-33 (The Metodologhy oft the Determination of the Effect of the Terrain Cover on the Movement of the Military Wheeled Vehicles), 45 p. (in Czech). The Czech Republic, Vyškov (2011)
16. Mazal, J.: Real time maneuver optimization in general environment. In: Recent Advances in Mechatronics., pp. 191–196. Springer, Heidelberg (2010)
17. Mazal, J., Stodola, P., Rybanský, M.: Traffic Management Optimization and Location Prediction in Context of Effectiveness Improvement of Cartography Analyses. In: Proceedings of the Joint 9th Asia-Pacific ISTVS Conference, 5 p., Sapporo, Japan, (2010)
18. Vala, M., Braun, P.: Vojenská kolová vozidla – teorie pohybu vozidel II., Military wheel vehicles – Theory of movement II), (in Czech). The textbook, 398 p. The Czech Republic, VA Brno, (1998)

Introduction of Human Views into Operational Capability Development within an Architectural Framework – March 2014

Robert A. Sharples

Airbus Expert - System Architecture
Airbus Defence and Space
The Quadrant, Celtic Springs,
Coedkernew, Newport, UK
robert.sharples@cassidian.com

Abstract. A. The current Enterprise Architecture (EA) philosophy within Airbus Defence and Space does not provide sufficient weight to the human aspects of our current architectures or any proposed changes to our existing systems/products. This R&D task was initiated to investigate the utility of adding Humans Views (HV) to complement the well known and understood Operational, System, Capability and Service Views of our EA philosophy. Following an initial examination of currently available Human View research the NATO Human Views templates were selected as the basis for consideration of the integration of humans into the System Engineering Lifecycle and Model Based System Engineering (MBSE) process

Keywords: Human Views, Architecture Frameworks, Architecture, Modelling, Systems Engineering, Dynamic Modelling, Experimentation, DoDAF, MoDAF, NAF, Defence Lines of Development.

1 Introduction

Based on our previous experience, principally for our Defence customer, we developed 10 hypotheses that the introduction of Human Views to the Architecture Framework would

- Identify immediately the impact of proposed changes to processes/systems on the people that have to implement/use them i.e. risk mitigation options
- Link with simulation to identify the effects over time on people, training requirements and organisation of proposed policy, process and system changes
- Increase the understanding and interactions of humans in the systems and systems of systems development
- Provide interfaces with advances of Human Computer Interfaces and introduce Human Psychology into the system architecture

J. Hodicky (Ed.): MESAS 2014, LNCS 8906, pp. 274–280, 2014.
© Springer International Publishing Switzerland 2014

- Expand the architectural footprint within the Airbus Defence and Space architectural, modelling, simulation and experimentation philosophy
- Expand the overall architectural footprint for the complete UK MoD, Defence Lines of Development (DLOD) – (Training, Equipment, Personnel, Information, Concept and Doctrine, Organisation, Infrastructure, Logistics and Interoperability)
- The inclusion of humans into the overall architecture should result in a large risk mitigation in terms of Training, Logistics and Personnel
- Mapping Services Views onto Human Views should increase the architectural integrity of the overall architectural philosophy
- Introduce the ability to provide Dynamic modelling of human behaviour in to the static Architecture Framework models

2   R&D Approach and Implementation

The initial task was to review the available literature on Human Views. This included.

Our initial research task focused on the MoDAF, Handbook Versions 1 and 2 [1,2], further research included detailed investigations of the NATO Technical Report [3] and a Canadian Human View Report utilising DoDAF [4].

The NATO approach to Human Views was selected as it mapped well to the Airbus Defence and Space Architecture, Modelling, Simulation and Experimentation philosophy.

One of our main goals was to define human interaction throughput the systems engineering lifecycle and system of systems and Model Based System engineering (MBSE) and not aimed specifically as Human Computer Interaction. (HCI)

The implementation involved creating detailed Logical Data models of Human Views within MoDAF, DoDAF and NAF together with all view interaction. The mapping of the NATO Human Views to the Framework Service Views was detailed as this was missing from the NATO Human View definition. The implementation was performed using IBMs System Architect as the tool provides very powerful logical data modelling.

The initial implementation was performed using IBMs System Architect, our aim was to produce a process that is architectural framework and tool agnostic. Future research will investigate the implementation with MOOD, Enterprise Architect, Mega and Rhapsody, as all these tools are used within Airbus Defence and Space.

Human View Implementation has been introduced in to the following projects.

- UK MoD Remotely Piloted Air System (RPAS) Study
- Internal Business Transformation
- ARTEMIS HoliDes (Holistic Human Factors and System Design of Adaptive Cooperative Human Machine System) R&D project [5]
- Emergency Response and Border Security systems
- Internal projects

3   NATO Human Views

To The NATO Human Views provide a viable method to identify and assess the human specific aspects of an architecture framework for the complete system lifecycle, Systems Engineering and Operational and Systems Architecture. Modelling and Simulation (M&S) extends this process to illustrate and capture the dynamic nature of human performance in a variable environment. Experimentation provides the data to populate the Human Views and their resultant models and then validate the modelled simulation.

Phase 1 introduced the following NATO Human views.

- HV-A – Concepts – facilitate the understanding of the human component in the overall operational / capability
- HV-C Tasks – Defines Human specific tasks (functions etc)
- HV-D Roles- All roles in all organisations (Image Analyst, UAV Pilot etc)
- HV-E Human Networks – Human to Human patterns
- HV-F Training – training needs for all organisations

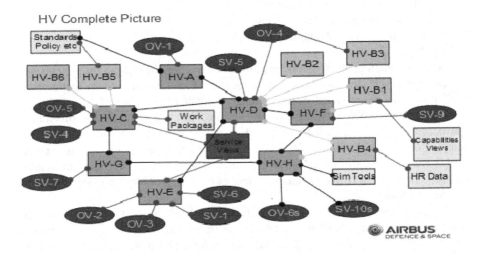

Fig. 1. Complete Human View interaction with Operational, System and Service Views together with some Airbus Space and Defence specific 'add ons'

Phase 2 implemented the rest of the NATO Human Views.

- HV-B Constraints (1 to 6)
- HV-B1 Manpower projections – all manpower requirements – forward loads
- HV-B2 Career Progression – career path for all Roles, departments involved
- HV-B3 Establishment History – historical load, forecast analysis, gap analysis
- HV-B4 Personnel Policy – HR policy and doctrine
- HV-B5 Health Hazard – Health and Safety etc

- HV-B6 Human Characteristics – any special needs, health issues, travel issues
- HV-G Metrics – human priorities, performance, criteria etc
- HV-H Human Dynamics – Dynamic Human Behaviour extracted from the static architecture model.

The complete HV picture also highlights the use of HVs allows the ability of placing Humans into the Systems of Systems concept and the transition into System Design.

4   Introduction of Human Views to Remotely Piloted Air System (RPAS) Operational Capability Development

The original architecture for a deployed RPAS followed our standard architectural approach and produced the standard high level operational view OV-1, Figure 2. This operational view together with a Capability Taxonomy was validated and verified with the Customer. The OV-1 defined the RPAS platform, the satellite communications links to Head Quarters in the UK and deployed in theatre, the RPAS control team, the launch and recovery team, the mission planners, troops on the ground and other aircraft communications links.

Typical High Level Operational View – Concept HV-A

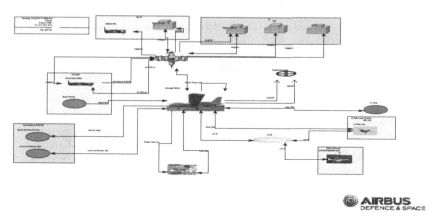

Fig. 2. Operational Concept (Produced via System Architect)

The Emphasis on Human Views Figure 3 compared with Figure 2 removed operational resources that do not directly interact with humans (for example Link 16), this highlighted the Human roles required to perform the operational task.

Figure 4 defines the architectural process followed to integrate Human Views in to overall architectural design. The operational and system views were re-used to define the HV-Concept, the HV-A Tasks from the operational scenarios, Resources (NOV-6c) and Functions (NSV-4), the HV-D Roles from the Organisational Charts (NOV-4) and

Resources (NSV-1), and the HV-E Human Networks from Resources (NOV-2, NSV-1 and HV-D).

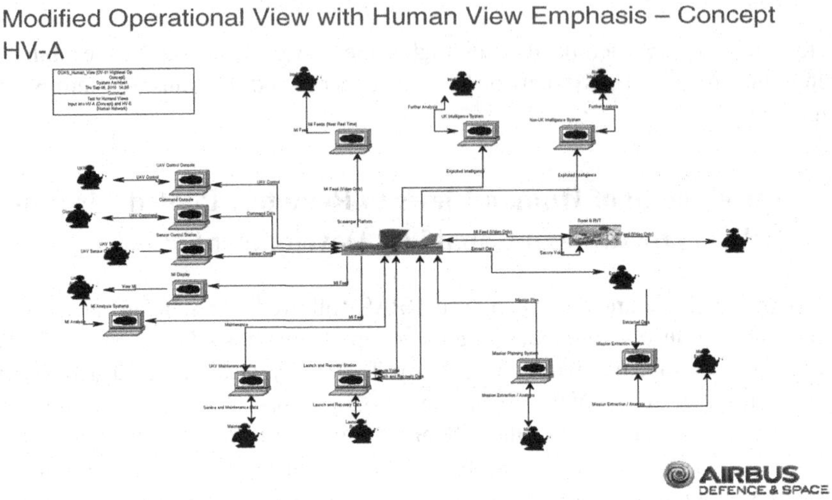

Modified Operational View with Human View Emphasis – Concept HV-A

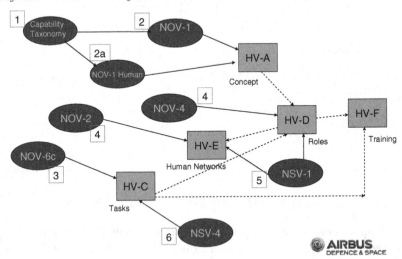

Fig. 3. Operational Concept with an emphasis on Human Interaction (Produced via System Architect)

High Level Process for Scavenger Human View Production

Fig. 4. High level process for the integration of Human Views into the Architectural model (Note the use of the NAF definitions for the Operational and System Views was used to make the model NATO consistent)

Hypothesis Re-visited

- Enable the identification of key drivers to transformation and provide the opportunity to achieve trade-offs between processes, systems and people

- Identify immediately the impact of proposed changes to processes/systems on the people who have to implement/use them i.e. risk mitigation options

- Link with simulation to identify the effects over time on people, training requirements and organisation of proposed policy, process and system changes

- Increase the understanding and interactions of humans in the systems and systems of systems development

- Provide interfaces with advances of Human Computer Interfaces a introduce Human Psychology into the system architecture

Fig. 5. AS high level ontology M&S

Hypothesis Re-visited

- Expand the architectural footprint within the System Design Centre architectural, modelling, simulation and experimentation philosophy

- Expand the overall architectural footprint for the complete MoD, Defence Lines of Development (DLOD) – (*Training*, Equipment, *Personnel*, Information, Concept and Doctrine, Organisation, Infrastructure, *Logistics* and Interoperability)

- The inclusion of humans into the overall architecture should result in a large risk mitigation in terms of Training, Logistics and Personnel
-
- Mapping Services Views onto Human Views should increase the architectural integrity of the overall architectural philosophy

- Introduce the ability to provide Dynamic modelling of human behaviour in to the static AF models

Fig. 6. AS high level ontology M&S

This second iteration culminated in the realisation that about 25 roles were not included in the original model, the focus on Human Views highlighted this significant deficiency in the original model. The majority of these 'missing' roles were identified as roles associated with the RPAS deployment into theatre. The compete definition of the aircrafts deployment allows us to perform what if scenarios with the equipment and personnel deployed; this is also having a direct impact on our deployment and logistic cost models.

This has led to a significant impact on our Systems thinking as the Human Viewpoint provides another way of looking at any system and is having a direct impact on our current Model Based Systems Engineering thinking.

5   Conclusion

The initial hypotheses were revisited following analysis of the introduction of Human Views. The conclusions are shown in Figures 4 and 5; all the hypotheses were verified with the exception of the incorporation of HCI into the system architecture. The prime reason for this exception was that the R&D tasks moved away from the MoD-AF based HCI view and moved into a System of Systems model, with the emphasis on Model Based System Engineering (MBSE).

References

1. The Human View Handbook for MoDAF First Issue (July 15, 2008)
2. The Human View Handbook for MoDAF (Draft Version 2) Second Issue (October 5, 2009)
3. NATO Technical Report TR-HFM-155 Human System Integration for Network Centric Warfare (February 2010)
4. Canadian R&D Contract Report Human Views Extensions to the Department of Defence Architecture Framework (September 2008)
5. HoliDes (Holistic Human Factors and System Design of Adaptive Cooperative Human Machine System) R&D project, http://www.holides.eu

Simulation Engineering Tools
for Algorithm Development and Validation
Applied to Unmanned Systems

Carlos Alejo, Irene Alejo, Yamnia Rodríguez, Jorge Stoilov, and Antidio Viguria

{calejo,ialejo,yrodriguez,jstoilov,aviguria}@catec.aero

Abstract. Nowadays, synthetic environments are considered a powerful tool to perform system testing. The use of virtual experimentation means results in a cost-effective option when facing large and/or complex system testing campaigns. Simulation-based testing reduces resources use, eliminates risks of failure on real experimentation and increments the safety level, especially when working with UAS/RPAS. Moreover, the use of simulation leads to a reduction of development costs and time to market. This work presents a set of simulation tools for UAV (Unmanned Aerial Vehicles) and UGV (Unmanned Ground Vehicles) systems that have been developed in the framework of the FP7 EC-SAFEMOBIL project. They are intended to be used as a tool to perform validation tests before real experimentation. The EC-SAFEMOBIL project is devoted to the development of sufficiently accurate motion estimation and control methods and technologies in order to reach higher levels of reliability and safety to enable unmanned vehicle deployment in a broad range of applications (landing on mobile platform, cooperative surveillance, etc.). These simulation tools allow testing the cited methods in a synthetic environment, using the exactly same estimation and control algorithms in the virtual world as those implemented for real systems. The comprehensive developed simulation environment has required the implementation of an optimized communication middleware, to provide flexibility, adaptability (allowing the addition or modification of control algorithms or UGVs, UAVs models, etc.) and scalability in order to fulfil the different needs of the specific scenarios. The development of a communication framework called ANIMO based on RTI implementation of DDS (Data Distribution Service) decouples the communication between modules or entities (UAV or UGV models, simulation core, etc.) from the simulation itself, and enables real-time communication of heterogeneous systems.

1   Introduction

The Simulation Tools for the EC-SAFEMOBIL project [1] consist of a set of tools that allows testing of critical software before being implemented in hardware and used in the project scenarios. These scenarios include the simulation of a UAV landing on a mobile platform, and the simulation of surveillance applications (tracking of UGVs).

J. Hodicky (Ed.): MESAS 2014, LNCS 8906, pp. 281–291, 2014.
© Springer International Publishing Switzerland 2014

A simulation is in essence a set of algorithms that represents the objects needed from the real world in a synthetic environment. Such objects could be the room, building or terrain the experiment is going to be held in, the UAVs and/or UGVs to be simulated, and the forces going on between entities, such as the gravity, the aerodynamics of the vehicles, etc. An "orchestra conductor" is also needed to synchronize every element in the simulation. Finally, if the user wants to see the evolution of the simulation, some tools for visualizing the environment both in 2D and 3D would be welcomed.

The tools used as the basis of the simulation framework have been VR-Forces [2] and VR-Vantage [3]. The former provides the synthetic environment along with the simulated forces, the simulation time synchronizer and the 2D visualization. The latter provides the 3D visualization. Using a plug-in architecture, the simulation tools are able to load precompiled software modules in the synthetic environment, incorporate them to the simulation and interact with it. The plug-ins added are basically controllers for every entity, including:

- A low-level navigation system for the UAV in the landing on ship scenario.
- A high-level navigation system for the ship, that makes the ship follow a predetermined route.
- A simulation of the DeckFinder sensor from Astrium [4] for the landing on ship scenario.
- A high-level navigation system for the UAVs taking part in the tracking scenario.
- A low-level control system for UGVs taking part in the tracking scenario.

The simulation tools also make use of a custom middleware to aid in the inter-systems communications in real time, developed at FADA-CATEC: the ANIMO framework.

The paper is organized as follows. Section 2 describes the simulation tools. Section 3 describes the integration with models from Matlab Simulink, sensor specifications and 3ds Max. Section 4 describes briefly the ANIMO framework. Section 5 comments the validation of results. Finally, the last section yields some final conclusions.

2   Simulation Tools

2.1   Scenario: UAV Landing on Ship

This scenario aims for a simulation in which a rotary-wing UAV is controlled via a low-level algorithm that controlled the servos of the UAV. Modifying the servos configuration the algorithm is able to guide it towards a moving platform –consisting of a ship–, and land it on a fixed point in the ship. The movement of the platform includes a predefined route and a simulation of the sea waves.

The following diagram shows in a simplified way the basic relationships between components:

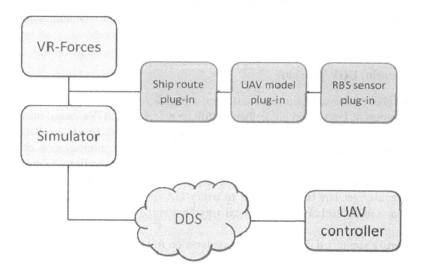

Fig. 1. Components in the landing scenario

Further explanations follow:

- The "simulator" is the main process. It consists of an application that uses the VR-Forces API to load a synthetic scenario and the plug-ins needed for the simulation (the ship route, the UAV model and the RBS sensor). The simulator is configured by an external configuration file that specifies several starting conditions, such as the UAV initial position and attitude. It is even possible to create a simulation with several UAVs and not only one, but then the simulation needs as many instances of the UAV controller running. The simulator creates an infinite loop that executes the simulation iterations. For each iteration, the simulator collects all the needed data and sends it to the UAV controller (or controllers) and waits for the response, which is sent to the UAV model.
- The "UAV controller" is a low-level controller that receives the data coming from the DeckFinder sensor, calculates the next configuration for the UAV servos and immediately sends the response back to the simulator.
- The "UAV model plug-in" receives the data from the UAV controller and calculates the next position and attitude of the UAV. When this is done, the simulator updates the position and attitude of the UAV in the scenario.
- The "ship route plug-in" is responsible for making the ship follow a path, defined in a separate file that contains a series of points indicating the latitude and longitude of every point in the path. By changing this configuration file the user can create different routes for the ship.

- The "RBS sensor plug-in" is a piece of software that simulates the behaviour of the Astrium DeckFinder sensor, as indicated by its specifications. The data taken into account have been the relative distance from the UAV to the ship, and the relative velocity between these two entities.

2.2   Scenario: UGV Tracking

The initial goal of this scenario is the testing of a high-level control algorithm able to manage a group of UAVs and guide them to follow a group of UGVs, based on variables such as the initial distance from every UAV to every UGV. This is a collaborative scenario, and the communication between entities and the minimization of the distance travelled by each UAV are more important that the optimization of the UAV controller or the simulation of the paths of the UGVs. So, unlike the previous scenario, once a target has been assigned to every UAV, the UAV controller is programmed at a high level and only the next waypoint is required for the UAV to start moving.

As before, a simplified diagram and its explanation follow:

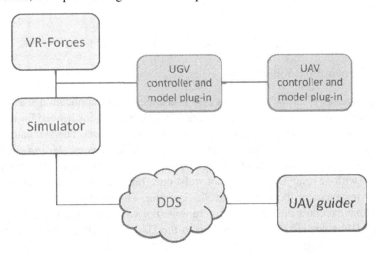

Fig. 2. Components in the tracking scenario

- The "simulator" is the main process. Same as before, but in this case the simulator collects all the needed data and sends it to the waypoint calculators and waits for the responses, which are sent to the UAV models.
- The "UGV controller and model plug-in" contains in one single module what was separated in the previous scenario (the UAV model and the UAV controller). While the previous UAV model needed to calculate the servo configuration, this plug-in just needs the point the UAV is headed to. The model then calculates the trajectory and makes the UAV fly towards the point until it is within a

predetermined radius, then the UAV reduces its speed and finally stops and waits until the next waypoint. This makes the UAV fly faster or slower, depending on the speed of the UGV.

- The "UGV controller and model plug-in" consists of a simple controller that receives the previously mentioned routes, along with the maximum speed the UGV can take in every stretch. The controller calculates the UGV heading and position for each iteration of the simulation, making it complete the route by taking the UGV to every waypoint in it. When a route is completed, the UGV starts over the route. Thus, the simulation is in an endless loop, as there is not a stop condition.
- The "UAV guider" is a dummy process that receives the position of the UGV assigned to a predetermined UAV and just sends it back, making the point the waypoint the UAV must head to. This part of the simulator is pending to be converted to a single module that holds the final collaborative algorithm.

2.3 Simulation Life Cycle

As has been mentioned before, every simulation is based on an infinite loop that runs as long as the user wants it to run. The actual code of the loop reads like this:

Table 1. Main loop of the simulation

```
1   void mainLoop()
2   {
3     timestampType simStepNumber = 0;
4     bool stop = false;
5     tickEverything();
6     while (!stop)
7     {
8       timeManager_->startCycle();
9       setSimStepToDependentModules(simStepNumber);
10      uavListener_->startJob();
11      sendData(simStepNumber);
12      waitAndCheckForReceivedData(simStepNumber);
13      if (!uavListener_->jobsPending())
14      {
15        tickEverything();
16        simStepNumber++;
17      }
18      if (checkForExit())
19      {
20        cgf_->pause();
21        stop = true;
22      }
23    }
24  }
```

The comments for the source code of the main loop follow:

- Line 3: The counter for the number of simulation steps is initialized.
- Line 4: The flag that tells the simulation to stop is initialized.
- Line 5: Every entity in the simulation is ticked before starting it.
- Line 8: The time manager is told to start a new iteration. This resets the iteration chronometer.
- Line 9: The simulation step number is sent to every module that needs it.
- Line 10: The UAV data listener is told to start a new job. A "job" is completed when all the data needed for the current simulation iteration has been received.
- Line 11: The simulator sends all the data needed by the dependant modules.
- Line 12: The simulator waits for all the needed data to arrive, or for the iteration chronometer to arrive its timeout. This function checks periodically whether the job is finished or not. Meanwhile, the call-back function receives the data and check if there are more data packets still to arrive. When all the data packets have arrived, the job is done.
- Lines 13-17: If the job is still unfinished, it means that a timeout has been reached and that the current iteration must be repeated. If the job has finished, every entity is ticked again and the simulation step number is increased.
- Lines 18-22: If the user has pressed the 'q' key in the console, the simulator is paused and the exit flag is set.

3   Integration with Other Software

Some parts of the simulator have been created using third-parties software. Among them there are the models created in Matlab Simulink [5] and the 3D objects created in 3ds Max [6].

Simulink models are needed for the VR-Forces plug-ins; see the brownish boxes in figures 1 and 2. Specifically, the UAV model plug-in in figure 1 is a model ported from Simulink, and wrapped to be called from VR-Forces.

The order is as follows: the model from Simulink implements a method called "step()", that does all the calculations needed in order to discover the next position of the UAV. VR-Forces implements a "tick()" method that calculates the next position for every entity in the simulation. To do so, VR-Forces needs to call the "tick()" method in every plug-in. In the case of the plug-in for the UAV model, this method calls internally to the "step()" method of the Simulink model.

3ds Max models are 3D objects that needed to be created, as these models were not in the object collection in VR-Forces. In order to import these objects and view them in VR-Vantage, first the models from 3ds Max have to be exported to the OpenFlight format. And only then is when the TDBTool and MedfTool from Mäk become useful. The former allows the user to load a terrain as a 3D object and visualize it in VR-Forces. The latter allow the user to load the 3D object in VR-Vantage.

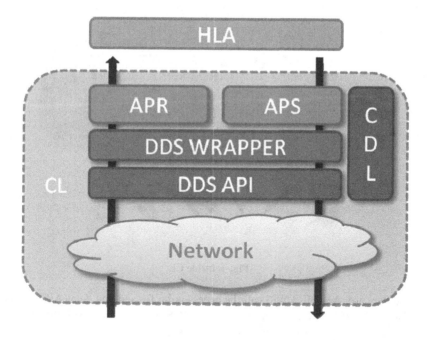

Fig. 3. A first glance at ANIMO

4   ANIMO Framework

An important part of the simulator is the communication layer, marked in figures 1 and 2 as "DDS". In order to make the communication easy, a communication framework has been developed and used in this project. This framework receives the name "ANIMO" [7], and consists of several abstraction layers. A first glance at ANIMO would yield something like shown in figure 3.

The previous diagram reads as follows: any high-level application (HLA) that needs to communicate with a device –whatever it may be and wherever in the network it is located– uses the API provided by the communication layer (CL) to read the data from the desired device as it were located in the same machine than the one running the HLA. The CL just communicates with the hardware abstraction layers (HAL) that wraps every device, which in turn reads the data directly from the device using its driver.

But where are DDS and the network in figure 3? They are inside the CL box. If the CL box is decomposed, the next diagram would show like this:

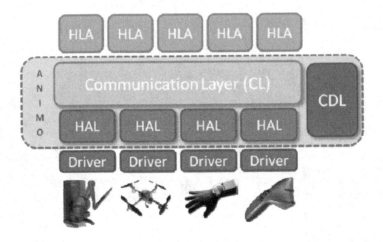

Fig. 4. Inside CL

Here they are. Any HLA will call the access point for sending data (APS) or for receiving data (APR), which in turn calls the DDS wrapper that uses the DDS API, which finally sends or receives the data via the network.

The CDL box that appears both in figures 3 and 4 stands for the common data library. The common data library contains all the data types that can be sent through DDS, and that are common to any HLA. This data types are the external interfaces needed for the communication with the every device in the network.

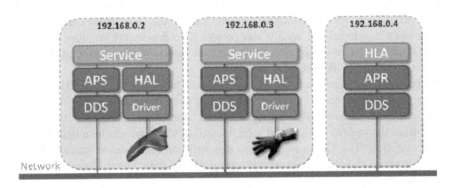

Fig. 5. ANIMO overall perspective

Thus, if the two previous diagrams are combined in one, the overall perspective of an application using the ANIMO framework is shown, as shown in figure 5.

The diagram in that figure shows, as an example, the architecture of the interface developed allowing the user to wirelessly control the point of view in VR-Vantage, using a IS900 tracking system and a Cyberglove. The figure shows how every device can be placed in a different machine (represented as the grey boxes and its theoretical IP addresses). Each device is governed by a service that just reads the data from the devices and sends it through the network converted into a data type from the CDL. A service is an application that keeps running endlessly in the background as long as the machine is on.

The way this interface works is like this:

- The service controlling the IS900 reads the attitude of the sensor in the wrist of the user and sends this data through ANIMO.
- The service controlling the Cyberglove reads the position of the hand and sends this data through ANIMO.
- The high-level application reads both datagrams. The data coming from the IS900 is used to simulate the mouse position. The data coming from the Cyberglove is used to simulate the mouse clicks. So, the user can be located in the centre of a virtual reality room and control the perspective without needing to have access to the mouse and keyboard of the PC controlling the room.

4.1 ROS Bridge

In case the simulator needs to access systems that do not have access to the ANIMO framework, or just needs to synchronize data with other kinds of networks, the ANIMO framework has an interface that can be implemented to create plug-ins that communicate with other systems.

One of these ANIMO plug-ins is the ROS Bridge, that allows the user to communicate the world of ANIMO with the world of ROS, and thus expanding the possibilities. The ROS Bridge implements a data parser that is able to translate the packages sent to and from the ANIMO network into packages the ROS network is able to understand. This is done by accessing the ROS API for publishing and subscribing to topics.

To make the ANIMO framework and the ROS Bridge even easier to use, the user can create "hubs", meaning that the data coming from a publisher in ANIMO is automatically redirected to a subscriber in ROS in a transparent way, and vice versa.

5 Validation of Results

The best part of the simulation tools is that the user can validate the behaviour of the algorithms tested just by watching the simulation running in the 3D world. Nonetheless, in case the simulation takes too long to execute, the user is given the chance to log any data wanted to a file, and then print the data saved or create plots or whatever.

Following are some plots with the data obtained in the landing scenario:

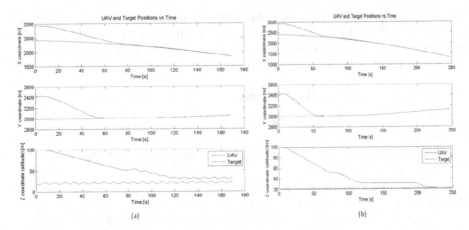

Fig. 6. Results of the landing scenario

The results in the right column –calmed sea– show the UAV landing properly in the platform after some time maintaining the right distance to it. The results in the left column –sea with some waves– show that the UAV never lands because the altitude is never maintained over time, due to a bug in the algorithm that must be fixed prior to the experiments with real UAVs.

6   Conclusions

In this paper, the work regarding the simulation tools of the Safemobil project has been introduced, along with some improvements that make the simulations able to communicate with models from Simulink and through the network through DDS and the ANIMO framework.

After working several months with VR-Forces and VR-Vantage as providers of the synthetic environment, it was discovered that these solutions were being used as mere visualization systems, while their whole potential was being discarded.

Future works include the possibility of creating custom synthetic environments by the use of 3D engines –like Ogre3D or Unity– and physics engines. Some steps are being already made in the Ogre3D direction, as it is the 3D engine contained inside ROS.

References

1. EC-SAFEMOBIL, FADA-CATEC (July 15, 2011),
   http://www.ec-safemobil-project.eu
2. VR-Forces simulation engine, VT Mäk,
   http://www.mak.com/products/simulate/vr-forces.html
3. VR-Vantage IG desktop visualization, VT Mäk,
   http://www.mak.com/products/visualize/vr-vantage-ig.html

4. DeckFinder - High-Precision Local Positioning System, Astrium,
   `http://deckfinder.net`
5. Simulink - Simulation and model-based design, MathWorks,
   `http://www.mathworks.com/products/simulink`
6. 3ds Max - 3D modelling and rendering software, Autodesk,
   `http://www.autodesk.com/products/autodesk-3ds-max`
7. Alejo, C., Alejo, I., Rodríguez, Y., Viguria, A.: ANIMO, Framework to simplify the real-time distributed communication. In: Proceedings of 5th International Workshop on Networks of Cooperating Objects for Smart Cities (2014)

Computer Models of Sensor and Weapon Systems: Assessing Model Utility Early in War-Game Development

Ronald T. Kessel

Defence Science & Technology, Waterloo, Canada
contact@ronaldkessel.com

Abstract. *"All models are wrong, but some are useful"* as the statistician George Box famously remarked (1979). Indeed, all computer models entail approximations that make them quantitatively "wrong" to some degree. Yet some models can be useful, likewise to a degree, for some applications but not for all. This holds when computer models of sensor or weapon systems are used to simulate actual system performance during the action of the game. In war gaming (broadly defined here as any application relying on models of sensor & weapon systems), a model is useful insofar as it supports the outcomes of the gaming, which may be education, training, tactical evaluation, force optimization, concept development, and so forth. To prove that a model suffices for given objectives is difficult, costly, and usually inconclusive. An alternate method for evaluating model adequacy early in a project in light of gaming objectives is described here. The method is based on well-known principles of hypothesis testing. It is therefore 1) objective and evidence based; 2) applicable to a wide range of computer models and gaming objectives; 3) requires moderate technical expertise, without requiring war-game developers to venture into the specialization of model developers. The method provides a framework for soliciting and evaluating the available evidence for model adequacy in light of gaming objectives, when allocating resources and exploring modeling options and suitability, early in a project.

1 Introduction

We may define "war gaming" broadly as *any* practical application of sensor and weapon system models, excluding the development of those models.

Models of sensor and weapon systems enable a virtual rendering of a limited set of actions of sensors and weapon systems during the course of the game; tasks such as the detection, classification, and identification of targets in the case of sensor systems, and engagement of targets in the case of weapon systems.

All computer models entail some degree of approximation, assumption, and simplification. *Accuracy* is the degree to which a model replicates essential phenomenon. Thus "all models are wrong" as the statistician George Box points out, but "some models are useful" as he goes on to say [1], in this way focusing our attention squarely on *utility* rather than on accuracy in its own right.

J. Hodicky (Ed.): MESAS 2014, LNCS 8906, pp. 292–307, 2014.

Models are *useful* insofar as they support the objectives of the war game. War-game objectives may include:

- teaching players about operational regulations, standards, or best practices;
- estimating the optimal placement or mix of sensors and weapon systems for force planning;
- validating concepts of use and virtual exercise of emerging *autonomous* systems;
- preliminary experimentation and de-risking of concepts of use for new sensor and weapon systems or combat scenarios; and
- much more (limited only by imagination).

In principle, the improvement of model accuracy has no stopping point. Ostensibly "better" models can *always* be developed to address a residual error that *always* remains. And experts working at the forefront of model development (*modelers*) can therefore always cite "serious" model shortcomings, even in the state-of-the art—otherwise they would be out of work.

But *serviceable* stopping points and digressions must have been reached along the way to the state-of-the-art; points at which admittedly imperfect models (frankly "*wrong*") could nevertheless be used successfully for one war-gaming application or another, without undermining the objectives of the application. Otherwise the models could *never* have be used responsibly. Success would be more a matter of luck than of design, leaving the developers of war games in a precarious position.

Ultimately the users of models must decide and prove to others when it is justified to allow admittedly imperfect models into critical applications. The justification is important. It strikes at the level of accountability and responsibility of those developing war games. It is the subject of VV&A cited earlier. The project team must ultimately justify why models, known to be imperfect, have nevertheless been brought into applications whose outcomes may have significant, even critical, consequences.

Too often the justification comes out of necessity and economics. A model is required for project delivery, but project resources and feasibility are limited, so one shops for a model that happens to fit the bill, literally. It is a matter of making do in a difficult situation. Limited resources are the reality that project teams generally face, but a justification based on them is arbitrary so far as the real issues of accuracy are concerned. Model choice stems from matters of funding, allocated project time and effort, system architecture, and so forth, rather than from the demonstrated adequacy for desired outcomes.

A justification for bringing admittedly imperfect models into critical applications should ideally include a proof that the accuracy required by the objectives is limited to a quantifiable degree by the objectives themselves. This amounts to deriving model-accuracy requirements directly from the war-game objectives. This is rarely done early in a project owing to its difficulty and the effort it requires, as discussed further in Section (2).

A project team is nevertheless obliged to show that they are acting responsibly, that at the very least they are using models that are known to be as accurate as can be determined in practice, using all of the information available for assessing accuracy in light of the given application.

This is generally *not* the same as using models that expert modelers have identified elsewhere to be their "best". The fact is that one accuracy assessment does *not* suit all applications. As we shall see in Section 3, quantitative accuracy assessments are not only a function of the quality of the model, but they also depend on (1) the objectives motivating the accuracy assessment (war gaming versus model development, for instance); on (2) the methodology used (quantitative metrics applied to the essential phenomenon at issue); and on (3) on the quality of the information by which the performance is judged (the empirical standard against which the model output is compared, including ground-truth data and uncertainty about operational conditions).

The accuracy assessment clearly changes in methodology and outcome if our application requires one essential phenomenon or another, such as from detection *probability* to detection *range*, for instance. These phenomenon are a related, of course, but they are incommensurate with each other. Thus the most accurate model for one is generally not the most accuracy for the other. And the assessment will change if our application faces a different degree of experimental error and uncertainty in the ground-truth data, and a different degree of control and knowledge of operating conditions. Accuracy assessments must in fact be re-evaluated for *each* application, in light of these and other factors.

The revaluation of accuracy easily changes the ranking of the "best" model. The expert modeler may compare the accuracy in a set of candidate models, in order to demonstrate that certain improvements made to modelling have been successful. Then the goal of demonstrating progress in modelling shapes both the methodology and the information used to assess model accuracy. In war-gaming, however, the goal of accuracy assessment is to demonstrate that at least one candidate model qualifies in some way for accomplishing the objectives of the war gaming. The two generally require different quantitative methodologies, with a different quality of information brought to bear as the standard for assessment.

The revaluation of model accuracy is perhaps the most important consequence and proof that one has shifted attention away from model accuracy in its own right, to model utility for the application at hand.

As we shall see, there are a number of factors that mitigate against high accuracy in modelling applications. These affect the power of the accuracy assessment to discriminate between different model accuracies, and between imperfect and perfect accuracy. They impose a limit of accuracy resolution—the limit of *practical perfection* for a given application—beyond which ostensible improvements in accuracy become meaningless; not because better accuracy is impossible, but because better accuracy cannot be recognized in practice owing to the limited quality of the information brought to bear as the standard for accuracy.

The possibility of *practical perfection* for model accuracy for a given application is a result of the combined effect of all of the allowances for model *inaccuracy* that naturally arise in any model application. These are described in Section (3). They are applied then in a hypothesis test for practical perfection in Section (4). The test consolidates the information available for evaluating model accuracy, objectively evaluating the evidence for accuracy in a framework that *all* parties—the war-game development team, expert model developers, project evaluators, and funding agencies—can accept. At the same time, it does not require one party to venture far into the expertise of another. Examples are given in Section (5).

2   Model Accuracy Requirements

Ideally we would like to translate war-gaming objectives directly into model-accuracy requirements, which, if met, would guarantee that a model's accuracy suffices for achieving those objectives. In practice, however, proofs of model sufficiency are very difficult to carry out. They generally require a significant work package in their own right. When attempted early in a project, moreover, they require a high degree analytic skill (much as proofs of sufficient conditions in mathematics generally do). Failing that, they are more straightforwardly addressed empirically, *late* in a project, well after models have been selected, as project outcomes come available for experimental validation, and insofar as the scope of the project allows for experimentation.

Thus models come to a project with their accuracy credentials in hand, while proofs of sufficiency generally come late in a project (if at all), as outcomes emerge in a process of experimental validation. The growing, very complex domain of model *verification, validation, and accreditation* (VV&A) [3, 4] is testimony to the challenge of proving the sufficiency of a model in a conclusive way.

In the absence of early top-down model accuracy requirements, the natural default is to opt for the most accurate models available, as a risk-mitigation measure; the *most* accurate models being the *least* likely to undermine the gaming objectives. This pressure for high model accuracy is opposed only by the added cost that better accuracy generally brings to a project—cost in terms of model complexity, computational burden, level of expertise required, proprietary licensing, the need for specialized data sets (for environmental, target, transducer & signal processing, etc.), expertise for quality assurance for scenario permutations, and so forth. So the war-game development team faces competing demands, from state-of-the-art in modelling and project risk on the one hand, and from limited project resources and overall feasibility on the other.

The project team naturally consults experts in state-of-the-art in modelling, but they are often frustrated to find that model developers are not in a position to give advice on accuracy requirements in light of the project's particular objectives. It is likely that the war-gaming (its methodology; objectives of education, decision making, and operational analysis; and hence its requirements) falls well outside the modeler's domain of expertise (computational physics and engineering). And it is more likely still that the modelers will focus on model accuracy as the goal, scarcely imagining that one could, in good conscience, settle for anything less than state of the art in accuracy, where they have so much professional capital invested. Their preoccupation with "all models are wrong" gives little ground to "some models are useful", and the project team will have to explore that ground of utility themselves, leading modelers much more than following them. Past experience along these lines motivates the present work.

3   Factors Mitigating against High-Accuracy in Computer Models

As experimentalists and expert modelers know, there are limits to degree to which model accuracy can be assessed. When models are validated against empirical observations of actual sensor or weapon system operation (*ground-truth data*), for instance, there are experimental errors of observation and uncertainties in the ground-truth data owing to imperfect methodology and imperfect control and knowledge of the operating conditions during the experiment. Indeed, much as "all models are wrong", so too all ground-truth data is "wrong", and therefore has a limits on the extent to which it can be used to validate model accuracy. These limits must be considered in any inferences drawn from an accuracy assessment. Their effect is to weaken the power of the ground-truth data to assess "true" model accuracy, limiting its ability to discriminate between the accuracy of two candidate models, and hence between imperfect accuracy and perfect.

There are a number of factors that create allowances for inaccuracy when evaluating models in light of a given application; namely, the:

1. limited objectives of the gaming,
2. essential dynamics required for those objectives,
3. quality of the ground-truth data,
4. inherent random variability of the essential dynamics,
5. level of use of a model needed to achieve the objectives, and the
6. proximity of the gaming objectives to critical real-world combat operations.

These all have the same effect and combine to weakening the power of accuracy assessments to meaningfully discriminate between imperfect accuracy and perfect. Each factor is reviewed in turn below.

3.1   Objectives of the War Gaming

Many objectives for training, education, concept development, and demonstration require a representative nominal realism in sensor and weapon models, but not a particular realism for very specifically defined operating conditions. The objectives may be largely indifferent to the particular operating conditions, and require only representative, plausibly realistic system performance expectations (in terms of coverage, speed and sequence of action in scripted or free play, realistic probabilities of success and failure, and so forth).

A game designed for teaching players about standard operating procedures, for instance, or about communication protocols, generally does not require a rich specification and exploration of environmental conditions affecting sensor and weapon system performance, and does not require high accuracy in dealing with them. Indeed, it is likely that the added richness and accuracy would detract or undermine the success and facilitation of the game.

Elsewhere, war gaming that pertains to future operations is generally uncertain about the particular geography, environmental, and operating conditions that may be faced in future operations. There is no doubt that these can have a significant impact on operations. Owing to the uncertainty, however, the modelling of future scenarios cannot avoid being only nominally representative regarding them—realistic in selected essential dynamics, but without representing future operations with what model developers would consider good or high accuracy. To insist on such accuracy would be misguided in the face of the uncertainty about future operations.

3.2   Essential Dynamics Required of a Sensor or Weapon System Model

It is impossible to speak of model accuracy without expressly identifying the essential dynamics for which accuracy is required. These must be determined by the developer of the war game and not by the developer of the model.

Essential dynamics are generally manifest as:

1. Quantitative parameters of deterministic physical system behaviour (e.g., the resonant flexural modes of ship structure determining its vulnerability to underwater blast, wind resistance on projectiles, or the attenuation of infrared radiation in fog, and so forth);

2. Quantitative statistical moments of system performance (e.g., average detection range and its variance, average dwell-time on target, mean-time to target track-loss, and so forth); or

3. Quantitative expectation (probability) of task completion (e.g., conditional probability of detection or false alarm, conditional probability of impact, confusion rates in target classification, kill probability, and so forth).

The objectives of the war gaming may require any subset of these from the model of a given sensor or weapon system. Usually they require only one. Different kinds of models are generally required for each kind of essential dynamic. Different standards of accuracy are certainly required for each.

The simplicity and quality of a model depends in large part on the essential dynamics it emulates. Expected performance probabilities (3) are generally the to model, because the focus is on outcomes of system action and the internal functioning of the system can be treated as a "black box", which is to say, ignored. Accuracy then depends much more on the quality of the ground-truth data for overall system performance than on the complexity of the model.

Next simplest are models of the statistical moments (2), usually the mean and variance, of system performance, which likewise focus on the outcome of system action rather than on its particular inner functioning. Higher order moments typically require greater model complexity for replicating them.

Most complex are the deterministic physical dynamics (1), because the model must then capture details of the physics and engineering of a system's many sub-systems. They also require the most detailed knowledge and specification of operating conditions. These kinds of model are generally only required very close to actual operations. Their methodologies are generally understood properly only by physicists and engineers. A high degree of specialized expertise is required to run such models with confidence.

The different kinds of models for each of the three different kinds of essential dynamics each entail a mixture of theory, approximation, and empirical validation.

In principle, none is more "realistic" or accurate than the other. Probabilistic phenomenon (3) may easily be more realistically and accurately modelled than physical (1) [5]. As with any model, the degree of realism and accuracy depends on particular approximations, assumptions, and empirical validation brought to bear on its particular implementation.

Essential dynamics can be identified at a more concrete level as well. Changing environmental conditions generally have a significant effect on sensor and weapon performance, for instance, and a war game may focus on one or another set of conditions of interest, on a subset of realistic conditions, or on the transition from one condition to another (day to night, for instance).

Focusing on the essential dynamics creates allowances for model accuracy inasmuch as a model's treatment of non-essential dynamics is largely a matter of indifference. Almost any plausible replication of non-essential dynamics is permitted provided that it is not out of the realm of physical possibility for the system being modelled. Only essential dynamics are of interest in the analysis of accuracy in a model for a given objective. One must not make the mistake of insisting on accuracy in a largely irrelevant set of essential dynamics.

3.3   Quality of Ground-Truth Data

Ground-truth data refers to the real-world empirical (experimental) observations made of the actual sensor or weapon system operating under realistic conditions, usually against controlled targets, by which model accuracy is validated. It is often forgotten that real-world empirical observations are subject to observation and measurement errors and uncertainties. Indeed, the ultimate standard of model validation—ground-truth data—is itself generally imperfect.

The quality of ground-truth data can be low if:

1. Staging trials of controlled targets (aircraft and ships, for instance) is costly, and the number of trials and range of operating conditions is low (small sample size);
2. Target aspect, speed, saliency, and vulnerability are difficult to control or are to some degree unknown during experimentation;
3. Essential dynamics must be estimated or inferred rather than straightforwardly measured (think of inferring muzzle velocity from projectile altitude or range when it cannot be directly measured, or of the effect of a field of internal ocean waves may have on long-range sonar sound propagation inferred from a few point measurements of the internal wave field);
4. Operating and environmental conditions are not controlled or fully known, as typically happens for long-range sensors and weapon systems, owing to spot sampling of distributed, changing variability.

Such imperfections widen the confidence limits of the ground-truth data in which a model's output must fall during validation. The larger the imperfections in ground-truth data, the easier it is for a simple model to be empirically validated, and the easier it is for a simple model to replicate them to within the confidence limits of the ground-truth data.

If one is not satisfied with the resulting uncertainty bounds on accuracy assessments, then the answer is not to improve the model or to opt for better models, but it is to collect more and better ground-truth data for model validation. This would be outside the scope of most war gaming projects.

3.4   Inherent Random Variability

Virtually all physical phenomenon are subject to a degree of unpredictable random variability. In sensor systems these are caused by scintillation, fluctuations in propagation conditions, and by aiming instability and errors for instance. They are also caused by unpredictable variation in target saliency, such as a target's signature, strength, aspect, speed, small-scale motion (heave, pitch, roll), or by occlusions, masking, shadowing, or clutter.

In weapon systems, random variability may be due to small-scale turbulence, and aiming errors or uncertainty, as well as variation or uncertainty about target vulnerability, aspect, speed, small-scale motion (heave, pitch, roll), and so forth.

Inherent random variability is present at all times during realistic sensor and weapon system operation. They are not imperfections in ground-truth data or in the model, but are an essential part of the phenomenon being modelled. Realistic models will therefore generally include inherent random variability of the same order as that in the ground-truth data.

It is difficult to discriminate between model inaccuracy and inherent random variability in system operation. The two can be discriminated in practice, but it generally requires large sample sets of ground-truth data to do so.

Inherent random variability creates allowances for model accuracy inasmuch as the larger the inherent variability, the less it matters in war gaming whether a model's output may be attributed to realistic rendering of inherent random variability or to inaccuracy. But the level of model usage must be considered at the same time.

3.5   Level of Model Usage

Assume for the moment that the objectives of a particular war-game will be accomplished after just *one* call for the output of a given model. Then one hardly needs a model at all to achieve the objectives. The model only needs to deliver a single plausibly realistic output, by reporting a single observation taken from an exercise of the sensor or weapon system in the real world. There is no question then of inaccuracy or inadequacy. The model is *practically perfect*.

At the other extreme, assume for the moment that war-game objectives will only be achieved after many thousands of calls for an output from a given model, as in Monte Carlo simulation for operational analysis for instance. Then inaccuracy and bias in the model will certainly impress itself on the progress and outcomes of the gaming. Extremely high model accuracy is generally required for such applications (and, incidentally, Monte Carlo simulation can be pathological for that reason).

It is in these ways that the level of model usage required to achieve the objectives of the war gaming create allowances or restrictions on model accuracy. Low levels of model usage generally imply greater allowances for model inaccuracy.

The level of usage must be determined by the developer of the war game, in light of its particular objectives, and not by the developer of the model. The quantitative allowances (or constraints) must be determined by analysts, but remains squarely in the domain of war-game development without venturing into the domain of expertise of sensor and weapon modelling.

3.6   Proximity of Actual Operations

By actual operations is meant present or immanent military operations, for which details knowledge of operating conditions are known (time, geography, environment, target characteristics, etc.).

If the objectives of the war-gaming have an immediate bearing on actual operations, then the degree of operational and environmental uncertainty is considerably reduced, and gaming outcomes are generally more critical that in other gaming applications. This increases the level of accuracy required and expected from models.

As a rule, the closer that war-gaming objectives are to actual operations, the more accurate its models must be. This would generally be true for applications of modelling & simulation regarding the use or operation of autonomous systems in actual operations.

4   Practically Perfect Models

A general outline of the concept of practical perfection in models is given here, with the mathematics addressed elsewhere. Just one equation is required, the condition for *practical perfection,* designated as

$$\left\| \begin{array}{c} Perfect\ Model \\ Accuracy \end{array} \right\| \leq \left\| \begin{array}{c} Inherent\ Randomness\ + \\ Imperfections\ in\ Ground\ Truth\ Data\ + \\ Uncerainty\ in\ Operating\ Conditions \end{array} \right\|_{\substack{Model \\ Utilization \\ Level}} \quad (1)$$

The vertical brackets in the equation $\| \quad \|$ indicate at quantitative measure of parameter indicated within.

$\| Perfect\ Model\ Accuracy \|$ is a measure of the difference between the output of a hypothetically *perfect* model and validating ground-truth data for the model. Given perfect ground-truth data and no uncertainty regarding an entirely deterministic phenomenon, we would have $\| Perfect\ Model\ Accuracy \| = 0$, signalling perfect accuracy.

In practice, however, all of the factors considered earlier introduce imperfection in the model accuracy assessment. This creates confidence limits (the right side of Equation 1) for the assessment of the accuracy of a hypothetically *perfect* model. But the same confidence limits apply then for the evaluation of the accuracy of *any* model.

In other words, if the accuracy assessed for a candidate model happens to fall within the confidence limits for the hypothetically perfect model, then the quality of the candidate model cannot be discriminated from the quality of a perfect model. The candidate model is practically perfect.

In practice, the combined allowances on the right side of the equation and be rather large. This is particularly true for complex, long-range sensor and weapon systems, whose exercise in real-world experimentation is severely limited owing to cost, and with environmental conditions difficult control or know.

4.1   Hypothesis Test for Accuracy

The test for practical perfection in (1) amounts to a hypothesis test in the usual sense of hypothesis testing at the foundation of the scientific method for objective knowledge.

Our (null) hypothesis is: *The given model is practically perfect for the given war-game application.*

The null hypothesis is set up as a challenge, to create a framework for evaluating the evidence for accuracy in models. It is tentatively accepted until it is contradicted by the available evidence.

Thus all of the factors mitigating against model accuracy (Section 3) must be examined by analysts, and the confidence limits that they together pose for an application-relevant assessment of model must be placed in the right side of Equation (1).

Then the model's actual accuracy, as determined by the deviation of its output from relevant ground-truth data, is inserted into the left side of Equation (1), as $\|Perfect\ Model\ Accuracy\|$, in order to see if it passes for practical perfection. If the inequality in Equation (1) is satisfied, then it means that there is *no* evidence that the model is *not* practically perfect for the given application. The model is presumably inaccurate to some degree, of course, but it is to a degree that is less than the quality of the information brought to bear on its accuracy assessment.

Hypothesis testing is perhaps the most widely used and widely accepted approach to objectively evaluating evidence. Much as the hypothesis-testing methodology applies generally within many scientific domains, so too the hypothesis test for practical perfection in models applies very generally to many different domains of war-gaming and sensor and weapon system models.

The full scope of hypothesis testing (its quantitative and statistical methodology, including significance, Type I and Type II errors, and so forth) can be brought to bear on practical perfection in sensor and weapon system models for a given application. This will not be done here for brevity. Analysts are required for the purpose, such as war-game development teams typically include.

4.2   Practical Implications

If there is no evidence that a given model is not practically perfect, then the project team is justified in proceeding as if the model were practically perfect. They are justified when deciding against investing in still "better" and more costly or burdensome models, or in further model development at project expense, and justified in allocating resources accordingly, early in the project. They are justified insofar as they are proceeding on the basis of the available evidence. One really cannot ask for more than that.

In practice, it may easily happen that the allowances for model inaccuracy (right side of Equation (1)) are much larger than expert model developers would accept for a standard of accuracy in their own work at the state-of-the-art in modelling. This difference is precisely the point that Box was making. The war-game project team must focus on utility, while expert modelers generally focus on accuracy in its own right, resulting in dramatically different standards for each.

If modelers are alarmed by grave "concessions" made in model accuracy (as they typically are), then they must have evidence that can be properly considered among the factors mitigating against accuracy. They can be invited to table their evidence so that it can be included in the test. Merely citing instances when a model was shown to be inaccurate or wrong will not do, because everyone already knows that models are wrong to some degree. The point is rather to justify the use of a given model that we know to be in error, for a given application.

If they are unable to turn their concerns into evidence for a hypothesis test like Equation (1), then it means that they have no objective evidence to bring to the table on the matter of model accuracy. Their evidence is at best subjective, and at worst biased by the prospect of bolstering the state-of-the-art in modelling.

Of most importance for project managers, then, practical perfection in modelling is a limit point for model quality, not because there is no room for improvement in a model, but because there is no way of recognizing further improvements in model accuracy owing to the limits of our empirical knowledge—owing to error and uncertainty in the available ground-truth data, and to uncertainties in operational conditions [2].

Two or more practically-perfect candidate models for a given sensor or weapon system are equivalent so far as accuracy is concerned. The choice between them for use in a given application can therefore be made on grounds of cost, simplicity, ease of use, computational burden, and so forth.

If a project's charter or resources rule out real-world experimentation, and if practically perfect models are available, then those models can serve applications much as they are. Resources spent improving or studying accuracy further would be wasted if resources were not also first spent on collecting better ground-truth data, or more certain information about operating conditions.

Testing for, and accepting practical perfection in a physical model lends credibility early on to war-gaming project inasmuch as it:

1. shows that the project team has done its homework, that it has explored and assimilated what can be known and applied regarding model accuracy, which bolsters its business case for funding and answers criticism (sometimes harsh) about model selection;

2. provides a framework for soliciting and evaluating further evidence regarding model quality in consultation with modelling experts early in a war-gaming project; and

3. where the existing standards of practical perfection are deemed to be inadequate for a broad range of applications, it helps programme leaders to justify and plan resource allocations for a campaign of experimentation and information gathering that is required for further improve models.

It is important to note that accepting the hypothesis does *not* generally guarantee that the model is adequate for the war gaming objectives. It only means that there is no evidence that it is *not* practically perfect. Such is the power of hypothesis testing generally. The tests are not positive assertions of truth (as a proofs of sufficiency would be, Section 2), but they are an objective evaluation of evidence. This must be borne in mind with some caution. Practical perfection in models is a hypothesis that stands until evidence to the contrary arrives. The hypothesis test given here enables the project team to make planning and resource allocation decisions based on the available evidence, at the time the decision is made. One cannot ask for more than that.

5   Examples

5.1   Timely Radar Detection of Fast Small Boat

War Game Requirement: We plan to develop a tactical game touching on response measures against small-boat attack on maritime forces (ships) in ports and harbours. It has been determined that, of importance for the objectives of the gaming, is a realistic probability of detecting the approach of a fast small boat by radar. The essential phenomenon, then, is the *expectation* of overall detection performance.

Ground-Truth Data: During realistic at-sea experimentation of the radar against small boat (controlled) targets, it was found that 6 out of $N = 8$ approaches of a distant small fast boat were detected and tracked by a given radar in a timely manner for stopping measures to be brought to bear on the small boat. Time and resources did not permit more than 8 trials.

Objective: Estimate the bounds of practically perfect model accuracy for radar-versus-small-boat models for use in the tactical game.

Fig. 1. X-band radar used in small-boat detection trials mounted at the bow of a passenger cruise ship (Source: Ronald Kessel)

Result: The parameter of interest is the probability of timely detection P_D of a distant, approaching, small fast boat. Appling the binomial distribution to the experimental data, it can be shown that the *true* probability of timely detection P_D' based on 6 successful detections in 8 trials lies in the range $0.52 < P_D' < 0.90$ with a 65 % confidence (the confidence level being roughly equivalent to the confidence level of ± one standard deviation if the relative frequency of occurrence of detection happened to be normally distributed.

Fig. 2. Small-boat detection trials. The orange RHIB is in fact an autonomous surface vessel, with driver standing ready on board as a precautionary measure. The exercises were to explore the use of the radar (background of image) to manage space for the unmanned vessel (Source: Ronald Kessel).

Discussion: Thus, *all* radar models that generate a probability of timely detection of $0.52 < P_D < 0.90$ are practically perfect for the application so far as the ground-truth data can establish. If we happen to nevertheless believe that this window of uncertainty regarding model accuracy is too large for our gaming application, then the answer it *not* to look for better models, but it is to first look for better (more) ground-truth data (sample size greater than $N = 8$).

In order to determine if the window of uncertainty is too large for accomplishing our objectives in the tactical war gaming, we must estimate the number of times that the detection of a distant, approaching, small boat must be simulated during the play of the war game in order to accomplish the objectives of the game.

If the purpose of the game is to teach players about rules of engagement or standard operating procedures, and this if can be accomplished in 8 or less simulated approaches of a small boat, then the uncertainty bounds are adequate for the objectives of the gaming. Based on observations made during the course of the game, that is, one could not find any evidence that one was using a model and not the actual diver detection sonar against actual divers.

On the other hand, if the purpose of the gaming is to optimize force deployment by Monte Carlo simulation of many thousands of repeated small boat approaches (many more than 8), then the window of uncertainty is too large, and better ground-truth data is required in order to establish whether a given model is adequate.

5.2   Detection and Response against Underwater Intruders

War-game requirement: Suppose that we would like to exercise concepts of detection, tracking, and non-lethal response against unauthorized entry into a security exclusion zone for maritime force protection. Players will exercise virtual sensors and effectors for rapid contact designation and response against underwater intruders, in order to prove concepts of emerging technology use, as well as to refine tentative rules of engagement, procedures, and communications among forces.

This was done in fact during the NATO Habour Protection Table-Top Exercises (HPT2E, Mar 2012) [6], featuring tactical war-gaming with emerging technologies for non-lethal rapid response against unauthorized entry of underwater (diver) small-boats into a waterside security exclusion zone (see Fig. (3)).

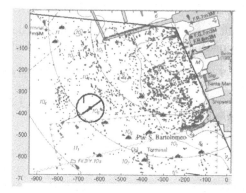

Fig. 3. Screen-shot from a diver-detection sonar with a diver approaching the sonar, detected in this case at about 700 m range. The range of first detection is highly variable in practice (not shown here) which naturally weakens the tolerance requirements for the physical model of detection (Source: Ronald Kessel).

Fig. 4. Blue-force command team in action at their OpenSea Tactical Theatre Simulator station (operations room on board frigate) during the Harbour Protection Table-Top Exercise (HPT2E) at NURC, March 2012 [6] (Source: Ronald Kessel)

But for illustration we focus here on just two essential phenomenon: (1) the expected detection range for underwater intruders, and (2) its inherent random variability, against which the technology, operating procedures, and rules of engagement must be robust. It was determined by game developers that the objectives of education and concept development could be achieved by 12 simulated diver intrusions distributed through vignettes of play.

Ground-truth data: Experimentation with diver-detection sonar (see sonar screen grab Fig. (4)) against divers found a very high probability of detection, but large variance in detection range. When divers were inserted into the field of view of the sonar at 400 m, the average observed detection range was roughly 300 m, with standard deviation of roughly 100 m (exact numbers immaterial here). The essential phenomenon, then, are the first two statistical moments (mean & variance) of detection performance.

Objective: Estimate the bounds of practically perfect model accuracy for diver-detection sonar versus underwater intruder for use in the tactical game.

Result: Using elementary statistics, is not hard to show that, as a rough estimate,

$$\left\| \begin{matrix} Modelled \\ Avg.\ Range \end{matrix} \right\|_{\substack{Model \\ Utilization \\ N \approx 12}} \approx 300 \pm \frac{100}{\sqrt{12}} = 300 \pm 29\ m$$

and

$$\left\| \begin{matrix} Modelled \\ Range \\ Variation \end{matrix} \right\|_{\substack{Model \\ Utilization \\ N \approx 12}} \approx 100 \left[1 \pm \left(\frac{2}{12} \right)^{1/4} \right] = 100 \pm 64\ m$$

Discussion: In other words, any diver detection model that had (1) a high probability of detection, (2) gave an average detection range of 300 ± 29 m for divers inserted at a range of 400 m (roughly 10 % accuracy in the mean), and (3) a standard deviation of 100 ± 64 m (roughly 64 % accuracy in the standard deviation) could not be distinguished from real-world operation before the outcomes of the war-game were accomplished. Any such model would be practically perfect so far as the gaming application was concerned.

This would *not* be true for *all* gaming applications of course. But the point is to be useful for the application at hand. Other, possibly better or worse models may be required to achieve different objectives in other gaming applications.

6   Conclusions

It was shown how war-game objectives and other factors mitigate *against* the pressure for high accuracy in model applications. They create a limit on model accuracy beyond which a model is *practically perfect*, at least so far as the given application is concerned. The test for practical perfection in models was framed quantitatively as a hypothesis test for evaluating the evidence regarding model quality early in a war gaming project.

The war-game developer joins the experimentalist in the test to provide model-independent conditions on model accuracy in light of the objectives and empirical uncertainties, and the model developer joins the experimentalist to provide model accuracy. The hypothesis test therefore provides a common framework for war-game developers, modelling experts, and experimentalists (sensor & weapon system specialists) to collaborate productively in model selection. Its concept should be familiar to all because hypothesis testing is part of any science or engineering curriculum. More importantly, it does not require each party to venture far into the expertise of the other.

The test takes the project team through the issues they face regarding model accuracy in light of their project objectives. If a project team is unable to frame and apply the hypothesis test for practical perfection, then it means that they are unprepared to discuss model accuracy for their war-gaming application.

Practical perfection is the best possible accuracy available to a project, not because more accurate models may not exist, but because accuracy is only useful and meaningful to a project in light of the particular application at hand. Investments acquiring or developing models with better accuracy than practical perfection will be fruitless without first collecting more and better ground-truth data or more certain information about the operating conditions.

If no candidate model satisfies the hypothesis of practical perfection, then it means that the state-of-the-art in modelling still has a way to go before its accuracy surpasses the current limits of accuracy assessment. It is in this way that the hypothesis test can help turn future model development toward specific applied objectives, with a quantitative stopping point (target) for further development in sight, because one is focusing then on model utility rather than on model accuracy.

References

1. Box, G.E.P.: Robustness in the strategy of scientific model building. In: Launer, R.L., Wilkinson, G.N. (eds.) Robustness in Statistics. Academic Press, New York (1979)
2. Kessel, R.T.: How ground-truth data can quietly stall your modelling & simulation programme, Technical Note TN-001-08Mar14 (2014)
3. Carson, J.S.: Model Verification & Validation. In: Yücesan, E., Chen, C.-H., Snowdon, J.L., Charnes, J.M. (eds.) Proceedings of the 2002 Winter Simulation Conference (2002)
4. Sargent, R.G.: Verification and Validation of Simulation Models. In: Jain, S., Creasey, R.R., Himmelspach, J., White, K.P., Fu, M. (eds.) Proceedings of the 2011 Winter Simulation Conference (2011)
5. Kessel, R.T.: Probabilistic versus Physical Models of Sensor and Weapon Systems, Technical Note TN-002-08Mar14 (2014)
6. Kessel, R.T.: Harbour Protection Table-Top Exercise (HPT2E): Final Report, CMRE-FR-2013 (February 2013)

Machine Learning for Parameter Screening
in Computer Simulations

Matteo Hessel[1], Fabio Ortalli[2], and Francesco Borgatelli[2]

[1] Politecnico di Milano, Milano, Italy
matteo.hessel@mail.polimi.it
[2] TXT e-solutions, Milano, Italy
{francesco.borgatelli,fabio.ortalli}@txtgroup.com

Abstract. The aim of this paper is to highlight the potential of Machine Learning for parameter screening in computer simulations, presenting alternative approaches to automatic parameter ranking and screening. This is indeed a fundamental step in the development of a simulator, because it allows reducing the dimensionality of the parameter set, making model tuning more efficient. With *parameter ranking* we denote the process of measuring the relevance of the parameters for accurately simulating a phenomenon, while with *parameter screening* we denote the choice of a specific subset of parameters to be used for model tuning. We will present ranking techniques based on Logistic Regression and Multilayer Perceptron, and a simple procedure for going from ranking to screening. Our techniques have been validated against a helicopter simulator *case-study* but the techniques do not rely on any domain-specific feature or assumption.

Keywords: Model tuning, parameter screening, machine learning, feature ranking, logistic regression, multilayer perceptron.

1 Introduction

The availability of reliable computer simulation has had many theoretical and practical implications. In first place, simulations have changed our way of considering the dynamics of complex systems and led us to a deeper understanding of chaotic behavior. Second, in many fields of Science, simulations have changed radically the research methodology; for example, it is extremely common to resort to modelling and simulation for understanding the evolution of biological or economical systems, as this provides a simple cheap environment to test hypothesis and theories. Finally, in all areas of Engineering, simulations are becoming the standard approach to Testing and Training: this is particularly true in all areas in which safety and costs are important factors (as it is in the aerospace, biomedical, pharmaceutical, and military industries). In order to develop computer simulations capable of accurately replicating the dynamics of complex systems in life-critical applications, the following steps are required: first, *mathematical modelling*, second, *numerical resolution* of the model and, finally, *tuning* of the model's parameters. The first two steps are the most

J. Hodicky (Ed.): MESAS 2014, LNCS 8906, pp. 308–320, 2014.

developed, with well-founded results and established methodologies, making *M&S* applicable to a wide range of different domains. The third step, Tuning, is the process of determining the best values for the parameters of a mathematical model. Such process can be extremely complex in force of high number of parameters in complex models and the non-linear interactions among parameters. Tuning is essential when the aim is not forecasting but the accurate replication in a simulated environment of some known phenomena. This is the case, for example, in the flight simulators industry (where legal constraints require a long tuning process to certificate a simulator for pilot Training) or in various medical contexts, such as simulation-driven training (Morgan et al, 2006, [1]) and accurate dose calculation in radiotherapy (Lewis et al, 2009, [2]). Tuning is, currently, the less developed step in *M&S* and it is mostly carried out by hand, by modifying the huge number of parameters by trial and error, until the required accuracy is obtained. The typical approach to tuning is therefore slow and human-intensive, making the identification of automatic techniques to support the process a relevant research topic. In our research, ultimately aiming at developing an entire novel methodology for model tuning, we have started by focusing on a first problem, automatic parameter screening: i.e. the process of identifying the subset of parameters most relevant for the simulation's output. It is a complex problem because of the non-linear interactions among different parameters, and because a good trade-off must be found: the smallest the set of parameters considered for tuning the easiest the tuning becomes, but, if relevant parameters are ignored, tuning can become impossible (because of the optimal solution may become unreachable modifying exclusively the remaining parameters).

2   Screening

Although screening is a process with a long tradition, most methods make relevant assumptions on the distribution of data or require significant domain knowledge. Example of classical techniques for parameter screening are *One-factor-at-the-time* Designs (Zhang, 2007, [3]), *Sequential Bifurcation* (Bettonvil et al, 1997, [4]), Pooled ANOVA (Last et al, 2008, [5]), *Design Of Experiments* (Fisher, 1935, [6]. Besides other specific assumptions made by each of these approaches, a common shortcoming in such methods is the assumption of the existence of some low-order polynomial relation between input and output variables; another limitation is the choice of a two-level scheme (as this choice implies linearity - or at least monotonicity - for the functional form of the output, and also makes the choice of the levels of the input variable a complex decision). When the assumptions made by each methods are satisfied and the required knowledge is available, traditional methods are very effective and in literature many successful examples can be found. However, we were looking for a more general approach capable of treating the model as a black-box, and capable of being as much as possible independent from the application domain. We thus chose to try to apply, in a peculiar application domain, the so-called Machine Learning techniques: with the term *Machine Learning* denoting the set of techniques and tools developed in different communities – *Statistics, Data Mining, Artificial Intelligence,*

Databases – for automatically learning relations in data). We first considered the existing *Feature Selection* algorithms, however, although apparently promising, these techniques focus mostly on eliminating redundancy, relying on learning the statistical dependencies among factors (which, in computer simulations, are independent). In order to exploit Machine Learning for our aims we have thus tried a less direct approach. First, we generate a database of <*parameter-set, simulation error*> tuples; secondly, we train a classifier on such database (using one of two alternative approaches); then we extract from the learnt classifier measures of relevance of the model's parameter; finally, we derive from the ranking of parameters a subset of "most" relevant parameters. The proposed techniques have been validated against a helicopter flight simulator case-study and our experiments have shown that, when applied to computer simulations, this indirect approach leads to higher quality results than *feature selection* algorithms (such as *rough set* based selection). Furthermore, when going from ranking to screening this approach allows to choose the number of parameters to be considered for tuning, allowing the engineers involved in the process to determine the preferred balance between dimensionality reduction and the necessity of not compromising the tuning process itself.

2.1   Database Generation

The *Machine Learning* techniques that we will present are traditionally applied in a very different context, as they are mainly used for learning relations in real world data (which is readily available, only needing to be appropriately collected). Instead our novel application of the same techniques in the context of computer simulations is rather peculiar, because we have to generate ourselves the data that we are going to analyze. This is obviously a very critical point, and we must be extremely careful in order to reduce as much as possible the *bias* that will be introduced. For this reason, we propose to generate the database of parameter assignments (and corresponding simulation errors) randomly, using a normal distribution centered in the initial assignment A_0. Such initial assignment consists in the "ideal" values of the parameters, as derived during the modelling phase through physical considerations. The standard deviation σ of the normal distribution must depend on the range of reasonable values for the parameters, a data easily estimated *a priori*. The value of the standard deviation is the parameter that sets the trade-off between the necessity of exploring as much as possible of the solution space and the need for remaining in the context of physically meaningful values. The choice of the value of σ is thus extremely relevant, but an appropriate choice should guarantee us to learn relations, which are both significant in the neighborhood where the optimal solution is likely to be, and not biased by the expectations of the analysts.

$$pnew_i = p_i + offset_i, p_i = (A_0)_i \tag{1}$$

$$offset_i \sim N(0, \sigma_i^2) \tag{2}$$

$$\sigma_i^2 = \frac{|R_i|}{6} = \frac{(b-a)}{6} \tag{3}$$

Assuming the range of the parameters symmetric with respect to the initial assignment, and following the previous policy, in average, only 1 out of 10 parameters will be sampled outside the range of feasible values (this can be trivially proved using from the Chebyshev's inequality). The outlier must then be set on the boundary in order to make all assignments *consistent* with the given ranges. After the database set up, we must then execute the simulation using the given assignments, simultaneously evaluating the performance of the simulator by comparing the dynamic of the system to the real observed behavior of the physical system that we want to replicate. The simulation error E(**A**) can then be stored, and, possibly, discretized. Discretization is necessary to apply many Machine Learning algorithms, as the first approach presented in this paper: Logistic Regression.

3   Ranking: Logistic Regression

Logistic Regression (LR) is a classical classification method, widely used to deal with discrete class variables. In this section we first present the relevant features of the Logistic Regression model, then we describe how to apply it and how to interpret the results, and finally we discuss pros and cons of this choice in the context of computer simulations. Implementations of this algorithm are available in most data-analysis packages (such as the *Matlab Statistical Toolbox*, *Weka* and *R*). More information on Logistic Regression are found in literature, e.g (Harrell 2001, [7]) or (Bishop 2006, [8]).

3.1   The Logistic Regression Model

Logistic Regression is the most famous and widely used *generalized linear model* (Nelder et al, 1972, [9]); in these kind of models the linear regression is applied to an arbitrary function of the response variable and not to the response variable itself. In the specific case of the LR model the link-function is given by the famous logit function:

$$logit(p) = \ln(\frac{p}{1-p}) \tag{4}$$

Given a binomial class variable (*Low_Error High_Error*) the LR model requires to approximate linearly the logit transformed probability of the event "output assuming one of the two values" and the model is therefore described by the following equations:

$$logit(P_{Low_{Error}}) = \beta_0 + \Sigma_i \beta_i * p_i \tag{5}$$

$$logit(P_{Low_{Error}}) = \vec{\beta}\vec{X} \tag{6}$$

By exponentiation of both sides of the previous equation, and by isolating the probability P of the output assuming the *Low_Error* value, we can transform in the model in a form suitable for computing the coefficients of the linear regression through either *maximum likelihood* or *maximum a posteriori estimation*:

$$\ln\left(\frac{P_{LowError}}{1-P_{LowError}}\right) = \vec{\beta}\vec{X} \tag{7}$$

$$\frac{P_{LowError}}{1-P_{LowError}} = e^{\vec{\beta}\vec{X}} \tag{8}$$

$$P_{LowError} = \frac{e^{\vec{\beta}\vec{X}}}{(1+e^{\vec{\beta}\vec{X}})} \tag{9}$$

If the N bin discretization has been used the previous must be modifies. However, the extension is relatively simple. Let's suppose K possible outcomes and let's assume the *independence of irrelevant alternatives* holds. Then a simple way to build the multinomial logit model is to run independently K-1 binomial logistic regressions, leaving out just the last outcome Y_K. With this approach, we obtain for each iteration, indexed from 1 to K-1, the following logistic regression models:

$$\ln\left(\frac{P_{outcome=Y_i}}{P_{outcome=Y_K}}\right) = \vec{\beta_i}\vec{X} \tag{10}$$

Again by exponentiation of both terms, isolating the different probabilities, and by further exploiting the fact that probabilities of all outcomes must sum up to one, we finally obtain the following relations, which once more allow us to determine the coefficients:

$$P_{outcome=Y_i} = P_{outcome=Y_k} * e^{\vec{\beta_i}\vec{X}} \tag{11}$$

$$P_{outcome=Y_k} = \frac{1}{1+\sum_j e^{\vec{\beta_i}\vec{X}}} \tag{12}$$

This is the basic idea, but there are many extensions to this model, among the many alternatives, we point out the model presented in (Cessie et al, 1992, [10]), which uses *ridge estimators* to improve accuracy in high dimensional parameter spaces. This slightly modified Logistic Regression algorithm is the one implemented in Weka (the open source package for Machine Learning and Data Mining) which we have used in our application of the techniques presented in this paper.

3.2   Ranking Extraction

Choosing *Logistic Regression* to learn the relation between the parameters values and the simulation's output makes it easy to extract the measures of relevance for the single parameter of the model: the regression coefficients βi of the different parameters directly provide us with the ranking. In a different setting, this approach might not supply us with a reliable measure of importance of the predictive power of each parameter, because, if the different factors are highly correlated, multi-collinearity makes computing the relevance of the single covariates much more complex. (For this reason, more complex metrics have been developed to extract from the Logistic Regression model the ranking of the parameters. Such metrics, among which we recall *Dominance analysis, Likelihood ratio and Wald statistics*, are capable of producing valid results also in circumstances in which the various factors are highly correlated). However, in the peculiar context of computer simulations, and given the way we have generated our database of assignments, we do not have to worry about multicollinearity. Indeed, the different parameters are totally independent, and our database is appropriately built in order to reflect such property, therefore, the ranking provided by the regression coefficients is valid and can be used to separate the relevant parameters from the others.

4   Ranking: Multilayer Perceptron

Neural computation is an innovative paradigm, biologically inspired, that has proved itself extremely powerful in a wide range of circumstances. A *neural network* is a directed graph of simple computational units, called neurons; each neuron, according to some rule, combines its inputs into an output, which is fed as input to its successors. A *Multilayer perceptron* (MP) is a feedforward neural network (a neural network described by a direct acyclic graph), in which the single neurons have a particularly simple behavior. The MP is widely used in classification problems, because is capable of dealing with both discrete and continuous class variables. Therefore, we can train the Multilayer Perceptron either on the original database of simulations or on the version with discrete class variable used for Logistic Regression. More information on neural networks in general (and more specifically on the multilayer perceptron) can be found in (Haykin, 1998, [11]), and implementations of the ideas

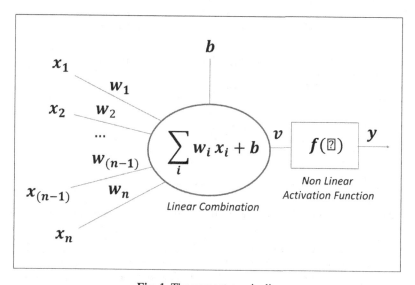

Fig. 1. The perceptron pipeline

presented in the following can be found in Weka (Hall et al, 2009, [12]), in the RSNNS (Bergmeir, 2012, [13]), and in the Matlab Neural Networks Toolbox. As done for Logistic Regression, we now briefly describe the MP model and define a heuristic strategy for parameter ranking.

4.1   The MP Model

The computational unit of a multilayer perceptron is the *Perceptron*. The perceptron was first proposed in (Rosenblatt, 1958, [14]) as the simplest model of the behavior of biological neurons in the brain, and its modifications are still widely used in computational neuroscience. As it is shown in Figure 1, such unit maps N inputs into a single binary or real-valued output variable y, computed applying an activation function f to a linear combination of the inputs and of a threshold b, weighted by coefficients w_i. Common activation functions are the step function, the sigmoids (such as the logit and hyperbolic tangent function), or the rectifier/softplus functions. A perceptron alone is quite limited and it can be used only for linearly separable classification problems. We can however combine many perceptron in a more complex feedforward network; if neurons are arranged in layers, with each neuron having as inputs the outputs of the previous layer we have the so called *Multilayer Perceptron*, shown in Figure 2:

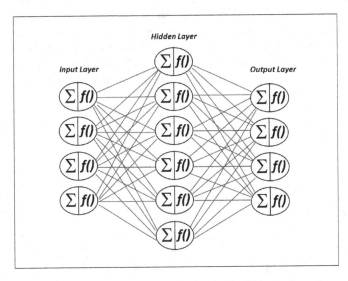

Fig. 2. A multilayer perceptron in the classical 3 layered topology

The first layer is called the input layer, the last one output layer, all other layers are called hidden layers, and to each edge of the graph a weight, w_i is assigned. In our case, we need in the input layer a number of perceptrons equal to the number of parameters of the model we need to screen, while, in the output layer, we will have either one perceptron (if we keep a continuous simulation error) or K perceptrons.

4.2   Computation

Assuming to have a multilayer perceptron, we now present how computation is managed, as this process is relevant to understand how a MP can be trained and how we can extract a ranking from a trained MP. Given L+1 node layers (counting input, output and hidden layers) and L edge-layers (the connection layers between the node layers), the computation of a multilayer perceptron can be described as a sequence of non-linear transformations from x^0 to x^L:

$$x_0 \overset{w^1}{\to} x_1 \overset{w^2}{\to} ... \overset{w^L}{\to} x_L$$

If N_j is the number of nodes at layer j, $x^j \in R^{N_j}$ for all j=0,...,L represents the input of layer j, and W^j is an $N_j \times N_{j-1}$ matrix for all j=1,...,L whose elements $W^j_{h,k}$ represent the weight of the edge connecting node h of layer j with node k of the previous layer j-1. The output value is computed applying in order, for all edge-layers for j=1 to j=L, the following expression:

$$x^j_h = f(v^j_h) = f(\sum_{k=1}^{N_{j-1}} W^j_{hk} x^{j-1}_k + b^j_h) \tag{13}$$

This paradigm of computation is the reference that must be kept in mind in order to understand all the following.

4.3   Topology

If a MP model is to be trained on our database, first the structure of the network must be chosen; the number of inputs and outputs is fixed thus the main design choices are the number of hidden layers and the number of nodes within those layers. The most widely used network topology has just one hidden layer. The reason is that convergence is usually faster for shallow architectures and it has been proved that the MP with a single hidden layer is a universal approximator (Cybenko, 1989, [15]), thus any function can be approximated with arbitrary precision if the weights of edges are properly chosen. In recent years, though, improvements in the training of deep networks (Hinton et al, 2006, [16]) have made other choices feasible, and some theoretical results imply that the universal approximation property of the three-layered MP is achieved at the cost of an exponential number of nodes with respect to networks with more hidden layers. Therefore, our approach to parameter ranking through the analysis of a trained MP applies to networks with any number of layers.

4.4   Training the Multilayer Perceptron

Once the network's topology has been devised, the best values for the network's weights must be found, this is done with the iterative back-propagation algorithm (Rumelhart, 1986, [17]) using the database of pre-classified simulations. Let η a parameter called learning rate. If the database with continuous class variable is used, training proceeds according to the following rules, applied each iteration (also called epoch) to all instances in the dataset (discrete classes can be dealt with likewise). 1) compute the difference between the expected output 'ex' and the actual output 'xL'; 2) propagate the error across the network from output to input layer; 3) update the weights and the thresholds values:

$$\delta_h^L = f'(v_h^L)(ex_h - x_h^L) \tag{14}$$

$$\delta_h^{j-1} = f'(v_h^{j-1}) \sum_{h=1}^{n_j} \delta_h^j W_{hk}^j, for\ j = L\ to\ 1 \tag{15}$$

$$\Delta b_h^j = \eta \delta_h^j, for\ j = 1\ to\ L \tag{16}$$

$$\Delta W_{hk}^j = \eta \delta_h^j x_k^{j-1}, for\ j = 1\ to\ L \tag{17}$$

This algorithm is the most widely used: although convergence is quite slow, it can be made more efficient resorting to batching and multithreading. It important to know that Back-propagation has been proved equivalent to the classical gradient descent procedure applied to an appropriate cost function. The algorithms shares therefore the known limits of such approach: convergence not guaranteed and result possibly just a local optimum.

4.5   Ranking

Extracting measures of relevance from a trained Multilayer perceptron is a complex task and there is no single way for doing so. Various approaches have been proposed in the past, all with their specific pros and cons; we present an alternative heuristic approach that is easily applicable to MPs with any number of hidden layers. Consider a network with L+1 node-layers and L edge-layers, with a single continuous outcome variable; given the previously defined notations, and denoted as R the array containing the parameters' ranks:

$$(\boldsymbol{R})_i := rank(p_i) \tag{18}$$

$$\boldsymbol{R} = W^L W^{L-1} \dots W^1 = \prod_{j=L\ to\ 1} W^j \tag{19}$$

If the network was made of linear perceptrons (having the identity function as activation function), each element of R would represent exactly the contribution to the outcome variable of the associated parameter when it takes unitary value. When applied to networks of non-linear perceptrons, the metric has just a heuristic value, yet it has proved itself very effective in our experiments on flight simulations, yielding to even better results than Logistic Regression. The extension of the method to N outcome variables or to a discrete outcome having N possible values is trivial (R is a matrix with obvious meaning).

5   Comparison: Pros and Cons

The Logistic Regression model can often achieve good classification performance, requiring a relatively low amount of training data; most potential shortcomings of this approach, such as the unreliability of the coefficients as measure of relevance of the single variables, are due to multi-collinearity, issue that, as we have seen, is not present in our peculiar context. The main problem with the use of Logistic Regression for parameter ranking is that the functional landscape that can be learned is limited; therefore, very complex objective functions might require more powerful classifier in order to be properly modelled and offer a valuable insight on the relevance of the different parameters. This is the reason for introducing an alternative approach. The multilayer perceptron's main strength is its representation power, due to its being a universal function approximator. Furthermore, the MP can be trained on the original simulation error values, and does not require discretization as LR, although it is still possible to train the network on the discretized dataset. However this approach has one big disadvantage when applied to our computer simulated environment: it usually requires a larger amount of data if compared to Logistic Regression. This can be a problem because we are responsible of generating all data to be analyzed and computer simulations can be computationally expensive and it is not always possible to speed up computation just adding resources. Indeed, this was the case in our case-study for validation: being a training flight simulator, was designed in such a way that simulations could only be executed in real-time). If a single function evaluation (i.e. a single computation of the simulation error for a given set of parameters) takes very long we therefore advise to try Logistic Regression first, and resort to the Multilayer Perceptron if needed.

6   Screening

We use *feature ranking* algorithms to evaluate all parameters of the model, assigning to each parameter a weight, measuring its importance. However in tuning we are often interested to completely ignore most of the parameters, leaving their default values fixed. Defining which parameters are to be retained for tuning process is obviously somehow arbitrary, and requires to find a trade-off. Considering for automatic tuning a high number of parameter implies the exploration a large solution-space. Instead, considering a too small set of parameters might make optimization impossible if the optimum falls in the portion of spaces that becomes unreachable. In order to use the ranks/weights of parameters to take a good decision, we suggest to sort the parameters according to their weights and then draw the cumulative function: the parameter set can be cut where the slope of the function slows down and at least a given percentage of the total weight is reached (e.g. at least 90-95%). The results of applying such procedure to our helicopter flight simulator were extremely satisfactory. Both the *Logistic Regression* based and the *Multilayer Perceptron* based techniques did identify all parameters which were known relevant by previous experience in tuning helicopter flight simulators; both also effectively screened the remaining parameters (with the ranking obtained through *Logistic Regression* and the ranking obtained with *Multilayer perceptron* being largely consistent with each other).

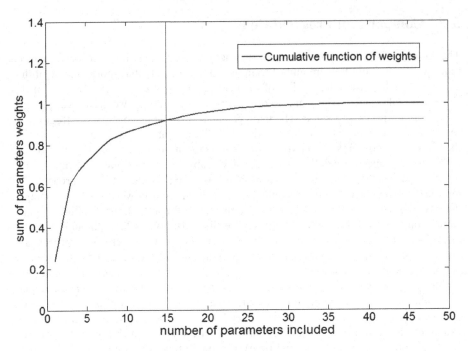

Fig. 3. Parameter screening for our helicopter case study, using the Logistic regression

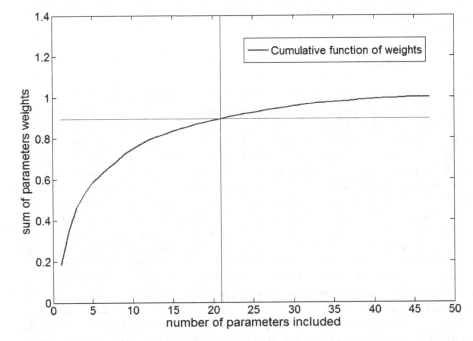

Fig. 4. Parameter screening for our helicopter case study, using the Multilayer Perceptron

On the reduced parameter set, computed either with LR or MP, we were even able to execute automatic tuning procedures capable of taking the simulation error almost to zero (solid lines in figure 5), and this shows that we had indeed identified the right parameters. The validity of our screening procedure is confirmed by the fact that, the same procedure, if execute with the complement set of parameters (those considered less relevant from our ranking procedure), was unable to achieve any improvement whatsoever in the performance of the simulation (green dashed line at the top of figure 5). As future research, we want to continue working on automatic tuning, making the previously shown parameter screening techniques the first step of a novel approach to the problem.

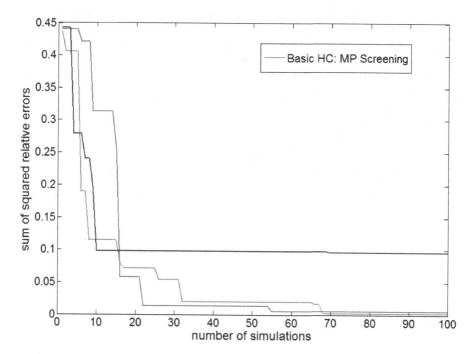

Fig. 5. Execution of the basic hill climbing optimization with different screening policies

References

1. Morgan, P.J., Cleave-Hogg, D., Desousa, S.: Applying theory to practice in undergraduate education using high fidelity simulation. Med. Teach. 28(1), e10–e15 (2006)
2. Lewis, J.H., Jiang, S.B.: A theoretical model for respiratory motion artifacts in free-breathing CT scans. Phys. Med. Biol. 54(3), 745–755 (2009)
3. Zhang, A.: One-factor-at-a-time Screening Designs for Computer Experiments, SAE Technical Paper 2007-01-1660 (2007), doi:10.4271/2007-01-1660
4. Bettonvil, B., Kleijnen, J.P.C.: Searching for important factors in simulation models with many factors: Sequential bifurcation. European Journal of Operational Research 96(1), 180–194 (1997)

5. Last, M., Luta, G., Orso, A., Porter, A., Young, S.: Pooled ANOVA. Computational Statistics & Data Analysis 52(12), 5215–5228 (2008)
6. Fisher, R.A.: The design of experiments, xi 251 p. Oliver & Boyd, Oxford (1935)
7. Harrel, F.: Regression Modeling Strategies. Springer (2001)
8. Bishop, C.: Pattern Recognition and Machine Learning, pp. 217–218. Springer Science+Business Media, LLC (2006)
9. Nelder, J., Wedderburn, R.: Generalized Linear Models. Journal of the Royal Statistical Society. Series A (General) 135(3), 370–384 (1972)
10. Le Cessie, S., Van Houwelingen, J.C.: Ridge estimators in Logistic Regression. Applied Statistics (1992)
11. Haykin, S.: Neural Networks: A Comprehensive Foundation, 2nd edn. Prentice Hall (1998) ISBN 0-13273350-1
12. Hall, M., Eibe, F., Holmes, G., Pfahringer, B., Reutemann, P., Witten, I.: The WEKA Data Mining Software: An Update. SIGKDDExplorations 11(1) (2009)
13. Bergmeir, C., Benìtez, J.M.: Neural Networks in R Using the Stuttgart Neural Network Simulator: RSNNS. Journal of Statistical Software 46(7) (2012)
14. Rosenblatt, F.: The perceptron: a probabilistic model for information storage and organization in the brain. Psychological Review 65, 386–408 (1958)
15. Cybenko, G.: Approximations by superpositions of sigmoidal functions. Mathematics of Control, Signals, and Systems 2(4), 303–314 (1989)
16. Hinton, G.E., Osindero, S.: Yee-Whye The: A fast learning algorithm for deep belief nets. Neural Computation 18(7), 1527–1554 (2006)
17. Rumelhart, D.E., Hinton, G.E., Williams, R.J.: Learning representations by back-propagatingerrors. Nature 323(6088), 533–536 (1986), doi:10.1038/323533a0

Human-Machine Communications for Autonomous Systems

Trevor Woolven, Phil Vernall, and Chris Skinner

Thales UK DMS/IMS
{trevor.woolven,phil.vernall,
christian.skinner}@uk.thalesgroup.com

Abstract. This paper explores some of the difficult issues associated with the ability of deployed, operational Autonomous Remotely Piloted Airborne Systems (ARPAS) to make decisions and then act upon the decisions made, particularly with regard to the dialogue with the Human Operator or Supervisor. We then look at how the use of operational analysis techniques can extend into Communications Modelling which, when coupled with a Synthetic Environment, allows developers to experiment with Autonomous capabilities against the backdrop of a high-fidelity communications landscape in a safe and secure environment, thus smoothing the path towards eventual integration and deployment

Firstly we explore what an Autonomous System needs in order to act autonomously by considering the question: How does the decision-making software decide what to do and what information does it need in order to do it? We then consider the role of the Human in such systems and how his/her role is becoming more Supervisory in nature, as described by schemes such as PACT (Pilot Authorisation and Control of Tasks) developed by Dstl [1], as the levels of autonomy increase in remotely operated systems.

Secondly we consider the circumstances under which the Human Supervisor may wish to control and/or change the type or level of decisions that the Autonomous Systems are allowed to make and/or act upon without recourse to the human in the loop.

Thirdly we consider some of the physical constraints under which an ARPAS might operate with particular regard to the interaction with the Human Supervisor and how they might be optimized. For example, in dealing with periods of time or geographic locations where communications might be restricted; how to assure that the ARPAS conforms to extant operating rules and how the use of an authorization framework can support the devolution of authority to make and act upon decisions.

Finally this paper examines how Modelling and Simulation techniques, methodologies and technologies can help understand and describe the ARPAS 'problem space' and be employed as a key enabler towards gaining Regulatory Authority trust, eventually leading to certification to fly, through a worked example using a Commercial off-The Shelf (COTS) toolset.

Keywords: UAS, UAV, Autonomy, Communications, Human-Machine Interface, Decision-Making, Autonomous Capabilities.

J. Hodicky (Ed.): MESAS 2014, LNCS 8906, pp. 321–332, 2014.
© Springer International Publishing Switzerland 2014

1   Introduction

The use of Remotely Piloted Air Systems (RPAS) is growing in both the Military and Civilian domains. As their use proliferates, an inevitable development is to expect them to do more. With the Human removed to outside the system more decisions will be devolved to the system itself and 'Autonomy' enables this to be realised.

We define Autonomy as the capability of a computer-based system to make decisions for itself with a varying degree of reliance upon the traditional Human Operator. In fact the role of the Human will become less 'operational' and more 'supervisory'. Many RPAS are already tasked to fly a route with the final decisions on how to get from A to B made by the on-board computers, rather than being controlled by a pilot using throttle and joystick.

As time goes by and as trust in the system to do the right things increases, the RPAS computers will make more and more decisions, reducing the currently routine workload of the human, thus allowing the human brain to concentrate on what it does best – achieving mission aims.

Clearly though there are issues to be solved, not least of which is how do the Regulatory Authorities certify an RPAS that can, to some extent think for itself, to fly in the same space as other air users? They need to understand how the Autonomy works, to believe in it and to trust that it will always 'do the right thing'.

Ultimately, any airborne system has to undergo flight trials before obtaining certification i.e. permission, to be flown. Modelling and Simulation has always played a part in this, from 6DoF flight models to wind tunnels through to a wide range of flight systems pilot trainers. The question to be answered now is: how are we to develop, test, verify, validate and certify Autonomous Systems that will make decisions we may not immediately understand?

We believe that Modelling Simulation & Synthetic Environment (MS & SE) has a key role to play in the certification of Autonomous Systems – helping the Regulators to gain trust in the systems by allowing the demonstration of adherence to certification requirements while simultaneously providing the requirements businesses will need to develop those systems in the first place.

2   What is Autonomy?

Autonomy (Ancient Greek: αὐτονομία *autonomia* from αὐτόνομος *autonomos* from αὐτο- *auto-* "self" and νόμος *nomos*, "law", hence when combined understood to mean "one who gives oneself one's own law"). [Collins English Dictionary – Complete & Unabridged 2012 Digital Edition]

Taking the definition of Autonomy presented above and applying it to the ARPAS arena, one could conclude that an ARPAS is one that is equipped to make its own decisions without recourse to the Human Supervisor, noting that the boundaries of these decisions and the circumstances under which they may be made would be under the control of the Human.

In this paper we choose to define Autonomy as "as the capability of a computer-based system to make decisions for itself with a varying degree of reliance upon the Human Operator." Furthermore, we consider that all significant-sized RPAS will require a minimum of Autonomous Sense & Avoid capability (also sometimes known as 'Detect & Avoid') in order to gain certification to fly in non-segregated airspace. This is in fact the stated position of several Regulatory Authorities.

3   Decision-Making

How do Computers Make Decisions?

Decision-Making Environment

When a decision needs to be made, it can only be made in full cognisance of the Environment in which the system is operating. For an RPAS this will include but not be limited to: the weather conditions that the air vehicle is currently experiencing or will soon experience; the current state of the system i.e. its ability to understand the immediate environment; proximity to other air users; the availability of the information required to be able to make the decision and the completeness and reliability of that information.

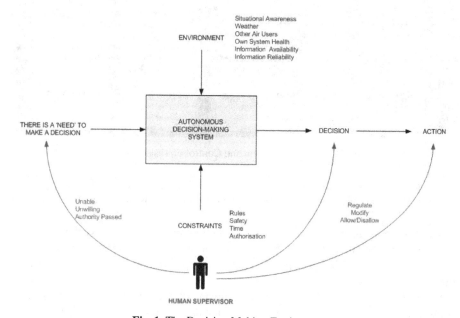

Fig. 1. The Decision Making Environment

Any decision can only be made within the set of **Constraints** acting on the system or upon the system's ability to make the decision. These include: operational rules such as the Laws of the Air or the Laws of Armed Conflict; the safety of the system itself and of other nearby air users; but perhaps most importantly the actions and decisions of the Human Operator/Supervisor himself.

The 'need' for a decision to be made by a computer in the first instance stems from the Human's inability or unwillingness to make the decision: he might not be able to tell the system what he wants, or he might not be able to make the decision fast enough or he may be perfectly comfortable letting the computer make the decision because he has gained a sufficient level of trust in its ability to do so safely and correctly.

The Human may also affect what is done with the Decision by modifying it in some way, asking for a different decision to be made or by disallowing or modifying how the Action resulting from the decision proceeds.

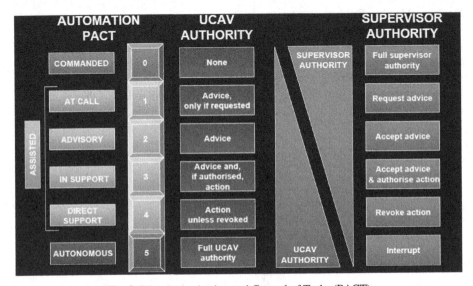

Fig. 2. Pilot Authorisation and Control of Tasks (PACT)

But still a question remains about the 'level' of decision. The PACT scheme developed in [1] illustrates the spectrum of Autonomous decisions over five different levels.

What we need to be careful of is that Autonomous Decision-Making is likely to occur as a continuous spectrum rather than one or more discrete steps or levels.

Figure 3 illustrates the concept of a continuous spectrum of Autonomy with an example:

In the low Autonomy phase all three Human roles are filled. The Tasking User sends tasks and information requests to the Planner who turns them into Missions for the UAVs in the RPAS to execute. These are then passed to the Pilot who will then either directly fly the UAVs to achieve the task request(s). In the high Autonomy phase only the Tasking User role is filled by a Human, the rest of the roles are performed by the Autonomous capabilities within the RPAS.

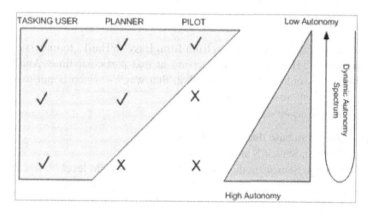

Fig. 3. Relationship between Autonomy Level & Human 'Role'

The main message is that the changes in Autonomy level will be dynamic and may occur at any time in any direction. The question is how and under what circumstances?

4   Human Supervision

4.1   The Role of the Human

So who is the Human in the loop? Where does he/she reside? How, when & why does the Human interact with an Autonomous System?

If the Human has sufficient 'trust' in a system he/she will be more likely to allow it to make decisions but the level of decision he/she allows the system to make may well vary over time as the situation the RPAS finds itself in changes. These may be pre-planned responses to certain parts of a Mission or reactions to expected or even unexpected changes in the RPAS operating environment – the reactive responses are the ones that get progressively more difficult to understand and these are the ones that impact upon the ability to achieve safe flight certification for ARPAS.

In order to gain trust in a system, all stakeholders including the regulatory authorities need to understand why it behaves in a certain way and, most importantly, to be able to predict how it will behave in all circumstances. We expect that an understanding of the logic will have already occurred; what, perhaps, they need is to be able to ensure is that the logic is valid under <u>all</u> circumstances where it will be invoked and this must especially include 'nested' logic It is a key facet of Autonomy that the decisions made may NOT be immediately understood by on-lookers and this is where the use of MS & SE will greatly aid the acceptance of Autonomy, by providing a safe environment in which to exercise the system and engage the regulators in integration, verification and validation (IV&V) activities.

4.2   Types of Decision

Types of decision also exist in a spectrum from Easy to Hard - to understand why the system has made THAT particular decision at that particular time. Another way to explain this is "I would not have done that, that way" – which is not to say that the chosen way is wrong, just different.

Example decisions on a Decision Spectrum:

- Return to base due to a fuel leak
- Turn on Sensor S at time T in mode M
- Change Sensor mode to mode N due to low light level
- Change Sensor Type in use due to weather conditions
- Change Air Vehicle position to nullify terrain obscuration or to avoid adverse weather
- Execute manoeuvre X to avoid collision
- Perform low priority task B before higher priority task A

5   Physical Constraints

The decision-making constraints generally involve extant Rules such as the Rules of the Air, the Rules of Engagement or the Laws of Armed Conflict. However, the key dimension that exercises the Regulatory Authorities is safety and ensuring that airborne systems do not pose a heightened or uncontrolled risk to human life or property.

The most important constraint on the decision-making capability of an Autonomous System is the interaction with the Human Supervisor and the most important physical element of that interaction is the ability to communicate.

Current Communications with manned aircraft are primarily by voice. For airspace management the pilot is required to respond to the ground based ATC operative within a predetermined time window to confirm receipt and understanding of the message sent and compliance with the suggested course of action.

The maintenance of communications continuity and mitigation strategies for 'lost or reduced communications' scenarios for manned and unmanned aircraft will need different solutions. Currently for manned platforms, in the event of a communications loss, the pilot will proceed with the pre-planned route but, for unmanned aircraft the solution is not that straight forward as (at low levels of autonomy) elements of flight management are carried out in non real-time (NRT) from the ground. Therefore, attempts at re-establishing communications must be undertaken.

As an example: the UK's WATCHKEEPER (WK) Unmanned Tactical Air System executes a pre-defined and certified sequence of actions whenever it detects an inability to communicate with its Pilot at the Ground Control Station: firstly manoeuvring trying to re-acquire communications capability and if that fails after a pre-determined period of time; flying a pre-determined route to a designated 'safe' area where the air vehicle may be crash-landed – while all the time attempting to re-establish communications with the Human-in-the-Loop.

The increased performance of platforms is leading to challenges in maintaining communications links during high rate manoeuvre which can be solved by both increasing autonomy and by using the knowledge of the manoeuvre in advance and preloading the communications manager to allow rapid repositioning of antennas and back up challenges prior to the event.

Similarly, the effects of terrain when flying "nap of the earth" trajectories to avoid detection are predicable, to a degree, and will also provide input to communications management to either request temporary autonomy uplifts, switch bearers to BLOS options or to provide opportunities for line of sight burst transmission.

Unexpected events such as interference (deliberate or otherwise) and atmospheric effects (such as precipitation, thunder storms and ducting) will require the system to provide fall back options either at mission or communications management levels. It may be acceptable at certain parts of a mission (transit phases for example) to uplift the level of autonomy or to select a more robust bearer with, usually, a more narrow data bandwidth. The latter would not be so acceptable during parts of the mission where the operator requires positive target identification from a video feed.

The Human needs to understand the Environment the RPAS is operating in and can only truly understand that through the ability of the RPAS to communicate. For the Human to be able to influence what the ARPAS does he/she needs to be able to communicate those commands or selections to the ARPAS and this may include Authorisation to make decisions at a certain (generally higher) level of Autonomy or the revocation of a previous commanded state change back to a lower or maximum level of Autonomy.

6   Regulatory Compliance

The Regulatory Authorities in the UK (Civil Aviation Authority (CAA) & Military Aviation Authority (MAA)) generally believe that Autonomy is a sound and realistic future goal. However, they will not allow RPAS to be integrated into non-segregated airspace without at least, a Sense & Avoid capability, which will, in extremis, have to be capable of making and acting upon decisions to keep the RPAS itself and all other air users safe at all times. The bare minimum capability is described as 'Pilot-Equivalence' where the RPAS must be certifiable to do whatever a pilot would normally do under similar circumstances.

The main issue with regulatory compliance is that the authorities will not certify a system that they cannot understand and test but have so far been unable to produce a robust and complete set of requirements for ARPAS to satisfy in order to gain that certification. Businesses wishing to supply ARPAS are thereby faced with a dilemma: develop an ARPAS with an 'assumption' of what it will take to achieve certification and run the risk of losing a considerable amount of money if it fails; or wait for the authorities to produce a set of requirements to meet and run the risk of being too late to market or of those requirements being too onerous to adhere to while remaining cost-effective.

We feel that the approach outlined in this paper sits in the middle of these two extremes and is the most pragmatic solution: engage the authorities at every turn, engender trust and confidence in them by sharing designs, ideas and solutions and use that process to assist the authorities in defining and writing down a suitable, robust set of ARPAS requirements, cognisant of the need to help business to affordably meet those requirements. To this end, Thales is working with the CAA and the European Aviation Safety Agency (EASA), on projects within the Single European Sky ATM Research programme (SESAR) and the Autonomous Systems Technology Related Airborne Evaluation & Assessment programme (ASTRAEA), supported by its own investment programmes.

Thales has developed a prototype Sense & Avoid system using a tiered level of sensors, aimed at supporting the integration of RPAS into non-segregated airspace over a series of 'baby steps' and has also developed a comprehensive Airspace Integration roadmap to further these aims. The plan is to engage further with the Regulatory Authorities to ensure that the solution increments are safe at all times via the MS & SE concepts described in this paper, then through a rehearsal stage leading finally to targeted flight trials.

7   Using Modelling Simulation and Synthetic Environment

7.1   Overview

Many Synthetic Environment experiments have succeeded whilst ignoring (or at least deferring consideration of) the key dimension of real-world communications. Several COTS tools are available which allow users to model how communications systems behave in both ideal and in less than ideal circumstances. It is essential to put the two together in order to optimise the possibilities for Computer-based Decision-making in RPAS through the engagement of the Certification Authorities. Accurate environmental Modelling and Simulation embedded within a Synthetic environment will become an essential tool.

The Regulatory Authorities are naturally unconvinced by Autonomy and yet without it RPAS will never routinely share non-segregated airspace with other, for example manned, air systems.

So, the best way to develop Autonomy software is in the laboratory where "flight" is safe and where the decisions made can be assessed without immediate concern. However, the role of the Human must also be considered and so communications between the system controller (the Human) and the ARPAS must be represented to the highest possible level of fidelity. In this way and through constant engagement with the regulatory authorities, trust in the ARPAS will grow to the point a t which ARPAS can be flown routinely as if they were manned systems with a pilot and/or flight crew on board.

7.2   Architectural Modelling

Architectural models of ARPAS operations have been produced by Thales, in its role as Design Organisation and made available to Regulatory Authorities to support early analysis of the possible operations, activities and functions of ARPAS in scenarios such as Sense and Avoid. These models have been used to identify the external entities and their required interactions with the ARPAS to understand the operational context. By using scenarios it has been possible to study the sequences of events, the decisions required by the relevant entities and the consequences of both correct and incorrect operation. This type of early analysis by modelling has then been used to inform the safety case and the design process in developing the System Architecture and requirements.

Furthermore, this design process has allowed engagement with the authorities to understand the issues and concerns regarding what are acceptably safe behaviours. Incremental development can be used to develop requirements (target levels of safety) to eliminate or mitigate hazards. Technical, operational and regulatory assumptions can be established and validated to underpin the evolving System Architecture. Dialogue and exploration of scenarios informs the design process in an iterative way leading to acceptable partitioning of hardware, software functions and subsequent algorithms.

Example: Communications Modelling for Unmanned Combat Air Vehicles (UCAV)

Several COTS modelling tools exist each with their own area of expertise. Thales has experience of Operational Analysis using AGI STK, Synthetic Environment scenario creation using MAK VR-Forces and communications modelling using Scalable Network Technologies' QualNet, amongst others. The current generation of tools are designed to fill a capability but also to operate together to provide a more comprehensive simulation environment. Communications protocol standards such as DIS and HLA usually form the 'glue' between the various tools. Understanding the terrain capabilities of each tool is also important to ensure that there is a common set of capabilities across the simulation environment.

Thales has conducted a modelling task to simulate and model communications on Unmanned Combat Air Systems (UCAS) to access future needs and capabilities. The task built on existing experience developed for Tactical UAS (e.g. WK) and incorporated the need for greater fidelity in communications simulation. The work utilised an existing terrain database for the VR-Forces tool derived from 30m Digital Elevation Model Data (DTED). DTED level 2 terrain data for the same geographical area was also imported into the QualNet tool. VR-Forces allows the simulation of vehicles and humans which interact with the terrain, follow roads, move in convoys, avoid obstacles, communicate over simulated radios, detect and engage enemy forces, and calculate damage. It is possible to configure VR-Forces to use an external communications effects server to control transmission of radio messages between entities. The communications effects server determines which entities are able to communicate with each other and how long it takes a message to be transmitted from the originator of the message to the receiver. Scalable Network Technologies, who develop the QualNet communications modelling tool, have created an Interface Control Document allowing any communications effects server that conforms to this interface to be used with VR-Forces.

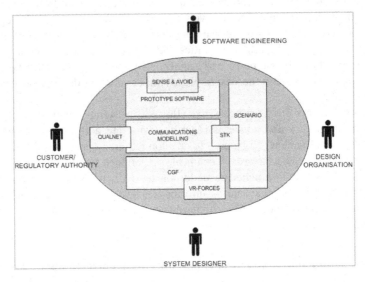

Fig. 4. MS & SE Example

Figure 4 illustrates the Synthetic Environment (SE) described in this section and how it is used. The Design Organisation uses the SE to engage with its Customer and/or the Regulatory Authorities to demonstrate the safe functionality of its prototype software – in this case a 'Sense and Avoid' algorithm. The underlying SE comprises a Computer-Generated Forces (CGF) package (e.g. VR-Forces) to present a real-time, dynamically varying and variable set of interacting entities. The Communications Modelling package (e.g. QualNET) sits on top of the CGF imposing realistic physical constraints on the communications paths within the overall Scenario. All parts of the SE are linked by a common Scenario that is developed to satisfy the requirements of all concerned:

- The Design Authority – to demonstrate their overall system solution performs as expected and is safe
- The Customer/Regulator – to be assured that the System is being exercised in a realistic manner
- The System Designer – to understand how to build the SE
- The Software Engineering team – to demonstrate to the Design Organisation AND the Customer/Regulator that their prototype software meets its requirements in a safe, robust and repeatable way

QualNet is designed as a communications simulator and normally runs faster than real time, however when coupled with VR-Forces via the Federation Interfaces library it is possible for QualNet to run in real time taking its simulation time from VR-Forces. DIS or HLA are used to link the tools allowing VR-Forces to handle the vehicle / human dynamics and QualNet to handle the realistic modelling of the communications network.

Creating the combined simulation as described allows use cases for various communication effectors to be run in a repeatable manor, including:

- Loss of communications due to terrain, weather and jamming.
- The effect of bandwidth restriction.
- The effects of SATCOM delay.
- Insertion of communication network faults in real time or at a specified time in the future.

8   Conclusions

Trust in the behaviour of RPAS is essential for their integration into regulated air space. Air Traffic Management is used to keep trusted air space users safe via separation in both time and space. The dichotomy for ARPAS is how to gain that trust without an extended period of prohibitively expensive flight trials.

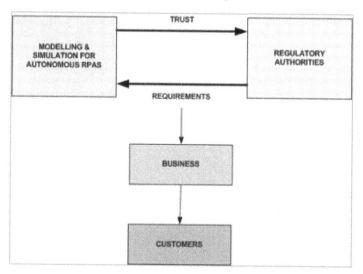

Fig. 5. The Regulation-Business Relationship

Figure 5 represents the relationships between MS&SE for ARPAS, the Regulatory Authorities, Businesses and Customers (note also that in this diagram the Business represents the Design Organisation).

Using Synthetic Environment experimentation, with a high fidelity representation of communications will allow Regulatory Authorities to be engaged from an early stage in the testing, integration, validation & verification of Autonomous systems. They will be able to experience the way in which Autonomy is applied and in which Autonomous Systems will behave in a wide variety of representative situations with realistic environmental conditions and constraints applied. It is, however, vitally important to use the right level of fidelity at the right time in the process as this can have a major effect upon both cost and schedule.

The Regulators will be able to assess, understand and approve such behaviours thus gaining trust and confidence in the system implementation and the Design Organisation's abilities. Once sufficient trust is achieved the system will be able to be deployed and ARPAS will become commonplace in our skies. Businesses will benefit and the Autonomy software will be able to be re-used or re-deployed into other systems.

References

[1] Taylor, R.M.: Technologies for Supporting Human Cognitive Control. UK Ministry of Defence, Dstl/ISS Human Science. Paper presented at the RTO HFM Specialists' Meeting on Human Factors in the 21st Century, Paris, France, June 11-13. RTO-MP-077 (2001)

Yarp Based Plugins for Gazebo Simulator

Enrico Mingo Hoffman[1], Silvio Traversaro[1], Alessio Rocchi[1], Mirko Ferrati[2],
Alessandro Settimi[2], Francesco Romano[1], Lorenzo Natale[1],
Antonio Bicchi[2], Francesco Nori[1], and Nikos G. Tsagarakis[1]

[1] Fondazione Istituto Italiano di Tecnologia,
Via Morego 30, 16163 Genova, Italy
{enrico.mingo,silvio.traversaro,alessio.rocchi,francesco.romano,
lorenzo.natale,francesco.nori,nikos.tsagarakis}@iit.it
[2] Research Center E.Piaggio
Faculty of Engineering University of Pisa
Largo Lucio Lazzarino 1, 56122 Pisa, Italy
{mirko.ferrati,alessandro.settimi,antonio.bicchi}@centropiaggio.unipi.it

Abstract. This paper presents a set of plugins for the Gazebo simulator
that enables the interoperability between a robot, controlled using the
YARP framework, and Gazebo itself. Gazebo is an open-source simulator
that can handle different Dynamic Engines developed by the Open Source
Robotics Foundation. Since our plugins conform with the YARP layer
used on the real robot, applications written for our robots, COMAN and
iCub, can be run on the simulator with no changes. Our plugins have two
main components: a YARP interface with the same API as the real robot
interface, and a Gazebo plugin which handles simulated joints, encoders,
IMUs, force/torque sensors and synchronization. Different modules and
tasks for COMAN and iCub have been developed using Gazebo and our
plugins as a testbed before moving to the real robots.

Keywords: Dynamic Simulation, Robotics, YARP, Gazebo, Open-
Source.

1 Introduction

In the past years, robotics researchers have been developing many robotics frameworks such as OpenRDK [1], YARP [11] or ROS [14] in order to ease the creation
of generic applications for robots and encourage code reuse. The performance
overhead introduced by these frameworks is balanced by the architectural benefits, for example they allow to build modular systems to execute one or more
assigned tasks.

In these frameworks, the *simulator* is a module that represents the real robot
at the interface level. Such simulator module accepts control input (desired joint
torques, desired joint position, ...) and outputs sensory feedback (cameras, joint
positions, ...) from the simulated world. These simulators usually allow to have
the human in-the-loop permitting to train a human operator. The most important aspect is that they allow to develop modules that directly will work in the

J. Hodicky (Ed.): MESAS 2014, LNCS 8906, pp. 333–346, 2014.
© Springer International Publishing Switzerland 2014

real robot without any need to rewrite code. In fact, when the real robot is used, there is a module that replaces the simulator by providing the same hardware interfaces. For instance, a module 'A' write desired joint position and read actual joint position without knowing if it is interfaced with the simulator (Figure 9) or the robot (Figure 7) since they expose the same interface.

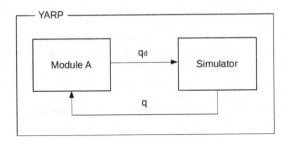

Fig. 1. Module A connected to the simulator

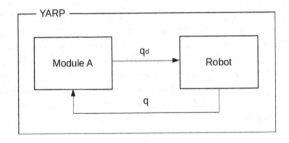

Fig. 2. Module A connected to the robot

By accurately simulating robots and environments, code designed to operate on a real robot can be executed and validated on the simulated equivalent system. This avoids common problems associated with hardware such as short battery life, hardware failures, and unexpected and dangerous behaviors, particularly during the initial stages of development and tuning of new modules and controllers. It is also much faster to have a simulation engine up and running than using a real robot, especially when the simulation engine can run faster than real-time. In this way the simulator becomes a fundamental part of the framework and the robot software development cycle as the first step to validate algorithms, thus minimizing the risks of hardware breaks.

With these concepts in mind we decided to extend one of the most known robotics simulator, Gazebo [10], to be compatible with one of the most used robotics framework, YARP (Figure 3), developed in the Italian Institute of Technology. YARP is supported by the iCub simulator (iCubSim, [19]) that is

Fig. 3. COMAN and iCub interacting inside a Gazebo simulation of a kitchen. Blue dots represent contact points.

dedicated to a specific platform. The needs of a more generic tool for simulating different robots rise up. Gazebo, which has been recently chosen as the simulator for the DARPA Virtual Robotic Challenge (VRC, [2]), allows the use of different dynamic engines, it is easily expandable through plugins and it has a strong and active community. Gazebo is maintained by the Open Source Robotics Foundation [13].

This paper is organized in the following sections: **related works**, discusses some of the most popular simulation environments in robotics, **structure** introduces in detail the Gazebo plugins developed in this work, **conclusions** summarize the outcome of this effort and finally **future works** discusses the follow up activities.

2   Related Works

A large number of simulators have been developed in the past two decades [8]. Such simulators range from dynamic solver libraries to complex simulation environments/systems. The latter are usually large projects that provide both rigid body dynamic simulations and tools such as graphical editors, planner libraries, visualization tools, controllers and so on.

The *Open Dynamics Engine* (ODE, [17]) is one of the most widely used rigid body dynamics engine in robotics simulation. ODE simulates chains of rigid bodies connected and constrained by different types of joints. It has a built-in collision detection system and implements hard contacts using non-penetration constraint whenever two bodies collide. Beside the large number of project that use it, at the moment the development has been paused. *Bullet* [5] is another dynamic engine. It implements different direct/inverse rigid body dynamic algorithms (eg. Featherstone articulated body algorithm, [6]) as well as different solvers (eg. Mixed Linear Complementarity Problem, MLCP) and contact models. Bullet is used for a wide range of projects and its community is active and continues to improve it constantly.

OpenRAVE [3] provides an environment for testing, developing, and deploying motion planning algorithms in real-world robotics applications. The main focus is on simulation and analysis of kinematic and geometric information related to motion planning. It provides many command line tools to work with robots and planners, and the run-time core is small enough to be used inside controllers and bigger frameworks. Industrial robotics automation is an important target application.

Webots [12] is a development environment used to model, program and simulate mobile robots. With Webots the user can design complex robotic setups, with one or several, similar or different robots, in a shared environment. A large choice of simulated sensors and actuators is available. The robot controllers can be programmed with the built-in IDE or with third party development environments. The robot behavior can be tested in dynamic simulated worlds (ODE based). The controller programs can optionally be transferred to commercially available real robots.

V-REP [15], similarly to Webots, embeds different tools that permit fast developing of algorithms, the code can be transferred inside real robotic hardware.

Gazebo [10] is a multi-robot simulator for outdoor environments. As Stage (part of the Player project, [7]), it is capable of simulating a population of robots, sensors and objects. It generates both realistic sensor feedback and physically consistent interactions between objects. It includes an accurate simulation of rigid-body physics and allows the user to select between multiple dynamics engines (ODE, Bullet, SimBody [16] and DART [18]). Gazebo has been used to compare algorithms for navigation and grasping in a controlled environment.

Finally, two notable softwares are the OpenHRP project used in Japan for the HRP series [9] and MuJoCo [20] used for model-based control.

Our decision to add a YARP interface to Gazebo is motivated by the following considerations. We want to switch between fast, not accurate simulations and slow, accurate ones, thus we need the capability of choosing among different dynamic engines. We also want a simulator which is both easy to use and to expand in order to add new robot models. Finally, we prefer an open-source software with an active community and money investments. Gazebo fulfills our requirements, in particular it is expandable with a plugin structure: in this work our YARP interface is a collection of Gazebo plugins.

3   Structure

It is useful to understand Gazebo plugins and YARP device drivers before describing the structure of our plugins (from now on *gazebo_yarp_plugins*).

Gazebo plugins are C++ classes that extend the functionalities of Gazebo, while YARP device drivers are C++ classes used in YARP for abstracting the functionality of robot devices. Usually, each class of gazebo_yarp_plugins embeds a YARP device driver in a Gazebo plugin.

3.1   Gazebo Plugins

A plugin is a piece of code compiled as a shared library and inserted into the simulator. A plugin has direct access to all the functionalities of Gazebo from the physics engine to the simulated world. Furthermore, plugins are self-contained routines that are easily shared and can be inserted and removed from a running system. There are 4 types of plugins in Gazebo: **world**, **model** and **sensor** plugins are attached to and control a specific simulated world/model/sensor respectively, while **system** plugin is specified on the command line and loads during the Gazebo startup.

3.2   YARP *Device Drivers*

YARP provides special devices that act as network proxies and make interfaces available through a network connection. This allows accessing devices remotely across the network without code change.

A device driver is a class that implements one or more interfaces. There are three separate concerns related to devices in YARP:

- Implementing specific drivers for particular devices
- Defining interfaces for device families
- Implementing network wrappers for interfaces

For example the Control Board device driver implements a set of interfaces that are used to control the robot (IPositionControl, ITorqueControl, etc.) and another set of interfaces to read data from the motors (IEncoders, etc).

3.3   Gazebo-YARP Plugins

The gazebo_yarp_plugins is made of:

- Gazebo plugins that instantiate YARP device drivers,
- YARP device drivers that wrap Gazebo functionalities inside the YARP device interfaces.

The plugins/devices already implemented are the *Control Board, 6-axis Force Torque sensor, Inertial Measurement Unit* (IMU) and a *Clock* plugin used for synchronization. The first three plugins are directly related to the simulated objects and sensors, while the last one is a system plugin that synchronizes all the other YARP modules with the simulation time.

Control Board. The Control Board plugin allows to control the robot using YARP Interfaces, it is implemented as a Gazebo Model plugin. Every control board allows the user to control one or more joints (a kinematic chain such as the arm or leg, etc.) as specified in a configuration file. For each controlled joint the control board opens different interfaces, permitting the use of different type of controllers for each joint. Such interfaces include position control, torque control, encoders reading, torque measurement and joint impedance control. Usually the number of instantiated control boards is equal to the number of kinematic chains. Each control board, during every cycle of simulation, reads position, velocity and torque values from the simulated joints and sends desired joints position or torques to the simulator. The values read from the simulator are broadcasted through YARP interfaces in the YARP network, in a similar way the desired joint values come from YARP interfaces (Figure 4). The following YARP interfaces are used to control the robot.

- **IPositionControl**: a position control with a linear trajectory generator considering a max joint speed
- **IPositionDirect**: a position control using Gazebo position PIDs
- **ITorqueControl**: a perfect torque follower
- **IImpedanceControl**: a joint impedance control with the following law

$$\tau_d = -P_d(q - q_d) - D_d\dot{q} + \tau_{offset} \tag{1}$$

where q_d is the desired equilibrium position, P_d is the desired joint stiffness and D_d is the desired joint damping. τ_{offset} is an extra signal that can be used for gravity compensation or inverse dynamics control.

Furthermore, the Control Board implements the **IControlMode** interface that allows to change the type of controller online. All these interfaces are also available on the robot and they have the same behaviour.

6-axis Force/Torque Sensor. A Force/Torque sensor measures a wrench in the robot structure. The sensor, at the time of writing, is simulated in Gazebo as if it was attached to the reference frame associated to a joint. On the YARP side, the reading of a generic sensor is implemented as a **IAnalogSensor** interface (Figure 5). The broadcasted data is a vector of six numbers representing the forces and the torques applied on that reference frame. Figure 9 shows CO-MAN interacting with an object in the ground. Figure 7 and Figure 8 shows the measured forces and torques from the simulation.

IMU Sensor. An IMU measures velocity, orientation, and gravitational forces, using a combination of accelerometers and gyroscopes, of the link where it is placed. It is also possible to add white Gaussian noise on the measurement (Figure 10). Similar to the Force/Torque sensor, it is implemented as a **IAnalogSensor** interface.

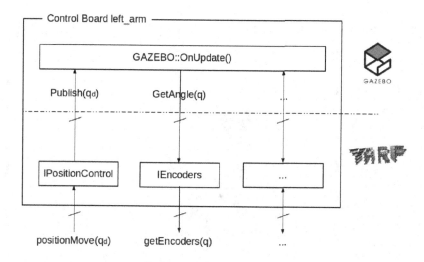

Fig. 4. Control Board plugin for the left_arm kinematic chain. yarp::IPositionControl interface has a method positionMove() that can be used to set joint values inside a YARP module. The plugin implements such interface by calling the Publish() method inside the Gazebo API to move the simulated joints at each OnUpdate().

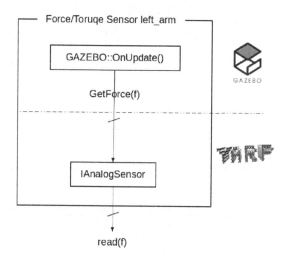

Fig. 5. The Force/Torque sensor in the left arm is implemented as a YARP IAnalogSensor interface. At every step the internal state of the plugin is updated with the last readings of forces and torques from the simulation.

Fig. 6. A Gazebo simulation running with COMAN interacting with an object in the ground

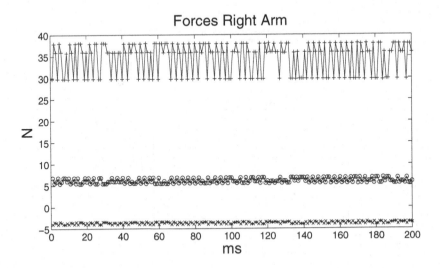

Fig. 7. Plot of forces measured at the Force/Torque sensor placed on the right arm (data logged during simulation). Forces along x,y and z are respectively crossed, circled and marked line.

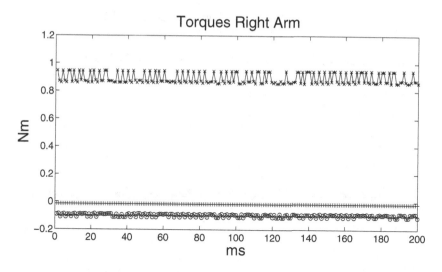

Fig. 8. Plot of torques measured at the Force/Torque sensor placed on the right arm (data logged during simulation). Torques along x,y and z are respectively crossed, marked and circled line.

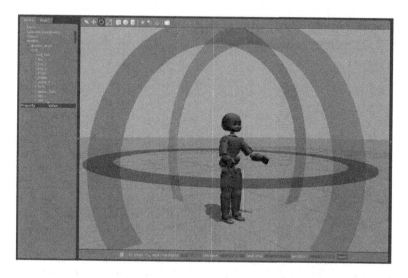

Fig. 9. A Gazebo simulation running with iCub

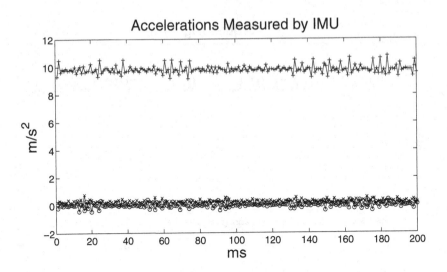

Fig. 10. Plot of accelerations measured by the IMU (data logged during simulation). Accelerations along x,y and z are respectively crossed, circled and marked line.

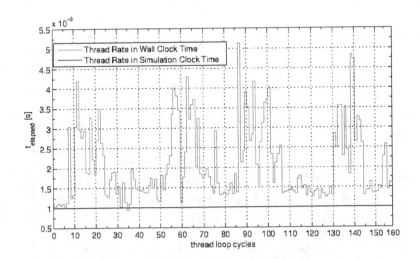

Fig. 11. Time elapsed between each execution of the control loop, measured in simulation clock time and in wall clock time. Desired thread rate is 1kHz and simulation time step is 1ms.

Clock. A fundamental aspect in simulations is the synchronization between YARP modules and the simulated robot. A YARP module is a process in which one or more threads are started. When such modules are used in the real robot, the thread rate is timed by the machine (system) clock, also called the *wall clock*. When the simulation is running we want the rate of such modules to be synchronized with the simulated time, otherwise the control loop could run faster or slower with respect to the simulated robot dynamics. The *real-time factor* (*RTF*) of the simulation is given by

$$RTF = update\_frequency \times step\_time \qquad (2)$$

and is kept to one when the desired update frequency is the inverse of the time increased at each step in the simulation. For instance if the simulation runs with a real time factor of 0.1, 10 seconds are needed to simulate 1 real second. Within this situation, the controller process should also be slowed down 10 times to be coherent with the simulation. To solve this issue we developed a *clock* plugin that synchronizes modules with the simulated time. The *clock* plugin is implemented as a System plugin and publishes on a YARP port the time information from the simulator. For every simulation step, the simulation time is incremented and the timestamp is sent via socket.

YARP functions that provide access to the computer internal clock and support thread scheduling can be synchronized with an external clock (this is enabled with the *YARP_CLOCK* environment variable). Classes supporting periodic threads (*RFModule* and *RateThread*) are therefore automatically synchronized with the clock provided by the simulator. The *yarp::os::Time* functionalities are also transparently working using the wall-clock or the simulation clock depending on the environment variable. Thread sleeps are performed using the right wall or simulated time.

When synchronized with the simulation clock the *yarp::os::Time* delay does not explicitly sleep on a wall clock, rather a scheduler is synchronized with the simulation clock by performing blocking reads on the *YARP_CLOCK* port. This scheduler wakes up the threads that required a delay just once, when they have slept for the desired duration. Compared to the ROS::Time implementation which uses small sleeps on wall clock to check synchronization with the simulated clock, this allows to run simulations both slower and faster than real time and still have synchronization between threads and controls. In any case, when accessing the simulated clock Experiments showed the approach to be successful in synchronizing 1kHz control loops against simulations running 1kHz, thus having a 1ms clock granularity.

A similar solution for synchronization has been consequently used also in [4].

Simulation Description Format (SDF). Gazebo uses an XML-style format, Simulation Description Format (SDF), to save and load information about a simulated world or model. An SDF encapsulates all the necessary information for a simulation such as:

- **Scene**: ambient lighting, sky properties, shadows.

- **Physics**: gravity, time step, physics engine.
- **Models**: collection of links, collision objects, joints, and sensors.
- **Lights**: point, spot, and directional light sources.
- **Plugins**: world, model, sensor, and system plugins.

Our Control Board, Force Torque sensor and IMU plugins are included inside the SDF file that describes our robots. For our humanoid bipedal robot, COMAN, we have five Control Board plugins (one for each kinematic chain), four Force/Torque sensor plugins (two in the legs and two in the arms) and one IMU sensor plugin (placed on the back of the waist). The SDF descriptions of COMAN and iCub are available in `https://github.com/EnricoMingo/iit-coman-ros-pkg` and in `https://github.com/robotology-playground/icub_gazebo` respectively. The clock plugin is loaded trough a command line parameter when the simulator is started.

4   Conclusions

In this work we have presented a set of Gazebo plugins, named *gazebo_yarp_plugins*, that allow to connect the robotics framework YARP to Gazebo itself. Gazebo was chosen since it is easy to use, it has the possibility to switch between different rigid multi-body dynamics engines, it is Open-Source and has an active community. Our plugins are based on YARP device drivers in order to have exactly the same interfaces in the real and simulated robot. This allows to write modules that will work both in the simulator and in the real robot without the need to change the code. This is a very important paradigm in robotics research and develop since it minimizes the presence of errors due to code porting. Furthermore the simulator becomes a tool that helps the developer in testing and validation before using the real platform. Such plugins consist in: a Control Board plugin to control the robot, a Force Torque sensor plugin and an IMU plugin. A special plugin dedicated to synchronization between modules and simulator was also implemented. The plugins were tested to simulate two humanoid bipedal robots, the COMAN and the iCub, both from the Italian Institute of Technology.

5   Future Works

Gazebo_yarp_plugins is a project at an early stage that is gaining more and more interest inside the YARP community. Beside the good results obtained up to now, some works are still missing in order to be able to have 100% compatibility with all the Gazebo functions. Furthermore we still need to implement plugins to connect YARP device drivers dedicated to cameras and RGB-D sensors to the simulated ones in Gazebo. We are also interested in multi-robot and human-robot simulation: we already have the possibility to easily simulate different robot models but it is still difficult to simulate multiple instances of the same robot. Furthermore, since our robots in IIT have flexible joints, we are investigating on how to simulate flexible joints without specifying extra joints/links inside the SDF of the robot. Finally we are planning an official release of our plugins inside the Gazebo community.

Acknowledgments. This work has been developed as part of a joint effort between three different European Projects "WALKMAN", "CoDyCo" and "SoftHands" aiming at implementing a common simulation platform to develop and test algorithms for our robotic platforms. This work is available as open-source to all the researchers in the YARP community (https://github.com/robotology/gazebo_yarp_plugins).

The research leading to these results has received funding from the European Union Seventh Framework Programme [FP7-ICT-2013-10] under grant agreements n.611832 WALKMAN, ERC Advanced Grant no. 291166 SoftHands and the CoDyCo project (FP7-ICT-2011-9, No. 600716).

References

1. Calisi, D., Censi, A., Iocchi, L., Nardi, D.: OpenRDK: a modular framework for robotic software development. In: Proceedings of International Conference on Intelligent Robots and Systems (IROS), pp. 1872–1877 (September 2008)
2. DARPA. Darpa robotics challenge (2013)
3. Diankov, R.: Automated Construction of Robotic Manipulation Programs. PhD thesis, Carnegie Mellon University, Robotics Institute (August 2010)
4. Eljaik, J., del Prete, A., Traversaro, S., Randazzo, M., Nori, F.: Wbi toolbox (wbi-t): A simulink wrapper for robot whole body control. In: ICRA, Workshop on MATLAB/Simulink for Robotics Education and Research. IEEE (2014)
5. Erwin, C.: Bullet (2003)
6. Featherstone, R.: Rigid Body Dynamics Algorithms. Springer-Verlag New York, Inc., Secaucus (2007)
7. Gerkey, B.P., Vaughan, R.T., Howard, A.: The player/stage project: Tools for multi-robot and distributed sensor systems. In: Proceedings of the 11th International Conference on Advanced Robotics, pp. 317–323 (2003)
8. Ivaldi, S., Padois, V., Nori, F.: Tools for dynamics simulation of robots: a survey based on user feedback. CoRR, abs/1402.7050 (2014)
9. Kanehiro, F., Hirukawa, H., Kajita, S.: Openhrp: Open architecture humanoid robotics platform. I. J. Robotic Res. 23(2), 155–165 (2004)
10. Koenig, N., Howard, A.: Design and use paradigms for gazebo, an open-source multi-robot simulator. In: Proceedings of 2004 IEEE/RSJ International Conference on Intelligent Robots and Systems (IROS 2004), vol. 3, pp. 2149–2154 (2004)
11. Metta, G., Fitzpatrick, P., Natale, L.: Yarp: Yet another robot platform. International Journal of Advanced Robotics Systems, Special Issue on Software Development and Integration in Robotics 3(1) (2006)
12. Michel, O.: Cyberbotics ltd. webots tm: Professional mobile robot simulation. Int. Journal of Advanced Robotic Systems 1, 39–42 (2004)
13. OSRF. Open source robotics foundation (2011)
14. Quigley, M., Conley, K., Gerkey, B.P., Faust, J., Foote, T., Leibs, J., Wheeler, R., Ng, A.Y.: Ros: an open-source robot operating system. In: ICRA Workshop on Open Source Software (2009)

15. Rohmer, E., Singh, S.P.N., Freese, M.: V-rep: A versatile and scalable robot simulation framework. In: IROS, pp. 1321–1326. IEEE (2013)
16. Sherman, M.A., Seth, A., Delp, S.L.: Simbody: multibody dynamics for biomedical research. Procedia IUTAM 2, 241–261 (2011)
17. Smith, R.: Open dynamic engine (2000)
18. Georgia Tech. Dart (2013)
19. Tikhanoff, V., Cangelosi, A., Fitzpatrick, P., Metta, G., Natale, L., Nori, F.: An open-source simulator for cognitive robotics research: The prototype of the icub humanoid robot simulator. In: Proceedings of the 8th Workshop on Performance Metrics for Intelligent Systems, PerMIS 2008, pp. 57–61. ACM, New York (2008)
20. Todorov, E., Erez, T., Tassa, Y.: Mujoco: A physics engine for model-based control. In: IROS, pp. 5026–5033. IEEE (2012)

Combining Complementary Motion Estimation Approaches to Increase Reliability in Urban Search & Rescue Missions

Vladimír Kubelka and Michal Reinstein

Center for Machine Perception, Department of Cybernetics, Faculty of Electrical
Engineering, Czech Technical University in Prague
{kubelka.vladimir,reinstein.michal}@fel.cvut.cz

Abstract. Precise motion estimation is vital for any mobile robot to
correctly control its actuators and thus to navigate through terrain. Basic approaches of motion estimation (e.g. wheel odometry) that can be
considered reliable in laboratory conditions tend to fail in real-world
search and rescue scenarios because of uneven and slippery surface the
robot has to cross. In this article, we pick some of the current localization and motion estimation techniques and discuss their prerequisites
in contrast with experience gathered during end-user evaluations and a
real-world deployment of our robotic platform in a town struck by an
earthquake (Mirandola, Italy). The robotic platform is equipped with a
set of sensors allowing us to combine various approaches to robot localization and motion estimation in order to increase the redundancy in the
system and thus the overall reliability. We present our approach to fuse
selected sensor modalities that was developed with emphasis on possible
sensor failures, which have been subsequently experimentally tested.

Keywords: Urban Search and Rescue, Mobile Robotics, Localization.

1 Introduction

Advances in technology of the recent decade have allowed mobile robotics (i.e.
robots that move around by their own means) to leave controlled laboratory environments and to start seeking for real-live deployments. This search is not unilateral, there are real-life problems that explicitly require such robotic technology—
the Fukushima power plant is planned to be decontaminated by means of mobile
robots, exploration of our neighbour planet Mars is performed (among others)
by robotic rover nicknamed Curiosity that is capable of collecting and examining
rock samples.

Development of powerful and efficient mobile CPUs allows robots to process
various data collected on-board immediately and use them to plan their actions
in order to accomplish their goals. Complementary, with the rapid advance in
sensor technology, it has been possible to embed richer sensor suites and extend
the perception capabilities and thus increase the environment awareness. Such
sensor suites provide multi-modal information that naturally ensure perception

J. Hodicky (Ed.): MESAS 2014, LNCS 8906, pp. 347–356, 2014.

robustness, allowing also better self-calibration, fault detection and recovery—given that appropriate data fusion methods are exploited.

In this paper, we focus on self-localization of mobile robots with respect to environment robot operates in. Self-localization is one of several key abilities a mobile robot needs in order to perform any kind of autonomous action involving movement through the environment. If omitted, the burden of navigation lies on human operator, who is required to interpret the sensor data (video stream is probably the most suitable for human operators) and decide what actions should the robot take. Of course in that case a stable broadband data link (wired or wireless) is necessary to transmit the data to the human operator and this is often found challenging or impossible due to real-life environments such disaster sites. Self-localization combined with mapping can lighten the amount of data transmitted or even make the human operator unnecessary if the robot can plan and execute actions by itself.

Fig. 1. The NIFTi/TRADR robotic platform with the distinct red Point Grey Ladybug3 omni-directional camera, the SICK LMS-151 laser range-finder on a rotary mounting and the black arm equipped with a depth camera and thermo camera

Experience with our robotic platform (developed during the EU FP7 NIFTi project and used within the TRADR project, see Figure 1) confirms these claims—thanks to end-user evaluations with Italian and German fire brigades (Corpo Nazionale dei Vigili del Fuoco, Das Institut für Feuerwehr- und Rettungstechnologie der Feuerwehr Dortmund), we have realized that combination of challenging environment and limited data link implies need for robust localization (and simultaneous mapping) that runs on-board and that is capable of exploiting as many sensors as possible.

The TRADR robotic platform is a tracked robot equipped with a suite of sensors and among those, track velocity encoders, an omni-directional camera and a laser range-finder are especially suitable for localization. The aim of this paper is to present development of the localization system of the TRADR robotic platform with emphasis on the difficulties of the real-life deployment. Our previous work concerning localization sensors and approaches to fuse their outputs is described in detail in [11, 15–17, 19, 10]. In section 2, we discuss in-field performance of the sensor suite the robot is equipped with, the state-of-the art algorithms available for these sensors and our implementation of these algorithms. In section 3, we present the current our fusion algorithm, that utilizes all the sensors we consider relevant to localization.

2   Sensors and Localization Algorithms

The simplest way a mobile robot can localize itself is by combining output of its wheel (or track) encoders with internal inertial measurement unit (IMU) that serves as an inclinometer and optionally as a compass. This technique is called dead reckoning and originates in marine navigation, when only velocity and azimuth of a vessel was known. In mobile robotics, dead reckoning provides the localization output with high sampling rate, since it is computationally undemanding. However, due to slippage of wheels (or tracks) and due to uncertainty in azimuth, localization error grows with distance traveled. This problem aggravates in the case of skid-steered robots—those ones that steer by introducing velocity differential between left and right row of wheels. In [1] and [23], improving the localization via estimating the actual slippage is proposed. It involves skid-steering odometry models and various constraints that (processed by the Kalman filter) decrease the localization error. Similar solution that models slippage in the case of tracked vehicles is presented in [5].

The very first implementation of the TRADR platform localization system was wheel odometry, that estimated position of the robot purely from sensors that measure track velocities. Since the TRADR platform is an example of the skid-steered vehicle, this simplistic approach works well only if the robot moves straight forward. Any turn the robot performs introduces significant error in estimated azimuth and therefore causes further position estimates to diverge quickly from the true value. We have addressed this problem in [16] and implemented an Extended-Kalman-filter based odometry system as described in detail in [19]. Our improved solution extracts only tangential part of the velocity indicated by the track encoders and replaces the rotational part by information provided by the IMU. It runs on-board the TRADR robot platform (Figure 1) and significantly improves its localization capability. Also, since it is possible to estimate attitude of the platform from the IMU measurements with reasonable accuracy [11], the resulting odometry works in 3D instead of 2D (6D instead of 3D if attitude considered). This implementation has proven to be sufficient for local navigation, yet globally, it still suffers from all the drawbacks of dead reckoning in general.

To suppress the undesired error accumulation while using dead reckoning, a GPS receiver may seem as a good choice. However, if we consider only standard GPS without any corrections (that would be—for example—differential GPS) its inaccuracy (6 meters is a good guess) exceeds any realistic limits our robotic solutions usually require—even with optimal GPS signal strength and number of satellites. Therefore, exteroceptive sensors (i.e. measuring properties outside the robot) are often exploited. State-of-the-art technique is visual odometry or visual SLAM (simultaneous localization and mapping) which utilizes digital camera images to track distinct landmarks the robot observes. A tutorial that gives an overview of the visual odometry is provided by Scaramuzza and Fraundorfer in [18, 6]; our implementation of the visual odometry was inspired by this paper.

Fig. 2. A panoramic image captured by the omni-directional camera in the earthquake scenario training site of the Prato fire brigade in Italy. Note that the black arm was not attached during this run.

In the case of a single camera setup (that is our case as well), visual odometry can estimate both rotation and translation of the robot between consecutive camera images yet scale of the translation is arbitrary; usually, a unit length is assigned to the first translation. Therefore, to express how many meters the robot has traveled, another source of information needs to be provided. It can be the dimensions of an object captured by the camera or it can be the IMU that measures linear accelerations and thus it is possible to estimate the scale the visual odometry works with [22, 8]. In case the platform is equipped with a stereo camera, scale is obtained implicitly because of the depth information the

Fig. 3. An example of a panoramic picture (cropped, showing approximately 190 degrees) being processed by the visual odometry algorithm running on-board the robot [4]. Grey circles denote all available features in the image, green circles stand for features that have been matched to some features in the previous image yet their displacement does not correspond to the robot movement hypothesis and finally, the blue circles mark matched features of the image whose displacement agrees with the movement hypothesis, indicated by the blue lines.

stereo camera provides. Visual odometry can be further augmented by adding a database stores selected features to be recognized when observed again in future. Such a solution leads to simultaneous localization and mapping—a broad area of research which is well out of scope of this paper.

The TRADR platform is equipped with the omni-directional Ladybug3 camera. The benefit of using this camera is the fact that the amount of landmarks that disappear from the field of view of the camera while moving is smaller compared to a single-lens camera. It synchronously captures 6 images covering the field of view and merges them into one panoramic image as shown in Figures 2 and 3. From this panoramic image, the body of the robot is masked out so the visual odometry concentrates only on the environment. While implementing and testing the algorithm, we have discovered that the mounting point of the camera strongly influences performance of the visual odometry. The omni-directional camera is attached to the top of the robot chassis (see Figure 1 once more), yet still the tracks and the body itself occludes significant part of the view field of the camera. Combined with the view point located close to the ground, the output of the visual odometry yields different accuracies for given axes (e.g. estimates of heading are significantly more reliable than the roll and pitch estimates); work on these issues is still in progress.

Apart from the visual information, depth is exploited as well. Our experience comes from utilization of the laser range-finder. It emits a laser beam and based on the time-of-flight, it computes distance of the illuminated object. This technology works fine even in direct sunlight with range over 100 meters, the SICK sensor we use reaches up to 50 meters. The laser beam can be swept around to collect multiple measurements to eventually construct whole 3D model of the environment (Figure 4 depicts the same scene as Figure 2 yet as a 3D scan). Commonly used approach to match these scans together is called Iterative Closest Point (ICP, [2]) which—similarly to visual odometry operating on a stereo camera images—estimates translation expressed in meters and rotation between two consecutive 3D scans. For robots operating only on a flat surface, the task of localization and navigation can be simplified by ignoring elevation and thus operating in 2D instead of 3D. For that case, frameworks that offer simultaneous localization and mapping have already matured enough to be used as a modules that take laser data as input and provide map and position as output (see [9] for an example of such a system).

The same task in the context of full 3D is more challenging—both in terms of memory and computational performance [13, 12]. The TRADR robotic platform is equipped with a robust industrial laser range-finder SICK LMS-151 which scans in a defined 2D plane. To obtain a full 3D scan of the environment, the whole sensor rotates so the it completely covers the space around the robot. The TRADR platform sensor setup generates a new 3D scan every three seconds, these scans are processed using ICP [14]. Outdoor experiments and simulated search&rescue scenarios proved our approach to be fairly robust even in forested areas and similar unstructured environments. Nevertheless, there are several weak points. Most of all, the environment is not completely static - during experiments, there are almost always persons moving around that appear in one scan but not in the next one. This problem of dynamic environments is a challenge for researchers to be solved, several approaches have been already proposed (e.g. [21]). The second issue is the fact that the laser range-finders usually consist of a high-velocity rotating mirror, in our case the whole sensor rotates as well. That makes then vulnerable to vibrations or worse—mechanical blockages (e.g. by hitting and obstacle or high grass). Apart from these issues, localization and mapping by means of laser range-finding provides precise localization estimates with a bonus of 3D model of the environment.

3   Multi-Modal Data Fusion

It is obvious that there is a need for a fusion system, which would exploit strong points of the various approaches we mentioned and which would made the localization less vulnerable to their weaknesses and possible faults. Sensor fusion is a broad research area; in context of localization, work of Sukumar et al. [20] proposes a way to detect faulty sensors by observing statistical characteristics of their output. An example of a fusion system, that utilizes one main sensor modality (digital camera) and fuses its output with several other support sensors, is given in [3]. Another way of utilizing multiple sensor modalities can be found in [7] where based on 2D laser scans, rough translation is estimated and

Fig. 4. Colored 3D point cloud created by stitching laser scans from the Sick laser range-finder together [14] and by coloring them by the panoramic image data. The model of the robot was added later during visualization.

then using an omni-directional camera, standard search for features is executed and the rough guess of the translation and rotation is refined.

We propose a fusion scheme, where all the exteroceptive sensor modalities (i.e. output of the visual odometry and the laser scanner matcher) are treated equally as velocity sensors and then the proprioceptive sensors provide support information to improve the output accuracy and to increase its sampling frequency. Structure of the system is shown in Figure 5: the left column of the blocks represents the available sensor suite; some of the signals get preprocessed (the middle column represents the visual odometry and the ICP algorithms). When fused by the Extended Kalman Filter, all measurements are treated as velocities (with the exception of acceleration). The output of the fusion algorithm is the currently estimated state (bold letters), which contains—among others—position, velocity and acceleration of the robot. The by-product of the Kalman estimation are also uncertainties of the elements of the state estimate. The fusion algorithm does not accept all measurements; those ones that significantly differ from the expectation are refused by the *Anomaly Detection* block.

We have decided to implement such a loosely coupled system to be able to add or remove sensors modalities without need to redesign the whole system. This way, the system is more resilient to several troublesome properties of the underlying algorithms we have described in the Section 2. For example: in the visual odometry output, incorrect measurements may occur because of mismatched features found in the panoramic image data. The fusion system tries to reject

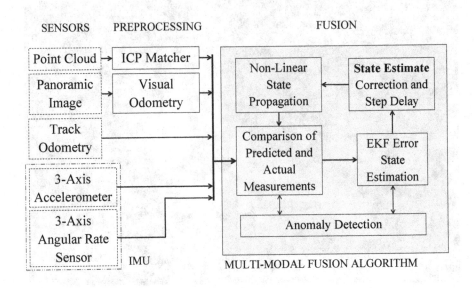

SENSORS   PREPROCESSING   FUSION

Fig. 5. Basic structure of the fusion system we propose [10]

these erroneous measurements by comparing them to the expectation based on the rest of the sensor suite. Even if the anomaly detection fails, the error that propagates into the state estimate is weighted by the reliability of the visual odometry—that is a native property of the chosen Extended Kalman filter approach. Similarly, in the case of the 3D laser scan matcher, blind utilization of its output may lead to incorrect localization of the robot because of several geometrical constraints laid on the observed environment. In that case, the localization errors accumulate over distance traveled yet by interpreting the output as a velocity measurement, this error is suppressed. Since our main goal is robustness against such sensor failures, we have performed a series of experiments both indoor and outdoor and induced sensor failures that we have encountered before during the end-user evaluations. During these experiments, ground truth data were recorded using the motion tracking system Vicon (with cooperation with the ASL, ETH Zurich) during experiments that took place indoors. For outdoor experiments, we used a precise theodolite that tracked a marker attached to the robot to record the reference.

The results confirm that we are able to overcome a significant amount of erroneous measurements originating in track slippage, laser scanner outages, visual odometry image features mismatches and camera occlusions. Also, these experiments uncovered several weak points, for example, the fusion system was found sensitive to laser scanner mismatches that produced incorrect indicated change of orientation of the robot platform. Based on this experience, we work on adjusting the anomaly detection block to better identify these cases.

4   Conclusions

We have presented several approaches to robot localization exploiting sensors measuring distinct physical properties and proposed a fusion system that combines inertial measurements, track velocities, omni-directional camera and laser range-finder measurements to estimate position and attitude of the TRADR robotic platform. This fusion system was designed to be able to overcome common sensor failures observed during end-user evaluations in real-world conditions. It was experimentally tested both indoors and outdoors with precise ground truth being recorded; the experiments confirmed its performance under challenging conditions and revealed possible weak points. The development is still in progress with emphasis on these weak points.

Acknowledgments. The authors were supported by the European Union FP7 Programme under the TRADR project No. 609763 and by the Czech Science Foundation (Project Registration No. 14-13876S).

References

1. Anousaki, G., Kyriakopoulos, K.J.: A dead-reckoning scheme for skid-steered vehicles in outdoor environments. In: Proc. IEEE Int. Conf. Robotics and Automation ICRA 2004, vol. 1, pp. 580–585 (2004)
2. Besl, P., McKay, H.: A method for registration of 3-D shapes. IEEE Transactions on Pattern Analysis and Machine Intelligence 14(2), 239–256 (1992)
3. Chiu, H.-P., Williams, S., Dellaert, F., Samarasekera, S., Kumar, R.: Robust vision-aided navigation using sliding-window factor graphs. In: 2013 IEEE International Conference on Robotics and Automation (ICRA), pp. 46–53 (2013)
4. Divis, J.: Visual odometry from omnidirectional camera. Master's thesis, Charles university in Prague, Faculty of mathematics and physics (2012)
5. Endo, D., Okada, Y., Nagatani, K., Yoshida, K.: Path following control for tracked vehicles based on slip-compensating odometry. In: Proc. IEEE/RSJ Int. Conf. Intelligent Robots and Systems IROS 2007, pp. 2871–2876 (2007)
6. Fraundorfer, F., Scaramuzza, D.: Visual odometry: Part ii: Matching, robustness, optimization, and applications. IEEE Robotics & Automation Magazine 19(2), 78–90 (2012)
7. Hoang, V.-D., Hernandez, D.C., Le, M.-H., Jo, K.-H.: 3d motion estimation based on pitch and azimuth from respective camera and laser rangefinder sensing. In: 2013 IEEE/RSJ International Conference on Intelligent Robots and Systems (IROS), pp. 735–740 (2013)
8. Kelly, J., Sukhatme, G.S.: Visual-inertial sensor fusion: Localization, mapping and sensor-to-sensor self-calibration. The International Journal of Robotics Research 30(1), 56–79 (2011)
9. Kohlbrecher, S., Von Stryk, O., Meyer, J., Klingauf, U.: A flexible and scalable slam system with full 3d motion estimation. In: 2011 IEEE International Symposium on Safety, Security, and Rescue Robotics (SSRR), pp. 155–160 (2011)
10. Kubelka, V., Oswald, L., Pomerleau, F., Colas, F., Svoboda, T., Reinstein, M.: Robust data fusion of multimodal sensory information for mobile robots. Journal of Field Robotics (early access, 2014)

11. Kubelka, V., Reinstein, M.: Complementary filtering approach to orientation estimation using inertial sensors only. In: 2012 IEEE International Conference on Robotics and Automation (ICRA), pp. 599–605 (2012)
12. Nagatani, K., Okada, Y., Tokunaga, N., Kiribayashi, S., Yoshida, K., Ohno, K., Takeuchi, E., Tadokoro, S., Akiyama, H., Noda, I., Yoshida, T., Koyanagi, E.: Multirobot exploration for search and rescue missions: A report on map building in robocuprescue 2009. Journal of Field Robotics 28(3), 373–387 (2011)
13. Nuchter, A., Lingemann, K., Hertzberg, J., Surmann, H.: 6D SLAM - 3D mapping outdoor environments. Journal of Field Robotics 24(8-9), 699–722 (2007)
14. Pomerleau, F., Colas, F., Siegwart, R., Magnenat, S.: Comparing icp variants on real-world data sets. Autonomous Robots 34(3), 133–148 (2013)
15. Reinstein, M., Hoffmann, M.: Dead reckoning in a dynamic quadruped robot based on multimodal proprioceptive sensory information. IEEE Transactions on Robotics 29(2), 563–571 (2013)
16. Reinstein, M., Kubelka, V., Zimmermann, K.: Terrain adaptive odometry for mobile skid-steer robots. In: Proc. IEEE Int. Robotics and Automation (ICRA) Conf., pp. 4706–4711 (2013)
17. Rohac, J., Reinstein, M., Draxler, K.: Data processing of inertial sensors in strong-vibration environment. In: 2011 IEEE 6th International Conference on Intelligent Data Acquisition and Advanced Computing Systems (IDAACS), vol. 1, pp. 71–75 (September 2011)
18. Scaramuzza, D., Fraundorfer, F.: Visual odometry [tutorial]. IEEE Robot Autom. Mag. 18(4), 80–92 (2011)
19. Simanek, J., Reinstein, M., Kubelka, V.: Evaluation of the ekf-based estimation architectures for data fusion in mobile robots. IEEE/ASME Transactions on Mechatronics, 1–6 (early access, 2014)
20. Sukumar, S.R., Bozdogan, H., Page, D.L., Koschan, A.F., Abidi, M.A.: Sensor selection using information complexity for multi-sensor mobile robot localization. In: 2007 IEEE International Conference on Robotics and Automation, pp. 4158–4163 (2007)
21. Tipaldi, G.D., Meyer-Delius, D., Burgard, W.: Lifelong localization in changing environments. The International Journal of Robotics Research 32(14), 1662–1678 (2013)
22. Weiss, S., Siegwart, R.: Real-time metric state estimation for modular vision-inertial systems. In: 2011 IEEE International Conference on Robotics and Automation (ICRA), pp. 4531–4537 (2011)
23. Yi, J., Zhang, J., Song, D., Jayasuriya, S.: Imu-based localization and slip estimation for skid-steered mobile robots. In: Proc. IEEE/RSJ Int. Conf. Intelligent Robots and Systems IROS 2007, pp. 2845–2850 (2007)

Safe Exploration Techniques for Reinforcement Learning – An Overview

Martin Pecka[1,*] and Tomas Svoboda[1,2,**]

[1] Center for Machine Perception, Dept. of Cybernetics, Faculty of Electrical
Engineering, Czech Technical University in Prague, Prague, Czech Republic
martin.pecka@fel.cvut.cz
http://cmp.felk.cvut.cz/~peckama2
[2] Czech Institute of Informatics, Robotics, and Cybernetics, Czech Technical
University in Prague, Prague, Czech Republic

Abstract. We overview different approaches to safety in (semi)auto-
nomous robotics. Particularly, we focus on how to achieve safe behavior
of a robot if it is requested to perform exploration of unknown states. Presented methods are studied from the viewpoint of *reinforcement learning*,
a partially-supervised machine learning method. To collect training data
for this algorithm, the robot is required to freely explore the state space
– which can lead to possibly dangerous situations. The role of *safe exploration* is to provide a framework allowing exploration while preserving
safety. The examined methods range from simple algorithms to sophisticated methods based on previous experience or state prediction. Our
overview also addresses the issues of how to define safety in the real-world
applications (apparently absolute safety is unachievable in the continuous and random real world). In the conclusion we also suggest several
ways that are worth researching more thoroughly.

Keywords: Safe exploration, policy search, reinforcement learning.

1 Introduction

Reinforcement learning (RL) as a machine learning method has been thoroughly
examined since 80's. In 1981, Sutton and Barto [3] inspired themselves in the
reinforcement learning discoveries in behavioral psychology and devised the *Temporal Difference* machine learning algorithm that had to simulate psychological
classical conditioning. In contrast with *supervised learning*, reinforcement learning does not need a teacher's classification for every sample presented. Instead, it
just collects rewards (or punishment) on-the-go and optimizes for the expected
long-term reward (whereas supervised learning optimizes for the immediate reward). The key advantage is that the design of the rewards is often much simpler
and straight-forward than classifying all data samples.

---

* Supported by the Grant Agency of the Czech Technical University in Prague under
Project SGS13/142/OHK3/2T/13.
** Supported by the EC project FP7-ICT-609763 TRADR.

J. Hodicky (Ed.): MESAS 2014, LNCS 8906, pp. 357–375, 2014.
© Springer International Publishing Switzerland 2014

Reinforcement learning proved to be extremely useful in the case of state-space exploration – the long-term reward corresponds to the value of each state [17]. From such values, we can compose a *policy* which tells the agent to always take the action leading to the state with the highest value. As an addition, state values are easily interpretable for humans.

Since the early years, a lot of advanced methods were devised in the area of reinforcement learning. To name one, *Q-learning* [25] is often used in connection with safe exploration. Instead of computing the values of states, it computes the values of state–action pairs, which has some simplifying consequences. For example, Q-learning doesn't need any *transition model* (i.e. dynamics model) of the examined system.

A completely different approach is *policy iteration*. This algorithm starts with a (more or less random) policy and tries to improve it step-by-step [16]. This case is very valuable if there already exists a good policy and we only want to improve it [11].

What do all of these methods have in common, is the need for rather large training data sets. For simulated environments it is usually not a problem. But with real robotic hardware, the collection of training samples is not only lengthy, but also dangerous (be it mechanical wear or other effects). Another common feature of RL algorithms is the need to enter *unknown* states, which is inherently unsafe.

As can be seen from the previous paragraph, *safety* is an important issue connected with reinforcement learning. However, the first articles focused on maintaining safety during exploration started to appear much later after the "discovery" of RL. Among the first, Heger [15] "borrowed" the concept of a *worst-case criterion* from control theory community. In 1994 he created a variant of Q-learning where maximization of long-term reward is replaced with maximization of minimum of the possible rewards. That basically means his algorithm prefers to never encounter a bad state (or, at least to choose the best of the bad states). This approach has one substantial drawback – the resulting policies are far from being optimal in the long-term–reward sense [10].

In this paper we show the various approaches to safe exploration that have emerged so far. We classify the methods by various criteria and suggest suitable use cases for them. To better illustrate some of the practical details, we use the UGV (Unmanned Ground Vehicle) robotic platform from EU FP7 project NIFTi [6] (see Figure 1) as a reference agent. It may happen that in these practical details we assume some advantages of UGVs over UAVs (Unmanned Aerial Vehicles), like the ability to stand still without much effort, but it is mostly easy to convert these assumptions to UAVs, too.

Further organization of this paper is the following: in Section 2 we discuss some basics of reinforcement learning (the reader may skip it if he is familiar with reinforcement learning); Section 3 is an overview of the safety definitions used in literature; Section 4 is the main part concerning the various approaches to safe exploration, and in Section 5 we conclude the findings and we suggest some further areas of possible research.

Fig. 1. NIFTi UGV robotic platform

2   Reinforcement Learning Basics

2.1   Markov Decision Processes

Markov Decision Processes (MDPs) are the standard model for deliberating about reinforcement learning problems. They provide a lot of simplifications, but are sufficiently robust to describe a large set of real-world problems.

The simplest discrete stochastic MDP comprises of: [17]

- a finite set of states $\mathbf{S}$
- a finite set of actions $\mathbf{A}$
- a stochastic *transition model* $\mathbf{P}$: $\mathbf{P}_t(s, a, s') = Pr(s_{t+1} = s' \mid s_t = s, a_t = a)$
  for each $s, s' \in \mathbf{S}$, $a \in \mathbf{A}$, where Pr stands for probability
- and the *immediate reward function* $\mathbf{R}$: $\mathbf{S} \times \mathbf{A} \to \mathbb{R}$ (or $\mathbf{R}$: $\mathbf{S} \times \mathbf{A} \times \mathbf{S} \to \mathbb{R}$
  if the reward depends on the stochastic action result)

To interpret this definition, we say that the at every time instant t the *agent* is in a state s, and by executing action a it gets to a new state s'. Furthermore, executing a particular action in a particular state may bring a *reward* to the agent (defined by $\mathbf{R}$).

The most important and interesting property of MDPs is the *Markov property*. If you have a look at the definition of the transition model, the next state only depends on the current state and the chosen action. Particularly, the next state is independent of all the previous states and actions but the current one. To give an example, the robot's battery level cannot be treated implicitly by counting the elapsed time, but rather it has to be modeled as a part of the robot's state.

Once the model is set up, everything is ready for utilizing an MDP. "The agent's job is to find a policy π mapping states to actions, that maximizes some long-run measure of reinforcement" [17]. The "long-run" may have different meanings, but there are two favorite optimality models: the first one is the *finite horizon* model, where the term $J = \sum_{t=0}^{h} r_t$ is maximized (h is a predefined time horizon and r_t is the reward obtained in time instant t while executing policy π). The dependency of r_t on the policy is no longer obvious from this notation, but this is the convention used in literature when it is clear which policy is used. This model represents the behavior of the robot which only depends on a predefined number of future states and actions.

The other optimality model is called *discounted infinite horizon*, which means we maximize the discounted sum $J = \sum_{t=0}^{\infty} \gamma^t r_t$ with $\gamma \in (0,1)$ being the *discount factor*. The infinite horizon tries to find a policy that is the best one taking into account the whole future. Please note the hidden dependency on the policy π (and the starting state s_0) – it is the policy that decides on which action to take, which in turn specifies what will the reward be.

Other extensions of MDPs to continuous states, time or actions are beyond the scope of this overview. However, some of the referenced papers make use of these continuous extensions, which proved to be useful for practical applications.

2.2   Value Iteration

Value iteration is one of the basic methods for finding the optimal policy. To describe this algorithm, it is first needed to define the essential notion of the *optimal value of a state*. In this whole subsection we suppose the discounted infinite horizon model, but analogous results can be shown for finite horizon, too. "The optimal value of a state is the expected infinite discounted sum of reward that the agent will gain if it starts in that state and executes the optimal policy." [17] Given a policy π, the induced value function is therefore defined as

$$\mathbf{V}_\pi(s) = E\left[\sum_{t=0}^{\infty} r_k \gamma^k\right], \tag{1}$$

where E denotes the expected value and r_k are the rewards for executing policy π. Taking the best value function over all policies then yields the *optimal value function* $\mathbf{V}^*$: [17]

$$\mathbf{V}^*(s) = \max_\pi \mathbf{V}_\pi(s). \tag{2}$$

Inversely, if we have the value function given, we can derive a policy from that. It is a simple policy that always takes the action leading to the most profitable neighbor state (with the highest value).

One useful formulation of the properties of the optimal value function is the formulation using the recurrent *Bellman equations* which define a dynamic system that is stable for the optimal value function. We can say a state's optimal value is the best immediate reward plus its best neighbor's optimal value: [17]

$$\mathbf{V}^*(s) = \max_a \left(\mathbf{R}(s,a) + \gamma \sum_{s' \in \mathbf{S}} \mathbf{P}(s,a,s')\mathbf{V}^*(s') \right). \tag{3}$$

Analogously, we can find the optimal policy using the same Bellman equation:

$$\pi^*(s) = \operatorname*{argmax}_a \left(\mathbf{R}(s,a) + \gamma \sum_{s' \in \mathbf{S}} \mathbf{P}(s,a,s')\mathbf{V}^*(s') \right). \tag{4}$$

The Value iteration algorithm is based on trying to compute the solution of Equation 4 using iterative Bellman updates (refer to Algorithm 1). In the algorithm, we use a structure called $\mathbf{Q}$ to store the "value" of state-action pairs. In Value iteration it is just a structure to save intermediate results, but it is the core of the Q-learning algorithm (described in Section 2.3). The stopping criterion of the Value iteration algorithm is not obvious, but Williams and Baird [26] derived an easily applicable upper bound on the error of the computed value function.

That said, after a sufficient number of those simple iterations, we can compute the almost optimal value function. The number of iterations needed for Value iteration to converge may be impractically high, but it is shown that the optimal policy converges faster [4], thus making Value iteration practical.

Algorithm 1. The Value iteration algorithm [17]

Input: an MDP (states S, actions A, rewards R, transition model P)
Output: the optimal value function $\mathbf{V}^*$, resp. the optimal policy π^*
    derived from the value function

1. $\mathbf{V}(s) :=$ arbitrary function
2. $\pi :=$ the policy derived from $\mathbf{V}$
3. while π is not good enough do
4.   for all $s \in \mathbf{S}$ do
5.   for all $a \in \mathbf{A}$ do
    Update:
6. $\mathbf{Q}(s,a) := \mathbf{R}(s,a) + \gamma \sum_{s' \in \mathbf{S}} \mathbf{P}(s,a,s')\mathbf{V}(s')$
7.   end for
8. $\mathbf{V}(s) := \max_a \mathbf{Q}(s,a)$
9.   end for
10. $\pi :=$ the policy derived from $\mathbf{V}$
11. end while
12. $\mathbf{V}^* := \mathbf{V}$, $\pi^* := \pi$

2.3   Q-Learning

Just a small change to the Value iteration algorithm results in Q-learning. The basic algorithm is the same as Value iteration, just the update step is done differently (refer to Algorithm 2). The consequence of this change is that no model of the system (transition function $\mathbf{P}$) is needed. It is sufficient to execute all actions in all states equally often, and Watkins [25] proved that if Q-learning were run for an infinite time, the computed $\mathbf{Q}$ would converge to the optimal $\mathbf{Q}^*$ (an analogue of $\mathbf{V}^*$).

Algorithm 2. The Q-learning algorithm (only the parts that differ from Value iteration when $\mathbf{V}$ is substituted with $\mathbf{Q}$) [17]

Input: an MDP (states S, actions A, rewards R, transition model may be
    unknown)
Output: the optimal state-value function $\mathbf{Q}^*$, resp. the optimal policy π^*
    derived from the state-value function

6. $\mathbf{Q}(s,a) := \mathbf{Q}(s,a) +$
    $\alpha\left[\mathbf{R}(s,a) + \gamma \max_{a'} \mathbf{Q}(s',a') - \mathbf{Q}(s,a)\right]$
8. line left out

2.4   Policy Iteration

Policy iteration is a completely different approach to computing the optimal policy. Instead of deriving the policy from the Value or Q function, Policy iteration works directly with policies. In the first step, a random policy is chosen. Then a loop consisting of policy evaluation and policy improvement repeats as long as the policy can be improved [17] (refer to Algorithm 3 for details). Since in every step the policy gets better, and there is a finite number of different policies, it is apparent that the algorithm converges [23].

Policy iteration can be initialized by a known, but suboptimal policy. Such policy can be obtained e.g. by a human operator driving the UGV. If the initial policy is good, Policy iteration has to search much smaller subspace and thus should converge more quickly than with a random initial policy [11].

3   Defining Safety

To examine the problems of safe exploration, it is first needed to define what exactly is the *safety* we want to maintain. Unfortunately, there is no unified definition that would satisfy all use cases; thus, several different approaches are found in the literature. An intuitive (but vague) definition could be e.g.: "State-space exploration is considered *safe* if it doesn't lead the agent to unrecoverable and unwanted states." It is worth noticing here that *unwanted* doesn't necessarily mean low-reward. In the next subsections we present the main interpretations of this vague definition.

Algorithm 3. The Policy iteration algorithm [17]

```
1. π' = arbitrary policy
2. repeat
3.    π := π'
   Policy evaluation: (system of linear equations)
```
4. $$\mathbf{V}_\pi(s) = \mathbf{R}(s, \pi(s)) + \gamma \sum_{s' \in \mathbf{S}} \mathbf{P}(s, \pi(s), s') \mathbf{V}_\pi(s')$$

Policy improvement:

5.
$$\pi'(s) := \underset{a \in \mathbf{A}}{\mathrm{argmax}} \left[\mathbf{R}(s, a) + \gamma \sum_{s' \in \mathbf{S}} \mathbf{P}(s, a, s') \mathbf{V}_\pi(s') \right]$$

```
6. until π = π'
```

3.1 Safety through Labeling

The largely most used definition of safety is labeling the states/actions with one of several labels indicating the level of safety in that state/action. What varies from author to author is the number and names of these labels.

To start with, Hans [14] has the most granular division of state/action space. His definitions are as follows (slightly reformulated):

- an (s, a, r, s') tuple (transition) is **fatal** if the reward r is less than a certain threshold (s is the original state, a is an action and s' is the state obtained after executing a in state s, yielding the reward r),
- an action a is **fatal** in state s if there is non-zero probability of leading to a fatal transition,
- state s is called **supercritical** if there exists no policy that would guarantee no fatal transition occurs when the agent starts in state s,
- action a is **supercritical** in state s if it can lead to a supercritical state,
- state s is called **critical** if there is a supercritical or fatal action in that state (and the state itself is not supercritical),
- action a is **critical** in state s if it leads to a critical state (and the action itself is neither supercritical nor fatal in s),
- state s is called **safe** if it is neither critical nor supercritical,
- action a is **safe** in state s if it is neither critical, nor supercritical, nor fatal in state s,
- and finally a policy is **safe** if for all critical states it leads to a safe state in a finite number of non-fatal transitions (and if it only executes safe actions in safe states).

Since we will compare other definitions the the Hans', it is needed to define one more category. A state s is called **fatal** if it is an undesired or unrecoverable state, e.g. if the robot is considered broken in that state. The fatal transition can then be redefined as a transition ending in a fatal state. Opposite to the precisely defined terms in Hans' definition, the meaning of words "undesired" and "unrecoverable" here is vague and strongly task-dependent.

Continuing on, Geibel [12] defines only two categories – *fatal* and *goal* states. "Fatal states are terminal states. This means, that the existence of the agent ends when it reaches a fatal state" [12]. This roughly corresponds to our defined set of **fatal** states. *Goal states* are the rest of final states that correspond to successful termination. Since Geibel only considers terminal states for safety, his *goal* states correspond to a subset of **safe** states. The other Hans' categories need not be represented, since they are meaningless for final states.

An extension of Geibel's *fatal* and *goal* states is a division presented by García [10]. His *error* and *non-error* states correspond to *fatal* and *goal* states, but García adds another division of the space – the *known* and *unknown* states, where *known* states are those already visited (and *known* have empty intersection with *error*). He then mentions a prerequisite on the MDP that if an action leads to a known *error/non-error* state, then its slight modification must also lead to an *error/non-error* state (a metric over the state space is required).

In Ertle's work [9], again the two basic regions are considered – they are called *desired* and *hazardous* (corresponding to **safe** and **fatal**). However, due to the used learning technique, one more region emerges – the *undesired* region. It contains the whole *hazardous* region and a "small span" comprising of *desired* states, and denotes the set of states where no training (safe) samples are available, because it would be dangerous to acquire those samples. In particular, he says that "The hazards must be 'encircled' by the indications of the undesired approaching so that it becomes clear which area [. . .] is undesired" [9].

A summary of the labeling-based definitions is shown in Figure 3. We examined the apparent imbalance between the number of categories Hans defines, and the other definitions, and that led us to the following observations.

The first observation is that creating labels for actions or transitions is unnecessary. If we need to talk about the "level of safety" of an action, we can use the worst label out of all possible results of that action (which retains compatibility with Hans' definitions). Moreover, as "it is impossible to completely avoid error states" [22], we can ignore the effects of the action which have only small probability (lower than a safety threshold) – we will call such effects the *negligible effects*.

A second remark is that the **fatal** and **supercritical** sets can be merged. In Hans' work we haven't found any situation where distinguishing between **supercritical** and **fatal** would bring any benefit. Specifically, in his work Hans states that: "Our objective is to never observe supercritical states" [14], which effectively involves avoiding fatal transitions, too. And since we avoid both supercritical and fatal, we can as well avoid their union.

Third, safety of a state does not necessarily depend on the reward for getting to that state. E.g. when the UGV performs a victim detection task, going away from the target area may be perfectly safe, but the reward for such action should be small or even negative.

Putting these observations together, we propose a novelty definition of safety for stochastic MDPs, which is a simplification of Hans' model and a generalization of the other models:

- A state is **unsafe** if it means the agent is damaged/destroyed/stuck... or it is highly probable that it will get to such state regardless of further actions taken.
- A state is **critical** if there is a not negligible action leading to an unsafe state from it.
- A state is **safe** if no available action leads to an unsafe state (however, there may be an action leading to a critical state).

To illustrate the definition on a real example, please refer to Figure 2. In 2(a), the UGV is in a **safe** state, because all actions it can take lead again to safe states (supposing that actions for movement do not move the robot for more than a few centimeters). On the other hand, the robot as depicted in 2(b) is in a **critical** state, because going forward would make the robot fall over and break. If the robot executed action "go forward" once more, it would come to an **unsafe** state. Right after executing the action it would still not be broken; however, it would start falling and that is **unsafe**, because it is not equipped to withstand such fall and therefore it is almost sure it will break when it meets the ground.

3.2 Safety through Ergodicity

An MDP is called *ergodic* iff for every state there exists a policy that gets the agent to any other state [20]. In other words, every mistake can be remedied in such MDP. Moldovan [20] then defines *δ-safe policies* as policies guaranteeing that from any state the agent can get to the starting state with probability at least δ (using a *return policy*, which is different from the δ-safe one). Stated this way, the safety constraint may seem intractable, or at least impractical – it is even proved, that expressing the set of δ-safe policies is NP-hard [20]. An approximation of the constraint can be expressed in the terms of two other MDP problems which are easily solved [20]; that still leads to δ-safe policies, but the exploration performance may be suboptimal.

In our view, safety through ergodicity imposes too much constraints on the problems the agent can learn. It sometimes happens that a robot has to learn some task after which it is not able to return to the initial state (e.g. drive down a hill it cannot go upwards; a human operator then carries the robot back to the starting position). But the inability to "return home" in no means indicates the robot is in an unsafe state.

3.3 Safety through Costs

Another definition of safety is to define a cost for taking an action/being in a state and minimize the worst-case cost of the generated policies (up to some failure probability). Such approach is presented in [15].

However, unless a threshold is set, this definition leads only to the *safest possible* policies, which are not necessarily *safe*. Expressing the safety using costs is natural for some RL tasks (e.g. when learning the function of a dynamic

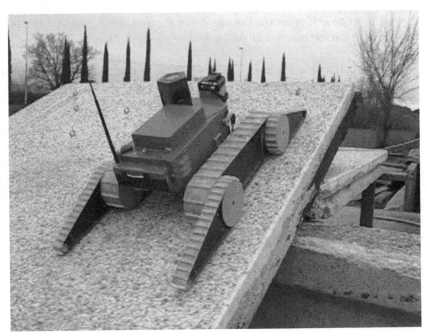

(a) A safe state

(b) A critical state – if the robot went still forward, it would fall down and probably break

Fig. 2. An illustration of safe and critical states

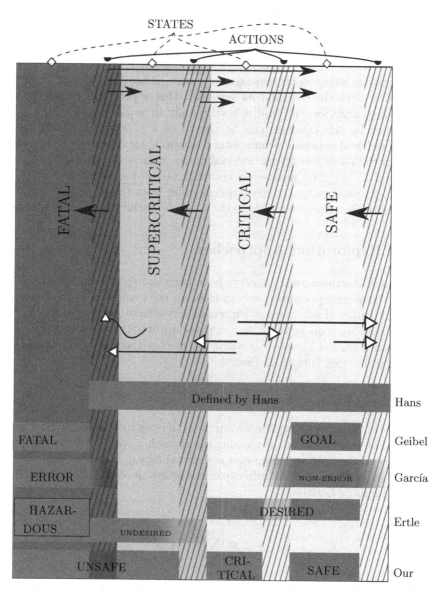

Fig. 3. *A summary of the definitions of safety.* The basic division is taken from Hans [14] and **fatal** states are added. States are drawn with solid background and white-headed arrows (→) denote the possible actions in the states. Actions are rendered with striped background and black-headed arrows (➤) end in states where it is possible to end up using the action.

controller of an engine, the engine's temperature can be treated as a cost). Unfortunately, not all **unsafe** states can be described using such costs in general. In addition, specifying the right costs may be a difficult task.

3.4 Safety as Variance of the Expected Return

An alternative to safety as minimization of a cost (either worst-case or expected) is minimizing both the cost and its variance. This approach is called *expected value-variance criterion* [15] and is used mainly in works prior 2000, e.g. [7]. A safe policy by this criterion can be viewed as a policy that minimizes the number of **critical** actions (because fatal transitions are expected to yield much larger costs than safe transitions, increasing the variance significantly).

As stated in [10], the worst-case approach is too restrictive and cautious. The other expected value-variance criteria suffer from the same disadvantages as safety through costs – mainly from the general difficulty to tune up the costs.

4 Safe Exploration Approaches

Finally, when the theoretical concepts have been shown and the various safety definitions have been presented, we can focus on the main part of this overview. Our categorization of safe exploration techniques is based on the work of García [10]. The basic division is as follows: approaches utilizing the expected return or its variance (Sec. 4.1), labeling-based approaches (Sec. 4.2) and approaches benefiting from prior knowledge (Sec. 4.3).

4.1 Optimal Control Approaches

Techniques in this category utilize variations of the *expected value-variance* safety criterion. The most basic one is treating the rewards as costs (when a reward is denoted by r_t, the corresponding cost is denoted by c_t). Standard RL methods can then be used to solve the safe exploration task, as described e.g. in [7] for discounted infinite horizon.

The RL objective function

$$J = E\left[\sum_{t=0}^{\infty} \gamma^t c_t\right] \tag{5}$$

is called the *risk-neutral objective*. To make this objective *risk-sensitive*, we specify a *risk factor* α and rewrite the objective as: [15]

$$J = \frac{1}{\alpha} \log E\left[\exp\left(\alpha\gamma^t \sum_{t=0}^{\infty} c_t\right)\right] \tag{6}$$
$$\simeq E\left[\sum_{t=0}^{\infty} \gamma^t c_t\right] + \frac{\alpha}{2} Var\left[\sum_{t=0}^{\infty} \gamma^t c_t\right],$$

which is also called the *expected value-variance criterion*. This approach is a part of theory using *exponential utility functions*, which is popular in optimal control [19]. To complete this section, the worst-case objective function (also called the *minimax objective*) is defined as

$$J = \sup \left[\sum_{t=0}^{\infty} \gamma^t c_t \right]. \tag{7}$$

As can be seen, the objective functions containing expectations cannot in fact assure that no unsafe state will be encountered. On the other hand, the minimax objective provides absolute certainty of the safety. However, it may happen that some of the unsafe states can only be reached with a negligible probability. In such cases, the α-*value* criterion defined by [15] can be used – it only takes into account rewards that can be reached with probability greater than α. In the work of Mihatsch [19], a scheme is presented that allows to "interpolate" between risk-neutral and worst-case behavior by changing a single parameter.

Delage's work [8] takes into account the uncertainty of parameters of the MDP. It is often the case that the parameters of the MDP are only estimated from a limited number of samples, causing the parameter uncertainty. He then proposes a possibility that the agent may "invest" some cost to lower the uncertainty in the parameters (by receiving some observations from other sources than exploration). A completely new research area then appears – to decide whether it is more valuable to pay the cost for observations, or to perform exploration by itself.

An approximation scheme for dealing with transition matrix uncertainty is presented in [21]. It considers a robust MDP problem and provides a worst-case, but also robust policy (with respect to the transition matrix uncertainty).

A theory generalizing these approaches can be found in [24]. The theory states that the optimal control decision is based on three terms – the *deterministic*, *cautionary* and *probing* terms.

> The deterministic term assumes the model is perfect and attempts to control for the best performance. Clearly, this may lead to disaster if the model is inaccurate. Adding a cautionary term yields a controller that considers the uncertainty in the model and chooses a control for the best expected performance. Finally, if the system learns while it is operating, there may be some benefit to choosing controls that are suboptimal and/or risky in order to obtain better data for the model and ultimately achieve better long-term performance. The addition of the probing term does this and gives a controller that yields the best long-term performance.[24]

To conclude this section, we think that these methods are not well suited for safe exploration – the expected value-variance and similar criteria provide no warranties on the actual safety. On the other hand, the worst-case approaches seem to be too strict.

4.2   Labeling-Based Approaches

The approaches utilizing some kind of state/action labeling (refer to Section 3.1 for the various labeling types) usually make use of two basic components – a *risk function* and a *backup policy*. The task of the *safety function* is to estimate the safety of a state or action. In the simplest case, the safety function can just provide the labeling of the given action; or it can return a likelihood that the action is safe; and in the best case, it would answer with a likelihood to be safe plus a variance (certainty) of its answer. The *backup policy* is a policy that is able to lead the agent out of the critical states back to the safe area. It is not obvious how to get such a policy, but the authors show some ways how to get one.

In the work of Hans [14], the most granular labeling is used, where fatal transitions are said to be the transitions with reward less than a given threshold. The safety function is learned during the exploration by collecting the so-called *min-reward samples* – this is the minimum reward ever obtained for executing a particular action in a particular state. The backup policy is then told to either exist naturally (e.g. a known safe, but suboptimal controller), or it can also be learned. To learn the backup policy, an RL task with altered Bellman equations is used:

$$\mathbf{Q}^*_{min}(s, a) = \max_{s'} \min \left[R(s, a, s'), \max_{a'} \mathbf{Q}^*_{min}(s', a') \right].$$

A policy derived from the computed $\mathbf{Q}^*_{min}$ function is then taken as the backup policy (as it maximizes the minimum reward obtained, and the fatal transitions are defined by low reward). He defines a policy to be *safe*, if it executes only safe actions in safe states and produces non-fatal transitions in critical states. To learn such safe policy, he then suggests a level-based exploration scheme (although he gives no proofs why it should be better than any other exploration scheme). This scheme is based on the idea that it is better to be always near the known safe space when exploring. All unknown actions from one "level" are explored, and their resulting states are queued to the next "level". For exploration of unknown actions he proposes that the action should be considered critical until proved otherwise, so the exploration scheme uses the backup policy after every unknown action execution. A disadvantage of this approach is that the agent needs some kind of "path planning" to be able to get to the queued states and continue exploration from them.

García's PI-SRL algorithm [10] is a way to safeguard the classical policy iteration algorithm. Since the labels *error/non-error* are only for final states, the risk function here is extended by a so called *Case-based memory*, which is in short a constant-sized memory for storing the historical $(s, a, \mathbf{V}(s))$ samples and is able to find nearest neighbors for a given query (using e.g. the Euclidean distance). In addition to the *error* and *non-error* states, he adds the definition of *known* and *unknown* states, where *known* states are those that have a neighbor in the case-based memory closer than a threshold. A safe policy is then said to be a policy that always leads to *known non-error* final states. To find such policy, the policy iteration is initialized with the safe backup policy and exploration is done via adding a small amount of Gaussian noise to the actions. This approach is suitable for continuous state- and action-spaces.

Another approach is presented in the work of Geibel [12], where the risk and objective functions are treated separately. So the risk function only classifies the states (again only final states) as either *fatal* or *goal*, and the risk of a policy (risk function) is then computed as the expected risk following the policy (where *fatal* states have risk 1 and *goal* states have risk 0). The task is then said to be to maximize the objective function (e.g. discounted infinite horizon) w.r.t. the condition that the risk of the considered policies is less than a safety threshold. The optimization itself is done using modified Q-learning, and the optimized objective function is a linear combination of the original objective function and the risk function. By changing the weights in the linear combination the algorithm can be controlled to behave more safely or in a more risk-neutral way.

A generalization of Geibel's idea to take the risk and reward functions separately can be found in the work of Kim [18]. In this work, the constrained RL task is treated as a *Constrained MDP* and the algorithm *CBEETLE* for solving the Constrained MDPs is shown. The advantage of this work is that it allows for several independent risk (cost) functions and doesn't need to convert them to the same scale.

A similar approach of using constrained MDP to solve the problem can be found in the work of Moldovan [20]. He does, however, use the ergodicity condition to tell safe and unsafe states apart (that is, safe are only those states from which the agent can get back to the initial state). Moreover, this approach is only shown to work for toy examples like the grid world with only several thousands of discrete states, which may not be sufficient for real robotics tasks.

The idea of having several risk functions is further developed by Ertle [9]. The agent is told to have several behaviors and a separate safety function is learned for each behavior. This approach allows for modularity and sharing of the learned safety functions among different types of agents. More details on this work will be provided in the next section, because it belongs to learning with teachers.

An approach slightly different from the previously mentioned in this section is using the methods of reachability analysis to solve safe exploration. Gillula in his work [13] defines a set of *keep-out states* (corresponding to **unsafe** in our labeling) and then a set called $Pre(\tau)$ is defined as a set of all states from which it is possible to get to a *keep-out* state in less than τ steps. Reachability analysis is used to compute the $Pre(\tau)$ set. *Safe states* are then all states not in $Pre(\tau)$ for a desired τ. This approach, however, doesn't utilize reinforcement learning, it computes the optimal policy using standard supervised learning methods with one additional constraint – that the system must use safe actions near the $Pre(\tau)$ set. On the other hand, the system is free to use whatever action desired when it is not near $Pre(\tau)$.

As was presented in this section, the labeling-based approaches provide a number of different ways to reach safety in exploration. They are, however, limited in several ways – some of them make use of the (usually hard-to-obtain) transition matrix, the others may need to visit the unsafe states in order to learn how to avoid them, or need the state-space to be metric.

4.3 Approaches Benefiting from Prior Knowledge

The last large group of safe exploration techniques are the ones benefiting from various kinds of prior knowledge (other than the parameters of the MDP). We consider this group the most promising for safe exploration, because "it is impossible to avoid undesirable situations in high-risk environments without a certain amount of prior knowledge about the task" [10].

The first option how to incorporate prior knowledge into exploration is to initialize the search using the prior knowledge. In fact, several works already mentioned in previous sections use prior knowledge – namely the approaches with a backup policy (Hans [14], García [10]). Also, García suggests that the initial estimate of the value function can be done by providing prior knowledge, which results in much faster convergence (since the agent does no more have to explore really random actions, the estimate of the value function already "leads it" the right way) [10].

Another option how to incorporate prior knowledge is by using *Learning from Demonstration* (LfD) methods. Due to the limited space, we will not give the basics of LfD – a good overview of the state-of-the-art methods is for example in [2]. For our overview, it is sufficient to state that LfD methods can derive a policy from a set of demonstrations provided by a teacher. What is important, is that the teacher does not necessarily have to have the same geometrical and physical properties as the trainee (although it helps the process if possible). It is therefore possible to use LfD to teach a 5-joint arm to play tennis, while using 3-joint human arm as the source of demonstrations (but the learned policy may be suboptimal; RL should then be used to optimize the policy).

In *Apprenticeship Learning* [1], the reward function is learned using LfD. The human pilot flies a helicopter at his best, and both system dynamics and the reward function are learned from the demonstrations. It is however apparent that the performance of the agent is no longer objectively optimal, but that it depends on the abilities of the human pilot.

Another way of incorporating prior knowledge into the learning process is to manually select which demonstrations will be provided, as in the work of Ertle [9]. In the work it is suggested that more teacher demonstrations should come from the areas near the unsafe set, in order to teach the agent precisely where the border between safe and unsafe is located.

The last technique described in our overview is interleaving autonomous exploration with teacher demonstrations. As in the previous case, some teacher demonstrations are provided in advance, and then the exploration part starts utilizing the teacher-provided information. After some time, or in states very different from all other known states, the agent requests the teacher to provide more examples [2,5]. The idea behind this algorithm is that it is impossible to think out in advance what all demonstrations will the agent need in order to learn the optimal policy.

Finishing this section, the algorithms utilizing prior knowledge seem to be the most promising out of all the presented approaches. They provide both a speedup of the learning process (by discarding the low-reward areas) and a reasonable way to specify the safety conditions (via LfD or interleaving).

5 Conclusion

In our work we have given a short introduction on the basics of *Markov Decision Processes* as well as the basic *Reinforcement Learning* methods like *Value Iteration*, *Q-learning* and *Policy Iteration*. In Section 3 we have summarized many recent approaches on how to define *safety* in the framework of optimal control and reinforcement learning. We have also proposed a novelty definition of safety, which divides the state space to *safe*, *critical* and *unsafe* states. We have shown that all other labeling-based safety definitions are covered by our new definition.

In Section 4 many different safe exploration methods are categorized into three basic groups – algorithms from optimal control theory, reinforcement learning algorithms based on state labeling, and algorithms utilizing extra prior knowledge. We have shortly summarized the advantages and disadvantages of the particular approaches. We have also stated that at least for difficult real-world problems, safe exploration without prior knowledge is practically impossible, and prior knowledge almost always helps to achieve faster convergence. Another observation has been that some of the safe exploration algorithms need to visit unsafe states to correctly classify them later, which might discard them from some usage scenarios where the unsafe states are really fatal.

It seems to us that the field of safe exploration in reinforcement learning has been very fragmented and lacks an all-embracing theory. However, the question is, if it is even possible to find such theory – the main problem may be the fragmentation and differences of various RL methods themselves. At least, the safe exploration community would benefit from a unification of the terminology (and our proposal of the novelty safety labeling would like to help that).

Other ways of possible future research are for example the following. New ways of incorporating prior knowledge into methods not utilizing it yet could bring interesting speed-up of those algorithms. There is also a bottleneck in the estimation of the results of unknown actions – some advanced function approximation methods should be explored (we aim to investigate Gaussian Processes this way). There are not enough experiments from difficult continuous real-world environments, which would show for example how large problems can be solved using safe exploration. The interleaved learning needs some guidelines on how to cluster the queries for the teacher to some larger "packs" and "ask" them together, possibly increasing the fully autonomous operating time. Last, but not least, the possibility to share some learned safety functions among different kinds of robots seems to be an unexplored area with many practical applications (maybe robot-to-robot LfD could be used).

Acknowledgments. This work has been supported by the Grant Agency of the Czech Technical University in Prague under Project SGS13/142/OHK3/2T/13, and by EC project FP7-ICT-609763 TRADR. We would like to thank Karel Zimmermann and Michal Reinstein (Center for Machine Perception, CTU in Prague) for their valuable insights into reinforcement learning methods.

References

1. Abbeel, P., Coates, A., Quigley, M., Ng, A.Y.: An application of reinforcement learning to aerobatic helicopter flight. In: Proceedings of the 2006 Conference on Advances in Neural Information Processing Systems, vol. 19, p. 1 (2007)
2. Argall, B.D., Chernova, S., Veloso, M., Browning, B.: A survey of robot learning from demonstration. Robotics and Autonomous Systems 57(5), 469–483 (2009)
3. Barto, A.G., Sutton, R.S., Brouwer, P.S.: Associative search network: A reinforcement learning associative memory. Biological Cybernetics (1981)
4. Bertsekas, D.P.: Dynamic programming: deterministic and stochastic models. Prentice-Hall (1987)
5. Chernova, S., Veloso, M.: Confidence-based policy learning from demonstration using Gaussian mixture models. In: AAMAS 2007 Proceedings, p. 1. ACM Press (2007)
6. Consortium, N.: NIFTi robotic UGV platform (2010)
7. Coraluppi, S.P., Marcus, S.I.: Risk-sensitive and minimax control of discrete-time, finite-state Markov decision processes. Automatica (1999)
8. Delage, E., Mannor, S.: Percentile optimization in uncertain Markov decision processes with application to efficient exploration. In: Proceedings of the 24th International Conference on Machine Learning, ICML 2007, pp. 225–232. ACM Press, New York (2007)
9. Ertle, P., Tokic, M., Cubek, R., Voos, H., Soffker, D.: Towards learning of safety knowledge from human demonstrations. In: 2012 IEEE/RSJ International Conference on Intelligent Robots and Systems, pp. 5394–5399. IEEE (October 2012)
10. Garcia, J., Fernández, F.: Safe exploration of state and action spaces in reinforcement learning. Journal of Artificial Intelligence Research 45, 515–564 (2012)
11. Garcia Polo, F.J., Rebollo, F.F.: Safe reinforcement learning in high-risk tasks through policy improvement. In: 2011 IEEE Symposium on Adaptive Dynamic Programming and Reinforcement Learning (ADPRL), pp. 76–83. IEEE (April 2011)
12. Geibel, P.: Reinforcement learning with bounded risk. In: ICML, pp. 162–169 (2001)
13. Gillula, J.H., Tomlin, C.J.: Guaranteed safe online learning of a bounded system. In: 2011 IEEE/RSJ International Conference on Intelligent Robots and Systems, pp. 2979–2984. IEEE (September 2011)
14. Hans, A., Schneegaß, D., Schäfer, A., Udluft, S.: Safe exploration for reinforcement learning. In: Proceedings of European Symposium on Artificial Neural Networks, pp. 23–25 (April 2008)
15. Heger, M.: Consideration of risk in reinforcement learning. In: 11th International Machine Learning Conference (1994)
16. Howard, R.A.: Dynamic Programming and Markov Processes. Technology Press of Massachusetts Institute of Technology (1960)
17. Kaelbling, L.P., Littman, M.L., Moore, A.W.: Reinforcement Learning: A Survey. Journal of Artificial Intelligence Research 4, 237–285 (1996)
18. Kim, D., Kim, K.E., Poupart, P.: Cost-Sensitive Exploration in Bayesian Reinforcement Learning. In: Proceedings of Neural Information Processing Systems (NIPS) (2012)

19. Mihatsch, O., Neuneier, R.: Risk-sensitive reinforcement learning. Machine Learning 49(2-3), 267–290 (2002)
20. Moldovan, T.M., Abbeel, P.: Safe Exploration in Markov Decision Processes. In: Proceedings of the 29th International Conference on Machine Learning (May 2012)
21. Nilim, A., El Ghaoui, L.: Robust Control of Markov Decision Processes with Uncertain Transition Matrices. Operations Research 53(5), 780–798 (2005)
22. Geibel, P., Wysotzki, F.: Risk-Sensitive Reinforcement Learning Applied to Control under Constraints. Journal Of Artificial Intelligence Research 24, 81–108 (2011)
23. Puterman, M.L.: Markov Decision Processes: Discrete Stochastic Dynamic Programming, 1st edn. John Wiley & Sons, Inc., New York (1994)
24. Schneider, J.G.: Exploiting model uncertainty estimates for safe dynamic control learning. Neural Information Processing Systems 9, 1047–1053 (1996)
25. Watkins, C.J., Dayan, P.: Q-learning. Machine Learning 8(3-4), 279–292 (1992)
26. Williams, R.J., Baird, L.C.: Tight performance bounds on greedy policies based on imperfect value functions. Tech. rep., Northeastern University,College of Computer Science (1993)

Improving the Ant Colony Optimization Algorithm for the Multi-Depot Vehicle Routing Problem and Its Application

Petr Stodola[*], Jan Mazal, and Milan Podhorec

University of Defence, Brno, Czech Republic
{petr.stodola,jan.mazal,milan.podhorec}@unob.cz

Abstract. This paper addresses our solution to the Multi-Depot Vehicle Routing Problem (MDVRP) based on the Ant Colony Optimization (ACO) algorithm. The first part introduces the basic concepts and principles of the algorithm along with its key parameters. The primary part of the article deals with the improvement of the original algorithm. The improvement consists in the distribution of algorithm's key processes, which can be executed simultaneously, to the individual cores of a multi-core processor. This part also includes several experiments (based on the Cordeau's test instances) we conducted to verify the value of improvement. The last part of the article presents the real application of the problem and our solution. Finally, the paper summarizes some perspectives of our future work.

Keywords: Ant Colony Optimization, Multi-Depot Vehicle Routing Problem, Speedup, Parallelization.

1 Introduction

The Multi-Depot Vehicle Routing Problem (MDVRP) is a well-known problem with many real applications in the areas of transportation, distribution and logistics. Many approaches and methods to this problem have been developed and implemented since it was formulated in 1959 for the first time by Dantzig and Ramser [1].

Very successful methods proposed for solution are based on heuristic or metaheuristic principles as this is an NP-hard problem, thus exact methods are not often feasible for more complex tasks.

In this paper, we address the solution to this problem via the Ant Colony Optimization (ACO) algorithm. It is a nature-inspired idea introduced in 1992 by Dorigo [2]. The first part of the article (Section 2) deals with the basic concepts and principles of the algorithm.

The primary objective is to introduce the improvement of our original approach which consists in parallel processing of crucial operations of the algorithm (Section 3).

---

[*] Corresponding author.

J. Hodicky (Ed.): MESAS 2014, LNCS 8906, pp. 376–385, 2014.

The value of improvement is validated via several experiments (based on Cordeau's test instances [3]).

In the last part (Section 4), the real application of our solution is presented. The goal of the application is the optimal planning of supply distribution and logistics (which is conducted via autonomous robots) in the real environment.

1.1   Literature Review

There are a lot of different approaches and methods proposed as a solution to the MDVRP problem. A broad overview of various methods is provided e.g. in [4, 5]. When taking into account only solutions based on the ACO theory, we can find several publications using this concept, see e.g. [6, 7, 8].

ACO theory is also used as a means of solution to various relating problems, e.g. Travelling salesman problem [9], Scheduling problem [10], Assignment problem [11], Set problem [12], and many others.

2   Concept of the ACO Algorithm

MDVRP is formulated as a problem of optimal distribution of goods or services delivered to multiple destinations (customers). Distribution is carried out by a fleet of vehicles starting from multiple depots, each located in a different place.

2.1   ACO Principle

ACO algorithm is a probabilistic technique adopted from the natural world where ants explore the environment to find food. The exploring starts randomly at first; when an ant finds food, however, it lays down a pheromone trail along its route. When other ants find such a trail, they are likely to follow it (and lay down their own trail if successful). Pheromone trails evaporate gradually, thus reducing its strength; is has an effect of avoiding the convergence to a locally optimal solution.

The principle of the algorithm is shown in Fig. 1. There, we can see a colony of ants; each ant explores the state space independently on one another to find a feasible solution. The process is carried out in successive generations. In the first generation, the searching for a solution is entirely random. After this process, each ant lays down the pheromone trail along its own solution found; the strength of such a trail corresponds to the quality of the solution. In the next generation, ants are likely to follow trails of better solutions than that of worse quality. In this way, the quality of the best solution found is improved steadily each generation. The detailed analysis of individual processes is beyond the scope of this article.

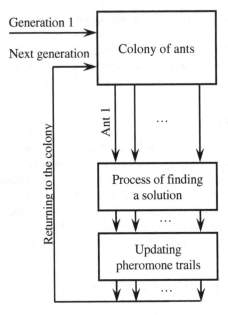

Fig. 1. ACO principle

2.2   Parameters

The algorithm works with a lot of parameters influencing the problem solution. These parameters are introduced very briefly below as the more detailed description is beyond the scope of this article. The most important parameters are as follows:

- **Number of ants in colonies**: this number represents the number of individual solutions found in each generation.
- **Method of updating pheromone trails**: the way in which pheromone trails are updated at the end of each generation.
- **Pheromone updating coefficient**: this coefficient controls the influence of individual solutions when updating pheromone trails.
- **Pheromone evaporation coefficient**: this coefficient determines the speed of evaporating pheromone trails at the end of each generation.
- **Coefficient to control the influence of pheromone trails**: this coefficient is used for computing probabilities for ants to visit a customer (based on the strength of pheromone trails) when searching for a solution.
- **Termination conditions**: it determines the total number of generations.
- **Optimization type**: it allows selecting the optimization criterion (minimization of total distance travelled, or total time of the whole process taken, or total fuel consumed).

3   Improvement of the Algorithm

The improvement consists in a parallelization of the key process of finding solutions by individual ants in a colony (see Fig. 1). In this process, every ant searches for a solution independently on one another, thus the computations have the potential to be distributed to more processors. There are two possibilities as follows:

- Distribution of processing to cores of a multi-core processor;
- Distribution of processing to more computers (to the GRID networks for instance).

3.1   Parallelization

We took advantage of the first possibility mentioned above, i.e. we distribute the process of finding ant's solutions to cores of a multi-core processor. Fig. 2 shows an example of the principle on a processor with 4 cores and 12 ants in a colony. As can be seen, computations are evenly distributed to available cores of a processor (the number of cores can be set arbitrarily according to user's requirements).

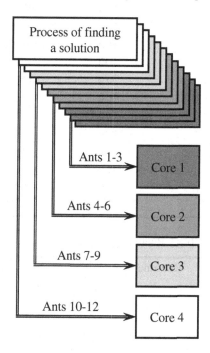

Fig. 2. Parallelization principle

The same principle of computational distribution is applied to the process of updating and evaporating of pheromone trails. It is also the process composed of parts independent on one another, so that the same approach can be used.

3.2   Experiments

The improvement, which consists in speeding up the whole time for optimization, is verified via set of experiments based on Cordeau's test instances, namely p01, p02, p03, p04, p05, p06, p07, p08, p09, p10, p11, p12, p15, p18, and p21.

First, Table 1 presents individual instances along with the best known solution for individual tasks, and best solution found by our algorithm. Next, Table 2 shows times needed for optimization depending on various numbers of cores used for computation (to be specific, we used 1, 2, 4, 6, 8, and 12 cores). All tests were executed on Intel Core i7 CPU X980 @ 3.33 GHz which is a 12-core processor.

Table 1. Experiment instances

Instance	Number of depots	Number of customers	Best known solution	Our best solution
p01	4	50	576.87	576.87
p02	4	50	473.53	475.86
p03	5	75	641.19	644.46
p04	2	100	1001.59	1018.49
p05	2	100	750.03	755.71
p06	3	100	876.50	885.84
p07	4	100	885.80	895.53
p08	2	249	4420.95	4445.51
p09	3	249	3900.22	3990.19
p10	4	249	3663.02	3751.50
p11	5	249	3554.18	3657.16
p12	2	80	1318.95	1318.95
p15	3	160	2505.42	2510.11
p18	6	240	3702.85	3741.80
p21	9	360	5474.84	5631.12

Table 2. Runtime for experiment instances

Instance	Runtime with various numbers of cores used					
	1	2	4	6	8	12
p01 (sec)	6.8	3.8	2.0	1.8	1.6	1.2
p02 (sec)	4.3	2.5	1.3	1.2	1.1	0.8
p03 (sec)	23.2	12.8	6.6	5.5	4.7	3.8
p04 (sec)	253.3	133.5	69.9	55.7	47.1	37.9
p05 (sec)	178.8	95.3	48.3	39.3	34.0	27.2
p06 (sec)	267.8	138.3	75.3	59.4	50.3	41.6
p07 (sec)	198.5	106.3	54.5	45.2	38.0	31.1
p08 (min)	111.4	58.4	29.7	24.9	20.7	17.0

Table 2. (*Continued*)

p09 (min)	117.2	60.6	30.9	26.3	22.0	17.7
p10 (min)	105.4	53.7	27.5	23.2	19.5	15.8
p11 (min)	115.0	58.9	30.0	25.2	20.6	17.3
p12 (sec)	61.0	32.9	16.9	13.7	13.8	10.8
p15 (min)	9.0	4.6	2.4	2.0	1.6	1.3
p18 (min)	84.3	43.5	22.0	18.6	15.6	12.8
p21 (min)	335.1	171.5	86.4	75.2	59.7	49.4

3.3   Experiments Evaluation

Fig. 3 depicts the results from Table 2 graphically. The runtime is expressed in % (the runtime of each task solved via 1 core represents 100%). In this figure, we can see that the improvement in runtime does not change much (for the given number of cores used) even when solving instances with very different complexity.

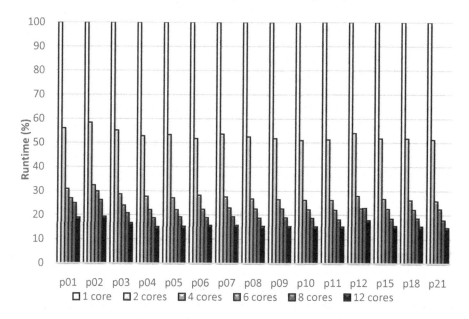

Fig. 3. Runtime for experiment instances

Table 3 presents the average values of runtime for different numbers of cores used along with the standard deviation and speedup values.

Table 3. Time saved by using various numbers of cores

Cores	1	2	4	6	8	12
Mean	100 %	53.0 %	27.6 %	23.2 %	19.9 %	16.0 %
Stdev	0.0 %	2.0 %	1.8 %	2.1 %	2.5 %	1.4 %
Speedup	1.00	1.89	3.63	4.31	5.02	6.26

Fig. 4 shows the speedup from Table 3. For 2 and 4 cores, the speedup corresponds to the number of cores linearly. For more cores, it is smaller due to the time management of threads and other reasons (based e.g. on the operation system and its process of threads distribution and memory management).

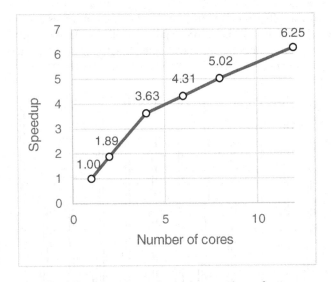

Fig. 4. Speedup when using various numbers of cores

4   Application

The improved version of the algorithm has been integrated to our system to support decision-making of commanders. This system has been proposed to plan the process of supply distribution from multiple depots on the tactic and strategic level.

It works with data of the real environment including relief, terrain, topographical objects, infrastructure, etc. The system provides a user friendly interface enabling to add, edit and delete nodes (depots and customers). Then, the MDVRP algorithm is executed. Subsequently, the optimal routes for all vehicles are displayed graphically.

The process of supply distribution might be carried out via manned vehicles or via autonomous robots. Each vehicle is loaded with the precise routes between individual customers in the correct order.

Fig. 5 shows this system with an example with 20 customers and 5 depots. Depots are shown as hexagons (labelled by letters), customers as circles (labelled by numbers). Black lines present the optimal routes for individual vehicles. Although the example is rather simple, the same system can be used for tasks with tens of depots and hundreds of customers.

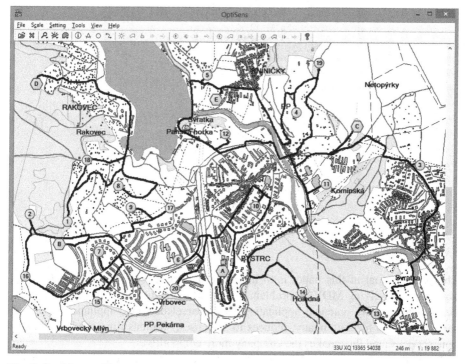

Fig. 5. Decision-making support system for commanders with the implementation of the proposed algorithm

Fig. 6 presents the results particularly for the vehicle (depot) B. There we can see the order of customers to be visited. The total distance travelled by this vehicle is 8.49 km; the total distance travelled by all vehicles is 41.71 km; the total time for the whole process of supply distribution is 9 minutes; and total fuel consumption is 4.2 liters.

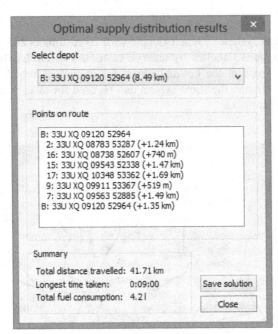

Fig. 6. Results for the depot B

5   Conclusions

The primary goal of this paper is to introduce the improvement of our ACO based algorithm for solving MDVRP problems. The optimal solution to this problem might be critical in many practical applications (e.g. parcel delivery, appliance repair). It saves resources for a company, reduces its expenses, shortens time needed to distribute services, and thus makes the company more competitive.

From the experiments conducted, we can draw a conclusion that the speedup achieved by parallelization of the algorithm is more than 6 when solved by all cores on a 12-core processor (regardless of the complexity of the task at hand). Furthermore, the solutions achieved by the algorithm are in all experiment instances of a high quality (not worse than 3% compared with the best known solution – see Table 1).

There are also some perspectives for our future work:

- The computation of processes of updating and evaporation of pheromone trails could be implemented on a GPU processor.
- Parallelization could be achieved not only on the cores of a multi-core processor but also by utilization of more computers (within the GRID networks for instance).
- The algorithm could be extended for solving other problems (for instance MDVRP with Time Windows or with Pick-up and Delivering).

References

1. Dantzig, G.B., Ramser, J.H.: The Truck Dispatching Problem. Management Science 6(1), 80–91 (1959)
2. Dorigo, M.: Optimization, Learning and Natural Algorithms. PhD thesis, Politecnico di Milano, Milan (1992)
3. NEO Web: Networking and Emerging Optimization. University of Malaga, Spain, http://neo.lcc.uma.es/vrp/vrp-instances/multiple-depot-vrp-instances/ (accessed March 10, 2014)
4. Hjorring, C.: The Vehicle Routing Problem and Local Search Metaheuristics. PhD thesis, University of Auckland, Auckland (1995)
5. Laporte, G.: The Vehicle Routing Problem: An overview of exact and approximate algorithms. European Journal of Operational Research 59(3), 345–358 (1992)
6. Caldeira, T.C.M.: Optimization of the Multi-Depot Vehicle Routing Problem: an Application to Logistics and Transport of Biomass for Electricity Production. Technical University of Lisbon, Lisbon (2009)
7. Ma, J., Yuan, J.: Ant Colony Algorithm for Multiple-Depot Vehicle Routing Problem with Shortest Finish Time. In: Zaman, M., Liang, Y., Siddiqui, S.M., Wang, T., Liu, V., Lu, C. (eds.) CETS 2010. CCIS, vol. 113, pp. 114–123. Springer, Heidelberg (2010)
8. Narasimha, K.S.V., Kivelevitch, E., Kumar, M.: Ant Colony Optimization Technique to Solve Min-Max MultiDepot Vehicle Routing Problem. In: American Control Conference (ACC 2012), Montreal, pp. 3980–3985 (2012)
9. Dorigo, M., Gambardella, L.M.: Ant Colonies for the Traveling Salesman Problem. Biosystems 43(2), 73–81 (1997)
10. Blum, C.: ACO Applied to Group Shop Scheduling: A Case Study on Intensification and Diversification. In: Dorigo, M., Di Caro, G.A., Sampels, M. (eds.) ANTS 2002. LNCS, vol. 2463, pp. 14–27. Springer, Heidelberg (2002)
11. Stützle, T.: MAX-MIN Ant System for Quadratic Assignment Problem. Technical Report AIDA-97-04, Darmstadt (1997)
12. de Silva, R.M.A., Ramalho, G.R.: Ant system for the set covering problem. IEEE International Conference on Systems, Man, and Cybernetics 5, 3129–3133 (2001)
13. Valis, D., Zak, L., Walek, A., Pietrucha-Urbanik, K.: Selected mathematical functions used for operation data information. In: Safety, Reliability and Risk Analysis: Beyond the Horizon, pp. 1303–1308 (2014)
14. Glos, J., Zak, L., Valis, D.: Possibilities of mathematical modelling of tribo-diagnostics data. Transport Means, Kaunas University of Technology, Kaunas (2013)

Author Index